NAVIGATING THE POLYCRISIS

NAVIGATING THE POLYCRISIS

MAPPING THE FUTURES OF CAPITALISM
AND THE EARTH

MICHAEL J. ALBERT

THE MIT PRESS   CAMBRIDGE, MASSACHUSETTS   LONDON, ENGLAND

The MIT Press would like to thank the anonymous peer reviewers who provided comments on drafts of this book. The generous work of academic experts is essential for establishing the authority and quality of our publications. We acknowledge with gratitude the contributions of these otherwise uncredited readers.

This book was set in Stone Serif and Stone Sans by Westchester Publishing Services.

Library of Congress Cataloging-in-Publication Data

Names: Albert, Michael J., author.
Title: Navigating the polycrisis : mapping the futures of capitalism and the Earth / Michael J. Albert.
Description: Cambridge, Massachusetts : The MIT Press, [2024] | Includes bibliographical references and index.
Identifiers: LCCN 2023021165 (print) | LCCN 2023021166 (ebook) | ISBN 9780262547758 (paperback) | ISBN 9780262378277 (epub) | ISBN 9780262378260 (pdf)
Subjects: LCSH: Forecasting. | Civilization, Modern—21st century.
Classification: LCC CB161 .A43 2024 (print) | LCC CB161 (ebook) | DDC 909.83/0112—dc23/eng/20230822
LC record available at https://lccn.loc.gov/2023021165
LC ebook record available at https://lccn.loc.gov/2023021166

155365110

To my parents,
who gave me a future

CONTENTS

ACKNOWLEDGMENTS ix

LIST OF ABBREVIATIONS xi

INTRODUCTION 1

1   THE PLANETARY POLYCRISIS 17

2   VISIONING AND SHAPING THE FUTURE: MODELS, SCENARIOS, AND CRITICAL SOCIAL SCIENCE FUTURES 63

3   PLANETARY SYSTEMS THINKING 87

4   THE SOCIOECOLOGICAL PROBLEMATIC: CLIMATE, ENERGY, FOOD, AND THE FUTURES OF CAPITALISM 113

5   FUTURES OF GEOPOLITICS, SECURITY, AND THE PLANETARY PROBLEMATIC 177

CONCLUSION 225

NOTES 243

INDEX 291

ACKNOWLEDGMENTS

There are many humans and nonhumans who made this book possible, though I'll focus mainly on the humans. This book was born from a dissertation project that would not have been possible without the support and guidance of Dan Deudney, Bentley Allan, and William Connolly. Few would have allowed such a sprawling and overambitious project to move forward under their supervision, and I have them to thank for believing in it and helping it come to fruition. Jane Bennett, Sam Chambers, and Jennifer Culbert had a significant influence on the evolution of my thinking during my time at Johns Hopkins as well, and I'm grateful to them for their input and support over the years. Beverly Silver, Simon Dalby, and David Scott also deserve thanks for their feedback and insights on the project. And I owe Mason Rayner, Jishnu Guha, Jay Mohorcich, Gregg Tourville, Nils Kupzok, Stephanie Erev, Jacob Kripp, Quinn Lester, CJ Higgins, Beth Mendenhall, Nathan Gies, and Casey McNeill deep gratitude for our friendship and wide-ranging conversations over the years, which made me a smarter human than I would have been otherwise.

This book was sharpened by workshops held at SOAS University of London in November 2021 and the University of Edinburgh in April 2023. I am deeply grateful to Meera Sabaratnam, Nick Srnicek, Alex Williams, Kerem Nisancioglu, Mathew Paterson, Phil Clark, Mathias Thaler, Troy Vettese, Claire Duncanson, and Thomas Homer-Dixon for taking the time to read and give feedback on the manuscript. Felix Berenskoetter and Fiona Adamson provided much-needed help on the book proposal, and I'm deeply grateful to them for their support during my time at SOAS. Conversations with Taylor Borowetz, Chris Smaje, Gabriela Cabaña, Iñigo Capellán-Pérez, John Barry, Nafeez Ahmed, Carolyn Baker, Mihaela Mihai, Elizabeth Bomberg, Oliver Turner, and Cedric Durand also shaped my thinking and made the book better than it would have otherwise been. I also owe a big thanks to Beth Clevenger for her support for the project, to the MIT Press editorial team, and to Benedikt Büchel for his assistance with the index.

To close, I first want to thank my parents. The unconditional love and support they gave me, and their encouragement for me to find my own path through all its twists and turns, has been all that any human could hope for. I also owe the world and more to Taylor, who is simultaneously a loving partner, intellectual companion, and artistic genius who gave detailed comments on the manuscript and provided much needed help with the visuals in this book. Finally, some of the key nonhumans whose inspiration and energy helped me get through the book-writing process include Thea, Cadbury, and Grahams; the oak trees of Primrose Hill and Hampstead Heath; the Water of Leith; and (last but not least) the Earth.

Michael J. Albert
June 2023

LIST OF ABBREVIATIONS

AI	Artificial intelligence
BAU	Business-as-usual
BECCS	Bioenergy plus carbon capture and storage
BIS	Bank of International Settlements
CCP	Chinese Communist Party
CDR	Carbon dioxide removal
CL	Climate leviathan
DAC	Direct air capture
EP	Existential problematic
EROI	Energy return on energy investment
FAO	Food and Agriculture Organization
FF	Fossil fuels
FIR	Fourth industrial revolution
GFANZ	Glasgow Financial Alliance for Net Zero
GM	Genetically modified
IAMs	Integrated assessment models
IEA	International Energy Agency
IoT	Internet-of-Things
IPCC	Intergovernmental Panel on Climate Change
LNG	Liquified natural gas
LtG	Limits to Growth

MEDEAS   modeling energy system development under environmental
and socioeconomic constraints

NAS   National Academies of Sciences

NC3   Nuclear weapons command, control, and communication

NDCs   Nationally Determined Contributions

NIC   National Intelligence Council

PBs   Planetary boundaries

RE   Renewable energy

SEP   Socioecological problematic

SRM   Solar radiation management

SSPs   Shared Socioeconomic Pathways

UBI   Universal Basic Income

VI   Violence-interdependence

VP   Violence problematic

WMD   Weapons of Mass Destruction

WMO   World Meteorological Association

INTRODUCTION

The 2020s have gotten off to a rocky start (to put it mildly). Words like "permacrisis" and "polycrisis" have become common currency, reflecting a broadening awareness that ours is an age of interconnected systemic crises with no clear end in sight.[1] The year 2021 was already a year of stress in global energy and food markets, ratcheting geopolitical rivalries, record levels of global military spending, and accumulating risks for the world economy—trends that were all turbocharged by Vladimir Putin's February 2022 invasion of Ukraine. It remains far from certain how these ongoing crises will unfold. But we know that deeper challenges loom on the horizon, from the climate and mass extinction crises to future pandemics, "net energy decline" for fossil fuels, an unsustainable and unstable global food system, the brewing new cold war between the United States and China, the simmering specter of far-right populism, the nascent threat of weaponized synthetic biology, and the destabilizing impacts of artificial intelligence on work, war, and human freedom.

This book asks where the world-system is headed as a result of these intersecting challenges. It makes three overarching arguments. First, I argue that that we must devote more systematic attention to the question of possible futures. "Business-as-usual" will come to an end—whether by choice or by disaster. Thus we need more future-oriented scholarship that can illuminate the possible roads ahead, their branching pathways, the dangers that lurk, and the opportunities that may emerge for progressive transformation. Second, I argue that to illuminate the space of possible planetary futures, we need a holistic approach that highlights the relations and feedbacks between the numerous challenges that compose our planetary predicament. As more and more analysts recognize, we confront not simply a climate crisis, nor simply a collection of numerous isolatable problems that can be studied by separate disciplines, but rather a "polycrisis" or nexus of reciprocally entwined crises characterized by complex feedback loops, blurred boundaries, cascade effects, and (in many cases) mutual amplification.[2] Third, I argue that a theoretical framework informed by complexity theory and world-systems theory can provide a new form of critical-futures analysis capable of grappling with the polycrisis condition. But the point here is not to claim superiority for a single theoretical approach, but rather to develop a conceptual framework that can facilitate synthesis across numerous disciplines and theoretical traditions—including international relations (IR), critical political economy, ecological economics, energy studies, the earth system sciences, critical security studies, and many others.

The goal of this book is thus to develop a new way of thinking about planetary futures that can help us create more useful and comprehensive maps of the possibility space. Such an approach must be planetary in scope, voraciously synthetic, and utterly indifferent toward disciplinary boundaries. In a word, it must be "transdisciplinary," in the sense of pragmatist scholarship that emerges directly from problems in the world demanding response (rather than from stale disciplinary debates) and that synthesizes knowledge across numerous disciplinary, theoretical, and methodological traditions.[3] In this sense, as Sanders van der Leeuw writes, transdisciplinary research analyzes "that which is at once between the disciplines, across the different disciplines, and beyond each individual discipline."[4] Transdisciplinary research has its risks (as I elaborate below). But it is also the necessary precondition of rigorous futures analysis that can inform contemporary strategies for progressive socioecological transformation. As the late Immanuel Wallerstein wrote more than forty years ago, our "ability to participate intelligently in the evolution" of the world-system is "dependent on [our] ability to perceive the whole. The more difficult we acknowledge the task to be, the more urgent it is that we start sooner rather than later."[5] In short, if we think the task is daunting, this is all the more reason to get started now.

PLANETARY FUTURES AND NAVIGATIONAL PRAXIS

In contrast to the vast majority of approaches in the social sciences, this book takes the future seriously as a focus of analysis. Most social scientific scholarship focuses overwhelmingly on the past and present, while occasionally making some speculations about the future (typically, if at all, in a book's conclusion). This tendency is reasonable to some extent, since we cannot corroborate or falsify our present-day hypotheses about the future, and our future speculations always run the risk of making us look foolish in the long run.[6] But this stance is far too limiting. Humans are temporally situated beings that act in relation to a future or set of possible futures that infuse the present and shape our hopes, fears, and projects.[7] As Jens Beckert argues, "'History matters,' but the future matters just as much."[8] Heikki Patomäki develops a similar argument: "Anticipation of the future is a necessary part of social action. . . . Consequently, if the social sciences are to be relevant they should be able to also say something about possible and likely futures."[9] The majority of social scientists who do investigate futures are typically less interested in "the future" itself than in techniques through which powerful actors imaginatively construct and act on possible futures.[10] This work is very important, and I also explore such futurological exercises (in chapter 2). But this book instead primarily follows Patomäki and others who develop what could be called a "realist" approach to planetary futures. From this view, the future is not solely made actual in the present through discursive construction, but also exists as a real though not-yet-actual possibility space composed of multiple possible trajectories and latent potentials.[11] The openness, uncertainty, and indeterminacy of the future is the main reason that social scientists tend to shy away from studying it directly, yet this indeterminacy is *precisely* why futures analysis is so important. As Patomäki writes, "Actions anticipating possible futures . . . shape the present and thereby also contribute toward the materialisation of a particular line of development in world history."[12]

Following Patomäki, this book is less concerned with "predicting" the future than with illuminating possible lines of world historical development in order to inform present-day strategies that can help shape the future in more progressive (or at least less catastrophic) directions. As I discuss in chapter 2, militaries, intelligence agencies, central banks, and corporations are all deeply engaged in various forms of future-scenario analysis, which they use to develop strategies that may "perform well under a range of future conditions."[13] Rather than allowing powerful actors to monopolize these techniques in their efforts to preempt and constrain the future possibility space, scholars and activists should engage in counter-hegemonic futures analyses in order to widen our imaginaries of possible futures and develop strategies to bring about more just futures. As John Urry says, the terrain of futures studies "is too important to be left to states, corporations and technologists, . . . and social science needs to be central in disentangling, debating and delivering those futures."[14]

There are at least two main tasks for counter-hegemonic futures analysis. The first is to illuminate the most likely futures that may emerge following current tendencies and trends. As Mathias Thaler discusses, this involves "if-this-goes-on"-style scenarios that are common in dystopian science fiction.[15] In the jargon of climate scientists and energy modelers, these are "business-as-usual" or "current-policies" scenarios in which trends in political economy, power relations, culture, energy consumption, greenhouse gas emissions, and technological change continue to follow their recent historical patterns.[16] As should be evident to any clear-sighted analyst of our planetary predicament, these pathways would result in increasingly "dystopian" futures over time—at least for the majority of humanity—whether they take the form of deepening climate apartheid, techno-authoritarianism, social and ecological collapse, or (at their worst extreme) human extinction. As I show in chapters 4 and 5, even more ambitious policy reforms and technological breakthroughs—if constrained within a profit- and growth-oriented "ecomodernist" framework—would likely push the world-system down a dystopian trajectory (or at best a "ustopian" future, in Margaret Atwood's sense, combining utopian and dystopian elements).[17] From a counter-hegemonic perspective, the purpose of exploring these futures is to understand the mechanisms and elite strategies that may prevent global capitalism from decisively shifting away from its increasingly catastrophic trajectory, anticipate the different kinds of systemic crises and disruptions that would emerge, highlight both the challenges and opportunities that these crises would create for progressive movements, and warn of the dangerous amplifying feedbacks that could make such trajectories self-reinforcing.

But this is obviously not the sole task of counter-hegemonic futures analysis. The second task is the work of developing "concrete utopias," which involves the imagination of desirable futures that are "genuinely possible"—or that may plausibly emerge through the conjunction of ongoing structural trends and counter-hegemonic struggles seeking to transform the world-system.[18] Concrete utopias are not idealized worlds in which all conflicts, inequalities, and forms of injustice have been eradicated. They are better understood, as Thaler puts it, as "temporary stations on a continuous, yet rocky journey" toward more just and sustainable futures.[19] In Wallerstein's terms, they are not "the face of the perfect (and inevitable) future, but the face of an alternative, credibly better, and historically possible (but far from certain) future."[20] Concrete utopian speculation must negotiate the tension between radical imagination and rigorous social, political, and ecological analysis of the possible. In other words, it emerges from the always fraught encounter between utopianism and realism.[21] The tension between utopianism and realism—or between our imagination of the desirable and clear-sighted analysis of the realistically achievable—is inescapable; it is simply impossible to objectively determine what is possible or impossible in any given political conjuncture.[22] But unlike many utopian scholars and visionaries, I place a bit more emphasis on the *realist* side of the equation. In particular, in this book I am less interested in the precise contours of concrete utopian destinations than the *processes and mechanisms* by which they might emerge in practice. In the words of Kim Stanley Robinson, we must "imagine the bridge over the Great Trench, given the world we're in and the massively entrenched power of the institutions that shape our lives."[23] This is easily the most challenging aspect of concrete utopian speculation, but it is nonetheless essential if we want to truly inspire belief in the potential for new worlds. To do this well, in a way that moderates (but does not entirely avoid) the risk of wishful thinking, we need a rigorous, transdisciplinary approach that can illuminate the constraints, obstacles, opportunities, and mechanisms of change that structure the future possibility space. As Erik Olin Wright emphasizes, "Any plausible project of emancipatory transformation must adopt a long time horizon" that explores "not simply the obstacles and openings for strategies in the present, but how those obstacles and opportunities are likely to develop over time."[24] In this sense, one of the key goals of this book is to provide a futures map and "methodology"—one whose affirmation of the role of intuition, imagination, and speculation would make it hardly count as a "methodology" for most social scientists—that can deepen our understanding of how the obstacles and opportunities for progressive transformation are likely to evolve over time in an age of intersecting crises.

The main function of the futures analysis developed in this book can thus be described as a form of "navigational praxis"—praxis in the sense of combining thought and action. This concept is influenced by the work of Nick Srnicek and Alex Williams,[25] who understand "navigation" as a praxis of mapping and exercising agency within complex socioecological systems, a praxis that must constantly update itself as events in the world unfold and new information comes to light. Navigation requires modifying and adapting not just our maps, strategies, and tactics, but also the specific goals of counter-hegemonic praxis as opportunities for transformative agency arise, subside, and reemerge. Counter-hegemonic movements must navigate a constantly evolving planetary-political possibility space, seeking either to dislodge hegemonic configurations and navigate toward concrete utopian potentials, or to mitigate harm and prevent the worst-case scenarios from materializing if it seems we are caught in the whirlpool of a dystopian pathway. In other words, even if we are unlikely to avoid the more dystopian regions of the possibility space, we can at least take steps to make these futures less catastrophic—for instance, by fighting for a 2.5°C rather than a 3°C or 4°C world, or by creating systems of mutual aid to reduce suffering among those of us whose lives are deemed "disposable" to the state and capital, or organizing across political differences to reduce the risks of untrammeled techno-authoritarianism or (eco)fascism. Thus, navigation is not all or nothing—not "revolution or bust"—but a praxis of continuously struggling to realize the best possible future that is within "our" power. Of course, this must transpire across a geographically and intersectionally differentiated landscape of social justice movements in the global north and south, with highly uneven degrees of vulnerability and at times conflicting values and strategies (including conflicts between more reformist and revolutionary, universalist and particularist, techno-modernist and degrowth factions or tendencies). To speak of social justice movements as a "we" is therefore both invitational and aspirational, expressing both potential and hope for a "movement of movements" that can become a planetary force capable of galvanizing and enacting global socioecological transformation.[26]

While future-oriented scholarship is depressingly sparse, I am of course far from the first to investigate planetary futures. It is therefore worth clarifying in general terms how this book builds on and differs from existing approaches. The different futures or "world-system pathways" I discuss in chapters 4 and 5—which include variants of green Keynesianism, collapse, ecosocialism, and what I call "techno-leviathan"—can in many ways be understood as variations of "archetypal" futures that occur in the realms of utopian/dystopian literature and transdisciplinary scenario work.[27] But this book goes further than existing approaches by developing a more deeply synthetic and transdisciplinary approach to planetary futures, perhaps in a way that may be too "eclectic" for some. Rigorously mapping the future calls for nothing less than a pluralist and synthetic methodology that can include as many problems, processes, and systems as possible in our analysis while carefully investigating the relations and feedbacks between them. Yet most futures analyses leave out one or more crucial elements of our planetary predicament—whether climate change, the evolution of capitalism, energy markets, energy "transition minerals" like lithium and copper, food systems, AI and synthetic biology, far-right populism, war and geopolitics, or others. Of course all futures analyses must be selective, and this book is no different. But it goes further than existing approaches toward a more comprehensive analysis of the intersecting problems that structure the future possibility space. (To those who would criticize me in turn for not including every relevant variable, I would merely say: I agree, go further please!) The core challenge of futures thinking is to follow the coevolution of many different variables simultaneously; if we leave out a crucial problem or process, our analysis of the future possibility space remains at best narrow and one-sided, and at worst compromised.

Existing work on planetary futures is also limited by inadequate integration between critical social theory and political economy, on one side, and quantitative modeling, on the other. On one hand, critical social theorists and political economists too often ignore quantitative modeling pro-jections of integrated climate-food-energy-economic trajectories, thereby limiting their understanding of how these systems may coevolve and the constraints they place on the future possibility space. Quantitative models, on the other hand, are by their very nature unable to integrate variables of interest to critical social theorists—particularly the evolution of power relations and counter-hegemonic struggles, as well as other qualitative factors like geopolitical conflict, militarization, police power, race and rac-ism, gender and hypermasculinity, emerging technological risks, identities and structures of feeling, and many others. Models also struggle to cap-ture complex systemic risks that emerge from nonlinear feedback processes in socioecological systems—such as the risk of "domino-like cascades" of earth system tipping points—which means that many if not most of them likely have a "gradualist" bias that underestimates the risks we face (though this should not always be assumed, since many models also leave out sociotechnical innovations and adaptations that may reduce these risks).[28] We should certainly not take the projections of climate, energy, and other models as holy writ: as the common refrain goes, *all models are wrong, but some are useful*. Rather, like science fiction at its best (which I also draw on), models can be a "machine for thinking."[29] In particular, they can deepen social scientific analyses of the climate, energy, food, land-use, and other parameters that constrain the future possibility space; the coevolutionary dynamics of different variables of interest; and the alternative futures that may unfold under a range of different "what if" assumptions and contin-gencies.[30] In sum, if we are to deepen our analysis of the future possibility space, we need to build bridges between seemingly incompatible theories and methodologies across the sciences and humanities.[31] A theoretical framework that can facilitate transdisciplinary synthesis is thus required.

MARXISM, COMPLEXITY THEORY, AND PLANETARY SYSTEMS THINKING

The theoretical framework developed in this book is situated at the intersec-tion of Marxism and complexity theory. It begins with the recognition that no comprehensive analysis of the polycrisis condition can be done without going through the Marxist tradition. Few thinkers have been as prescient as Marx in anticipating the broad contours of the evolution of capitalist modernity and its tendency toward cumulative political-economic and ecological crises. Rather than reducing Marxism to a teleological and economistic reading of history, or a rigid theoretical framework with a set of pre-established theses, we should instead view it as an open-ended investigation of the dynamics, historical patterns, internal tensions and struggles, mechanisms of reproduction, and possible futures of global capitalism.[32] Marxists instinctively grasp the fact that, as Nancy Fraser puts it, we face "not just a set of discrete punctual problems, but a deep-structural dysfunction lodged at the very heart of our form of life."[33] Furthermore, with its synthetic ambition to study the "totality" of global socioecological relations—or the overarching system of planetary metabolism shaped and constrained by global capital—a Marxist framework alerts us to the inherent limits of isolationist analyses and proposed "solutions" that merely defer or displace various problems and contradictions, both in space and time, without genuinely resolving them.[34]

However, while Marxist approaches are vital to the analytic task before us, they are insufficient on their own. Too often they perpetuate a form of what William Connolly calls "socio-centrism," or the tendency to focus on political and economic factors alone—at best acknowledging but without deeply engaging with the earth system sciences, energy studies, ecological economics, and other fields that highlight the geophysical parameters that will constrain the possible futures of capitalism.[35] Ecological Marxists, on the other hand, go much further in this direction by foregrounding the socioecological relations of capitalist (re)production and their planetary consequences. Yet they give us only part of the story. At best these approaches analyze the links between the crises of capitalism and the earth system, at times integrating other problems like pandemic disease and the global food crisis. But they rarely investigate *how* these multiple crises will converge and amplify each other, instead focusing primarily on how capitalism fuels crises in different subsystems.[36] Furthermore, ecological Marxists typically ignore problems like net energy decline, digital surveillance, policing, and emerging technological risks in the realms of AI, synthetic biology, and nuclear weapons. This gives them only a partial glimpse of the planetary predicament as a whole, which is fine for the purposes of more isolationist studies, but not if we want to rigorously investigate planetary futures.

In sum, while Marxist approaches are indispensable, I suggest that an alternative theoretical approach that is nonetheless indebted to Marxist frameworks can provide deeper insight into planetary futures. In particular, our framework should enable us to do the following: (1) situate global capitalism as merely one complex system that coevolves with a broader landscape of self-organizing systems (including ecological, security, ideological, and technological systems or assemblages), (2) map competing hegemonic and counter-hegemonic projects that advance opposed framings of and solutions to the crises we confront, and (3) develop a "methodology" (if that is the right word) that combines theory, history, modeling projections, and imagination to project a range of possible futures for the world-system.

These are the key goals of the theoretical framework that I call "planetary systems thinking." This approach falls under the broad umbrella of what is often called "complexity theory." But we should emphasize that there is not one single form of complexity theory, but rather a set of related approaches aiming to transcend the analytic reductionism, disciplinary isolationism, human/nature dualisms, and assumptions of linear change and causality that dominate the Newtonian scientific worldview.[37] Planetary systems thinking can thus be considered a variant of complexity theory—one that is particularly inspired by world-systems theory, ecological Marxism, Manuel Delanda's framework of "assemblage theory,"[38] Edgar Morin's notion of "planetary thinking,"[39] and the neo-Gramscian "complex hegemony" approach developed by Alex Williams.[40] Planetary systems thinking is the subject of chapter 3, but for now I'll briefly elaborate two of the key concepts that form the foundation of this approach.

The first is the concept of a *complex system*: an open and dynamic system that emerges from a set of feedbacks between component parts but without negating the autonomy of the parts. Rather than the closed or tightly controlled homeostatic systems conceived in the traditions of cybernetics, Parsonian social theory, and Hegelian Marxism,[41] complex systems should be understood as open systems or "dissipative structures" that are continuously exchanging matter and energy with their surrounding environments.[42] They exhibit provisional and often fragile forms of stability that are reproduced through negative feedback mechanisms, though they are liable to rapidly shift between alternative states in response to external shocks or slow shifts in key system parameters.[43] Complex systems also range on a *spectrum of systematicity*: from more heterogeneous and net-worked "assemblages" on one side, in which the parts retain a high degree autonomy (e.g., ecosystems), to more tightly integrated and hierarchically ordered systems on the other (e.g., biological organisms).[44] Throughout this book I often use the term *assemblage* to refer to complex systems that are on the more loosely integrated and heterogeneous side of the spectrum (such as when I speak of security and ideological assemblages). But all complex systems in reality fall somewhere between these two poles, and over time they may shift in one direction or other. The capitalist world-system, for instance, became a more tightly integrated global system during the corporate-led hyperglobalization drive of the 1990s, though rising geopolitical tensions and calls for "decoupling" between the US and Chinese economies may be starting to reverse this trend.[45]

The second key concept is less familiar but equally important to the argument of this book as a whole. This is the concept of the *problematic*, which refers to a nexus of problems that shape and constrain the possible trajectories of a complex system. My use of this concept comes from the work of Manuel Delanda,[46] though he borrows it from the philosopher Gilles Deleuze. I am interested in how Delanda's reworking of this concept can deepen our understanding of the widely used but undertheorized notion of "problematique." The Club of Rome, for instance, in its infamous *Limits to Growth* report spoke of a "World Problematique": a conjunction of intersecting ecological and economic problems that constrains the possible trajectories of the world-system.[47] As William Watts wrote in his foreword to the report, "We continue to examine single items in the problematique without understanding that the whole is more than the sum of its parts, that change in one element means change in the others."[48] Edgar Morin shares this notion of problematique when he writes that there "is no single vital problem, but many vital problems, and it is this complex intersolidarity of problems, antagonisms, crises, uncontrolled processes, and the general crisis of the planet that constitutes the number one vital problem."[49]

Following Delanda, Morin, and the Club of Rome, the concept of the problematique or problematic gives us a way to think about problem-spaces composed of numerous reciprocally determining dimensions. This is exactly the sort of concept we need to analyze the unfolding polycrisis and understand the constraints it places on the possible futures of global capitalism and the earth system. The planetary polycrisis—or what I later call the "planetary problematic"—is the simultaneously singular and multiple crisis that emerges from the interlocking challenges we confront. It is the field of problems that collectively structure the future possibility space, though the future that ultimately emerges will be determined by struggles between competing hegemonic projects to frame, narrate, and provide "solutions" to the problematic. Like the Marxist concept of "totality," the planetary problematic is an abstraction that can guide theoretical and empirical analysis, though its substantive content can emerge, as in Marx's method, only by "ascending from the abstract to the concrete," thereby elaborating the problematic as a "rich totality of many determinations and relations."[50] This book will illuminate the intricate architecture of the planetary problematic in order to inform a counter-hegemonic praxis of navigation. The point is not to try to include everything in our analysis, but rather to highlight the key dimensions of the problematic that are most causally relevant to the planetary future, analyze the positive and negative feedbacks between them, and explore future trajectories that are "coherent" in the sense of following the feedback structure that entangles them.[51]

We should, however, acknowledge that this sort of transdisciplinary futures analysis carries risks. On one hand, there is the risk of oversimplification and mistakes as we venture into fields beyond our disciplinary expertise. The risks are real, but I make no apologies for taking them. To use an expression popularized by Dan Gardner,[52] the "foxes" among us (rather than the "hedgehogs") are more likely to successfully anticipate the broad contours of the future. In other words, rather than ultra-specialized experts, it is the agile and curious—those who venture far outside their disciplinary comfort zones, seeking out new insights from other fields and opposing perspectives that challenge their thinking—who are best placed to connect the dots and develop more realistic maps of the future.[53] Martin Wolf—the chief economics commentator at the *Financial Times*, and a recent convert to systems thinking—makes the point well: "We need to analyse within the [disciplinary] siloes, while also analysing across them. . . . It is bound to irritate professional experts working comfortably in their silos. But . . . it has become clear that such narrowness is folly. It is to be precisely wrong rather than dare to be roughly right."[54] In other words, specialization is still necessary; it provides the raw material with which the foxes among us can build a more synthetic narrative. But to develop more useful and comprehensive maps that will help us navigate the planetary polycrisis, we must get outside of our disciplinary comfort zones, remain agile, take risks, and be willing to continuously address our blind spots—no matter which fields of knowledge this forces us into—and revise our maps accordingly. If we "dare to be roughly right" about the future, then there is no other option.

But there is also a second key risk we must be mindful of: that by focusing on the "big picture" of world-system and planetary-scale futures, we may ignore or subsume diverse experiences and temporalities within a homogenized planetary narrative. As Carl Death writes, the risk is that analyses of planetary futures produce "visions of universal, homogeneous time," which can close down "a sense of hetero-topic time, in which multiple timescales and trajectories exist simultaneously."[55] Put differently, we do not want to pretend as if "the future" will involve one universally shared trajectory, or that the planetary problematic means the same thing for all peoples and places. Far from it. Instead we must emphasize, following Alex Anievas and Kerem Nisancioglu, that global historical processes "are always the outcome of a *multiplicity of spatially diverse nonlinear causal chains* that combine in any given conjuncture."[56] In other words, the future—like the history of global capitalism—will be spatiotemporally uneven *and* combined, involving a multiplicity of local struggles and trajectories across the world-system *as well as* a planetary trajectory that emerges from the combination between them. This means, as Stefanie Fishel and company write, that our analysis of the planetary problematic should be "simultaneously singular and plural, combining the universality of a common entangled existence on planet Earth and the particular and multiple differences of culture, gender, privilege, location, species and temporality."[57] Of course, in practice this is easier said than done. This book places a bit more accent on the *combined* rather than the *uneven* nature of the planetary problematic, which is in part simply the result of my own cognitive constraints, though it is also justified by the globally integrative tendencies of capitalism and the deepening reality of planetary entanglement. I also focus primarily on developments in the world-system "core"—mainly the US, China, and Europe—since what happens in the core will probably have the most influence over the planetary future as a whole. I counterbalance this by showing how trajectories in the core will be shaped and constrained by political struggles across the periphery and semi-periphery (or global south). But this is a limitation of the present study, and further scholarship is needed to develop more fine-grained narratives of possible futures in diverse states, regions, and localities across the world-system.

OUTLINE OF THE BOOK

Chapter 1 explains the concept of the "planetary polycrisis" and provides an overview of its key dimensions, including crises of the earth system, capitalism, energy, food, global security, and identity (or what I call "existential crises"). It provides an empirical foundation that the subsequent tasks of theory construction and future-scenario analysis build upon.

Chapter 2 explores different approaches to the study of planetary futures. It begins by examining the use of quantitative models to develop scenarios—focusing in particular on the *Limits to Growth*, integrated assessment models, and the shared socioeconomic pathways. Next, it explores the role of qualitative scenario exercises in the military, intelligence, and corporate sectors—focusing mainly on the National Intelligence Council's *Global Trends* reports. Finally, it engages with what I call "critical social science futures," or approaches that use the tools of social science and critical theory to explore possible, probable, and desirable futures. The chapter argues that we need a theoretical approach that allows us to develop more synthetic and transdisciplinary futures methodologies, bringing together quantitative modeling projections with qualitative analyses of global political economy, power, and resistance.

Chapter 3 develops the conceptual foundations of planetary systems thinking. The chapter elaborates the book's key concept—the planetary problematic—while also analytically distinguishing between three sets of problems within the overarching problematic: (1) the "socioecological problematic," which refers to the nexus of problems encompassing the earth system crisis, the structural crisis of capitalism, net energy decline, food crises, and pandemic risk; (2) the "violence problematic," which refers to the nexus of war, militarism, policing, "terrorism," and emerging technological risks; and (3) the "existential problematic," referring to the problem of creating shared meaning and belonging, which is generative of problems like nationalism, race and racism, gender and hypermasculinity, and far-right populism. The chapter concludes by describing the futures "methodology" that I call "mapping," which involves qualitative analysis of the key parameters and relations that structure the planetary problematic, using theory and model projections to anticipate how these parameters may coevolve, and imaginatively constructing possible future trajectories that are coherent in the sense of respecting the relations and feedbacks among these parameters. Readers who are less interested in theory may skip this chapter, but they would run the risk of confusion regarding my use of particular concepts in subsequent chapters.

Chapter 4 shifts to a direct investigation of the future possibility space by focusing on the socioecological problematic (SEP). The chapter unfolds in a way analogous to system dynamics models: First, it creates a qualitative "model" of the SEP by describing the relations and feedbacks between ecological, political-economic, energy, and food crises. Second, it develops multiple scenarios for how these crises may unfold following a series of "what if" questions. The chapter shows that both business-as-usual as well as green Keynesian reform trajectories would most likely end up in global collapse—that is, *unless* dramatic technological breakthroughs occur. On the other hand, if revolutionary technological breakthroughs *do* occur, then this would likely drive the emergence of what I call techno-leviathan[58] (elaborated more in chapter 5). The chapter thus challenges the conventional wisdom, at least among mainstream analysts, that policies to accelerate the renewable energy transition and catalyze a "green industrial revolution" would be sufficient to resolve our planetary predicament, even if they help stabilize global temperature increases at 2°C or below. It concludes by shifting to the concrete utopian mode by exploring how deepening crises of capitalism could also create the conditions for ecosocialist transitions, whether in the next fifteen to twenty years or later this century.

Chapter 5 investigates the intersections between the violence, socioecological, and existential problematics. As in chapter 4, I begin by describing the causal relationships between their key components and then explore how they may coevolve in the future. The chapter shows that worsening geopolitical tensions, militarization, and police repression would coincide with socioecological crises to push business-as-usual trajectories further toward collapse. On the other hand, if both green Keynesian reforms *and* revolutionary technological innovations occur, I show that this would likely fuel the emergence of techno-leviathan by unleashing a vicious spiral between increasing insecurity (driven mainly by "democratized" weapons of mass destruction) and intensified military-police repression. Finally, the chapter again shifts to the concrete utopian mode by exploring the potential for what I call "abolitionist" security assemblages in an ecosocialist trajectory, which would entail new practices of security that focus on reducing the root causes of violence rather than relying on military-police responses.

The conclusion summarizes the trajectories sketched in chapters 4 and 5 by encapsulating them in seven main scenarios (what I call the "uneven and combined world-system pathways"), considers their implications for counter-hegemonic praxis, and concludes with some reflections on the role of hope and pessimism in collectively navigating our planetary predicament.

1

THE PLANETARY POLYCRISIS

In philosophical terms, the planetary polycrisis transcends the distinction between the one and the many.[1] In other words, it is not a single crisis that can be reduced to, say, a crisis of capitalism.[2] Nor is it merely a collection of "disparate crises" or unrelated shocks that contingently interact (as World Economic Forum analysts believe).[3] Rather, it forms a set of inextricably entangled systemic crises that are nonetheless irreducible to each other, or that cannot be reduced to a single system or agency (even if we agree that global capitalism is the "ecologically dominant" driver, which I'll elaborate in chapter 3).

The term "polycrisis" was reportedly first used by former European Commission President Jean-Claude Juncker to describe the convergence of crises facing the EU in the wake of the 2008 financial crisis.[4] Largely thanks to the work of Adam Tooze, it has since become a widely used shorthand to capture the basic insight that the totality of political-economic, ecological, energy, and other crises we confront is "more dangerous than the sum of its parts"[5]—that is, more destabilizing, perplexing, and difficult to address than any individual crisis in isolation. The term is also contested. Some claim that the notion of polycrisis is an "illusion," or that the concept means little more than "lots of bad stuff happening simultaneously."[6] A bit more thoughtfully, others argue that it exaggerates the existence of positive feedback mechanisms that lead to mutual crisis amplification while downplaying the role of dampening negative feedbacks (such as energy price inflation triggering economic recession and demand destruction, thus bringing down energy prices and restoring economic growth).[7] As this book will show, the planetary polycrisis no doubt has a complex architecture composed of both positive and negative feedback loops. But it is also unquestionably the case that, as chapters 4 and 5 in particular will demonstrate, the mutually amplifying feedback mechanisms outweigh the dampening negative feedbacks, making the whole far more destabilizing than the sum of the parts. In short, there is no question that the term polycrisis captures something essential about our planetary conjuncture; the real issue is how we understand it and how we analyze the specific crises, intersections, and feedback mechanisms in play.

There are at least two ways to define polycrisis. On one hand, we could follow Thomas Homer-Dixon, Michael Lawrence, and Scott Janzwood by defining it as *a* specific crisis event combining shocks in at least two or more systems—the COVID-19 crisis, for instance, or the 2022-2023 energy-food-inflation crisis precipitated by the Russian invasion of Ukraine.[8] On the other hand, we could follow Tooze by speaking of *the* polycrisis in a broader sense: as a longer-term world historical condition of global turbulence driven by the intersecting crises of capitalism, energy, and the earth system. The former approach may have the advantage of analytic specificity, as Homer-Dixon and company argue. But it downplays the reality that individual polycrises are structurally caused by—and thus expressive or symptomatic of—a broader world-systemic and planetary polycrisis condition.[9] When I speak of *the* planetary polycrisis, my usage is thus closer to Tooze's, though I also occasionally refer to specific polycrisis events.

But to grasp the meaning of polycrisis, we must also clearly define what we mean by "crisis," which should not be overextended to describe "everything bad" (so to speak). In the ancient Greek understanding, *krisis* refers to the critical turning point in a disease, which thrusts the urgency of decision-making upon us.[10] Similarly, through a complexity theory and Marxist lens, crises are "critical transitions" or periods of "far-from-equilibrium" turbulence in which the structures, functions, and feedbacks that define a system's "identity" are ineluctably transformed, though a system may persist in a prolonged "interregnum" for many years before settling into

a new equilibrium.[11] Following this meaning of crisis, the planetary polycrisis can be understood as a protracted phase of critical transition and
turbulence that is unfolding simultaneously across multiple sub-systems
of the world-earth system[12]—from political economy and finance to climate, biodiversity, energy, food, disease, global security, and identity. It
is not (or at least not necessarily) a "permanent" crisis, since a transition
to a new world-earth system configuration could resolve the underlying
tensions fueling the seemingly constant barrage of systemic shocks. But to
imagine and politically construct a new world-earth system equilibrium
requires a sufficiently holistic analysis of the planetary polycrisis; otherwise
we risk merely shifting problems around, or "solving" one crisis by causing
or exacerbating another, thereby perpetuating systemic turbulence.

This chapter begins the process of analyzing the planetary polycrisis by
focusing on its main constituent elements. It focuses on the earth system
and climate crises, the structural crisis of global capitalism, the global energy
crisis, the global food crisis, the potential crisis of automation-induced
technological unemployment, what I call (following Daniel Deudney) the
"crisis of violence-interdependence," and identity or "existential crises."
All of these problems can be understood as crises in the sense described
above, or periods of critical transition and turbulence in particular sub-
systems of the world-earth system. Other global challenges—including
pandemic disease, disinformation, worsening geopolitical rivalries, aging
populations, and population growth—can in contrast be viewed as *stressors*
that converge with and risk amplifying the above crises. I acknowledge
that others would parse the planetary polycrisis in different ways with different emphases (e.g., some would contest the claim that we confront a
"crisis of violence-interdependence," while others would argue that global
health or the US-China rivalry constitute systemic crises).[13] I do not claim
to provide an exhaustive survey that covers every dimension of the polycrisis in this chapter, but I argue that the (sub)systemic crises discussed here
will have the deepest implications for our unfolding predicament and its
possible futures. The relations and feedbacks between these crises, and the
myriad stressors that will make them more fiendishly difficult to address in
practice, are explored in more depth in chapters 4 and 5.

THE EARTH SYSTEM CRISIS

We begin with the earth system crisis, which refers to the rapid (in geological time) disruption of the multiple subsystems of the earth—encompassing the atmosphere, oceans, biosphere, and cryosphere—and the risk of a "state shift" toward a radically new planetary configuration.[14] One of the most useful frameworks that can help us illuminate the multidimensional nature of this crisis is the concept of planetary boundaries (PBs), which refers to biogeochemical processes in the earth system that regulate its overall stability and resilience. Earth system scientists identify nine PBs—including climate, biodiversity loss, interference with the nitrogen and phosphorous cycles, stratospheric ozone depletion, ocean acidification, global freshwater use, land-use change, chemical pollution, and atmospheric aerosol loading. Transgressing each boundary can lead to destabilizing planetary shifts—for example, by undermining the capacities of the earth's oceans, rivers, and forests to support life and regulate the earth's carbon balance.[15] But Will Steffen and colleagues argue that climate change and biodiversity form the key boundaries with the most influence over the earth system as a whole.[16] I therefore focus here first on the biodiversity crisis, including the entwined problem of deforestation, and next on the climate crisis.

Debate is still unfolding about the severity of what is often described as the "sixth mass extinction," but there is little question that the earth's biodiversity is under threat. A broad survey of the evidence by the Intergovernmental Science-Policy Platform on Biodiversity and Ecosystem Services suggests that the global rate of species extinction "is already at least tens to hundreds of times higher than it has averaged over the past 10 million years."[17] The World Wildlife Fund estimates that mammalian, bird, fish, and amphibian populations have on average declined 69% since 1970, with the highest depletion rates observed in Latin America (94% average declines).[18] Extinction rates are even faster for insects—eight times the rate of mammal, bird, and amphibian extinctions—with total insect mass falling 2.5% per year.[19] The full extent and severity of the "insect apocalypse" remains uncertain, due to limited data in many parts of the world.[20] But we know that it is already having negative impacts on pollinator-reliant agriculture, leading to an estimated 3%–5% losses in global fruit, vegetable, and nut production and 427,000 additional annual deaths from malnutrition-related diseases.[21] And we know that these impacts will only worsen if insect extinctions continue unchecked.

The problem of deforestation cuts across the biodiversity and land-use boundaries. The earth continues to lose roughly 4.7 million hectares of forests each year in *net* terms (i.e., deforestation minus reforestation elsewhere), and since 1990 the global forest area has declined by 178 million hectares in absolute terms—an area roughly equivalent to the size of Libya.[22] The continuous loss of old-growth forests and their species assemblages poses a direct existential threat to the Indigenous inhabitants and stewards of these ecosystems, and it may also pose catastrophic risks to humanity and the earth more broadly. For one, an increasing number of scientists fear that many of the earth's tropical forests are now transitioning from carbon *sinks* to *net carbon sources*, in the sense that they release more carbon into the atmosphere than they sequester each year.[23] In particular, the Amazon rainforest, which stores somewhere between 150 and 200 billion tons of carbon, is nearing a point of no return (somewhere between 20% to 40% of forest loss, compared to roughly 17% or even 33% today), beyond which positive feedbacks may push it toward a dry savannah with far less carbon-sequestration potential.[24] The result, were this to occur, would be a massive pulse of additional annual emissions that amplifies our warming trajectory.

Additionally, the COVID-19 pandemic has raised the profile of zoonotic spillover risks, and scientists agree that deforestation and biodiversity loss are among their leading drivers. This is because there may be as many as 600,000 species of mammalian viruses circulating in forest ecosystems, most of them harbored in opportunistic species like bats and rodents that are more likely to thrive in disturbed and denuded habitats.[25] Land-use changes associated with urbanization, infrastructure developments like building new roads, and extractivist activities that encroach on wildlife habitats expand the interface between humans and these massive viral reservoirs, thereby increasing the risk of zoonotic spillovers.[26] It is therefore no coincidence that animal-originating viruses have made the jump to infect humans with increasing frequency over the past fifty years, leading David Morens and Anthony Fauci to claim that "we have entered a pandemic era."[27] So long as our current trajectory of deforestation and biodiversity collapse continues, these spillover events will occur with greater frequency.

In sum, mass extinction represents a crisis for the earth system that will pose significant risks to food production and global health. Many scientists argue that "zero future land conversion of natural ecosystems," including a "half earth" strategy that protects about half of the earth's surface from direct human interference, will be necessary to reverse the tide of mass extinction and reduce these risks.[28] The new Global Biodiversity Framework agreed at biodiversity COP15 in Montreal, which aims "to halt and reverse biodiversity loss" by 2030, may help stimulate more ambitious policies and action to pursue these objectives.[29] But the immediate outlook is not promising: the global finance needed to achieve conservation targets falls short by an estimated $700 billion per year;[30] there is no viable (i.e. profitable) green capitalist strategy to mobilize such funds on the needed scale, let alone one that could also avoid detrimental social impacts (e.g., dispossessing Indigenous communities of their land and resources); and the land-use demands of global agriculture and raw material extraction—the primary drivers of global land-use change and mass extinction—are projected to keep rising in the absence of radical policy, technology, and behavior shifts.[31] More broadly, we must ask: What are the odds that "zero future land conversion" is compatible with a continuously growing capitalist economy? The short answer: not impossible in theory, but highly unlikely in practice (a point I return to below).

THE CLIMATE CRISIS

The climate is the key boundary for the earth system as a whole. The international policy consensus is that warming must be limited to an average rise of 1.5°C or 2°C above preindustrial levels in order to ward off the risks of catastrophic and potentially irreversible climate impacts. The Intergovernmental Panel on Climate Change (IPCC) claims that to give us a fifty-fifty chance at stabilizing global warming at 1.5°C requires reaching "net zero" emissions by 2050, which means the point at which remaining emissions are offset by carbon removal techniques, whereas a fifty-fifty shot at 2°C would require reaching net zero emissions by 2070.[32] Unfortunately, despite a recent wave of net zero pledges by governments, corporations, and investors, current policies have us nowhere near on pace to meet the 2°C (let alone the 1.5°C) target.

Compared to where things stood right after inking the Paris Agreement—when government policies and fossil fuel production plans put the earth on track for at least 3.6°C by 2100—the climate situation today is looking less apocalyptic (at least taken by itself).[33] But there remains little to celebrate: Climate Action Tracker estimates that even with new climate and energy policies adopted in 2022 (e.g., the Inflation Reduction Act in the US, and the EU's Fit for 55 package), a current-policies scenario still puts the earth on track for 2.7°C by 2100.[34] If the Nationally Determined Contributions (NDCs) adopted by states under the Paris Agreement were translated into concrete policies, we would be on pace for 2.4°C of warming by the end of the century, whereas an optimistic scenario—in which the US, China, and 129 other countries fulfill their recent pledges to reach net zero by mid-century—could put us on track for 1.8°C.[35] Some are thus hopeful that the global wave of net zero pledges means the 2°C target may remain in reach. But these net zero targets, at least so far, are little more than what Hayley Stevenson calls "bullshit," or empty promises that are not backed up by concrete policies and interim targets, and which betray indifference to the actual scale of near-term policy and behavioral changes needed to put us on pace to meet the 1.5°C target.[36]

Far from 2°C, our most likely climate trajectory at present lies somewhere between the current-policies and NDC scenarios (i.e., between 2.4 and 2.7°C). This is not good. Yet things are probably even worse than these projections suggest. This is because the climate models used by Climate Action Tracker and the IPCC almost certainly underestimate the risk of positive feedbacks in the earth system—including from forest dieback, terrestrial and subsea permafrost melt, methane from wetlands, and weakening arctic albedo.[37] For example, as previously noted, multiple studies suggest that most climate models have unrealistic assumptions about the capacity of forests to continue sequestering CO_2 in the future. One study predicts that the Amazon will become a net carbon source by the mid-2030s, which would be "decades ahead of even the most pessimistic climate models" used by the IPCC.[38] Another shows that we will likely reach a global-scale tipping point in which land-based ecosystems worldwide become net carbon sources potentially as early as the 2040s.[39] As the authors write, "Failure to account for this results in a gross overestimation of climate change mitigation provided by terrestrial vegetation."[40] Wildfires pose another feedback risk that is not accounted for in IPCC projections. The summer 2021 fires that burned across Eurasia and North America, for instance, released a record 1.76 tonnes of CO_2—comparable to the annual emissions of Russia—showing that these fires are already having massive climate impacts.[41] Additionally, many scientists argue that the risk posed by carbon and methane release from the terrestrial permafrost has been underestimated by mainstream climate science, since recent studies show that it is already thawing much faster than IPCC models anticipate, and the same is true of methane release from wetlands across the planet.[42]

As Mark Lynas suggests, these positive feedbacks together mean that "we could be seeing half a degree or more of additional warming by the end of the century."[43] In other words, it means that current policies likely put the planet on pace for closer to 3.2°C rather than 2.7°C of warming by 2100. Even more worrying, it means that failure to meet the 2°C target could plausibly push us down what Will Steffen and colleagues call a "Hothouse earth" pathway, defined as a trajectory in which "biogeophysical feedbacks in the Earth System . . . become the dominant processes controlling the system's trajectory," which would raise temperatures ever-higher by triggering a "domino-like cascade" of tipping points.[44]

Stepping back for a moment, we should remember that even if we do not confront the imminent threat of tipping-point cascades, this is no reason for complacency: a 2.7°C rise by 2100, even 2°C, would be bad enough. We are already witnessing dangerous impacts at the current 1.2°C average rise, seen in the two- to threefold increase of category 4 and 5 hurricanes and typhoons; record-shattering heatwaves and flooding events across the planet, including the summer 2022 flood in Pakistan that killed 1,739 and affected more than 33 million people; worsening drought conditions across the American West, Southern Europe, the Amazon region, and most of the African continent; historically unprecedented wildfires across North America, Europe, Australia, and even the Arctic; and accelerating polar ice melt, which may have already triggered irreversible collapse of the West Antarctic Ice Sheet and be putting us on track for 6–7 meters of sea level rise over the coming centuries.[45] At 1.5°C, an estimated 16% of the population will be vulnerable to at least two or more potentially deadly climate impacts, and this would rise to 29% in a 2°C world (affecting about 2.7 billion people), with by far the highest levels of vulnerability seen in Africa, the Middle East, and South Asia.[46] And, again, things will probably be even worse than climate models are projecting, given that climate shocks—such as the summer 2021 heatwave in the Pacific Northwest, and the horrific summer 2021 floods in Central China—have been occurring in recent years that are "simply 'off scale' compared with what atmospheric models forecast." This suggests, as Michael E. Mann says, that models are "underestimating the magnitude of the impact of climate change on extreme weather events."[47] It goes without saying that things would only get worse as the earth gets hotter. If or when the planet nears 3°C, as Lynas describes, we would witness a "globe-girdling region of drought engulfing a substantial majority of the world's current population and land area," which would mean unprecedented water stress, crop production failures, and a "new era of escalating food commodity price shocks" capable of triggering "large-scale civilizational collapse."[48] In other words, while 2°C would pose an existential risk to much of the global south—particularly to populations in sub-Saharan Africa and low-lying island states—compound climate-economic-food system risks could threaten the stability of even rich countries and the world economy as a whole if/when we near 3°C. And the positive feedbacks unleashed at 3°C could push the earth to 4°C (highly unlikely before 2100, but possible over the course of the twenty-second century), which would mean agricultural collapse across the world's major breadbaskets and increasingly regular heat extremes that exceed the limits of human survivability, thereby rendering much of the earth's midlatitude regions uninhabitable.[49] Depending on how political systems respond, the threat of human extinction would become very real, especially if titanic carbon-cycle feedbacks are unleashed at 4°C that trigger a "runaway warming process"—a low-likelihood but human extinction-level event that cannot be discounted.[50]

In sum, the climate crisis poses a clear existential threat to humanity and the earth, and current policies *may* be setting us up for a hothouse-earth trajectory, but certainly at least for an era of worsening climate damages. What must be done to stop it? Liberal policymakers and pundits tell us that the problem is primarily one of technology and political will: axe the fossil fuel subsidies, raise the price on carbon, force corporations and banks to disclose their climate-related financial risks, ramp up investments in renewable energy and other green technologies, and markets will get the job done. But what if the challenge is far more structural, as ecological Marxists and post-growth ecological economists claim? In other words, even in the best-case green capitalist scenario in which the above policies are adopted, would this be enough to put us on pace to meet the Paris Agreement targets and reduce stress on other planetary boundaries—in this way achieving "green growth"?

THE DECOUPLING CHALLENGE

The question of whether truly "green growth" is possible can be boiled down to the feasibility of "decoupling." In other words, can continuous compound GDP growth be decoupled from carbon emissions, rising material and energy consumption, deforestation, and other environmental impacts? Decoupling can take different forms. First, as indicated, there is the question of *what* growth is decoupling from, which can focus on specific environmental impacts like deforestation and carbon emissions, or from specific forms of resource consumption like energy and raw materials.[51] Second is the question of whether decoupling is *relative* or *absolute*: relative decoupling occurs when the indicator in question *grows more slowly* than GDP, whereas absolute decoupling occurs when the indicator plateaus and eventually *declines* even as GDP continues to increase.[52] For our purposes, the key question is whether global GDP can *absolutely* decouple from carbon emissions, material and energy consumption, and land-use conversion, since this would be necessary to stabilize the earth system.

The belief that absolute decoupling *is* possible is foundational to the philosophy known as ecomodernism,[53] which can be considered the dominant approach to environmental policymaking across the world-system. The evidence that ecomodernists draw on to support this belief comes from a number of empirical indicators and modeling projections. For instance, eighteen rich countries have achieved absolute decoupling between GDP and CO_2 emissions, while many have also achieved absolute decoupling from energy and "domestic material consumption" (which measures total raw material consumption within a nation's territory).[54] The global economy has also steadily improved the "energy intensity" of economic growth—from roughly 2.21 kilowatt hours of energy for every dollar of GDP (kWh/$) in 1990 to 1.62 kWh/$ in 2012—though total world energy consumption grew from roughly 106,000 terawatt hours to 158,000 terawatt hours during the same period.[55] In other words, we have so far only observed *relative* decoupling between energy and GDP at the global scale, though some models appear to illustrate the feasibility of *absolute* decoupling in the future: the International Energy Agency (IEA), for example, in its *Net Zero by 2050* scenario suggests that global energy demand by 2050 could be 8% smaller than in 2020 even as it "serves an economy more than twice as big."[56] Taken together, decoupling proponents claim that the evidence supports their contention that there is no irreconcilable contradiction between growth and sustainability, so long as the right policies are in place to steer markets away from fossil fuels toward low-carbon technologies, nature protection, and greater resource efficiencies.

Unfortunately for the green growthers, a burgeoning intellectual cottage industry of critiques of decoupling arguably refutes or at least significantly weakens the evidential basis of their claims.[57] These critics make two key arguments: first, that the evidence used to support the feasibility of absolute decoupling from material and energy throughput at the *global* scale is flawed at best; and second, that there is even weaker evidence that absolute decoupling, from both emissions and overall material throughput, could occur *fast enough* to meet the Paris targets and stabilize the earth system.

First, as we have seen, proponents of the absolute decoupling narrative tend to fixate on local examples of relative or absolute decoupling in rich countries, claiming that these national-scale examples prove the potential for absolute decoupling at the global scale. The problem is that this narrative tacitly assumes a world of separate "national" economies, which hardly captures the interlocking socioecological relationships that inextricably entwine "national" economies in the era of neoliberal globalization.[58] Thus they ignore not only the way in which rich countries have offshored much of their material- and energy-intensive manufacturing processes to the global south, but also the broad shadow of energy and materials embodied in their imports (not just those directly present in the goods consumed, but also the broader web of materials, energy, land, and infrastructures needed to mine, manufacture, and transport these goods to their destinations). For instance, Thomas Wiedmann and colleagues show that while the EU, the United States, and Japan have grown their GDP while stabilizing or even reducing domestic material consumption, a broader analysis of their "material footprint"—which includes this broader shadow of energy and materials embedded in their imports—demonstrates that material and energy consumption levels have kept pace with GDP growth. They conclude that "no decoupling has taken place over the past two decades for this group of developed countries."[59] Focusing on the global economy as a whole, Giorgos Kallis and Jason Hickel show that resource intensity improved over the course of the twentieth century, though the early twenty-first century has seen a faster rate of growing resource consumption than global economic growth. Thus the global economy as a whole, far from "dematerializing," has actually been "rematerializing" in recent decades.[60]

Proponents of decoupling would respond that even if absolute decoupling in material and energy consumption has not yet occurred at the global scale, more ambitious policy reforms would make it possible in the future. However, several studies show that even the most optimistic modeling scenarios fail to prove the possibility of absolute decoupling at the global scale. For example, in a "high-efficiency" scenario modeled by the UN Environment Programme—which combines a high and rising carbon price plus a doubling in the rate of material efficiency improvement—absolute decoupling remains out of reach: global resource use grows more slowly but steadily to reach 132 billion tons in 2050 (compared to roughly 100 billion tons in 2020).[61] Focusing specifically on energy, while scenarios developed by the IEA and IPCC assume that absolute decoupling between growth and global energy consumption is possible, Paul Brockway and company show that their models ignore or underestimate "rebound effects" (both direct and indirect[62]), which can "erode more than half" of the gains from energy efficiency improvements as the overall scale of economic activity increases.[63] In other words, these modeling projections are highly unrealistic, and in a high efficiency scenario we would witness accelerated relative decoupling at best.

Second, given the time-sensitive nature of the climate crisis, there is the question of how quickly absolute decoupling of growth from emissions might occur. Among ecological economists, practically no one says that absolute decoupling between global economic growth and emissions is impossible. But the critical question is whether this could occur fast enough to meet the 1.5°C or 2°C targets. A number of analysts project that

3%–4% annual emissions reductions at the global scale are roughly the fastest rates possible in a context of continuous economic growth, due to both the lack of mature technological options to decarbonize the "hard-to-abate" sectors (more on this below) and the difficulties of decarbonizing a continuously growing energy supply.[64] However, reaching *zero* emissions by 2050—that is, without the aid of carbon dioxide removal (CDR) techniques—would require annual declines of about 8%. This is widely viewed as impossible short of a massive World War II–style mobilization that would entail unprecedented disruption to the world economy (comparable to the effects of the COVID-19 lockdowns).[65] Therefore, nearly all the 1.5°C scenarios developed by the IPCC and IEA rely on a *massive and rapid* deployment of CDR by 2050. The IEA, for example, in its net zero scenario, projects that CDR would need to mop up about 7.6 gigatons (gt) of CO_2 per year by 2050.[66] Given the IEA's unrealistic projections about absolutely decoupling global GDP from energy, 7.6gt of annual CDR is almost certainly an underestimate, but we must appreciate the scale of the challenge posed by even such relatively small figures. The problem is that these techniques are either immature or unproven at scale, or would entail massive land, energy, and water requirements—with major consequences for food production, biodiversity, and social justice.

Bioenergy plus carbon capture and storage (BECCS), for example, has become the "savior technology" for many climate modelers and policymakers, which could hypothetically provide a carbon *negative* source of energy that removes 10gt–20gt of carbon per year.[67] But an Oxfam report warns that even just 11gt of BECCS-based CDR would mean "devoting an area up to twice the size of India—to growing bioenergy crops," which would have massive consequences on forests, biodiversity, water consumption, and food prices.[68] Because of the limited land area that would be available for BECCS if we want to avoid competition with food production and biodiversity protection, one study estimates that BECCS deployment should be limited to just 100 million tons of carbon removal per year (this does not, of course, preclude the possibility that it *will* be scaled up beyond such limits, regardless of the social and ecological impacts).[69] The obvious problems with BECCS have caused other scientists to put their faith in direct air capture (DAC), which is much less land intensive and wouldn't entail similar trade-offs with food production. But the problem here is not only that DAC technology remains unproven at scale; large-scale DAC plants can capture about 1 million tons of CO_2 per year, which means that to capture 5 *giga*-tons per year by 2050 would require building five thousand plants between now and then, or *166 per year for the next thirty years* (to put this in perspective, as of 2022, just eighteen DAC facilities were operating in the world, capturing less than 0.01 mt of CO_2/year).[70] Such a rapid buildup is not impossible in theory, but Ryan Hanna and company show that this would require an "extreme crash deployment program," mobilizing about 2% of global GDP per year, starting in the next few years.[71] And even in this case, Hanna and company (who, it is worth highlighting, are advocates rather than critics of DAC) suggest that such a program would likely be able to remove only 2.2gt–2.3gt per year in 2050.[72] And this is all under very optimistic assumptions. We fundamentally do not know if large-scale deployment of CDR technologies will work, not only because these techniques are not yet proven at scale, but also because scientists fear they could weaken the earth's land and ocean carbon sinks—meaning that the carbon removed may be largely offset by weakening sinks elsewhere.[73] Thus the risk here is that CDR promotes "mitigation deterrence" in the short run—that is, reducing the urgency of near-term mitigation due to faith in future CDR deployment—and fails to capture and sustainably store carbon in the long run,[74] meaning a double whammy of wasted resources and worse-than-expected climate chaos.

In contrast to these more technological options, the best hope for large-scale CDR appears to be a massive global-scale program of reforestation and carbon-sequestering agroecology, along with restoring carbon-sequestering ecosystems like grasslands and mangroves, which could potentially remove 10gt per year by 2050.[75] But this brings us back to the question of whether growth can be absolutely decoupled from land-use conversion and biodiversity depletion, since this would be necessary to realize the potential of rewilding and reforestation: Even if global capitalism accelerates the renewable energy transition and brings down carbon emissions, can it roll back the broader earth system crisis?

As previously mentioned, many scientists believe that to reverse biodiversity loss and make rewilding goals achievable, "zero future land conversion of natural ecosystems" would be necessary, which would mean halting the key drivers of land-use change: agricultural expansion, raw material extraction, and infrastructure development.[76] Among these drivers, agricultural land expansion may be the easiest *in principle* to reverse, since global meat consumption—by far the biggest driver of agricultural land use—could be reduced without necessarily constraining global economic growth (e.g., by shifting to plant-based diets and/or lab-grown meat).[77] We must not downplay the difficulties of halting agricultural land expansion while producing food for a growing population, particularly given projections of continuously rising meat consumption and the technical, economic, and cultural obstacles to scaling up alternative proteins.[78] But *absolutely* decoupling from raw material extraction at the global scale is most likely an insurmountable challenge: at current rates global material throughput—including minerals, metals, and biomass for nonfood uses—is likely to rise from 100 billion tons in 2020 to between 170 and 184 billion tons by 2050.[79] Yet preventing further degradation of land and biodiversity would require *at least* stabilizing if not radically shrinking this material footprint before 2050 in order to reduce the risks of irreversible biodiversity collapse in sensitive ecosystems.[80] In other words, total resource consumption would need to remain at least stable, if not decline dramatically, even as global GDP *triples* by 2060 and *continues to grow exponentially*. As discussed earlier, the modeling evidence suggests this is not possible.[81] Even in a best-case scenario, in which the land footprint of the global food system declines from reduced meat consumption while circular economy policies lead to dramatic increases in recycling rates, it is very unlikely that global GDP could be absolutely decoupled from land use and biodiversity loss. The evidence from history suggests that, while such decoupling between growth and land use could occur in rich countries that offshore much of their material footprints, continuous exponential increase in the overall scale of economic activity would at least temper if not wipe out these gains at the global scale: for instance, increased recycling would moderate but not reduce the rate of primary material extraction, while much of the land saved from reduced meat production would be put to other commercial uses (e.g., for new mega-infrastructure projects, solar and wind farms, bioenergy, mining, data centers, and so forth) in order to support the needs of a world economy that is two to three times larger than today—and still exponentially growing.[82]

In sum, it appears extremely unlikely that global capitalism is capable of achieving the 1.5°C target, and it is even less likely if not impossible that it could roll back the broader earth system crisis. And this does not even touch on the question of whether it could do it in a way that promotes social justice rather than fueling continued displacement and dispossession of already marginalized communities to scale up solar and wind energy, BECCS plants, afforestation, lithium/cobalt/copper mines, and other green capitalist projects—creating what Matthew Paterson and Peter Newell call a "decarbonized dystopia."[83] This is what ecological Marxists and environmental justice activists have been arguing for decades, and their conclusions appear to be borne out by contemporary ecological economics. And, as we'll see later in this chapter, while technological innovations could make these challenges more manageable for global capital, they would do so at the cost of creating or exacerbating other problems.

THE STRUCTURAL CRISIS OF GLOBAL CAPITALISM

In addition to provoking crises in the earth system, global capitalism is also facing its own internal crisis. Many economists have argued in recent years that global capitalism confronts a condition they call "secular stagnation," or a long-run trend toward weakening GDP growth—particularly in the "advanced" economies of the global north, but now increasingly in China as well.[84] A number of trends support this perspective: the declining rate of global GDP growth, from 5.5% in 1967 to 2.5% annually in 2016; steadily increasing reliance on public and private debt to deliver growth, rising from about 100% of global GDP in 1965 to 360% in 2021; declining labor productivity growth, falling from roughly 4% in 1970 to 1.5% in 2015; weakening rates of capital investment in production and R&D, falling from over 20% of global GDP in the 1970s to between 14%–18% over the past decade; and a corresponding increase in financial speculation and "rent-seeking" activities among capitalists (i.e., strategies to profit from control over scarce assets rather than investing in production).[85] Marxists share much of this analysis, but they often describe this condition as a "structural crisis," or a situation in which a particular mode of accumulation—in this case the "neoliberal" regime, defined by the weakening power of labor relative to capital, the dominance of finance capital in the accumulation process, and an ideology of market liberalization and unrestricted capital mobility—is no longer able to provide a secure foundation for capital accumulation.[86]

One way to articulate the root of the problem is that the neoliberal assault on working-class power, by creating a situation of skyrocketing inequality and stagnant wages, created immense pressure to rely on financial deregulation and easy credit in order to "sustain demand in an economy suffering from demand-deficiency syndrome."[87] In the lead-up to the 2007–2008 financial crisis, for instance, US consumer demand—a key driver of global economic growth—was largely propped up by the wealth effect generated by an unsustainable housing boom, which was itself fueled by an opaque and brittle financial superstructure underpinned by mortgage securitization. In this sense, the 2007–2008 crisis, while originating in the financial system, was the symptom of a deeper structural malaise in global capitalism: a condition, as Tooze writes, in which it must continuously rely on "abnormal financial bubbles" in order to "achieve no more than a 'normal' rate of growth."[88] The 2007–2008 financial crisis led to stronger regimes for supervising financial systemic risk and ensuring adequate capital buffers for systemically important financial institutions, thus reducing the risks of banking crises. But the quantitative easing programs and near-zero interest rates pursued by central banks had the primary effect of funneling more money into financial speculation; propping up asset prices for the investor class; and fueling increased risk-taking among hedge funds, pension funds, asset managers, and others seeking higher returns in a near-zero or negative interest rate environment.[89] As a result, during the period between the 2008 financial crisis and the 2020 pandemic, inequality only increased—with the top 1% capturing 95% of the gains from economic growth since 2009—and growth remained precariously reliant on near-zero interest rates, unprecedented debt levels, and asset bubbles.[90] These problems only got worse as a result of COVID-19 and the crisis-fighting measures pursued by rich countries: inequality reached new heights, with the richest 1% capturing nearly two-thirds of wealth generated since 2020; corporations were holding over $5 trillion in cash by the end of 2020, which they were funneling mainly into speculation more than productive investment (e.g., on real estate, tech stocks, and cryptocurrencies); central banks brought interest rates back to near-zero after a brief trend toward "normalization" between 2017 and 2019; and total debt levels reached a historically unprecedented 360% of global GDP.[91]

Global capitalism has thus been limping along thanks in large part to an unsustainable regime of low interest rates and easy credit, which may now be coming to an end via the 2022 inflation shock. The world economy experienced a rapid yet uneven recovery from the pandemic lockdowns in 2021, with global GDP rising 6% after a 3% contraction in 2020. This rapid recovery, along with lingering supply-chain difficulties and a convergence of stressors in global food and energy markets (more on this below), set the stage for the largest surge of worldwide inflation in nearly forty years, which peaked at an annualized rate of 12.1% in October 2022.[92] Mainstream economists typically view this as a problem of "excess aggregate demand" or "too much money chasing too few goods," driven in large part by the COVID-19 stimulus spending. But in reality, while pandemic stimulus played a role, the inflation surge has been far more a problem of energy, food, and supply chain shocks, followed by profiteering by powerful corporations—who react to upstream cost increases either by protecting or *amplifying* profit margins—followed in turn by struggles among workers to prevent real wage declines.[93] Non-financial corporations across the global north have thus reaped record profits, while wages among workers have on average failed to keep up with cost-of-living increases.[94] Despite this, while some European countries have turned to unconventional policy measures like windfall taxes and even price caps, for the most part the inflation-fighting response remains dominated by interest rate hikes to put a damper on consumer demand, investment, employment levels, and wages—thereby risking recession, financial instability, and further misery for workers. The blunt tools of central banks have struggled to get inflation under control, which is projected to continue declining but at a slower rate than previously expected: from 8.7% in 2022 to 7% in 2023 and 4.9% in 2024.[95] But the social, economic, and political consequences of interest rate hikes—meaning higher debt-servicing costs for a massively overindebted world economy—are highly uncertain and a source of trepidation for many.

Nouriel Roubini, for one, argues that the world economy is headed for a period of unprecedented turbulence. This could take the form of cascading debt crises and a deep global recession triggered by interest rate hikes, or sustained long-run inflation as central banks pull back in order to prioritize financial stability.[96] As Cedric Durand puts it, central banks confront a choice between financial collapse and "slow-motion agony," with the more likely scenario being "a real devaluation of financial assets through a [slow-motion] crisis . . . in the form of permanent mid-level inflation."[97] Many analysts, including the World Bank, agree that while inflation is likely to decline in the near term, there is nonetheless a "growing risk that it may remain elevated" for years to come as a result of several headwinds—including persistent energy and food supply shocks (exacerbated by climate change); rising geopolitical tensions and associated deglobalization trends (e.g., the trend toward "reshoring" and/or "friend-shoring" manufacturing in critical industries, leading to rising labor and production costs); and a shrinking labor supply due to aging populations.[98] While the outlook is far from certain, the reemergence of inflation may thus signify a structural shift in the world economy rather than a transitory blip resulting from the COVID-19 crisis and subsequent war in Ukraine. At best this would make it more challenging for technocratic elites to manage the deepening contradictions of capitalism, given the trade-offs between reducing inflation, ensuring financial stability, protecting growth and jobs, and keeping the lid on populist unrest.[99] At worst, it may set up global capitalism for what Roubini calls the "the worst period of stagflation the world has ever seen": a period of stubbornly high inflation, high unemployment, and stagnant growth punctured by increasingly severe recessions.[100]

It is possible that Roubini (widely known as "Dr. Doom") may be downplaying the capacities of rich countries to contain the fallout of rising debt and inflation without necessarily provoking a crisis of epic proportions. But his argument becomes more persuasive—and global capitalism's predicament more challenging—when we take a closer look at the energy problem, which goes much deeper than Putin's war.

THE GLOBAL ENERGY CRISIS

As of mid-2021, few would have claimed that we face something like a global energy crisis—in the sense of a crisis of fossil fuel *supply*, not simply of its climactic effects. But February 2022 changed all that. Putin's invasion of Ukraine triggered what the IEA describes as "the first truly global energy crisis": a series of price shocks in natural gas, oil, coal, and electricity markets that rocked most of the world-system, with Europe and import-dependent states in the global south bearing the brunt.[101] European natural gas prices rose tenfold between February 2021 and August 2022 as Russian gas deliveries fell by 80%. Rising demand for liquified natural gas (LNG) and coal to meet shortfalls helped push up coal and LNG prices around the world. Brent crude briefly reached over $123 per barrel—tripling above its lows in early 2020 and reaching its highest levels since 2008—and remained well over $100 for months before declining to $76 as of June 2023 (due to looming recession fears). The social and political consequences were immense: 70 million people across the global south lost access to electricity; low-income populations in rich countries were forced to choose between "eating or heating;" oil and gas companies enjoyed record profits; and rich countries (particularly in Europe) considered or adopted previously unthinkable measures—including windfall taxes on energy companies, price caps, and energy rationing.[102]

How should we explain this crisis? It is clear that energy price inflation was merely turbocharged, not caused, by the Ukraine war: oil, gas, and coal prices had been steadily climbing over the course of 2021, the result of rapidly rebounding energy demand following the COVID-19 lockdowns, along with regionally specific exacerbating stressors (e.g., a brutal 2020–2021 winter and low gas storage in Asia and continental Europe, drought-induced constraints on hydropower production in China and Brazil, coal shortages in India, and slow summer wind speeds across Europe).[103] Beyond these proximate causes, many analysts agree that underinvestment in oil and gas was a deeper structural cause: after a period of elevated prices between 2008 and 2014, the "shale revolution" led to an oil and gas supply glut in 2014–2015 that forced oil and gas companies to scale back on investment in exploration and production; investment in renewables, meanwhile, was far from sufficient to compensate for any potential shortfall in fossil fuel supplies.[104] This was only made worse by the pandemic shock, which temporarily demolished oil demand by a third and plunged oil prices to historic lows in April 2020, leading to a 30% contraction of capital expenditures in the oil and gas sector.[105]

There is no question that "underinvestment" is a key cause of the crisis. But it begs the question of *why* this has become such a problem in the first place, leading many in the oil and gas sector to speak of "structural supply under-investment."[106] Periods of low prices by themselves are an insufficient explanation, especially given recurrent projections from the IEA and others of continuously rising oil and gas demand plus depletion from existing fields. Some analysts put the blame on net zero climate policies: as the fossil fuel lobbyists have recently argued, by calling for the eventual phaseout of fossil fuels, governments are disincentivizing oil and gas investment in the present and thus exacerbating supply shortfalls.[107] The argument has logic, but so far little evidence: as the IEA shows, net zero pledges across sixty-eight countries plus the EU are "not yet correlated with changes in fossil fuel spending" relative to countries that have not adopted such pledges.[108]

Rather, to make sense of structural underinvestment and gain a deeper understanding of the current energy crisis, we should turn to a concept developed by ecological and biophysical economists: energy return on energy investment (EROI), or net energy. EROI refers to the net or surplus energy that is left over after subtracting the amount of energy used to obtain that energy, which includes the energy used directly in the extraction process (e.g., to pump oil and gas out of the ground), as well as the energy used indirectly in various stages of its lifecycle (e.g., the energy used to manufacture a power plant or oil rig, or to deliver the energy to its point of use).[109] For example, *conventional* oil flowing from the giant "elephant" fields like Ghawar in Saudi Arabia has a high EROI (estimated at about 40 units of energy extracted for every unit of input, or 40:1) and relatively low production costs, whereas *unconventional* oil sources like US shale, the Canadian and Venezuelan oil sands, offshore and arctic oil have significantly lower EROI (estimated at about 7:1 for offshore and between 2:1 and 3:1 for shale and oil sands).[110] While mainstream energy analysts typically neglect the framework of EROI, they are at least partially aware of its implications when they highlight the increased capital intensity and higher break-even price of unconventional oil and gas compared to conventional sources—that is, the fact that oil prices must be around $60–$80 per barrel or higher to turn a profit for shale and oil sands, compared to $20–$40 for conventional fields (though different analysts come to widely different estimates).[111] By itself, the more conventional focus on break-even prices goes a long way toward understanding the current energy crisis: as the world economy becomes more reliant on unconventional oil and gas reserves that require larger upfront capital expenditures, the investment case for new oil and gas exploration steadily weakens—particularly given the poor financial performance of US shale companies, who are now being disciplined by investors to focus on boosting shareholder returns rather than increasing production, as well as the large uncertainties about future demand and price trajectories in an era of energy transitions.[112]

But this does not give us the whole story. From a mainstream economic perspective, the only significant constraint on fossil fuel supply is economic or financial, not geological: that is, a shortage of investment to extract the earth's vast reserves of burnable carbon. Indeed, when viewed through the lens of *total* resources, the amount of oil and gas that remains to be extracted is enormous. But net energy analysis shows us that what really matters is the total energy extracted *minus* the energy needed to extract and deliver that energy to its point of use. Thus even though total fossil fuel resources remain huge, global EROI decline can constrain economic growth by reducing the net energy available for the rest of the economy, since this means a greater share of energy and capital must be devoted to the energy sector.[113] Indeed, this is what the historical record shows: for most of the twentieth century up until 1960, when (according to Charles Hall) average EROI for fossil fuels was approximately 60:1, energy spending as a share of global GDP averaged about 3%–4%. Yet, in the past decade, when Hall estimates that average fossil fuel EROI declined to about 17:1, energy spending doubled, to roughly 6%–8% of GDP on average—reaching a record 13% of GDP in 2022.[114] Thus it is likely no coincidence that the peak-EROI era coincided with the "golden age" of Keynesian capitalism, while declining average EROI in the past thirty years has been associated with the era of "secular stagnation."[115]

Furthermore, a crucial point, which EROI scholars often emphasize, is that net energy decline is a *nonlinear process*, since the net energy available for the rest of the economy decreases in a nonlinear fashion once EROI dips to between 10:1 and 5:1—a phenomenon they call the "net energy cliff."[116] In other words, the difference between an EROI of 10:1 and 5:1 is larger than the difference between 50:1 and 10:1, and there is an *even larger* difference between 5:1 and 3:1. The concept of *percentage net energy gain* can help provide more clarity on this phenomena: an EROI of 50:1 means that 98%

of the energy created is made available to (or "gained" by) the non-energy sectors of the economy, which falls to 90% with an EROI of 10:1; subsequently, the net energy gain falls to 80% with an EROI of 5:1, to 75% with an EROI 4:1, to 66% at 3:1, and to 50% at 2:1.[117] Notably, it appears that the world economy may already be moving down the slope of the net energy cliff: when using an "EROI final" methodology that accounts for the total energy invested in refining and delivering energy to the point of use, Paul Brockway and colleagues show that average EROI for all fossil fuels falls to somewhere between 5:1 and 6:1.[118] While such calculations should be taken with a grain of salt, considering major uncertainties and methodological disagreements regarding EROI calculations, they nonetheless suggest, as the authors write, that "we may already have entered this zone of highly nonlinear change, where further modest declines in [EROI] lead to increasingly rapid reductions in the net energy available to society."[119]

The theory that we may be nearing a net energy cliff for fossil fuel EROI is no doubt speculative. Furthermore, average global EROI estimates can only teach us so much, since they overlook important differences between different fuels and their production costs in different regions. But if the theory is roughly accurate, then it means we may be confronting a period of nonlinear decline in the *net* fossil energy available for the world economy, which would manifest in the form of an increasingly large share of global GDP and energy consumption being devoted to the energy sector—meaning less energy and capital available for the rest of the economy—and a long-run trend toward rising energy costs, elevated supply risks, and economy-wide inflation that may get continuously worse as fossil fuel EROI continues to decline at a nonlinear rate.[120]

Even if we are not really facing a net energy cliff, but simply a period of structural underinvestment caused in part by EROI decline, then this still bodes ill for energy security in the coming years (particularly for oil security, the dominant energy source globally). As the IEA projects in its "stated policies" scenario, oil demand will grow to 103 million barrels per day (mb/d) by the mid-2030s and then very slowly decline until 2050. Yet low investment in recent years means "there are relatively few new resources under development and a dwindling stock of discovered resources in the non-OPEC world available to be developed," while "persistent under-production" among OPEC producers relative to their targets "may be a harbinger of the risks that lie ahead."[121] As the IEA concludes (in uncharacteristically stark terms), "Something has to change in order to avoid an energy-starved world characterised by continued price volatility."[122] The situation may be less critical if oil demand tracks more closely with British Petroleum's (BP) projections, which, in their post-Putin shock "new momentum" scenario, anticipate oil demand plateauing around 100 mb/d until 2030 before slowly declining.[123] But (as I elaborate in chapters 4 and 5), the energy security situation may be even worse come 2030 than both BP and the IEA anticipate, due to their unrealistic assumptions about US shale production, unexpected headwinds that may constrain OPEC production, their limited incorporation of energy rebound effects,[124] their neglect of increased demand pressures from ramped-up militarization, and ignorance of the impacts of worsening climate chaos on energy infrastructure. In sum, the net energy cliff hypothesis is not essential to the argument that we confront significant fossil fuel supply risks in the coming years. But it suggests that the energy problem may be deeper and less tractable than most analysts realize. It would mean that we may be facing not just a series of transitory price spikes, but rather a looming contradiction between the growing energy demands of global capitalism and the shrinking net fossil energy that will be available in the coming years.

Yet all of this depends on the speed and ultimate course of the renewable energy transition. As the IEA says, given the looming contradiction between underinvestment in fossil fuels and projected rising demand, a "surge in spending to boost deployment of clean energy technologies and infrastructure provides the way forward, and this needs to happen quickly or global energy markets will face a turbulent and volatile period."[125] In short, if business-as-usual is leading us toward a future of worsening climate-energy-economic polycrises, then an accelerated energy transition appears to be the "poly-solution" we need.[126] Is renewable energy up to the challenge?

RENEWABLE ENERGY TO THE RESCUE?

There is no question that renewable energy (RE) is on a roll. Solar photovoltaics and wind energy costs have fallen 73% and 22%, respectively, since 2010, and numerous analysts claim that we are on the cusp of an exponential

RE takeoff driven by a "Learning-By-Doing" feedback.[127] Thanks in part to the 2022 energy shock and new policies adopted—including the EU's REpowerEU plan, the US Inflation Reduction Act, and China's fourteenth Five-Year Plan—the IEA projects that global solar and wind generation will double between 2022 and 2027—a 30% increase above its 2021 forecast—with solar PV poised to surpass coal as the world's largest electricity source by 2027.[128] Solar PV is already the least costly option for new electricity in a majority of countries worldwide, and it will likely be the cheapest option nearly everywhere by 2030.[129] From this view, the relentlessly declining cost curves of solar, wind, and battery storage technologies will soon lay waste to the fossil fuel industry and enable states to simultaneously resolve the climate, energy, and inflation crises.[130]

Others, on the other hand, argue that renewable energy will unlikely be able to power industrial consumer capitalist societies on their own (at least for a long time). In this view, the intermittency challenge (i.e., the fact that RE sources are variable and must be supplemented by large amounts of storage, baseload power, and/or new transmission lines); the existence of difficult-to-electrify sectors that currently lack technologically mature low-carbon alternatives; and the intensive land-use requirements, mineral demands, and (arguably) low EROI of solar and wind energy make deep decarbonization a much larger challenge than assumed by techno-optimists.[131] Thus rather than an imminent era of RE abundance, the pessimists claim that the limits of RE technologies mean they will be unable to replicate the historic energy bounty provided by fossil fuels. If they are right, then the contradiction between growing energy demands and net energy decline may be fatal for global capitalism—forcing the world economy down a trajectory of energy demand destruction, deindustrialization, and economic contraction.[132]

Because of its technical nature, this debate has been ignored by the vast majority of social scientists, even by energy IPE scholars.[133] But it is an incredibly important one, since the technical potential and limits of renewable energy will critically shape the possibility space of world-system futures. In certain respects, the evidence favors the more optimistic position: RE technologies are rapidly expanding, continuously improving, and most likely face no absolute geophysical limits to how far they could expand in the long run. However, at the same time, a number of political, economic, and technical barriers may critically constrain the RE transition and prevent it from solving the entwined crises of climate, energy, and inflation. In this section, I do not provide an exhaustive survey of each and every obstacle, but focus on a few that will be most relevant to my scenario analysis in chapter 4: (1) scaling up finance for renewables; (2) the hard-to-abate sectors; (3) transition mineral bottlenecks; (4) land-use conflicts; and (5) the EROI question.

Starting with finance, the challenge is to rapidly scale up public and private investment in renewables, which is needed both to achieve climate targets and "avoid an energy-starved world" in an era of structural fossil fuel supply underinvestment.[134] Yet, despite rapidly falling costs, the IEA shows that "clean energy investments"—which for them includes not only solar and wind energy, battery storage, EV chargers, grid modernization, and end-use efficiency, but also carbon capture, nuclear energy, biofuels, and hydrogen-based fuels—remain far too slow and would need to triple, from $1.4 trillion in 2022 to $4.2 trillion in 2030, in order to meet these objectives.[135] At the same time, despite underinvestment relative to projected future demand, upstream investment in new oil, gas, and coal expansion—estimated at $520 billion in 2022, merely a small decline from the 2015–2019 average—remains remarkably resilient (arguably horrifyingly so) despite rapidly falling costs for solar and wind.[136] The problem, as Brett Christophers shows, is that RE investments on average continue to offer less attractive returns than oil and gas projects—typically 8%–10% for renewables, and 15% or higher for oil and gas.[137] Even though renewables will create cost savings in the long run through both lower electricity bills and avoided climate damages, their higher upfront costs and weaker returns for capital in the short run form a critical constraint on mobilizing the necessary finance. As Christophers says, "investment decisions are not determined by price. The nub of investment is profit."[138] Thus, according to McKinsey, only 40%–50% of the needed investments in RE come with a "positive investment case," that is, sufficient returns for capital, while the rest must be met by either public spending or policies to unlock private finance (e.g., through higher carbon pricing, scaling up subsidies for RE technologies, and policies to "derisk" RE investments for private capital).[139] The problem is particularly acute in the global south, which (excluding China) faces higher capital costs for RE projects due to their perceived risks and weaker returns.[140] This makes it clear that—contrary to some techno-optimistic assumptions—cheapening solar and wind electricity on their own will not save us. Only a public investment and policy push among the major emitters, and global financial reforms that dramatically increase RE investments in the global south, could plausibly do so.

The second key challenge involves the so-called "hard-to-abate" sectors, or those that cannot be easily (if at all) electrified—including shipping, aviation, steel, cement, fertilizers, plastics, aluminum, and other heat-intensive industries—and thus cannot be decarbonized using mature technologies.[141] These sectors are responsible for roughly 20%–25% of annual global emissions, and the IEA acknowledges that decarbonizing them will "depend on technologies that are at the prototype or demonstration stage," including next-generation batteries and biofuels, "green" hydrogen produced by electrolysis, and CDR technologies like DAC.[142] While we should expect cost declines along with occasional breakthroughs in the coming decades, neither should we underestimate the challenges. I have already discussed the problems with CDR. Additionally, policymakers and business leaders are increasingly putting their faith in green hydrogen (or "blue" hydrogen, using natural gas plus carbon capture), which is touted as a clean energy carrier that can be used for heat-intensive industries and long-distance transport sectors that are difficult to electrify. Yet hydrogen produced by renewables was three to five times more expensive than fossil fuel–based hydrogen in 2021, and aligning with the IEA's net zero scenario would require electrolyzer production to expand *6,000-fold by 2050*.[143] As Adrian Odenweller and colleagues conclude, this will not happen *even if* rapid cost declines allow green hydrogen production to expand at the same rate that solar and wind have over the past decade. And in the absence of much greater public investment in green hydrogen supply chains, private investment and production will remain constrained by a "vicious cycle of uncertain supply, insufficient demand and incomplete infrastructure."[144] Furthermore, while many are bullish on the future of hydrogen, others view it as an inefficient and wasteful way to use renewable electricity: as Jorgen Henningsen claims, green hydrogen may face energy conversion losses of up to 50%, and it makes little sense from an efficiency standpoint "to waste half, or more, of the green electricity for producing hydrogen," especially if it proves more challenging than expected to rapidly scale up renewable electricity (because of the other obstacles discussed here).[145] In sum, decarbonizing the hard-to-abate sectors by 2050, while producing comparable quantities of "green" steel, cement, plastics, and aviation fuel at affordable prices, would likely require "near-miraculous technical advances," as Vaclav Smil says.[146] Such advances are plausible (indeed, they happened with solar), but it would be unwise to assume they are inevitable or even the most likely scenario, particularly within the time frame needed to hit the Paris targets.

Transition metals are the third challenge. As is commonly recognized, building up RE infrastructures will require a massive mining expansion: the IEA estimates that meeting net zero targets would require increasing lithium extraction rates by forty times, graphite by twenty-five times, cobalt by twenty-one times, nickel by nineteen times, and rare earths by three to seven times above contemporary levels, alongside huge increases in copper, manganese, iron ore, bauxite, silicon, and other minerals.[147] Mining for these metals is already producing "green sacrifice zones" across the planet—such as the toxic landscapes surrounding China's rare earth mines—which are set to accelerate in the coming years.[148] But from the perspective of "green" capital—for whom these sacrifice zones are a necessary evil—the primary challenge concerns how rapidly mining can be scaled up to meet rising demands. The IEA, for instance, projects that, in an accelerated energy transition, rising demands for copper, lithium, and cobalt would outpace expected supply: existing mines and projects under development would "meet only half of projected lithium and cobalt requirements and 80% of copper needs by 2030."[149] High prices would of course incentivize new mining projects to meet rising demands, but this would take time: on average, between 2010 and 2019, it took twelve years to complete exploration and feasibility studies for new mines, and four to five years to complete construction.[150] A key challenge for mining companies (as for oil and gas companies) is future demand uncertainty: on a "stated policies" pathway, current projects will nearly meet future demand, thus obviating the immediate need for scaling up upstream investments; but if policies unexpectedly shift, then it will take time to ramp up production.[151] High prices would also incentivize enhanced recycling and technological substitutions (e.g., shifts to solid-state or sodium-ion batteries that use alternatives to lithium). But it would similarly take time, investments, and proactive policy to scale up recycling infrastructure. And the substitutes—even if manufacturing capacities can be rapidly scaled up—would entail lower-performance batteries (unless there are further technological breakthroughs).[152] In a context of rapidly rising RE demand, there would most likely be no easy or quick solution for mineral bottlenecks, and this could plausibly, in conjunction with other obstacles, derail the transition or at least slow it down considerably.

Fourth comes the issue of land-use conflicts during the transition. Because of the low "power densities" of renewables compared to fossil fuels,[153] the transition will require devoting large swathes of land to solar and wind farms, transmission lines, and energy storage infrastructure. For instance, one study estimates that the "visual footprint" of RE infrastructures needed to hit net zero in the US may take up between 3% to 14% of the US land area in the lower 48, and this percentage would be much higher in densely populated small countries.[154] In short, the land-use implications of the RE transition will be big, but the main issue is not land scarcity but rather politics. Both onshore and offshore wind energy expansion has been fought and often delayed across Europe—sometimes fueled by legitimate social and ecological concerns, but also by right-wing populists who view turbines as "symbols of monstrous, pointless waste, and futile political correctness" (to quote Roger Helmer of the UK Independence Party).[155] Similarly, as solar energy projects have proliferated across the rural US, they are often fought tooth and nail by organized conservative opposition fueled by a mix of legitimate concerns, misinformation, and culture-war sentiments, leading to lengthy permitting delays across the country.[156] As the RE transition advances, with new RE projects tripling or even quadrupling above current levels, we can expect that organized resistance and permitting delays will persist if not worsen significantly. This provides a necessary reality check: it is easy to project accelerated RE deployment as costs come down in the abstract world of energy models. But in the real world of politics, as Tooze writes, "the energy transition will have to be won, community by community."[157] Intelligent land-use planning (e.g., designating go-to areas where RE development would have low environmental and social impacts, as the European Commission has proposed) can moderate these conflicts.[158] But the sheer mass of land required, as well as coastal seas for offshore wind, means they cannot be circumvented.

Finally, there's the EROI problem, which is a more uncertain, contested, and lesser-known obstacle compared to the others. Energy researchers have traditionally argued that solar and wind energy have low EROI compared to fossil fuels, but recent studies have begun to complicate this calculus. For instance, as discussed earlier, Brockway and company show that average fossil fuel EROI falls to between 5:1 and 6:1 when using an "EROI final" methodology.[159] This is much lower than traditional "EROI standard" estimates and suggests that solar and wind—often estimated to have an average EROI of 10:1 or higher—may provide similar or even greater net energy levels, especially as fossil fuel EROI declines.[160] But Brockway and company (as they acknowledge) do not apply a similar methodology to RE sources to provide a fair comparison—one that accounts for the energy costs of manufacturing, transporting, installing, and mining and refining the materials for solar panels and wind turbines. By developing a methodologically consistent comparison of fossil fuels and renewables that builds on Brockway et al., Carlos de Castro and Iñigo Capellán-Peréz show that average fossil fuel EROI declines to roughly 4:1, though solar and wind continue to have even lower energy returns on average: approximately 2.9:1 for onshore wind, 2.3:1 for onshore wind, 1.8:1 for solar PV, and 0.8:1 for concentrated solar power.[161] These estimates—like all EROI calculations—should be taken with a grain of salt. But they show that, despite ongoing net energy decline for fossil fuels, current solar and wind technologies most likely continue to provide even lower energy returns on average. And while innovation will improve the energy yields of individual RE technologies, other factors may counterbalance these gains—such as the need for scaling up battery storage and building out new transmission lines as the share of intermittent renewable electricity expands; the "decreasing returns in the potential of renewables" as the sunniest and windiest locations are progressively occupied; and increasing energy requirements to extract minerals as the highest quality ores deplete; among others.[162]

Most importantly, when using a "dynamic" rather than "static" model of EROI, Capellán-Peréz and colleagues show that the EROI of RE systems will be even lower during the early to middle phases of the transition because of their *high upfront energy and mineral costs*.[163] In other words, even if RE technologies end up having higher energy returns over their lifetimes than fossil fuels, the problem is that they would deliver significantly lower levels of net energy in their early phases, when huge quantities of energy and minerals are needed to rapidly build up low-carbon energy systems. And the faster the speed of transition, the higher the upfront energy and mineral demands, meaning a larger share of energy must be diverted from other economic uses toward the energy and mining sectors.[164] This problem, while studied primarily by energy scholars and ecological economists, has also been recognized by Isabel Schnabel of the European Central Bank: "The faster and more urgent the shift to a greener economy becomes, the more expensive it may get in the short run," which may "exert upward pressure on prices of a broad range of products during the transition period."[165] In other words, as multiple studies show, the risk is that an accelerated transition—while critical to meet the Paris targets—would shrink the net energy available for the rest of the economy, thus increasing the risks of energy shortages, mineral bottlenecks, and economy-wide inflation—or what some have called "greenflation."[166]

While the implications of EROI analysis for the RE transition are contested, the evidence suggests that net energy will most likely decline at least in the early to middle phases of the RE transition. The end-point of the RE transition would be a more sustainable and affordable energy system with lower operating costs, but there are two key dangers that may prevent us from getting there: continuous and possibly fatal delays, or backlash against an accelerated transition. On one hand, the combination of inadequate finance, mining bottlenecks, land-use conflicts, and permitting delays may continue to constrain the pace of transition. This would not only be detrimental to the climate, but would also threaten global energy security, since insufficient investment in RE systems would leave renewables unable to make up for fossil fuel supply shocks if/when such shocks materialize. Even worse, net energy decline for fossil fuels, which are critical inputs in RE supply chains, may constrain the fossil energy supplies that are available for the *RE transition itself.*[167] We already saw this to some extent in 2022–2023, when rising costs for energy, aluminum, steel, and polysilicon increased solar, wind, and battery costs by 10%–20%—ending their decade-long streak of continuous cost declines.[168] Such disruptions could persist or even get worse as fossil fuel EROI continues to decline, thus foiling techno-optimistic predictions of continuous exponential cost reductions for solar and wind (as I discuss in chapter 5, worsening geopolitical tensions between the US and China could be an even bigger source of disruption). On the other hand, if the RE transition *does* accelerate, the danger is that the net energy available for the global economy would plummet, creating a high-risk greenflation and a right-wing populist backlash against the transition.

In sum, while the optimists are most likely right about the immense energy potential of renewables, others show that political, economic, and technical obstacles will make the transition far from smooth and painless. To the contrary, it would need to cross a turbulent river to reach the destination, and precisely what this destination will look like remains far from certain. "Energy descent" or "collapse" is one possible future, but so is an RE-powered green industrial revolution. Given the uncertainties, in chapter 4 I explore different scenarios for how the RE transition may unfold.

THE GLOBAL FOOD CRISIS

In one sense of the term, "crisis" is simply a *normal* condition of the global food system, given that roughly 2.3 billion people suffer from at least moderate food insecurity, while 828 million suffer from acute hunger and malnutrition.[169] This has been further exacerbated by the war in Ukraine, which raised food costs by 12.7% on average in G7 countries over the course of 2022, and pushed them even higher in the global south (e.g., between 20%–30% in Egypt, and up to 100% in Turkey).[170] But as climate change, aquifer depletion, soil erosion, net energy decline, and other stressors combine with a growing global population, the currently "normal" condition of global food system pathology may be pushed toward further breakdown. As the Food and Agriculture Organization (FAO) claims, at "no other point in history has agriculture been faced with such an array of familiar and unfamiliar risks," and the "growing frequency and intensity of disasters, along with the systemic nature of risk, are jeopardizing our entire food system."[171] Thus there is no question that the global food system is confronting a systemic crisis, but the question is how the crisis is framed, what causal drivers are emphasized, and which solutions are proposed.

To start, we know that the global food system is a key driver of the earth system crisis. First, it is a direct contributor to climate change: agriculture is responsible for about 18% of emissions, whereas the broader food system (including transportation, packaging, processing, and retail)—is responsible for somewhere between 26% and 35% of total emissions.[172] Second, agriculture is the primary driver of land-use conversion, since it is responsible for clearing or transforming roughly "70 percent of the world's prehistoric grasslands, 50 percent of the savannas, 45 percent of the temperate deciduous forests and 25 percent of the tropical forests."[173] As a result, agriculture is not only a dominant force behind the biodiversity crisis but also a key driver of zoonotic spillover risk. One study estimates that agricultural drivers since 1940 have been responsible for more than 50% of all zoonotic disease events, which is largely the result of land-use change but also the product of large-scale livestock operations that facilitate rapid viral mutation.[174] The persistent, aggressive evolution of avian influenzas, which have frighteningly high case-fatality rates, are of particular concern in this context.[175]

Beyond the risks it poses to humanity and the earth, the globalized industrial food system is itself facing a host of converging stressors. Productive topsoil is being steadily eroded much faster than new soil is forming, leading to moderate or severe degradation of roughly one-third of the world's farmland.[176] Water-based "food bubbles" are also forming in more than eighteen countries—including major global producers like the United States, China, and India—where food production depends on depleting local aquifers faster than they can regenerate.[177] These problems already appear to be stifling efforts to raise agricultural yields: for maize, rice, wheat, and soybeans—which together account for nearly two-thirds of global calorie consumption—the rate of growth in annual yield increases has been slowing since the early 1980s.[178] This means that while global crop production continues to grow in absolute terms, it is "doing so at an ever slower rate."[179] By itself this is not necessarily a problem, since the world already produces enough food to feed a population of 10 billion. But in the context of a continuously growing population (projected to reach between 9 and 10 billion by mid-century), globally rising demand for meat and animal products, and the dominance of a neoliberal or "corporate food regime" that relies primarily on ecologically damaging yield increases to maintain affordable food prices, such trends are indeed alarming.[180]

And this is before we bring climate change into the picture. The IPCC shows that temperature and precipitation trends, while raising yields in certain high-latitude regions, have already contributed to declining yield growth rates globally and will continue to do so in the future. It projects that, for each degree Celsius of temperature increase, wheat yields may be reduced between 2.9% and 6%, rice by 3.2%–3.7%, maize by 4.5%–7.4%, and soybeans by 3.1% relative to a world without warming.[181] Given techno-productivist claims that food production must increase 50%–70% by 2050 to feed a growing population,[182] these projections are not insignificant, but still fairly moderate. However, as the IPCC acknowledges, they only account for the effects of average temperature increases and changing precipitation patterns—ignoring the impacts of intensified drought, extreme weather events like flooding and hurricanes, pollinator declines, land and soil degradation, aquifer depletion, and increased stress from pests—all of which are set to get worse as the climate warms.[183] One study shows that these yield decreases would be much higher even when just accounting for the conjoined impacts of rising temperatures and worsening pests, which together could diminish key staple yields by 10%–25% for each 1°C of warming.[184] It is impossible to anticipate precisely how yields will evolve in the future, given the difficulties of modeling complex cascading risks and anticipating future adaptations.[185] However, if current trends in production and power relations in the global food system go largely unchanged, then we will at best be entering a world with incrementally yet continuously rising rates of hunger and food insecurity, and at worst a world of agricultural breakdown with dramatic consequences.

To get a deeper understanding of the world we may be entering, it is important to highlight not just average yield changes but also the changing probabilities of more extreme production failures that could occur in any given year. In particular, we should highlight the risks posed to the world's main breadbasket regions—particularly the United States, China, India, Brazil, and Argentina, which collectively account for roughly 72% of global maize, wheat, rice, and soybean production.[186] The problem is that the neoliberal food regime—based on principles of agricultural specialization, free trade, and reduced emergency storage to draw on in times of stress—has undermined agricultural self-sufficiency around the world (particularly in the global south) and made most states heavily reliant on these major breadbaskets. In other words, as Anthony Janetos and colleagues explain, the global food system has been "highly optimized for efficiency in peacetime under relatively stable environmental conditions."[187] But we are entering a world of highly unstable environmental and geopolitical conditions, which will threaten the world's breadbaskets and increase the risks of major production shocks in these regions (i.e., 10% declines or higher in a given year).[188] Monica Caparas and company, for instance, project that by mid-century these breadbaskets will face production shocks at least every other year—seven times more frequently than at present—whereas "synchronous breadbasket failures," involving shocks that simultaneously strike two or more of the world's key breadbaskets, may occur once in every three or eleven years (depending on assumptions about future irrigation potential).[189] Again, these projections are subject to major uncertainties, which could make them overly pessimistic or optimistic, but if roughly accurate this would have immense implications: an unprecedented global food crisis—far worse than either the 2011–2012 or 2022 food shocks—occurring once every three or eleven years by mid-century. And these events would become even more frequent and severe if/when the planet nears 3°C.

In sum, the conjunction of land and soil degradation, pollinator collapse, worsening climate shocks, population growth, and slowing yield increases means that the world-system is likely headed for unprecedented food system turbulence. The unsustainability of the current food system is widely recognized, even among agribusiness firms, and it is thus extremely unlikely that there will be no reforms or adaptations to improve its sustainability and resilience. But dominant framings of the global food crisis continue to advance quite similar policies and technologies that have produced this crisis in the first place—for example, increased specialization and reduced trade barriers, genetically modified seeds that improve drought tolerance, and "climate smart agriculture" methods that involve marginally less resource-intensive versions of the same industrial agricultural model.[190] At best these efforts represent moderate tweaks to the global food system, and an important question is whether these limited reforms and technological adaptations—that is, those that are compatible with the neoliberal food regime power structure—would be able to do more than "soften" global food system breakdown (which I address in chapter 4).

TECHNOLOGICAL PROBLEM-SHIFTING

There is no doubt that technological innovation can help moderate the crises discussed above. Advances in RE technologies, battery storage systems, biofuels, and next-generation nuclear reactors may reverse the trajectory of net energy decline. Genetically modified seeds, lab-grown meat, vertical farming, and the application of drones and AI to agriculture could boost the resilience and sustainability of industrial farming in a climate-changed world. Advances in AI, synthetic biology, 3D printing, the "internet of things" (IoT), and robotics may enhance labor productivity while improving material and energy efficiencies—thereby rejuvenating economic growth, creating new outlets for profitable productive investment, and powering the "green" industries of the future.

In particular, many believe that a new threshold of exponential technological advance—sometimes called the fourth industrial revolution (FIR)—is imminent, referring to mutually reinforcing innovations in AI, biotechnology, nanotechnology, robotics, the IoT, 3D printing, quantum computing, and other emerging technologies. Klaus Schwab, the founder and executive chairman of the World Economic Forum, articulates these hopes when he claims that we "have yet to grasp fully the speed and breadth of this new revolution. . . . Many of these innovations are in their infancy, but they are already reaching an inflection point in their development as they build on and amplify each other in a fusion of technologies across the physical, digital, and biological worlds."[191] These technologies form a key pillar of what William Robinson describes as an "emerging post-pandemic capitalist paradigm" based on enhanced digitalization, automated production of goods and services, and investment in FIR technologies.[192] Powerful forces are converging to drive this agenda across the world-system, including the rising power of the American and Chinese technology giants, green capitalist reformist efforts (seen in calls for a "digital revolution for sustainable development"), and the pressures of geopolitical competition in the domains of AI and digital infrastructure between the United States, China, and Europe.[193]

Whether or not such technologies will allow global capitalism to muddle through the above crises remains to be seen. However, we can anticipate that many if not all of them will give rise to a host of other problems.[194] For one, digital and AI technologies can themselves reinforce the earth system crisis because of their unavoidable reliance on energy, mineral, and water-intensive data centers and server farms, which may consume fifteen times more energy in 2030 relative to 2020 levels.[195] In short, they are not the engines of "dematerialization" that many take them to be. But in this section I highlight other forms of what we can call "technological problem-shifting," or ways in which technological "solutions" to ecological crises may create or exacerbate other problems. I focus on three entwined problems: technological unemployment, a nascent crisis of violence-interdependence, and rising risks of techno-authoritarianism.

The first key problem is how the FIR will drive automation and technological unemployment across the global economy in the coming decades. Most economists continue to play down the risk of technological unemployment, claiming that the same mechanisms that compensated for job losses in past automation waves will continue to operate in much the same way.[196] But others, like Daniel Susskind, convincingly demonstrate why these assumptions are flawed (at least if the "exponential" dreams of techno-optimists turn out to be true). Simply put, they ignore how advances in AI and robotics would "relentlessly" become capable of performing more and more tasks done by humans today. As a result, any overall expansion of economic activity, which in the past would have compensated for lost jobs, will eventually simply lead to more work being taken up by machines, with human labor pushed into "an ever-shrinking set of activities."[197] This would undoubtedly be a qualitatively novel situation relative to previous waves of automation in the history of capitalism, but the question is how rapidly and to what extent it would drive technological unemployment. Kai-fu Lee, for one, anticipates that around 38% of jobs will be *automatable* (not necessarily *automated*) by the early 2030s, and 40%–50% by 2040, whereas actual levels of structural unemployment could reach 20%–25% between 2040 and 2050 (compared to a global unemployment rate of 5.8% in 2022).[198] A survey of nearly three hundred experts in the AI field came to similar conclusions, anticipating on average 24% unemployment by 2050.[199] Susskind, in contrast, expects automation to unfold more gradually, suggesting that structural technological unemployment may reach 15%–20% later this century—but he also emphasizes that it would exacerbate job precarity, wage suppression, and inequality well before then, since more and more workers will be competing for more poorly paid and insecure positions.[200] Even if the more gradualist and lower end projections are correct, this would still create the risk of "tremendous social disorder and political collapse stemming from widespread unemployment and gaping inequality," as Lee remarks, and it is questionable to what extent 20%+ structural unemployment would be compatible with the survival of capitalism (at least as we know it).[201] The extent to which automation proceeds will be contingent on numerous factors, including working-class struggles over wages, investment patterns, and the pace of technological innovation in AI and robotics.[202] We should not assume an ineluctable automation-driven crisis, but the risk teaches us that global capitalism may be trapped between a rock and a hard place: protracted stagnation on one side, and technological unemployment on the other.

A second problem is how FIR technologies may trigger what I call, following Daniel Deudney, a "crisis of violence-interdependence."[203] Violence-interdependence (VI) refers to the capacity of states and non-state actors to inflict physical violence across geographic distance. A "crisis" of VI can be thought of as a situation where technological advances in the forces of destruction can no longer be effectively constrained by existing security practices—leading to a situation of accelerating violence potential that forces states to adapt. In this sense, if the nuclear revolution created a crisis of VI for the Westphalian state system, then we can say that emerging FIR technologies may similarly unleash unprecedented levels of VI that push the world-system toward a "crisis" point.[204]

The weaponization of biotechnology is arguably the most alarming dimension of the crisis. Biotechnology refers to a broad category of technologies that "exploit biological processes for industrial, medical, or other production purposes," which includes synthetic biology and genome editing techniques (e.g., CRISPR-Cas9) that can tinker with biological organisms or even design new ones from scratch.[205] The promise of synthetic biology is vast—and we can largely thank it for the mRNA vaccines that helped save millions of lives during the COVID-19 pandemic[206]—but by the same token so is its destructive potential. As a National Academies of Sciences (NAS) report puts it, "It is possible to imagine an almost limitless number of potential malevolent uses for synthetic biology."[207] For example, existing pathogens can be modified, or new ones designed from scratch, with much higher virulence and resistance to vaccines.[208] Furthermore, CRISPR gene editing can be weaponized in ways that go beyond modifying pathogens: disease-carrying insects could be modified to transmit diseases more easily, formerly harmless insects could be altered to carry dangerous diseases, and pollinating insects could be infected with "gene drives" to propagate genetic variants that induce population collapse—thus disrupting agricultural systems.[209] At present, as biosecurity experts emphasize, bioweaponization risks are overwhelmingly posed by states and state-sponsored groups, since these capabilities remain highly dependent on advanced technologies and laboratory equipment.[210] However, the NAS report shows that improvements in DNA synthesis technologies "have followed a 'Moore's Law–like' curve for both reductions in costs and increases in the length of constructs that are attainable," and that "these trends are likely to continue."[211] The result—as Gaymon Bennett and colleagues aptly suggest—is a "black swan waiting to happen."[212]

Emerging bioweaponization capacities may be the most alarming dimension of the emerging crisis of VI, but they aren't the only one. Digitalization across the world economy has unleashed cybersecurity vulnerabilities that will intensify further as the IoT dramatically increases the number of networked devices and sensors in cities, homes, cars, electricity grids, food supply chains, and other critical infrastructure systems in the coming years, which may triple from 11.7 billion networked devices in 2020 to 30.9 billion in 2025 and even reach into the trillions in subsequent decades.[213] Nuclear weapons remain an ever-present apocalypse waiting to happen, which may become more dangerous in an age of digitally networked vulnerabilities, technological advances in hypersonic missiles and outer space–based weapons, and pressures to automate nuclear decision-making—creating what has been described as a destabilizing "cyber-AI-nuclear nexus" (which I discuss in chapter 5).[214] Furthermore, military-grade drones are also becoming more widely accessible to nonstate actors as their manufacturing costs decline, which could be used to target political leaders, indiscriminately attack crowds, or even deploy aerosolized bio-agents.[215] In conjunction with advances in 3D printing, which could make it easier for nonstate actors to acquire weapons systems that "previously required expertise and industrial capabilities exclusive to more-advanced states"—including killer drones, bioweapons, and possibly even nuclear weapons—these converging technologies will exacerbate bio, nuclear, and cybersecurity risks while creating new kinds of risks that are impossible to anticipate.[216]

In sum, while we should be not oversensationalize the risks, it is evident that FIR technologies will increase the destructive power available to nonstate actors, perhaps dramatically. But the key danger here is arguably not the threat posed by nonstate actors, but rather the reactions it will trigger among governments and security apparatuses—particularly given the unprecedented powers of surveillance, policing, and military force projection that these same technologies will also bring into existence. This brings us to the third and arguably most pressing risk posed by FIR technologies, which is that they may unleash a vicious spiral between worsening VI and techno-authoritarian state power.[217]

Technological advances are already empowering militaries, security agencies, and police forces with uniquely extensive and intensive methods of surveillance and lethal force projection. For example, facial recognition technologies, which can match stored or live video footage of individuals with a database, are creating new systems of "digital enclosure" that make it easier for states to monitor, track, and detain citizens.[218] Emotion recognition algorithms are another emerging technology that can be paired with facial recognition cameras to monitor crowd sentiment and identify potentially "risky" individuals, which for the world's security agencies and corporations hold "the promise of reliably filtering friend from foe, distinguishing lies from truths, and using the instruments of science to see into interior worlds," as Kate Crawford describes.[219] AI-based predictive policing is another emerging practice already being deployed across China, the United States, and Europe, which includes location-based algorithms that mine data on the links between places, events, and crime rates to predict when and where crimes are more likely to happen, as well as algorithms that "draw on data about people, such as their age, gender, marital status, history of substance abuse, and criminal record" to anticipate which individuals will commit future crimes.[220] The problem of racial bias here is obvious, since the algorithms are themselves trained on racially biased police data that emerge from a structurally racist political economy, thus reinforcing policing practices in the US that disproportionately harass, detain, and kill Black people—as well as Chinese policing practices that disproportionately target Uyghurs.[221] These practices have thus far reached their apogee in China's Xinjiang region: as Darren Byler shows, the Chinese state has constructed a "digital enclosure of unprecedented scale and depth" that envelops Uyghur life, involving dense networks of biometric cameras, GPS tracking, checkpoints, facial recognition systems, and emotion recognition systems designed to "eliminate the ideological problems of prisoners" detained in so-called "reeducation camps."[222] While it is undeniable that such systems are developing with unique intensity in China, it would also be wrong to fixate on China while ignoring how similar systems of predictive policing, facial recognition, digital enclosure, and apartheid-like systems of racialized border and mobility controls are also slowly enveloping Western liberal democracies.[223]

This brief survey merely gives us a small taste of the techno-authoritarian powers that may emerge as FIR technologies advance. For example, future innovations may enable the rise of robot soldiers and insect-sized killer drones; data-mining algorithms that can more effectively monitor, analyze, and police the oceans of big data that currently overwhelm analytics capacities; militarized nano and neuro-technologies that can monitor brain activity and (according to their developers) read human thought itself; and other technologies of violence and repression that we cannot yet imagine.[224] The FIR will thus enable historically unprecedented forms of techno-authoritarian power that even relatively progressive governments will feel increasingly compelled to deploy in an era of "democratized" weapons of mass destruction. Such techno-authoritarian trends have of course been evident since the 9/11 terrorist attacks, and they were further bolstered by the COVID-19 pandemic. But the truth may be that we have not seen anything yet.

EXISTENTIAL CRISES: THE POLITICS OF FEAR
AND FAR-RIGHT POPULISM

So far we have been focusing on the ecological, political-economic, and technological dimensions of the planetary polycrisis. But the polycrisis also reaches into the most intimate realms of the human psyche or subjectivity. Subjectivity is itself a key subsystem of the capitalist world-system, referring to patterns of individuality, identity, and cognitive-affective dispositions. Thus we should not be surprised that contemporary subjectivities are themselves a site of crisis and transition, which is largely the product of the multiple crises we have surveyed, but also in part irreducible to them. Different terms have been used to describe these crises—for example, crises of meaning, ontological security crises, identity crises, even spiritual crises—but I will use the term "existential crises," referring to destabilizing shifts that erode or undermine individual and collective structures of identity, feeling, and belonging.[225]

While we should be wary of universalizing narratives, a number of trends suggest that existential crises are a global yet uneven phenomenon: a global epidemic of depression, which affects up to 350 million people worldwide and has been worsened by the pandemic; rising deaths from suicide, alcoholism, and drug abuse in many countries (particularly in the US, which has seen a tripling of these "deaths of despair" since 1990); reports of unbearable loneliness for large numbers of people in atomized neoliberal cultures; and the increasing virulence of nationalism, racism, and religious fundamentalism across the world-system.[226] To a large extent these trends can be attributed to the mesh of neoliberal economic and cultural globalization, which has brought diverse cultures into greater proximity while simultaneously undermining economic security for working-class populations, eroding union support structures, displacing and fragmenting rural communities, intensifying inequality, and creating a widely shared affect of being subject to forces beyond one's control.[227]

It is no secret that these economic and existential anxieties have in turn triggered aggressive and often violent reactions. Michael Kimmel, for instance, argues that religious extremism and nonstate terrorism across the global north and south can be understood as efforts to recover a sense of manhood from "the devastatingly emasculating politics of globalization," which appeals to "young men whose world seems to have been turned upside down."[228] Existential crises can in this sense trigger "hypermasculine" reactions, which arise, as Cara Daggett explains, "when agents of hegemonic masculinity feel threatened or undermined, thereby needing to inflate, exaggerate, or otherwise distort their traditional masculinity."[229] Such hypermasculine tendencies can also be seen in the gendered and racialized politics of the far-right across North America, Europe, India, Brazil, Israel, the Philippines, and elsewhere. While they take different forms and emerge from variable circumstances, most if not all of these movements share a common set of discursive and affective tendencies that Ruth Wodak calls the "politics of fear": scapegoating minorities as responsible for the woes of "the nation" (typically ethnic or racialized minorities, but also "globalist elites"), construing them as "a threat to *us*, to 'our' nation," desiring a strong-armed "law and order" agenda, and reasserting patriarchal gender norms (often through intense antipathy to feminist, LGBTQ+, and reproductive rights movements).[230] The "politics of fear" that these movements share is often seeded by economic factors like stagnant wages, rising inequality, and youth unemployment. Yet some of the most successful far-right parties in Europe (e.g., the Swiss People's Party and Austrian Freedom Party) have thrived in countries that were largely unscathed from the 2008 crisis and that have relatively low levels of inequality and unemployment.[231] Thus these trends cannot be explained by economic insecurities alone, but also require taking account of existential anxieties shaped by cultural globalization, migration, and demographic shifts—hence the rise of white supremacist paranoia about the so-called "great replacement" taking place across Europe and the United States.[232]

The rise of religious fundamentalism and far-right populism across the world-system is therefore best understood not solely as a symptom of capitalism's structural crisis, but also as a reaction against a broader range of real and perceived threats to a "way of life" or mode of existence. The climate crisis in this sense poses an existential crisis to many on the right, signaling the unsustainability of a way of life in which they are deeply ideologically and emotionally invested, leading to either outright climate denial or acknowledging the problem even while denying the need for rapid emissions reductions (an approach becoming more common among European far-right movements).[233] At a time when the conjoined crises of capitalism and the earth demand decisive transformative action, such crises are thus sowing existential anxieties that often militate *against* such actions. As Albena Azmanova claims, this can be the case simply by reinforcing support for centrist parties (i.e., the devil one knows best), since conditions of uncertainty can reinforce conservative instincts even when this entails "clinging to the very dynamics that create general material and psychological precarity" in the first place.[234]

But in the worst-case scenario, these existential anxieties can facilitate the rise of "fascist" regimes, defined by Robert Paxton as hypernationalist regimes "in which a mass-based party of committed nationalist militants, working in uneasy but effective collaboration with traditional elites, abandons democratic liberties and pursues with redemptive violence and without ethical or legal constraints goals of internal cleansing and external expansion."[235] Paxton argues that one of the key "mobilizing passions" that characterizes fascism in all its manifestations across history is "a sense of overwhelming crisis beyond the reach of any traditional solutions," thus driving its adherents into the arms of authoritarian leaders and legitimizing violence against racialized Others.[236] Far-right movements across the world-system are in this sense at least "proto-fascist."[237] But even well short of full-blown fascism (in Paxton's sense), it is clear that the convergence of political-economic and existential crises can facilitate the rise to power of authoritarian leaders, weaken popular support for democratic institutions, and harden self/other relations. And as converging political-economic, climate, energy, food, security, and existential crises worsen in the coming years, the risks of fascism could be much greater than they are today, creating a potentially devastating positive feedback that would force the world-system down a trajectory of full-blown catastrophe.

In sum, existential crises are a critical dimension of the planetary polycrisis that may amplify (and be amplified by) the other crises surveyed above. But by no means do such crises always or automatically trigger regressive reactions. They can alternatively create the preconditions for the emergence of more ecological and compassionate values, subjectivities, and solidarities, as we have also witnessed in conditions of crisis.[238] Regressive tendencies appear to have predominated over the past two decades, owing largely to the weaknesses of leftist movements around the world, but also to the inherent frailties of atomized neoliberal subjectivities that predispose populations to conservative reactions in times of crisis.[239] Moving beyond the politics of fear toward a politics of solidarity that can adequately and equitably respond to the planetary polycrisis is arguably the most difficult dimension of the predicament we face.

CONCLUSION

This chapter has provided merely a narrow portrait of the planetary polycrisis and the feedbacks that compose it. These feedbacks, and the risks of
problem-shifting that emerge when we fail to address the polycrisis as a
whole, are further explored in chapters 4 and 5. But it is enough for now
to demonstrate that we confront a predicament that is more than the
sum of its parts—a multiplicity of intersecting crises that should be studied as holistically as possible in order to illuminate its possible futures.
How well have existing analyses of planetary futures grasped the complexity of our unfolding predicament? This is the subject of chapter 2.

2

VISIONING AND SHAPING THE FUTURE: MODELS, SCENARIOS, AND CRITICAL SOCIAL SCIENCE FUTURES

It is no coincidence that periods of crisis and turbulence, as Ariel Colonomos says, tend to be those when "ideas about the future are most highly sought after and could have the most impact on reality, when the course of history seems to oscillate between various possible worlds."[1] It is not hard to see why this is the case: reflection on possible futures is an essential, inescapable dimension of individual and collective agency—particularly in times of crisis when temporal horizons are compressed, the urgency of decision arises, and we must grapple with the possible futures that may result from our decisions.

The concern for futures has (unfortunately) had less impact on the social sciences. Yet it is possible to identify a minor tradition of research and speculative imagination called "futures studies," defined by Wendell Bell as "a transdisciplinary, unifying social science" that aims "to discover or invent, examine and evaluate, and propose possible, probable, and preferable futures."[2] Far from detached observations of the historical process, exercises in futures studies—as Silke Beck and Martin Mahony argue—are inherently political: future scenarios "do not just represent possible futures, but also help to bring certain futures into being," for instance, by shaping the cognitive-affective dispositions of political actors; constraining or widening the range of imagined possible futures; motivating efforts to ward off futures perceived as undesirable; and/or inspiring new activist, policy, or investment strategies to bring desired futures into being.[3]

I situate this book squarely within the broad tradition of futures studies, and this chapter provides a survey of existing efforts to model, anticipate, and shape the possible futures of the world-earth system. Rather than pretending to be comprehensive, the goal of this chapter is instead to critically engage scenario analyses that are most relevant to the approach I develop in this book. In particular, I am interested in approaches that are planetary in scope and synthetic in their ambition: not scenario studies that focus on one or two trends (e.g., in emissions, energy demand, technology) but that analyze something like the Club of Rome's "World Problematique."[4] The goals here are threefold: (1) to survey the landscape of futures scenarios developed to model global futures in an era of planetary crises, focusing mainly on quantitative modeling, qualitative scenario exercises, and what I call critical social science futures; (2) to highlight their strengths and weaknesses; and (3) to lay the groundwork for the alternative theoretical approach and scenario analysis that I develop in subsequent chapters.

MODELING FUTURES: THE LIMITS TO GROWTH

The rise of digital computation in the 1950s and 1960s made possible a new technique of scenario analysis that would change the face of futures studies: computer models and simulations. At its core, computer modeling and simulation is a way to perform lab-like experiments on virtual systems: the model is itself a simplified, restricted representation of a complex system that quantifies its key variables and their relationships, and simulation runs showcase how a system might evolve following different sets of initial conditions or tweaks to the model's parameters.[5]

Advances in computational modeling in the 1960s enabled what would arguably become the most (in)famous exercise in futures research of the twentieth century: the Club of Rome's *Limits to Growth* (LtG) report, conducted by Donella and Dennis Meadows, Jorgen Randers, and William Behrens. Meadows and company were informed by the emerging paradigm of "system dynamics" pioneered by Jay Forrester. As they explain, this approach "focuses not on single pieces but on connections, looking at demography, economy, and the environment as *one planetary system* with innumerable interactions."[6] System dynamics formed the basis of the World3 model used by Meadows and colleagues to simulate the possible trajectories of the world-earth system. The model is based on an incredibly complex structure of negative and positive feedback loops that mathematically represents the relationships between industrial output, population growth, nonrenewable resource depletion, pollution, and food production—though these parameters are subdivided into more than two hundred variables.[7] The goal of the model, as Meadows and company describe, is to "extend our intuitive capabilities so that we can follow the complex, interrelated behavior of many variables simultaneously," while exploring how policy changes and other parametric tweaks would alter the possible trajectories of the world-earth system.[8]

The final product of the original LtG study was twelve representative scenarios, nine of which eventually ended in either "collapse" or gradual decline in industrial output and population levels. Scenario 1, the "standard run" or business-as-usual (BAU), was the most famous: an abrupt collapse starting around 2020 caused by rapidly rising costs of nonrenewable resources, leading to a collapse in industrial output, food production, and population levels.[9] Scenario 2 tweaked the model by doubling the total stock of nonrenewable resources from a 250- to 500-year supply (following 1970 usage rates). In this case, growth continues for longer, but worsening pollution leads to rising death rates, accelerated capital depreciation, and dwindling food production, while the doubling of nonrenewable resources delays the depletion crisis by only a couple of decades (due to the relentless demands of exponential growth), leading to collapse between 2040 and 2050.[10] Scenarios 3 through 9 introduced a combination policy and technological tweaks. In scenario 3, for instance, they assume breakthroughs in nuclear fast breeder reactors that extend the lifetime of uranium supplies and enable access to deep-sea minerals and more diffuse mineral ores, while also adding recycling initiatives that reduce the resource intensity of industrial output by three-quarters; in this case a depletion crisis is avoided, but growth comes to an end between 2060 and 2070 because of rising pollution exceeding the absorption capacities of the earth.[11] Only scenarios 10 through 12—model runs involving technological innovations to boost resource efficiency, soil conservation measures, global population control policies, and caps on material-energy throughput levels—produce a sustainable "steady-state" for the world-earth system that avoids overshoot and collapse.[12]

It is little wonder that the LtG generated such rancor among economists and policymakers committed to the dream of endless growth. The report has attracted constant streams of commentary and critique ever since its publication—much of it misplaced and demonstrating little serious engagement with the text. For instance, critiques claiming that the LtG authors ignored the role of technological innovation and market signals, or that they wrongly predicted we would "run out" of resources, are based on gross misrepresentations of the actual report.[13] Meadows and company, for example, emphasize that the collapse scenarios are not triggered by "running out" of resources but rather by the "growing cost of exploiting the globe's remaining sources and sinks," in this way anticipating later developments in EROI and net energy analysis.[14]

Yet there are obvious limitations with the LtG analysis. For one, while Meadows, Randers, and Behrens do not view population growth as *the* core ecological problem, their study still tends to place excessive emphasis on this parameter. Thus their model runs rely heavily on stringent and highly problematic population control measures to enable more sustainable outcomes rather than redistributions of wealth. In other respects the LtG is simply dated and requires updating in light of contemporary knowledge. For example, while the original study presciently recognized the climate threat posed by fossil fuel combustion, the limited knowledge of the time means that carbon emissions and other planetary boundaries are not included in the pollution parameter.[15] Furthermore, the LtG—while recognizing the potential for breakthroughs in solar and wind energy—did not anticipate that they could become a major new energy source in the twentieth century, which gives more hope to global capital that it can avoid the twin pitfalls of depletion and pollution crises (though transition minerals for RE technologies, as we've seen, pose their own depletion and pollution risks). More broadly, the inherent limits of the World3 model, and of modeling more generally, means that Meadows et al. give no account of power relations and resistance in shaping the different trajectories, overlook the specifically capitalist drivers of exponential growth, and occlude other processes and shocks that will have important ramifications for the future of growth (such as war, pandemics, and economic crises).

Despite these limitations, one thing is for sure: more than fifty years after its publication, the LtG retains its relevance. For one, multiple studies show that its projections have tracked closely with recent data.[16] More importantly for the future, its arguments on why exponential economic growth may lead to collapse or (at best) gradual decline remain salient. On one hand, the dynamics of net energy decline and the risk of a "net energy cliff" means that something like the LtG's standard run collapse scenario could still plausibly materialize, though delayed by a decade or two by breakthroughs in unconventional oil and gas extraction (thus following scenario 2 more closely). On the other hand, the nascent climate emergency and broader assault on planetary boundaries lends credence to the LtG's longer-term collapse scenarios triggered by "pollution crises," though the causal mechanisms and feedbacks would need updating based on current knowledge.

As we will see, I do not think economic growth will *inevitably* come to an end during this century. But any futures methodology must be informed by key insights of the LtG's system dynamics framework, particularly its emphasis on thinking in terms of a "problematique" rather than individual problems, tracing the positive and negative feedback loops that link different problems and systems, and anticipating "problem-shifting" risks in which efforts to solve one problem give rise to others. The LtG authors, as they readily acknowledge, were hardly able to capture the whole of the World Problematique. But their system dynamics methodology provides a productive framework for exploring planetary futures, one that can be enriched using the tools of Marxism and complexity theory (as I elaborate in chapter 3).

INTEGRATED ASSESSMENT MODELS AND THE SHARED SOCIOECONOMIC PATHWAYS

While it retains its relevance, the LtG was an early and now in many respects dated effort to model the World Problematique. Today other modeling approaches with much greater computational power—enabling them to integrate far more variables—have been developed by scientists and transdisciplinary knowledge networks. Most notably, integrated assessment models (IAMs) have become a key tool among scientists and policymakers, which model the feedbacks between earth and human systems and project a range of future trajectories based on different "what if" assumptions and policy interventions. The many types of IAMs are often broadly categorized into two classes. The first are cost-benefit IAMs, which refer to simplified climate-economy models (e.g., William Nordhaus's DICE model) that attempt to calculate the costs and benefits of different climate mitigation pathways.[17] These models have been extensively critiqued for being overly simplistic and downright dangerous: Nordhaus's model, for example, infamously projects that mitigation pathways to stabilize global temperatures at 3.5°C would be "optimal" from a cost-benefit calculus, whereas a 6°C rise—deemed by most climate scientists to be a potentially human-extinction-level event—would reduce global GDP by only 10%.[18]

Process-based IAMs, on the other hand, are more ambitious modeling efforts to represent the interactions between climate, economy, energy, food, land use, and/or other subsystems. As the IPCC explains, process-based IAMs "combine insights from various disciplines in a single framework, resulting in a dynamic description of the coupled energy–economy–land-climate system."[19] These models are the methodological foundation of climate and energy scenarios developed by the IPCC and IEA. In turn, these scenarios are increasingly used by policymakers, central banks, and corporate actors to anticipate the economic and financial implications of different decarbonization pathways (e.g., their fossil fuel demand trajectories, investment requirements, and risks to existing fossil fuel assets) and inform present-day policies and investment strategies.[20]

IAMs also form the basis of a widely used set of scenarios known as the shared socioeconomic pathways (SSPs). The SSPs were developed through interdisciplinary collaboration between climate scientists and economists, and since 2017 they have been deployed in more than 1,370 studies, including the IPCC's special report on 1.5°C and its most recent Sixth Assessment Report.[21] The scenarios combine qualitative storylines, which include political and economic developments that cannot be easily quantified or modeled, with quantitative projections of trends in population,

economic growth, energy consumption, emissions, land use, urbanization, and other variables.[22]

The creators of the SSPs developed five core scenarios. The first represents
a "sustainable development" scenario (SSP1) in which the world economy
shifts gradually to a sustainable path: resource efficiency improves dramatically, leading to an overall reduction in material-energy throughput; the
world is put on pace to meet the Paris targets, though reliant on significant
CDR expansion; and economic growth, while slower than the BAU baseline,
quintuples the size of the global economy by 2100 (with global GDP rising
to more than $500 trillion, compared to roughly $100 trillion today).[23] The
second (SSP2) represents a "middle of the road" scenario in which socioeconomic and technological trends "do not shift markedly from historical patterns." Progress toward sustainability is steady but slow, technology advances
but without fundamental breakthroughs, GDP (like in SSP1) rises to $500
trillion by 2100 but is less evenly distributed, and population reaches 9.4
billion.[24] The third scenario (SSP3) is called "regional rivalry": in this world,
resurgent nationalism, geopolitical competition, and security concerns constrain global cooperation on environmental problems. Economic growth
is slower, at only 1%–2% annually (still doubling the size of the global
economy by 2100), inequalities worsen, material-intensive consumption
patterns persist, and the global population grows to 12.6 billion by 2100.[25]
In SSP4 ("inequality"), mitigation efforts are more successful—enabled by
strong progress in renewable energy and digital technologies. But highly
uneven investment and development patterns lead to worsening inequality
and social stratification.[26] Finally, in SSP5 ("fossil fueled development"), the
world "places increasing faith in competitive markets, innovation and participatory societies to produce rapid technological progress."[27] Global GDP
soars to $1,000 trillion by 2100, but this comes at the expense of contin-
ued exploitation of fossil fuels and emissions-intensive development—with
total energy demand tripling from 2020 levels and emissions continuously
rising until 2100. The result is a more equal world, both within and between
countries, but one that must rely on high deployment of CDR and solar
geoengineering to defend itself from a carbon-loaded climate.[28]

It is not difficult to pick holes in these scenarios. Indeed, it is questionable whether any of them represents a genuinely plausible future. This

is not to say that the qualitative storylines are without merit. On their own they provide plausible (if bland and apolitical) descriptions of alternative futures. But the quantitative projections accompanying them are highly flawed. For one, the IAMs on which they are based—as the authors acknowledge—"do not consider feedbacks from the climate system" on socioeconomic trends.[29] The authors believe this is needed to provide a set of baseline scenarios that can later be amended by including climate impacts. But, in the meantime, it provides an incredibly misleading set of scenarios, such as the hellish emissions trajectory in SSP5 that leads to only "low challenges" for climate adaptation—a ludicrously implausible future. Furthermore, unlike the system dynamics model that informs the LtG, the general equilibrium-based IAMs that primarily inform the SSPs only weakly capture the feedbacks between material-energy throughput and economic growth. As a result, they assume that a "sustainable development" trajectory is compatible with continuous exponential growth via absolute decoupling from rising material-energy use—despite evidence to the contrary (discussed in chapter 1). In striking contrast to the LtG, the models also ignore energy and mineral supply risks: fossil fuel and mineral abundance is a "default assumption" of the IAMs on which the SSPs are based, regardless of the demand trajectory.[30] Perhaps most importantly, continuous economic growth is also a default assumption of these IAMs, making it impossible for them to anticipate future constraints on growth or model post-growth futures.[31]

Compared to the LtG, the SSPs represent two steps forward and two steps backward. Rather than opening up imagination, analysis, and evaluation of a wide range of plausible futures, instead they close down futurological speculation to a narrow range of scenarios that have questionable plausibility, at best, and are downright impossible, at worst. The SSPs are used extensively across the science and policy worlds, not only informing the IPCC's mitigation pathways (SSP5, for instance, forms the basis of the IPCC's most CDR-intensive "1.5°C-compatible" scenarios)[32] but also climate mitigation, adaptation, and investment strategies being developed by policymakers, planning authorities, businesses, and cities around the world. For example, the Net-Zero Asset Owner Alliance—an influential consortium of investors and asset managers aiming to push companies toward Paris-compatible business models, which has been described as the "gold standard" of sustainable capital management—allows its members to develop net zero targets based on SSP5, scenarios that involve a most likely implausible 20gt of annual CDR deployment by 2050.[33] The SSPs can in this way have a beguiling influence on the contemporary imaginations of capitalists and policymakers, facilitating greenwashing and delay by making more gradualist decarbonization pathways appear compatible with 1.5°C. It is thus critical that we subject them to more rigorous scrutiny. Otherwise the narrow range of scenarios, and inclusion of perniciously implausible futures like SSP5, may constrain contemporary imaginations and expectations in ways that risk "locking-in technologies, infrastructure and policies that are undesirable" from an ecological and social justice standpoint.[34]

Still, we should highlight that others have done valuable work with IAMs to open up the scenario imagination. For example, researchers using the MEDEAS (modeling energy system development under environmental and socioeconomic constraints) framework have developed a series of scenario studies that—unlike mainstream IAMs—integrate the impacts of climate change, energy use, net energy decline, and geological depletion on future economic growth, in this way building more directly on the system dynamics framework used by the LtG.[35] In one study they show that by integrating these geophysical feedbacks, global GDP begins to plateau in the 2040s and declines gradually in subsequent decades—driven mainly by liquid fuel scarcity in the 2040s and intensifying climate damages after mid-century—producing a protracted global recession that would upend world order and drive the self-organization of post-growth political economies.[36] Like with all models, such results must be interpreted cautiously: for instance, the model excludes technological innovations in CDR, nuclear energy, green hydrogen, and renewables. It may also overestimate climate damages, though their assumptions are plausibly more realistic than mainstream IAM representations of climate damages (given the notorious limitations of the latter).[37]

In sum, IAMs are a necessary and valuable tool that can be used in ways that challenge rather than reinforce the political-economic status quo.[38] There are of course inherent limits to quantitative modeling, but this does not mean models should be rejected tout court by more critical and qualitative social theorists. Instead they can be used cautiously—mindful of their underlying theoretical assumptions, limits, and blind spots—to anticipate future trends in variables of interest, particularly those that can be expected to follow more or less linear trajectories (e.g., trends in GDP growth, energy demand, population growth, emissions, and warming levels), at least up to certain "critical" inflection points. But the social sciences and humanities are needed to deepen our investigation of the global political-economic dynamics, power relations, and counter-hegemonic struggles that will shape the possible futures of the world-earth system. We need more of what Andreas Malm and the Zetkin Collective call "political climate modelling,"[39] or exploration of alternative futures based on deep theoretical understanding of how political-economic systems like global capitalism actually function, and which opens up speculative yet disciplined imagination of possible discontinuities in the power relations and structures of the global political economy. I shortly explore approaches within the social sciences that do this—which I call critical social science futures—but first it is worth briefly exploring how powerful actors have developed comparable scenario methodologies.

BEYOND MODELS: SCENARIOS IN THE CORPORATE AND INTELLIGENCE WORLDS

An influential report from the Bank of International Settlements warns policymakers that modeling-based scenario methodologies, while necessary, are insufficient to deal with risks characterized by "deep uncertainty, nonlinearity and fat-tailed distributions."[40] Climate risks in particular, it writes, emerge from "multiple nonlinear dynamics (natural, technological, societal, regulatory and cultural, among others) that interact with each other in complex ways," while IAMs "are inherently incapable of representing all these interactions."[41] The report suggests that more qualitative scenario methodologies are thus needed to account for a broader range of causal forces, cascade effects, extreme events, and possible futures.[42]

The approach called for follows a tradition of scenario analysis that can be genealogically traced back to Herman Kahn and the RAND Corporation, whose strategy of "thinking about the unthinkable" would inspire a wide range of scenario planning and war-gaming exercises in the halls of national security.[43] A similar approach was also pioneered by Royal Dutch Shell in the 1960s and 1970s. Pierre Wack, the "father of Shell scenarios," pushed its leaders to go beyond linear modeling of demand and supply trends to account for potential surprises—using "intelligence and intuition to sharpen their understanding of a complex world"—which (reportedly) enabled the company to "anticipate, adapt, and respond" to the oil shocks of the 1970s.[44] Similar methodologies have informed climate-security scenarios developed in the military and intelligence worlds, which have the explicit goal of looking beyond conservative climate projections in order to consider "the full range of what is plausible."[45]

But these scenario exercises tend to be fairly narrow in scope rather than integrating a wider range of socioeconomic, technological, and ecological parameters (as the SSPs do). In contrast, a more synoptic and synthetic set of qualitative scenario analyses comes from the US National Intelligence Council (NIC) and its *Global Trends* reports. These reports have been published every four years since 1997, and their goal is to provide a framework of analysis and set of scenarios for each incoming administration to help it "craft national security strategy and navigate an uncertain future."[46] They integrate data (and implicit theory) on what they call the core "structural forces" shaping future dynamics, including demography, the environment, economics, and technology; explore how these forces intersect to affect "emerging dynamics" at different scales; and construct alternative scenarios, typically taking place fifteen to twenty years in the future, that follow different "what if" assumptions for how these dynamics might unfold.[47]

The most recent *Global Trends* report, developed for the Biden administration, projects five possible futures for the year 2040. The first scenario is called "renaissance of democracies," which is clearly the (utopian) dream of the liberal internationalists: technological innovations in AI, biotechnology, and other fields produce a "series of ground-breaking advances, enhancing productivity and leading to an economic boom" in the US and allied nations.[48] Meanwhile, China—because of its "inefficient state-directed economic model" and high debt levels—fails to escape the middle-income trap, while Russia also confronts decline caused by overreliance on energy exports and "post-Putin elite infighting."[49] By the mid-2030s, the US and its allies are global leaders in new technologies, in position to set global standards to limit their negative implications (e.g., disinformation and privacy concerns), and able to promote democratic revival worldwide. The second scenario—"a world adrift"—provides one of the more "dystopian" futures feared by the US foreign policy establishment. In this world, stagnant economic growth, widening social divisions, and political polarization plague the US and its allies. China, on the other hand, is able to exploit their troubles to expand its global influence, and by 2035 it is strong enough to force Taiwan to begin talks on reunification. Overall this is a world in which "international rules of behavior are no longer followed, global cooperation is limited, and technology fails to provide solutions."[50] The third scenario—"competitive coexistence"—falls somewhere between the first and second: economic growth is strong both for the West and China, and they reestablish strong economic interdependence while continuing to compete over political influence, governance models, and dominance in new technologies. The risks of great-power war are diminished and global problems like climate change are more manageable, but inequalities persist, and poor countries are less able to adapt to worsening climate disasters and other challenges over time (similar to the SSP4 "inequality" scenario).[51]

The final two scenarios present more "discontinuous" futures. The fourth scenario—"separate siloes"—is a more dramatic version of the second scenario, which echoes SSP3 ("regional rivalry"). In this future, the world by 2040 is "fragmented into several economic and security blocs of varying size and strength, centered on the United States, China, the European Union (EU), Russia, and a few regional powers."[52] This appears to result from rising protectionist measures taken in the 2030s, as converging problems like worsening unemployment, trade disputes, transnational health and terrorist threats, and populist surges pressure states to increase trade barriers and protections for local populations and industries (to a large extent what we are witnessing today in the wake of Putin's invasion of Ukraine).[53] In contrast, the fifth and final scenario—"tragedy and mobilization"—depicts a future not unlike the one hoped for by social justice movements, but one triggered by catastrophe: synchronous breadbasket failures in the early 2030s lead to global famine and skyrocketing food prices. Social unrest and protest intensifies around the globe, including an outbreak of violence triggered by disinformation in which thousands are killed in Philadelphia, and youth movements join together worldwide to force political and economic reforms.[54] Green parties are swept into power across Europe, the EU and China join together in an "unlikely partnership" to support a worldwide Marshall Plan–style effort to meet the sustainable development goals by 2050, and corporate charters are reformed to "embrace serving a wider range of stakeholders." The United States, Canada, and Australia are initially resistant but slowly follow such initiatives, while Russia, some OPEC countries, and extremist groups resort to violence and disinformation to challenge these efforts.[55]

While the NIC's scenarios lack quantitative precision relative to the SSPs, they make up for this with their relatively rich descriptions of future trends in geopolitics and technology. The geopolitical futures they describe largely reflect debates in IR about the evolving contours of world order—for example, between those anticipating liberal internationalist revival under US leadership or shifts to more bipolar or multipolar world orders—but they are much richer than the restricted mono-disciplinary accounts typically found in IR.[56] It is clear, and not surprising, that the US intelligence community understands the need for a holistic, synoptic lens in order to "look into the future and then shape it . . . to the advantage of the United States" (as one National Security Agency researcher describes their mandate).[57]

But their scenarios, while occasionally insightful, are also (as we might expect) constrained by questionable assumptions and oversights. Among those are modernist assumptions about the intrinsic links between economic growth, democratization, and improved capacities to solve social and environmental problems, rather than viewing growth as *itself* a key cause of such problems.[58] Furthermore, while the report is synoptic in scope, it is also less than systematic regarding its analysis of the key scenario drivers and the feedbacks between them. For example, while it celebrates technological innovation as the engine of economic revitalization and "democratic renaissance," it does not acknowledge the resulting forms of technological problem-shifting that would plague this scenario—including worsening technological unemployment and democratizing weapons of mass destruction, which would likely counteract the scenario's assumptions about "boosting public trust" and making global challenges more manageable.[59] In this sense, like many of the IAMs underlying the SSPs, it provides inconsistent scenarios in which "one part of the forecast contradicts another," since they fail to consider the wider web of feedback loops that link these parameters.[60]

To its credit, the NIC does countenance the possibility of an EU-China centered world order that would be far more enlightened than the US-led order. But the NIC is obviously not constructing this scenario as a performative intervention intended to make such futures more attainable. To the contrary, given the US intelligence community's notorious history and continuing practice of monitoring, infiltrating, and sabotaging social justice movements—from the civil rights and Black Power movements of the 1960s to the environmental and antiracist movements of the present—we can say that this is a future the NIC would like to prevent from materializing. Like the scenario analyses developed by Shell, which in part aimed to inform strategy on how to preempt resistance to its extractivist projects around the world,[61] as well as Pentagon-funded research on the dynamics of large-scale social movement mobilization and possible tipping points,[62] so can the NIC's fifth scenario be viewed as part of a strategy of anticipation and preemption.

In sum, the NIC's *Global Trends 2040* provides a synthetically rich map of possible futures, yet one with clear limitations. As an exercise in qualitative futures modeling, it falls short because of its limited analysis of the feedbacks between the scenario drivers it identifies. Given the NIC's aim of shaping the future to the geostrategic advantage of the US, it is perhaps not surprising that it gives disproportionate attention to the US-China rivalry while only superficially addressing the climate crisis and other problems like inequality, pandemic risks, far-right populism, and technological unemployment—which (from its perspective) need only be "solved" to the extent that this boosts the relative power of the US and its allies. Critical scholars and activists can learn from the NIC's scenarios, in terms of both their insights on possible futures and the example they provide on how scenarios can be used to inform strategic planning in the present. But to develop a truly transdisciplinary futures analysis that can inform a counter-hegemonic praxis of navigation, we need critical theory and the social sciences.

CRITICAL SOCIAL SCIENCE FUTURES

Related to, yet distinct from, the other approaches we have surveyed, critical social science futures can be defined as scenario studies that use the tools of social science and critical theory to explore possible futures from the standpoint of movements struggling for social justice. While such approaches are relatively rare among critical theorists and social scientists, we should also recognize that critical theory has always been inherently futural. As Azmanova explains, critical theory identifies "antinomies (tensions, contradictions) that are constitutive of a given historical form of social relations," which "are both sources of suffering and emancipatory openings toward attainable possibilities for a less unjust world."[63] In other words, critical theorists aim to illuminate future possibilities that are *immanent* to the present, or contained as latent potentials within current tendencies and trends.[64] John Urry, in this sense, suggests that Marx can be thought of as a kind of futurist: a theorist who identified the key contradictions and tendencies (or "laws of motion") of his age and extrapolated these tendencies to explore the probable futures of capitalism—anticipating, for instance, the globalization of capital and its relentless assault on all non-capitalist forms of production, the continuous revolutionizing of the forces of production and replacement of human labor with machines, the centralization of capital in financial and corporate oligopolies, and the degradation of the soil by capitalist agriculture—and highlighted the potential for an emergent revolutionary movement led by the working class.[65]

As Urry indicates, a good place to start when exploring existing critical social science futures is with the Marxist tradition. Unlike the other approaches surveyed above, Marxist analyses of possible futures are informed by theoretical and historical understanding of global capitalism: its dynamics of accumulation, exploitation, and dispossession; its world historical patterns of expansion, crisis, and systemic restructuring; and the conflicts it generates both between and within social classes (i.e., not just conflicts between workers and capitalists, but also between different factions of the capitalist class, and between workers conditioned by systems of gender, race, and imperialism). Using the tools of political economic theory, history, conjunctural analysis, and (occasionally) speculative imagination, Marxists help illuminate how capitalism may evolve and adapt in response to contemporary crises, the increasingly dystopian futures that lie in wait if capitalism goes unchallenged, and the (eco)socialist futures that may become possible through sustained counter-hegemonic struggle. "Ecosocialism or barbarism" is the common refrain that structures most Marxist thinking on the future, putting it in direct contrast to the approaches surveyed earlier, which believe (whether explicitly or implicitly) that perpetual, exponential growth is compatible with sustainability.

Few Marxists explicitly view themselves as engaged in future studies, yet many of their analyses can be read in this way. For example, Marxist analyses of the structural crisis of neoliberal capitalism often speculate on how this crisis may evolve in the coming years and decades, with some claiming that we may be witnessing the beginning of the end of capitalism. Wallerstein, for one, claims that "the only certainty is that the existing system—the capitalist world-economy—cannot survive. What is impossible to know is what the successor system will be."[66] He suggests that the crisis of neoliberalism may go on for decades, but that the capitalist world-system will at some point, likely between 2030 and 2050, "bifurcate" and evolve down one of two possible postcapitalist trajectories: either a noncapitalist but still highly exploitative, hierarchical, and polarized system representing the "spirit of Davos," or a relatively democratic and egalitarian postcapitalist system representing the "spirit of Porto Alegre."[67] Wolfgang Streeck also believes that we are witnessing the beginning of the "terminal" phase of capitalism—the result of mutually reinforcing dynamics between skyrocketing inequality, debt, stagnant growth, geopolitical anarchy, and elite corruption. But unlike Wallerstein, Streeck does not think we are on the cusp of a new world-system so much as what he calls a "prolonged period of social entropy," or a "breakdown of system integration" that shifts the "burden of ordering social life, of providing it with a modicum of security and stability, to individuals themselves"—in short, a "collapse" future.[68] David Harvey, while cognizant of the potentially "fatal contradictions" that capitalism confronts in the twenty-first century, has a more open-ended analysis of its possible futures. He concludes that capitalism "can probably continue to function indefinitely but in a manner that will provoke progressive degradation on the land and mass impoverishment"—unless a global counter-hegemonic movement emerges that can at least neutralize its worst excesses.[69]

This is merely a brief survey of Marxist analyses of the structural crisis of neoliberalism and its possible futures, which is vast. But the main limitation that most of these approaches share is their very limited integration of ecological and geophysical processes. They often recognize climate and energy as important variables, but they make minimal effort to integrate theory and data on emissions and possible mitigation pathways, the socioecological consequences of unmitigated warming, net energy decline, food system risks, transition mineral demands, pandemic risks, and other socioecological problems. Nor do they attempt to integrate technological trends in renewable energy, AI, synthetic biology, and other developments with important systemic consequences. While they take us well beyond the LtG and SSPs by foregrounding relations of power and resistance within capitalism and their possible futures, this comes at the cost of losing the climatological and geophysical context that will shape and constrain these futures. Transdisciplinarity is not yet in sight.

Other Marxists, however, go further in this direction. In particular, the work of Geoff Mann and Joel Wainwright is unique for its explicit and systematic exploration of planetary futures. In their words, "The Left needs a strategy . . . for how to think about the future. . . . The goal is not a mechanistic model of the future but a complex, theoretically informed lens through which to speculate coherently."[70] I wholeheartedly agree.

Mann and Wainwright foreground what they call the "climate/political change complex" as the key object of futurological analysis, which brings together an analysis of the possible trajectories of climate change with speculation on how the capitalist world-system may respond to its effects.[71] In particular, they identify three key trends or "logics" that they claim will be most salient in shaping the planetary future: (1) the logic of capitalism's crisis tendencies; (2) the logic of ecological catastrophe; and (3) the logic of weaponry, particularly nuclear and space-based weapons of mass destruction.[72] The different futures they sketch are driven by the intersection between these global trends. To start, Mann and Wainwright argue that the intensifying contradictions of neoliberal capitalism can be resolved only by a "Keynesian world state," since nationally based Keynesian approaches are bound to be crushed by the power of globally footloose capital.[73] At the same time, they anticipate that intensifying climate chaos will reinforce calls for a global green Keynesian solution while also heightening pressures for emergency climate interventions like solar radiation management (SRM). Additionally, they claim that the militarization of outer space, and the rise of space-based nuclear weapons in particular, will either motivate the emergence of a world government that can prevent an out-of-control arms race or enable a single state (most likely the US) to impose an imperialist world order backed by unprecedented force-mobilization capabilities.[74]

Mann and Wainwright argue that these three trends together mean that the most likely scenario for our planetary future is the emergence of what they call "climate leviathan" (CL), defined as "a regulatory authority armed with democratic legitimacy, binding technical authority on scientific issues, and a panopticon-like capacity to monitor the vital granular elements of our emerging world."[75] The designation of this entity as a "leviathan" is inspired by Thomas Hobbes: for Hobbes, the leviathan of the state creates order and security, thus banishing the chaos or "war of all against all" that defines the so-called "state of nature." Similarly, for Mann and Wainwright, CL can be considered an emergent form of planetary-scale sovereignty that is able to "seize command, declare an emergency, and bring order to the Earth, all in the name of saving life."[76] They claim that this would not necessarily entail a world government but could involve either a US- or China-led imperial order, though a world government of some sort may also emerge in the wake of a future world war between the United States and China.[77] But while they view CL as our most likely future, they sketch three other scenarios that comparatively receive less attention. The first is "climate Mao," which envisions an authoritarian world order (most likely led by China) that "expresses the necessity of a just terror in the interests of the future of the collective"—in short, a socialist version of climate leviathan.[78] Second is what they call "climate behemoth," or reactionary populist coalitions that seek to perpetuate fossil fueled consumption indefinitely. Mann and Wainwright argue that climate behemoth is less likely than CL to become hegemonic, since most sectors of the capitalist class now support some form of climate action, but that it still represents a potent disruptive force.[79] Third is the utopian scenario that they describe, mostly in the negative, as "climate X." This refers to a world in which both capitalism *and* state sovereignty have been abolished—a world based on the principles of equality, inclusion for all, and solidarity in "composing a world of many worlds" (following the Zapatistas).[80] Mann and Wainwright's core thesis overall is that "the future of the world will be defined by Leviathan, Behemoth, Mao, and X and the conflicts between them," though they view CL as most likely to prevail in this struggle.[81]

Mann and Wainwright give us a plausible and thought-provoking map of our planetary future(s). The four main scenarios they sketch help us look beyond the ecosocialism/barbarism dichotomy that structures most Marxist thinking about the future, while also capturing important dynamics and potentials that are occluded by the SSPs and other scenarios described earlier. I describe some comparable scenarios in chapters 4 and 5 that build on Mann and Wainwright's analysis. But these authors only go so far toward the transdisciplinary synthesis we need to develop more systematic, rigorous, and realistic analyses of the future possibility space.

For one, Mann and Wainwright largely neglect the problem of energy, instead uncritically accepting the "shale revolution" narrative at face value and ignoring the challenge of surmounting net energy decline (for both fossil fuels and renewables).[82] Thus, unlike more perceptive energy analysts,[83] they failed to anticipate the energy security challenges now plaguing global capital. Nor do they discuss the challenge of absolutely decoupling capital accumulation from emissions and other planetary boundaries, nor do they discuss the challenge of transition minerals, even though these are arguably *the key challenges* that green capitalism must surmount. These oversights weaken their argument that CL is the most likely future and lead them to downplay the threat of climate behemoth while ignoring the potential for global "collapse" scenarios. Furthermore, while Mann and Wainwright are right to highlight the "logic of weaponry" as a key parameter shaping the planetary future (part of what I later call the violence problematic), their focus on space weaponry is a bit odd. What about advances in AI, algorithmic surveillance, synthetic biology, and the broader FIR? As I show in chapter 5, these are really the key technologies that would make something like CL possible, though they are almost entirely ignored by Mann and Wainwright.

Finally, their discussion of "climate X," while laudable in some respects, is not the kind of concrete utopian analysis we need to build toward better futures. They make no serious effort to describe how a "ragtag" formation of climate justice communities could plausibly present a political challenge to global capital and the state, nor do they consider how they could organize the rapid transformation of the world economy needed without the resources and coordinating power of states. While there is a role to play for utopian "regulative ideals" like climate X, the risk, as E.O. Wright says, is that they provide "vague utopian fantasies [that] may lead us astray, encouraging us to embark on trips that have no real destinations at all."[84] Additionally, Mann and Wainwright claim that other ecosocialist visions are merely slightly different versions of CL,[85] making it seem as if leftists must choose between the "just terror" of climate Mao or the mysterious abstract utopianism of climate X. I agree that an authoritarian form of eco-socialism is a real risk, but their argument ignores the rich middle ground of concrete utopian potentials that are far more plausible than climate X (if still unlikely) and much less totalitarian than climate Mao.

In sum, while Mann and Wainwright make valuable contributions to the task of mapping our planetary future(s), they do not provide the transdisciplinary approach we need to develop a more systematic and realistic analysis of this possibility space. They remain too constrained within their disciplinary comfort zones (political economy, geography, and political theory) and are unable to think beyond the "climate/political change complex" toward the broader planetary problematic that will determine the future(s) of capitalism and the earth. They take us further than other Marxists, but we have not yet reached a genuinely transdisciplinary form of critical social science futures.

The thinker who has arguably gone furthest in this direction is Paul Raskin. Raskin's scenario work—developed through interdisciplinary collaborations with the Global Scenario Group in the 1990s and the Great Transition Initiative since 2003—is unique for its transdisciplinary impetus that spans the sciences and humanities, and the scenarios that he and his collaborators have developed are highly influential among futures researchers.[86] Raskin recognizes that we confront an epochal crisis induced by the contradictions of global capitalism, which is forcing a protracted era of turbulence and transition on us with multiple possible futures. And he grasps the need for a synthetic and multidimensional analysis of this crisis: "Experts illuminate various parts of the global elephant, but fail to apprehend the whole beast."[87] Raskin proposes three main scenario "archetypes," each with a couple of different variants. "Conventional worlds" are futures of incremental adjustment, with two variants: one that continues to be dominated by market forces, and another that sees a shift toward global Keynesian reform.[88] Raskin suggests that both variants of conventional worlds—especially the "market forces" scenario—will most likely end up in what he calls "barbarization" worlds, or futures of political-economic fragmentation and ecological collapse. Barbarization worlds also have two variants: in "fortress worlds," political-economic elites retreat into protected enclaves and declare a "planet-wide state of emergency" in order to suppress social rebellion, institutionalize an apartheid-like separation between the haves and have-nots, and siphon critical resources for the reproduction of elite lifestyles.[89] "Breakdown," on the other hand, is a more extreme collapse scenario in which "a coherent authoritarian intervention fails to materialize (or proves inadequate)," war and conflict intensify, institutions collapse, and a "new Dark Age descends."[90]

Raskin's "great transitions" archetype, in contrast, signifies the utopian hope for a more egalitarian, sustainable, and postcapitalist "planetary civilization."[91] Unlike most utopians, Raskin provides a relatively detailed account of how this transition might emerge: in the mid-2020s a "general emergency" unfolds in which political-economic and ecological crises gather "into a mighty chain reaction of cascading feedbacks and amplifications."[92] An era of global reform thus emerges (between 2028 and 2048) in which world leaders implement a "New Global Deal" that channels and constrains markets to function within socially and ecologically prescribed limits.[93] The emergent result is a "planetary social democracy," but by the 2040s, revanchist campaigns and capitalist forces reassert themselves, provoking a powerful "global citizen's movement" to push further toward more far-reaching global transformation. They succeed, and in 2048 the "Commonwealth of Earthland" is established, creating a postcapitalist world federation.[94] Emissions are brought down to zero by mid-century, GDP is replaced by alternative measurements of well-being, and the incomes of the richest are capped so that they exceed those of poorest by a factor of only ten. A nascent culture of postmaterialist values, global solidarity, and "planetary consciousness" forms the existential foundations of this new world.[95]

Raskin provides a glimpse of transdisciplinary futures research at its best. Perhaps more than any other scenario analysis to date, his work brings modeling projections together with social theoretical analysis of political-economic, governance, cultural, and social movement trends.[96] The scenario archetypes he develops are an inescapable reference for all subsequent planetary futures studies, even anticipating Mann and Wainwright's climate leviathan to some degree.

But there are weaknesses in Raskin's narrative. A critical limitation is its hazy analysis of the "global problematique." Raskin lists many of the key problems, but he does not show us *how* they may amplify each other or *why* they may pose a systemic crisis for global capitalism. As a result, the crisis scenarios he sketches are quite vague and provide little insight into how these crises may unfold, the problems they will create for states and global capital, and how the latter may respond in turn. The main issue is that Raskin does not provide a clear "model" of the global problema-tique that grounds his analysis of the possibility space, or an articulation of the key causal mechanisms and feedbacks that will shape and constrain the futures of the world-earth system. Thus, while his narrative is strong on imagination, intuition, and mythos, there is no explanatory model or framework that allows us to understand why "conventional worlds" are likely headed for collapse, why global Keynesian reform would likely be both insufficient and unstable, and how postcapitalist alternatives might emerge in the time frame needed to head off climate catastrophe.

Still, there is no question that Raskin provides one of the richest works on planetary futures to date. Many of the scenarios I develop in chap-ters 4 and 5 can be considered elaborations and refinements of Raskin's scenario archetypes, though my techno-leviathan scenario is closer to Mann and Wainwright's CL. Other critical social science futures that I have not yet touched on will also play a role in informing these scenar-ios.[97] But in order to get there, a theoretical detour is needed.

CONCLUSION

This chapter has provided a broad survey of existing efforts to model, vision, and shape the possible futures of the world-earth system. My goal in the rest of this book is to develop a critical and transdisciplinary approach to plane-tary futures that builds on chapter 1's analysis of the planetary polycrisis—developing a more synthetic rather than isolationist approach—while also building on and enriching the scenarios explored in this chapter. While I locate myself within the Marxist tradition (broadly defined), mapping the planetary-political possibility space requires a theoretical framework that goes beyond Marxist approaches—a broader complex systems ontology that can integrate theory and data across the domains of political economy, ecology, energy and food systems, technology, and global security. Just as Donella Meadows and company's World3 model synthesized knowledge about cause-and-effect relationships from numerous disciplines, so do we need a more qualitative and critical theory-informed variant of system dynamics modeling that brings together insights across the sciences and humanities. The conceptual and methodological foundations of an alternative approach to planetary futures—which I call planetary systems thinking—are the subject of chapter 3.

3

PLANETARY SYSTEMS THINKING

It has been said that futures analysis is inherently a work of synthesis or bricolage: picking up heterogeneous components from diverse fields of knowledge and stitching them together to form a tapestry that is more than the sum of its parts.[1] Thus it requires a framework of analysis that, as Edgar Morin says, is "capable of unifying concepts which repel one another," or making seemingly opposed approaches and methodologies appear in a more complementary light.[2] As we saw in chapter 2, neither modeling nor critical social science futures are sufficient by themselves to illuminate the future possibility space. How can we synthesize insights from earth system science, IAMs, energy studies, IR, political ecology, critical security studies, and other fields in a way that allows us (as Mann and Wainwright say) to "speculate coherently" about planetary futures?

Complexity theory is a useful starting point. It is the transdisciplinary paradigm par excellence, the theoretical "home" that attracts many of us who have become disillusioned with the disciplinary divisions that structure the natural and social sciences. As Kenneth Boulding once wrote, complexity theory can be described as a "skeleton of science . . . on which to hang the flesh and blood of particular disciplines."[3] It is not by accident that complexity theory has been deployed across knowledge traditions as diverse as physics, biology, ecology, earth system science, sociology, economics, IR, agroecology, neo-Gramscian theory, psychoanalysis, and neuroscience.[4] Complexity theory also provides a useful set of concepts—such as possibility spaces, attractors, bifurcations, tipping points—that can facilitate speculation on possible futures and the dynamics that may drive different scenario trajectories. If the future is an obscure "terra incognita,"[5] complexity theory can help us map this not-yet-actual territory, but such maps must be provisional, partial, and subject to continuous revision as we proceed ever-more deeply into this terrain.

Complexity theory thus forms the conceptual backbone of the futures analysis developed in this book. But we should remember, as Erika Cudworth and Stephen Hobden point out, that there is not one single complexity theory but rather a diverse set of articulations of complexity concepts informed by different theoretical assumptions, methodologies, and disciplinary traditions.[6] Planetary systems thinking can be understood as a specific form of complexity theory that aims to facilitate bridge-building or bricolage across the sciences and humanities—forming what could be considered a more qualitative, critical theoretical, and imaginational (rather than computational) variant of systems dynamics modeling. Just as any computational model entails a set of assumptions about the nature of the world being investigated, the key systems and variables that must be included, the causal relationships that link these variables together, and the agencies or forces that drive their coevolution, so do we need an explicit theoretical and conceptual framework that can guide our more qualitative analysis of the future possibility space.

Chapter 3 thus elaborates the philosophical assumptions and conceptual architecture that I use in subsequent chapters to develop a more synthetic analysis of the planetary polycrisis and its possible futures. I begin at the highest level of abstraction by briefly explaining the concept of the problematic and its relationship to complex systems. From there we put more concrete flesh on these concepts by elaborating the core conceptual elements of planetary systems thinking: the planetary problematic, the socioecological problematic, the violence problematic, and the existential problematic. I conclude with a brief discussion of the futures "methodology" that I call "mapping."

PROBLEMATICS AND COMPLEX SYSTEMS

As we have already seen, numerous scholars speak of a world or global problematique that emerges from the feedbacks between numerous global challenges. Manuel Delanda, drawing on both Deleuzian philosophy and the mathematics of chaos and dynamic systems theory, can help us develop a deeper understanding of this concept. For Delanda, a problematic is more than just a nexus of intersecting problems: it also constitutes a structure of reciprocal relations that shapes and constrains the possible trajectories of a complex system.[7] A problematic emerges from the encounter between the core goals of a system—for example, to survive and flourish—and the intersecting challenges, tensions, and obstacles that force the system to creatively adapt or transform in order to pursue these goals. It is a structure in the sense that it constrains the range of possible behaviors and trajectories that are available to a system, but this is a dynamic and open-ended structure that can shift as the system evolves and its environment changes. A problematic thus determines the "possibility space" for a given system, and each possible trajectory for that system can be understood as a "solution" to its problematic—a solution *not* in the sense of a "fix," but as a way of responding to these problems that creates a particular trajectory for the system. For example, as explored in chapter 2, Meadows and company analyze the world-system's problematic in terms of the feedbacks between industrial output, depletion, pollution, and so forth, and the multiple scenarios they discuss can be thought of as "solutions" to this problematic.[8] As we saw with system dynamics, to analyze a system's problematic and explore its possibility space requires that we first identify the key problems or parameters that are most relevant to the system's possible trajectories, and then analyze what Delanda calls the "dependency relations" that will determine how these problems evolve together.[9] In other words, dependency relations refer to the causal relationships and feedbacks that link the components of a problematic, signaling that they are all reciprocally dependent and coevolving—though some parameters may be loosely integrated, and others more tightly coupled.

The concept of "attractor" can also help us map out a system's possibility space. Each possible trajectory for a complex system is governed by a particular attractor, or a set of emergent negative feedback mechanisms that tend to reproduce a particular set of behaviors and patterns and prevent the system from shifting (or "bifurcating") toward an alternative trajectory.[10] For instance, Steven Bernstein and Matthew Hoffman use the concept of attractor to think about the negative feedback dynamics that reproduce "carbon lock-in," referring to the "overlapping political, economic, technological and cultural forces that reinforce fossil fuel energy use."[11] Similarly, we can think of BAU trajectories as maintained by an attractor or set of negative feedbacks that tend to prevent global capitalism from decisively changing course—including the structural power of finance and fossil capitalists to lobby against policies that conflict with their short-term interests, the limited profitability of RE investments relative to fossil fuels and high upfront costs of the transition, the (waning but still potent) ideological power of neoliberal economics, elite and popular anxieties about the impacts of climate policies on jobs and energy security, and police repression of climate activists and environmental defenders. But complex systems always have multiple attractors that populate their possibility spaces. Bifurcation events or tipping points occur when the negative feedbacks that reproduce a particular attractor are disrupted or overwhelmed by contrasting positive feedbacks, thereby allowing the system to shift to a qualitatively novel set of behaviors, patterns, and trajectories.[12] For instance, the improving economics of RE technologies vis-à-vis fossil fuels, rising geopolitical competition over nascent "green" industries, the growing intensity of climate impacts and rising concern among populations, growing support for radical state interventions to address climate and cost-of-living crises, and numerous other factors can weaken the negative feedbacks reproducing BAU trajectories and allow the world-system to shift toward an alternative attractor. In particular, systemic shocks—such as energy and food supply shocks, pandemics, or financial meltdowns—can trigger bifurcation events, or periods of crisis and turbulence in which formerly taken-for-granted norms, routines, and expectations are disrupted; broader swathes of a population are politicized or radicalized; and previously unthinkable policy responses become thinkable, if not common sense. But crises are no guarantee that a system will shift to an alternative attractor: as we saw with the 2008 financial crisis and 2020 COVID-19 crisis, systems can also settle back into preexisting patterns after a brief window of opportunity.[13] Still, these are periods when alternative possibilities are revealed and new courses can be pursued, which requires the agency of counter-hegemonic movements to push the system toward alternative attractors in the possibility space.[14]

In sum, a problematic determines the possibility space of a complex system—creating a space of possible future trajectories, attractors that govern or constrain these trajectories through negative feedback mechanisms, and bifurcations between them. For Delandian complexity theory (like with system dynamics), the aim is to identify the key parameters that collectively compose a system's problematic, map the relations between them, "compute" or creatively imagine its possible trajectories, and illuminate the multiple attractors that appear to structure its possibility space. But in order to move from the abstract world of theory to the concrete realm of global politics and its possible futures, we need to creatively rework this framework and synthesize its insights with the work of world-systems theorists, ecological Marxists, critical security scholars, and others.

THE WORLD-EARTH SYSTEM

I start here with what we can call, following Levi Bryant, a "topographical map" of the world-earth system through the lens of planetary systems thinking; in other words, a map of its currently existing structure, as opposed to a "vector" map of its future possibility space.[15] As previously mentioned, the world-earth system refers to the broadest scale of analysis: the nexus that inextricably entwines the rhythms of global capitalism with the earth system, which forms a multiscalar structure of "nested" socioecological systems—from individual bodies to cities, nation-states, regions, the capitalist world-system, and the earth system as a whole. These systems are "nested" in the sense that systems at lower scales (e.g., local communities and cities) collectively compose higher-level systems at national, regional, and planetary scales.[16] States, for instance, can be understood as socioecological systems that are constrained by (while also co-constituting) the higher-scale dynamics of global capitalism and the earth, while cities and local communities are similarly constrained by while also co-constituting the higher-scale dynamics of territorial states and the broader earth system.[17] Different analyses can focus on planetary, regional, national, or more localized scales of the world-earth system, though these different geographic scales are always co-constitutive—with "causal powers running in all directions."[18]

Following world-systems theory, the capitalist world-system can be understood as an emergent planetary-scale formation that simultaneously integrates, constrains, and pressures all lower-level systems to pursue the function of endless capital accumulation—that is, by rewarding states, firms, and individuals who pursue capitalist goals and punishing those that do not.[19] Capitalism does not functionally subsume all other systems, as Marxists sometimes imply with the concept of "totality," but it can be considered the "ecologically dominant" structure governing the world-earth system. As Bob Jessop explains, ecological dominance refers to "the capacity of one system in a self-organizing ecology of self-organizing systems to cause more problems for other systems than they can cause for it."[20] Another way to put it, as E. O. Wright says, is that the functions of these other systems (e.g., law, security, media, education) are subordinated to the capital accumulation function, which prescribes "functional limits" within which these other systems operate.[21] For instance, while legal systems help moderate the worst excesses of capitalist exploitation, they rarely infringe on the "sacred" right of private property—even when this gives corporations license to extract and burn fossil fuel assets well in excess of the 2°C carbon budget; furthermore, in rare cases when they *do* infringe on private property rights, such as through eminent domain, this is most commonly done in the broader interests of capital (e.g. to build pipelines).[22]

The capitalist world-system also tends to produce and reproduce a "core-periphery" structure, or a pattern of uneven development between high-, low-, and middle-income countries and regions.[23] Core-periphery relations are inherently socioecological: multiple studies demonstrate that the global north benefits disproportionately from flows of embodied labor, land, energy, and raw materials coming from the global south—receiving eleven times more value-added per ton of raw materials embodied in its exports and up to twenty-eight times more value-added per unit of embodied labor.[24] In thermodynamic terms, core regions are spaces in which the "work-energy" of both humans and the earth tend to accumulate and crystallize in the form of resource-intensive infrastructures and technologies, while peripheries suffer disproportionately from the "entropy" that these flows of work-energy generate (e.g., in the form of air pollution, waste streams, and denuded landscapes).[25] Unlike earlier forms of dependency theory, we should highlight that core-periphery relations are dynamic rather than static: former peripheries can become semi-peripheries and eventually cores, and vice versa (made evident by the rise of China, India, and Brazil).[26] And rather than focusing only on relations between the global north and south, core-periphery relations operate not only between but also *within* nation-states, regions, and cities, forming a kind of "fractal" pattern of uneven development at all geographic scales—seen, for instance, in metropolitan regions exploiting their rural hinterlands, or rich neighborhoods in cities controlling resources while racialized low-income neighborhoods suffer from underinvestment.[27]

Planetary systems thinking also follows neo-Gramscian theory by viewing the state as a critical node of self-organization and counter-hegemonic struggle in the world-system. Rather than the image of a unified "actor" so common in IR theory, the state is better thought of as a terrain of competing hegemonic projects, with a given hegemonic ordering of the state based on an "unstable equilibria of compromise" within a power bloc and between this bloc and the broader population.[28] In this sense, the state is a complex system combining social, ecological, infrastructural, and institutional elements that can shift between different attractors (e.g., between more center-left and right-wing regimes). Counter-hegemonic struggle can shift states in more progressive directions that counteract the imperatives of capital accumulation—for instance, through Keynesian demand management, redistribution, and environmental regulation.[29] But the possibility space of state action is constrained under the pressures of global capital, since states are structurally reliant on capital accumulation to raise tax revenues, deliver public services, and mitigate social unrest. The state-form thus has a certain "strategic selectivity," as Jessop puts it,[30] that biases the interests of capital, though there is no *structural necessity* that it must forever remain capitalist. We can thus speculate on how states may evolve as ecological, political-economic, technological, demographic, and other parameters change over time. This could entail the rise of new state-forms that have not yet existed, as well as the "collapse" of existing state-forms—or a breakdown in their former structures and functions, leading to a "feudalized" landscape of competing sovereignties—which will be contingent on the outcome of struggles between competing hegemonic projects.

THE PLANETARY PROBLEMATIC

The foregoing conceptual analysis of the world-earth system gives us a way of mapping the current planetary conjuncture. The concept of the planetary problematic, in contrast, allows us to develop a "vector map" that illuminates the crises, stressors, and feedbacks working to destabilize current structures.[31] The planetary problematic is the nexus of intersecting problems that impels and constrains the self-organization of the world-earth system, creating a possibility space composed of not-yet-actual trajectories, attractors, and bifurcations between them. It represents the totality of relations and feedbacks between ecological, energy, food, political-economic, technological, and existential parameters—a much broader version of the Club of Rome's World Problematique. But unlike the LtG and other apolitical modeling approaches, we must emphasize that "solutions" to the planetary problematic will be determined by counter-hegemonic struggles between states, fractions of the capitalist class, intellectuals, and social movements to discursively frame these problems and mobilize power to control or shape how they are addressed in practice. While we can speak of more localized problematics at different scales—referring to the intersecting problems, vulnerabilities, constraints, and potentials confronting different states and regions across the world-system—the concept of the planetary problematic signifies that all of these local problematics are entangled, creating an emergent problematic that is more than the sum of its parts. Counter-hegemonic struggles over the planetary problematic will thus take place at multiple sites and scales across the world-earth system—from local communities and towns to cities, states, regions, and global institutions—with every struggle having both an intimately local and planetary significance.[32]

While the problems that compose the planetary problematic are all entwined through complex dependency relations, it is also useful to analytically distinguish between three key sets of problems within the overarching problematic, which are "solved" through the creation of political-economic, security, and ideological systems or assemblages: the socioecological problematic, the violence problematic, and the existential problematic.[33] Each set of problems forms a relatively autonomous problematic that is not reducible to the others, though they are all inextricably entangled. To paraphrase Kojin Karatani, they form a "Borromean knot," such that struggles and transformations in one field of problems necessarily entail conjoined transformations in the others.[34] Marxists have historically tended to focus on the economic or socioecological problematic while treating ideological and security apparatuses as "superstructural" phenomena. But each system or assemblage forms a solution to a relatively autonomous problematic, and breaking from the present trajectory of the world-earth system will require novel solutions for all three.

THE SOCIOECOLOGICAL PROBLEMATIC

The socioecological problematic (SEP) refers to the problem of producing and reproducing the metabolic foundations of a society: the flows of labor, energy, food, and raw materials that sustain a "way of life" while simultaneously transforming its ecological conditions. When the Club of Rome analyzed the World Problematique, they were really in this sense talking about the global SEP while sidelining the violence and existential problematics. Each "solution" to the SEP forms a socioecological or political-economic system (these terms, for me, are interchangeable, since political economies are always inextricable from ecological processes). Following the Marxian concept of "modes of production," these involve both *forces* and *relations* of production: the technologies and techniques through which labor practices (our metabolic relations with the earth) are configured, and the class-race-gender hierarchies through which collective labor, both "productive" and "reproductive," is organized, utilized, and constrained.[35] Every socioecological system or political economy is structured by a problematic that emerges from the relations between parameters like climate, geography, soil, microbes, water, energy sources, mineral deposits, and relations of power and resistance between social forces. These parameters are all entangled, some via tighter and others through more indirect feedback processes. This makes socioecological systems vulnerable to what Thomas Homer-Dixon calls "synchronous failure," or cascading crises in which shocks originating in one subsystem propagate through other subsystems—such as the COVID-19 shock cascading across financial, energy, food, climate, public health, and supply chain systems.[36] But there can be no climate or geophysical determinism: how socioecological systems respond to crises—whether through transformation, adaptation, or "collapse"—is always the product of political struggles, though the range of possible responses is necessarily constrained by the intersections among climactic, geological, and technological parameters.

While there is a "universal possibility space" that involves all possible solutions to the SEP across history,[37] capitalism can be understood as a historically specific solution to the SEP. Capitalism was itself born from the fires of socioecological crisis that ruptured the feudal era—shaped by the end of the Medieval Climate Optimum, overconsumption by the feudal classes, insufficient investment in productive innovation, soil degradation, population growth, and the bubonic plague—and has periodically adapted and transformed in response to changing socioecological parameters throughout its history (e.g., the depletion of local resource-complexes, requiring constant geographic expansion to resume capital accumulation on an expanded scale).[38] The result has been the continuous reproduction and expansion of a globalized political economy that constrains solutions to the SEP within capitalist parameters—that is, by constraining global patterns of land use, agriculture, energy-material consumption, and manufacturing in ways that are primarily concerned with sustaining capital accumulation and economic growth indefinitely. To what extent this particular historical solution can survive the twenty-first century is open to question. In other words, does a viable attractor exist in global capitalism's possibility space that would allow it to simultaneously sustain compound growth, mitigate or at least manage the consequences of ecological crises, and "at least partially [meet] the demands for livelihood protection emanating from mass movements," as Beverly Silver and Corey Payne say would be necessary to construct a more sustainable world capitalist hegemony?[39] Or, as Jason Moore suggests, might we witness "the breakdown of the strategies and relations that have sustained capital accumulation over the past five centuries"?[40] As I elaborate in subsequent chapters, my own view is that we are not necessarily facing the end of capital accumulation as a whole, especially if we agree that something like "capital" has existed in precapitalist societies.[41] But we may very well witness the end of capital-*ism* in the sense of a world-system in which capital accumulation forms the *ecologically dominant* organizing principle (a point I elaborate in chapter 5).

As with all socioecological systems throughout history, the ultimate trajectory of global capitalism will be determined not just by the coevolution of climate, energy, food, microbes, and other ecological parameters but by the success or failure of competing hegemonic projects to frame, manage, and navigate this nexus of problems. The dominant axis of struggle at present is between competing capitalist factions within the intersecting fields of climate, energy, finance, and food systems: on one side are the states and factions of the capitalist class most aligned with "fossil capital": mainly the fossil fuel industry and petro-states whose revenues are directly reliant on burning fossil fuels, but also the emissions-intensive cement, steel, automotive, arms manufacturing, and agribusiness firms whose profitability is (at least for now) inextricably bound up with fossil fuel combustion, along with the largest banks, asset managers, and hedge funds that finance their operations.[42] On the other side are the "green" reformist factions of the capitalist and state managerial classes rallying behind the Net Zero by 2050 agenda, including the Glasgow Financial Alliance for Net Zero (GFANZ); green capitalists like solar, wind, electric vehicle, and battery manufacturers; the tech giants seeking a renewable energy-powered high-tech utopia; central bankers concerned with the financial risks posed by climate change; public-private coalitions like the Global Alliance for Climate Smart Agriculture seeking to reform (or marginally tweak) industrial food systems; and pro-decarbonization centrist or center-left political parties.[43] Finance capital occupies an ambivalent middle position between the fossil and green capitalist blocs, with many of the world's largest banks and asset managers joining GFANZ while also continuing to finance fossil fuel projects (according to one estimate, fifty-six of the biggest banks in GFANZ have provided $270 billion for new fossil fuel projects since joining the alliance in 2021).[44] And even much of the "green" capitalist bloc—including the tech sector, finance capital, philanthro-capitalists like Bill Gates, and centrist NGOs like the Environmental Defense Fund—appears doubtful that capitalist efforts to stabilize the climate will succeed: hence their provision of millions in financial support for solar geoengineering research— which, as Kevin Surprise and JP Sapinski argue, is increasingly viewed by green (not just fossil) capital as "a *near-term supplement* for emissions cuts in alignment with [their] long-term vision of incremental, market-driven climate transitions."[45]

In contrast to these capitalist factions, there are a range of counter-hegemonic movements proposing postcapitalist solutions to the SEP, though these movements remain weak in the current conjuncture. On one hand, we can identify ecomodernist movements on the left that advocate maintaining or even radically advancing the productive forces unleashed by capitalism while subjecting them to a socialist rationality and more equitably distributing their fruits.[46] As we will see in subsequent chapters, while these approaches would provide the potential for a more ecologically rational world-system relative to contemporary capitalism, they would also encounter some of the same forms of technological problem-shifting explored in chapter 1. In contrast, more radical approaches—including degrowth, ecofeminism, postextractivism, and postdevelopment—directly challenge capitalist relations of production as well as the ideologies of "progress," consumerism, and "the good life" on which they're based. These approaches would be better placed to avoid technological problem-shifting and pursue genuinely sustainable and just solutions to the SEP, though they confront difficult questions about political feasibility in the foreseeable future.[47] We should not sugarcoat the obstacles these movements are up against, and it is understandable that many consider their programs to be little more than "abstract" rather than concrete utopian dreams.[48] But given the polycrisis storm bearing down on global capitalism, which could make it increasingly challenging to sustain material and energy intensive modes of living over time, these movements may be less utopian than their critics typically think (as I show in chapter 4).

THE VIOLENCE PROBLEMATIC

Entwined with the SEP, though relatively autonomous, is what I call the violence problematic (VP). As critical security theorists have long recognized, the problem of violence—how to regulate, constrain, and organize the exercise of interpersonal physical violence, both within and between societies—is one of the foundational genetic conditions of political order.[49] In other words, the problem of violence creates pressures that drive the self-organization of systems and practices for regulating, constraining, and responding to violence—including systems of war and military organization, diplomacy, law, and policing. Like the SEP, the VP can be considered a structure of dependency relations and feedbacks that morphs over time as its key parameters shift—for instance, through geopolitical realignments, technological changes, and shifts in the intensity of political-economic "structural violence" or exploitation (we can also include socioecological shifts like climate change, food system disruption, and energy transitions, which intersect with and shape patterns of conflict). Thus, like with the SEP, we can "model" the possible futures of violence by analyzing the feedbacks between these parameters.[50] But we must again avoid determinist assumptions (e.g., that worsening climate change will necessarily provoke increased conflict) and emphasize that these futures will be coproduced through counter-hegemonic struggle and contestation.

Modeling the futures of "violence" is complicated, however, by the fact that "violence" is itself a multidimensional and "essentially contested" concept. In other words, as Willem de Haan writes, "who and what is considered as violent varies according to specific socio-cultural and historical conditions."[51] But I focus mainly on two categories of "violence" (though in practice they sometimes blur together). The first category is "state violence," which refers to institutionalized practices of direct physical coercion and force projection that governments carry out against other societies as well as their own people. It includes military violence between states and police violence used to enforce social order within a state's territory, as well as military-police operations that project force against individuals and groups beyond a state's borders (e.g., through counterterrorism, counternarcotics, and migrant policing operations). The second category—"nonstate violence"—refers to "violence" as understood through the eyes of states and their networks of elites, security agencies, police forces, and intellectuals—hence its designation in the negative (*non*state) rather than receiving a positive signifier. Nonstate violence can thus potentially include everything from physical violence that directly causes bodily harm for human individuals or groups—such as violent "crime," nonstate "terrorism," violence against women, and violent insurgencies—to disruptive and transgressive acts that challenge the legal order and authority of the state and capital—including strikes, civil disobedience, sabotage, property destruction, and written or verbal statements seen to incite violence or revolution. This categorization may be confusing for some, since it includes acts of resistance typically thought of as "nonviolent." But it has two advantages: (1) it allows us to make sense of how states and their military-police forces define the "problem" to which they are tasked with responding, which encompasses threats to political-economic order more broadly rather than merely direct bodily harms; and (2) it captures the ambivalent, subjective, and essentially contested nature of the concept of violence. The key point is that concepts like "violence," "security threats," "crime," and "terrorism"—while not without objective referents—are inherently perspectival and subject to counter-hegemonic contestation over how they should be defined and addressed in practice.

Following Michael Williams, we can use the term "security assemblages" to describe "solutions" to the VP. As Williams explains, global security assemblages can be defined as "complex structures" that "inhabit national settings but are simultaneously stretched across national boundaries in terms of actors, knowledge, technologies, norms and values," and which encompass both public and private security agencies.[52] While security governance is to a large extent institutionally crystallized within specific national contexts, security assemblages complicate and exceed dichotomies like national/global, public/private, and war/policing. For instance, Caroline Holmqvist and colleagues use the concept of security assemblages to highlight the intersections between military power and policing. This follows Mark Neocleous's argument that "war and police are *always already together*," signifying "processes working in conjunction" to pacify populations and secure social order at simultaneously local and global scales.[53] Similarly, Didier Bigo shows that the post-9/11 field of global security has witnessed "the interlocking of internal security agencies and the subordination of both military and police to 'intelligence' services."[54] The result can be described as an emergent global "surveillant assemblage" that integrates different national security agencies under the leadership of the US and its NATO allies—what Giuseppe Zappala calls the "Fourteen Eyes" (an expansion of the original "Five Eyes" intelligence alliance).[55] Private companies increasingly play a critical role in these global security assemblages, both as providers of "security" services themselves (e.g., private military and security firms like Wagner Group and G4S) and as developers and operators of the technological platforms that militaries and intelligence agencies rely on (e.g., Amazon's provision of cloud computing services to the US Department of Defense).[56] Following these scholars, I use the term "military-police assemblages" to describe the particular form of security governance that relies on military and policing logics and institutions to manage "violence" by means of violence. Military-police assemblages are thus a particular kind of security assemblage, whereas the latter is a broader category that can in principle involve practices for regulating and constraining violence that do not involve military and police institutions (a point I return to below).

One important question concerns the extent to which military-police assemblages today form an emergent global system, or whether they are better understood as connected yet nationally distinct security apparatuses. Michael Williams takes the latter position, arguing that global security assemblages have a more heterogeneous or networked structure rather than forming a tightly integrated global system.[57] Hence his use of the term *assemblage* rather than *system*. In contrast, Catherine Besteman argues that we may be witnessing the emergence of a "totalizing system" that she calls "militarized global apartheid," understood as a racially segregated world order that integrates systems of surveillance, biometric tracking, militarized borders, criminalization, and incarceration in order to secure spaces of privilege while constraining the mobility of racialized populations.[58] Besteman suggests that militarized global apartheid is divided between relatively autonomous "security empires" that emanate from different states—particularly the United States, the EU, and Israel, but also China, India, and Saudi Arabia—which can be thought of as distinctive projects of racialized control that link "domestic carcerality to extra-state forms of military intervention, counterinsurgency, and border control."[59] But these security empires are also inextricably entwined through shared discourses (e.g., the threat of Islamic terrorism), techniques (e.g., mass incarceration, militarized borders), and technologies (e.g., AI, big data, facial recognition and other biometrics technologies).[60] William Robinson goes even further by claiming that global military-police assemblages can today be described as an emergent "global police state," or a "repressive totality" in which "omnipresent systems of mass social control, repression, and warfare [are] promoted by the ruling groups to contain the real and the potential rebellion of the global working class and surplus humanity."[61] His analysis is broadly similar to Besteman's, though it draws more attention to how privatized security firms and services—from private mercenary armies and police forces to privatized prisons, immigrant detention and deportation services, border technology firms, and surveillance firms—form a crucial investment outlet for overaccumulated capital in an era of structural crisis for global capitalism.[62]

The truth lies somewhere between these two poles. Because of geopolitical rivalries and often opposed (but overlapping) national articulations of the key threats to global security, global military-police assemblages are less of an integrated global system compared to global capitalism—hence my designation of them as *assemblages*. But this may change over time, whether in the direction of fragmentation (e.g., in a "regional rivalry" scenario) or deeper global consolidation.

Despite the disciplinary divisions that frequently sever security studies from political economy, the relations between political economies and security assemblages in practice are deep and inextricable. Some might therefore ask whether it makes sense to distinguish between the SEP and the VP in the first place. In particular, by making this distinction, there is a risk that my approach falls into a sort of dualism that obscures their underlying entanglements. This critique is often made of Weberian state theorists and Marxists who identify distinct economic and geopolitical "logics" of power. As Andreas Bieler and Adam Morton argue, such an approach risks reifying the state, or a "military-industry moment," as "distinct and separate from world capitalism," rather than dialectically *internalizing* their relations.[63] I acknowledge that this is a risk, but I believe it is worth taking this risk to move beyond the limits of existing Marxist approaches.

This analytical distinction is valuable for at least two reasons. The first, simply put, is that the interests of global capital and security agencies don't always coincide. Rather, following Bob Jessop, we can say that they form intersecting hegemonic projects that are "strategically coupled" yet irreducible to each other.[64] For example, as Didier Bigo explains, militaries and security professionals (or "securocrats") have their own interests that are not simply beholden to those of transnational capital; rather, they struggle to enhance their autonomy to police the field of security governance, determine which "threats" get prioritized, and constrain the range of possible responses.[65] However, it is also true that the interests of trans-national capital, intelligence agencies, police institutions, and militaries are deeply entangled. For instance, as Peter Phillips shows, global capitalist elites and security professionals often share similar worldviews and pursue convergent policies that support each other's interests. They do this in part through global fora such as the Atlantic Council—the key advisory group that "sets the parameters of US–NATO operational expectations and global security priorities"—which lists many of the world's leading asset managers, defense contractors, and former NATO commanders on its board of directors.[66] But it seems more accurate to frame this relationship as one of *strategically coupled hegemonic projects*, rather than a *singular* hegemonic project with transnational capital at the helm and global military-police assemblages reduced to the function of executing its will. As Jessop writes, hegemony can "never be constructed by just one set of social forces anchored in just one sub-system. . . . It rather emerges from the interaction of various social forces rooted in different orders so that they share common programmatic objectives despite their differing codes."[67] Following Jessop, even if we agree that transnational capital is the "ecologically dominant" power in the capitalist world-system, it is nonetheless true that there are differences in the "programmatic objectives" of capitalists and security professionals that arise from the relatively distinct problematics to which they respond. Thus it is valuable to distinguish between hegemonic projects on the conjoined but irreducible terrains of the SEP and VP, which can also allow us to anticipate possible futures (as I discuss in chapter 5) in which solutions to the VP become ecologically dominant—thereby constituting one possible path, though not an ideal one from the perspective of social justice, by which the capitalist world-system may cease to be primarily "capitalist."

The second, and arguably more important, reason that it is valuable to make this distinction is because it brings more attention to counter-hegemonic struggles on the terrain of the VP—including struggles against militarization, policing, mass incarceration, surveillance, and militarized borders. Marxist theorists, even those like Robinson who foreground the relations between global capital and military-police assemblages, have traditionally ignored or at best viewed these struggles as secondary to struggles on the terrain of political economy. As George Rigakos argues,

this has produced two limitations in Marxist theory: (1) an explicit critical theory of security is never developed, and (2) no "programmatic ideas
about security after capitalism" are ever entertained.[68] Fortunately, while
struggles against militarism and policing are nothing new, they have risen
to prominence in recent years largely thanks to the success of Black Lives
Matter and allied movements, which draw inspiration from the work of
"abolitionist" scholars like Angela Davis and Ruth Wilson Gilmore.[69] Adam
Elliot-Cooper provides a useful and succinct articulation of the abolitionist
position: "Policing and prisons are forms of state violence which add more
violence to the problems they claim to solve. . . . Abolitionist reforms . . .
would erode society's reliance on the police and prison systems, and
instead empower community-led and social solutions to the inequalities
which lead to violence and harm in the first place."[70] Abolitionist reforms
in this sense may include providing secure housing and free education,
guaranteeing secure and unionized employment, investing in educational
programs to "dismantle sexist assumptions" and reduce violence toward
women and non-binary people, decriminalizing drugs while improving
mental health services for those struggling with addiction, and expanding
community-led practices for managing public safety.[71] Taking inspiration
from these movements, Arun Kundnani develops an abolitionist approach
to "national security," one that "advocates building institutions that foster the social and ecological relationships needed to live dignified lives,
rather than reactively identifying groups of people who are seen as threatening."[72] The aim in both cases is to navigate toward a future in which the
VP is no longer primarily addressed through military, policing, and carceral
"solutions," but rather by nonpunitive, nonviolent, and restorative justice
and public safety practices that emerge in tandem with more equitable
political economies.

Another way to articulate the challenge for counter-hegemonic theory
and strategy, as Rigakos puts it, is to develop a "socialist police science" that,
like the "capitalist police science" of the eighteenth and nineteenth centuries, takes "seriously the legal, economic, and security planning necessary for
the transition from one mode of production to another. . . . A post-capitalist
future depends on systematically re-purposing this apparatus and harnessing
its technological potential for a democratic security at the core of a democratic economic social order."[73] Many abolitionists may view the concept of

a "socialist police science," as well as calls for "repurposing" existing security apparatuses, with skepticism if not alarm. But these two approaches may not be so opposed as appears at first glance. If we take a navigational counter-hegemonic approach, which emphasizes (as many abolitionists do) that abolition is an inherently long-term project—a "regulative ideal" that can inform activism and policy in the present—this means new narratives and practices of "security" (or "safety," if one prefers) will be needed in the near-term to create the conditions for longer-term abolitionist transitions. The scars of war, police brutality, capitalist exploitation, and inequality that fuel geopolitical tensions and drive cycles of violence-begetting-violence— both between and within states—will not heal overnight. Progressive strategies for managing geopolitical tensions, ensuring public safety, protecting critical infrastructures, and preventing nonstate terrorism (particularly but not solely from the far-right) would thus be needed by left-wing regimes that may come to power in the future. As Stephen Wertheim rightly claims, by "avoiding conventionally defined security questions, the left cedes this terrain to the establishment," and democratic constituencies "need to hear how a different approach will make them safer."[74] It will ultimately be challenging to escape the gravitational pull of hegemonic militarization-policing attractors, since the fear of real or perceived threats creates immense pressure to perpetuate current institutionalized solutions, while future outbreaks of violence (e.g., from nonstate terrorist attacks, worsening gun violence, or military aggression) can form negative feedbacks that reinforce military-police institutions if/when particular localities or states begin to navigate beyond them. We are seeing this today, for instance, in European states like Germany who are remilitarizing in response to the war in Ukraine, as well as in American cities like Los Angeles where surges in gun violence have reversed efforts to reduce police forces.[75] Still, we can speculate that an "abolitionist attractor" exists in the possibility space, which will require patient, long-term transformation in political economies and security (as well as ideological) assemblages.

THE EXISTENTIAL PROBLEMATIC

While the existential problematic (EP) receives less attention than the first two in this book, it is nonetheless necessary to include it. The EP refers to the problem of creating forms of collective meaning, identity, and belong-ing. It is the source of what Michael Mann calls "ideological power," which "derives from the human need to find ultimate meaning in life, to share norms and values, and to participate in aesthetic and ritual practices with others."[76] I use the concept of ideological assemblages to describe "solu-tions" to the EP, but we should emphasize that ideologies are much more than just systems of ideas or beliefs: rather, they include the unconscious, affective, and emotional attachments through which identities and ways of life are reproduced. In this sense they are similar to what Raymond Wil-liams calls "structures of feeling," described by Alex Williams as "something looser, more pervasive, and less conceptual or semantic than 'ideology,' a kind of affective register of lived experience."[77] Ideological assemblages emerge from relations between neurobiological, social, technological, institutional, and discursive components—including brains, bodies, social-ization processes, media networks, education institutions, and forms of knowledge.[78] I use the term *assemblage* here to indicate that these are not logically coherent networks of ideas and beliefs (which the concept "ideological system" would imply), but rather looser configurations that nonetheless tend to produce distinctive patterns of thinking and feeling. Like with all complex systems, we can say that ideological assemblages are governed by attractors or negative feedback mechanisms that main-tain them within particular parameters, but they can also bifurcate or shift toward alternative configurations—whether within a single human indi-vidual or across a society more broadly. Similarly, Thomas Homer-Dixon and colleagues suggest that a "cognitive-affective belief system constitutes a basin of attraction in the state space of possible belief systems," and that ideological transitions often involve "more a jump into a new coherent cognitive-affective state [or attractor] than a gradual adjustment of some convictions."[79] Solutions to the EP are always complex and multilayered: each human individual is a specific "solution," a way of creating meaning, identity, and belonging that is shaped by their particular history as well as their location within a matrix of power relations.[80] But it is possible to identify dominant ideological or cognitive-affective patterns that govern global politics today.

Alex Anievas and Kerem Nisancioglu, for instance, show that the birth of capitalism was inextricably bound up with the "ideological apparatus" of race, white supremacy, and Eurocentric notions of "progress," which would "serve both to legitimise the horrors of colonialism and spur the development of capitalism."[81] This ideological assemblage formed a "solution" to a relatively autonomous problematic—the problem of creating meaning and belonging for a European psyche disturbed by the interlinked crises of feudalism and Christendom—rather than emerging solely because of its instrumental legitimizing function for the nascent colonial-capitalist world-system. But we can say that it coevolved in a "strategically coupled" way with the emergence of capitalism and its military-police assemblages, giving birth to the structural formation that is often called "racial capitalism."[82] This ideological assemblage would continuously evolve and adapt over time, taking on a more secular character in the nineteenth century, shaped by the emerging ideologies of liberalism and social Darwinism, and a less *explicitly* racist character in the mid-twentieth century under the aegis of US hegemony and its promise of "development" and shared consumerist abundance.[83] Rather than a monolithic entity, this "solution" to the EP, like capitalism, takes on unique articulations in different national-cultural contexts and contains its own internal struggles (e.g., between more secular cosmopolitan and religious or ethnonationalist tendencies). But these articulations share certain features: ideologies of "progress" based on economic growth and techno-scientific mastery; desires for consumerism as the path to the "good life"; and Darwinian ideas about competition and superiority/inferiority based on relations of class, race, gender, and ethnicity.[84] Even those of us who intellectually repudiate such ideas are nonetheless conditioned by them, showing that ideological assemblages go much deeper than mere ideas and beliefs.

Despite its fluidity and adaptability, this ideological assemblage clearly forms a constraint on the solution-space for the planetary problematic. It serves to delegitimize Indigenous and peasant-based forms of knowledge and socioecological practices by framing them as "backward"; reinforce racialized military-police solutions to the VP; at best (e.g., among ecomodernist leftists), constrain the political imagination within more egalitarian forms of modernist "monoculture;"[85] and, at worst, fuel ethnonationalist and hypermasculine rage toward Others who threaten increasingly fragile forms of identity and belonging. But counter-hegemonic challenges to this ideological assemblage are becoming more widespread, seen in calls to "decolonize the imaginary" of growth, rethink ideologies of "progress," and revive Indigenous and other ancestral solutions to the SEP—not as nostalgic yearnings for the past but for the purposes of constructing decolonial futures.[86] We can expect that the coming decades will be an era of cognitive and affective turbulence, with shifts in climate, political economy, technology, and other parameters sparking or reinforcing existential crises that further destabilize these dominant structures of meaning and identity. As discussed in chapter 1, such crises can have the effect of triggering aggressive reassertions of identity based on hardened self/other relations. But they can also enable ideological transitions toward new forms of solidarity and belonging beyond the capitalist, racist, and nationalist patterns of modernity.

This is arguably the most difficult dimension of the planetary problematic: we know, for instance, what needs to be done to stop climate change, but no one seems to have yet figured out how to stop far-right populism, or how to galvanize psychosocial tipping points toward more progressive subjectivities and solidarities. I do not pretend to provide answers to this conundrum. All we can say is that the success of counter-hegemonic movements will be contingent on the capacities of activists, intellectuals, and progressive policymakers to formulate compelling narratives that resonate with people during the "far-from-equilibrium crisis" situations that will emerge with greater frequency in the coming years, thereby nudging them toward alternative worldviews.[87] But how this can be done at scale, and whether it can overwhelm or neutralize the tide of ethnonationalist reaction, remains to be seen.

NAVIGATING PLANETARY FUTURES: FROM MODELING TO MAPPING

I briefly conclude this chapter by elaborating the futures "methodology" that is informed by planetary systems thinking, showing in particular how it overlaps with and differs from quantitative modeling approaches. One way to articulate this difference is via the distinction between modeling and "mapping": whereas computational models develop restricted portraits of systems that focus on quantifiable variables that can be represented via differential equations, mapping is a more qualitative exercise that grapples with a wider range of relations and feedbacks—a practice of situating and orienting ourselves in an inexhaustibly complex planetary reality.[88] It encompasses what Levi Bryant describes as topographical, vector, and modal forms of mapping: topographical maps provide a "snapshot" of complex systems in a given historical conjuncture; vector maps "chart trajectories along which worlds are unfolding," thus providing a glimpse of futures based on the "gravitational tendencies of the present"; and modal maps provide what we could call "concrete utopian" maps of "futures that *could* exist" if counter-hegemonic movements are able to reshape these systems in particular ways.[89] But to develop vector or modal maps of possible futures requires more than linearly extrapolating key trends; rather, as Patomäki emphasizes, we must also imagine "crises and other possible nodal points of world history" (i.e., bifurcation events) that may rupture these linear trajectories, thus setting up a subsequent set of possible alternative pathways.[90]

In this sense, the "methodology" of planetary systems thinking involves analyzing the dependency relations between the key parameters that compose the SEP, VP, and EP; bringing together theory, data, and modeling projections to anticipate how these parameters may coevolve over time; and imagining multiple future trajectories—along with potential bifurcation events—that are *coherent* in the sense of following the dependency relations between the parameters. Constructing future scenarios in a way that integrates these numerous parameters and rigorously respects the dependency relations between them is of course a major challenge. Climate models and IAM projections can aid us, but to account for the qualitative, nonlinear complexity of real-world systems—as well as the role of human agency and counter-hegemonic struggles in determining their futures—we must rely in part on what I call "synthetic intuition": a way of intuitively grappling with complexity that is informed by a combination of theory, historical understanding, conjunctural analysis, modeling projections, and futurological imagination. While some would view this as an "unscientific" approach that lacks the rigor of quantification, in reality it recognizes that imagination and intuition are as critical to the sciences—particularly to IAMs and climate scenario work—as to the arts and humanities, though "they remain buried in practices and intuitive forms of testing that are not properly acknowledged."[91] In this sense, the task of grappling with planetary futures is not a question of modeling versus intuition, quantification versus qualitative narrative, but is instead a matter of developing frameworks that can facilitate bricolage among seemingly disparate methods, theories, and forms of knowledge—in this way developing a "complex, theoretically informed lens through which to speculate coherently" about the future, as Mann and Wainwright call for.[92] This is the promise of planetary systems thinking, as well as its challenge.

CONCLUSION

In sum, the world-earth system is the multiscalar structure linking global capitalism and the earth system. The planetary problematic, in turn, is the structure of intersecting problems, tensions, and feedbacks that is destabilizing the world-earth system and driving the emergence of alternative futures. It can be analytically parsed into the socioecological problematic (SEP), the violence problematic (VP), and the existential problematic (EP), each of which forms a site of competing hegemonic projects and counter-hegemonic struggles—involving struggles over the organization and direction of socioecological, security, and ideological systems or assemblages. But they are all inextricably linked—the parameters of each problematic forming parameters for the others—as figure 3.1 shows. Mapping the possible futures of global capitalism and the earth requires us to identify the most relevant parameters both within and between these three problematics, analyze their dependency relations and feedbacks, extrapolate the most likely trajectories or scenarios for how these assemblages may coevolve, identify potential "nodal points" or crises that would rupture these trajectories, and imaginatively construct multiple diverging pathways that may unfold following these bifurcation events.

I should emphasize that planetary systems thinking, like complexity theory more broadly, is simply a "meta-theoretical" orientation, a conceptual scaffold or "skeleton" (to use Boulding's term) that can facilitate transdisciplinary analysis of the future possibility space.[93] By itself it cannot tell us much about what the actual futures of the world-earth system might be. For this, as I have repeatedly emphasized, we need to do the work of synthesizing theory and data across numerous disciplinary and

The planetary problematic

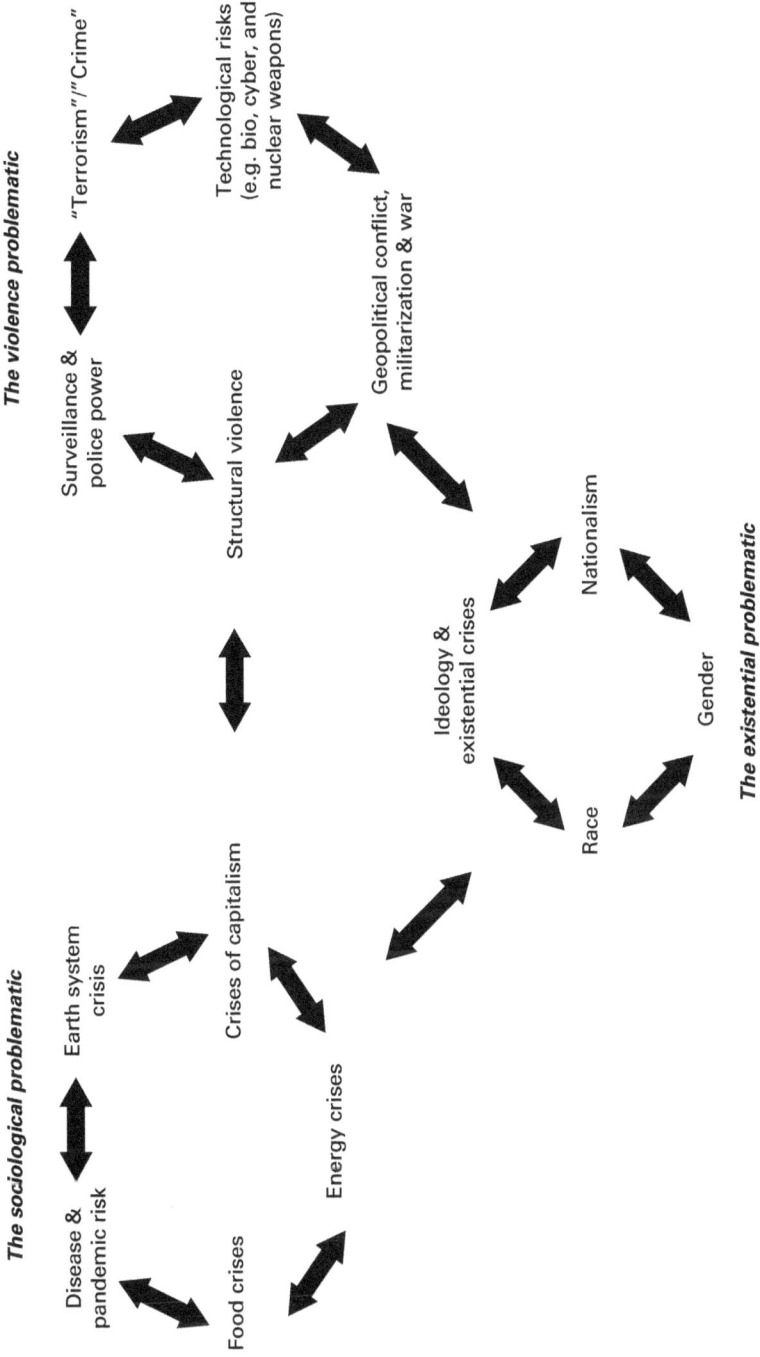

The sociological problematic

The violence problematic

The existential problematic

Food crises

Energy crises

Disease & pandemic risk

Earth system crisis

Crises of capitalism

Structural violence

Surveillance & police power

"Terrorism"/"Crime"

Technological risks (e.g. bio, cyber, and nuclear weapons)

Geopolitical conflict, militarization & war

Ideology & existential crises

Race

Gender

Nationalism

3.1

methodological traditions. My own analysis in the chapters to come inevitably entails a partial and selective synthesis. But my hope is that other analysts—who may have different evaluations of the most important problems or parameters, come from different disciplinary and theoretical perspectives, and highlight other crucial feedbacks that I do not account for—may build on and enrich planetary systems thinking and the futures analysis developed in the following chapters.

4

THE SOCIOECOLOGICAL PROBLEMATIC: CLIMATE, ENERGY, FOOD, AND THE FUTURES OF CAPITALISM

This chapter begins our direct investigation of the future possibility space by focusing on the socioecological problematic (SEP). As discussed in chapter 3, to analyze the SEP we must begin in a way analogous to system dynamics models. That is, we first identify the most relevant parameters or elements of the problematic under investigation and explore the dependency relations and feedbacks between them. As is common in systems modeling diagrams, I will often represent these relationships using bidirectional arrows (e.g., climate ←→ energy, climate ←→ food). The arrows refer to dependency relations through which events, crises, and policies adopted in one subsystem impact and cascade across the others. These can be the direct result of geophysical processes, such as extreme weather shocks disrupting energy and food systems, while others involve the intentional or unintentional results of policy, such as the effects of energy security strategies on the climate crisis or the effects of climate policies on energy and food systems. Feedback loops occur when these cascading impacts on other systems circle back and impact the sub-system where the policy or shock originated, which can either amplify or dampen the initial stimulus.[1]

The key parameters I focus on in this chapter include climate, biodiversity, energy, food, pandemic disease, political economy, and ideology, though all these parameters are composed of numerous sub-parameters that are connected through complex causal chains and feedback loops. I begin by briefly describing some of the key dependency relations within the earth system, and then broaden the analysis to investigate the earth system ←→ political economy nexus. From there I expand to first integrate the energy parameter, then food, and finally the nexus between the SEP and the existential problematic. The next step will be to linearly extrapolate current trends in these conjoined parameters while respecting the dependency relations between them. Subsequently, we can identify possible crises or "nodal point" conjunctures that may create the conditions for discontinuous ruptures, explore the counter-hegemonic struggles that will determine how governments respond to such crises, and then examine the subsequent trajectories that would unfold following such responses. I do not claim to provide an exhaustive survey of all possible world-earth system trajectories in this chapter. But by bringing together critical social theory with IAM projections and other forms of knowledge, the goal is to construct a richer, more realistic, and comprehensive set of scenarios than would be possible in the absence of transdisciplinary synthesis. To quote Wallerstein again, "The more difficult we acknowledge the task to be, the more urgent it is that we start sooner rather than later."[2]

CLIMATE ←→ EARTH SYSTEM → PANDEMIC DISEASE

I begin briefly with the links between the climate crisis, earth system change, and pandemic risk, which involve feedbacks that can take on their own momentum beyond human influence. Climate and earth system models tend to ignore or only weakly capture the complex feedbacks between cumulative atmospheric carbon, ocean acidification, ice sheet dynamics, forest dieback, permafrost melt (both terrestrial and subsea), and methane from wetlands, as well as other tipping elements like the Atlantic Meridional Overturning Circulation (AMOC).[3] As discussed in chapter 1, this means that the IPCC and Climate Action Tracker's warming projections associated with different emissions pathways will almost certainly prove to be conservative. Following Mark Lynas and others who take more account of recent studies suggesting faster-than-expected feedbacks, I therefore assume we should add an extra 0.3°C–0.5°C to more linear warming projections.[4] This would, for example, give us a best median estimate of 3°C–3.2°C rather than 2.7°C by 2100 from a current-policies trajectory, and a median estimate of 2.7°C–2.9°C rather than 2.4°C for a scenario in which all states meet their NDCs under the Paris Agreement.[5] But we should also acknowledge the potential for more gradualist—as well as even more rapid and catastrophic—warming trajectories.

Additionally, we should briefly highlight how the climate crisis will intensify other disruptions in the earth system. For one, climate change is a key driver of mass extinction by undermining the temperature niches to which different species have adapted, which can trigger abrupt collapse in particular ecological assemblages when they pass a given temperature threshold.[6] In turn, this can not only feedback on the climate crisis by releasing carbon from degraded ecosystems, but also intensify pandemic risk by denuding habitats and altering the migratory patterns of zoonotic disease vectors like bats and rodents, thereby forcing them into closer proximity with humans.[7] While politically and economically driven land-use change is the key driver of zoonotic spillover risk, the convergence between climate change and collapsing species assemblages would further amplify these risks if/when we cross tipping points in these ecosystems. In short, while we may have already "entered a pandemic era,"[8] this may be nothing compared to what is in store for us by mid-century and beyond if current trends continue.

POLITICAL ECONOMY ←→ CLIMATE/EARTH SYSTEM

These feedbacks show that earth system trajectories will not be entirely determined by human agency. But at least for the foreseeable future, political struggles over the future of global capitalism will have the most influence on climate and earth system futures.

Political economy is of course a hugely complex and internally differentiated parameter with numerous sub-parameters. But to simplify things, beginning with the political economy → earth system dependency relation, I focus on how competing hegemonic projects over the organization and direction of the global political economy will shape climate and earth system trajectories. This approach is analogous to the IPCC's association of the SSPs with specific emissions trajectories (e.g., SSP1 leading to a 1.5°C or 2°C compatible trajectory, SSP2 leading to a 2.7°C trajectory, and so on).[9] But unlike the IPCC, we must provide a deeper understanding of the power relations, political coalitions, and global political-economic transformations (or lack thereof) that would correspond with each earth system trajectory.

As I elaborate further in the scenarios below, we can identify four political-economic attractors or trajectories that populate the world-system possibility space: (1) a "neoliberal drift" trajectory, in which the world-system, despite the critically weakened legitimacy of neoliberalism, continues to drift along its current trajectory, with no sufficiently powerful coalition emerging that is able to enact or sustain the policies needed to decisively change course; (2) a "green Keynesian" trajectory, in which coalitions of green finance and manufacturing capitalists, center-left political parties, and social movements in core states are able to accelerate the transition away from fossil capital toward more sustainable energy and food systems; (3) a "fossil nationalist" trajectory (which, in its more extreme forms, could be called "fossil fascism"[10]), in which the factions of the capitalist class most aligned with fossil capital ally with right-wing populist movements to defend endless fossil fuel combustion;[11] and (4) an "ecosocialist" trajectory, in which increasingly powerful climate justice and labor movements, most likely in a context of deep capitalist crisis, succeed in reshaping the global political economy to prioritize sustainably and equitably meeting human needs (rather than profit and growth).[12]

While it is possible to imagine many different geographically uneven and combined variations of these scenarios, we can also roughly anticipate that each one, if globally dominant, would correspond with a particular emissions trajectory: neoliberal drift, for example, would perpetuate a gradualist, half-hearted approach to climate mitigation, leading to somewhere between the current-policies and NDC scenarios (i.e., between 2.7°C and 3.2°C by 2100). Green Keynesianism would accelerate mitigation, but given constraints on the speed of emissions reductions in a context of rising GDP and energy consumption (discussed in chapter 1), this would likely at most enable global emissions reductions of about 3%–4% per year.[13] This could give us a shot at the 2°C target if it happens soon enough (e.g., following an "announced pledges" scenario in which states follow through on their net zero pledges), though this would likely require significant carbon removal efforts by 2070.[14] Fossil nationalism, if it becomes globally dominant (an unlikely but plausible scenario), would ensure a hellish climate future even worse than a current-policies scenario, whereas an ecosocialist transition that breaks from the GDP growth-constraint would enable a far more rapid emissions reduction and planetary rewilding trajectory that could bring the 1.5°C target within reach. Furthermore, I will assume—following the arguments of ecological economists discussed in chapter 1—that all three of the capitalist trajectories would involve continuously rising material-energy throughput, leading to intensifying pressure on land use and biodiversity as GDP continues to exponentially expand, but with more significant relative decoupling in the green Keynesian scenario. Only the ecosocialist scenario could bring a stop to this broader assault on the earth system.

This gives us a schematic overview of how global political-economic struggles will shape the futures of climate and the earth, but things are further complicated by the fact that earth system changes will *themselves* feedback on and shape the ultimate trajectories of global capitalism. I focus here primarily on what economists call "physical risks," that is, the literal physical impacts of climate change on economic growth, as well as "transition risks," which refer to the risks of stranded assets and financial instability resulting from the RE transition.[15] Starting with physical risks, climate change will impact economic growth by shifting capital from production to infrastructure repair and adaptation, increasing health-care costs, dampening consumer and investor confidence, diminishing labor productivity (particularly for outdoor workers), devaluing real estate in coastal regions that over time become uninsurable, and (potentially) provoking financial crises (e.g., if extreme storms trigger widespread insurance claims and debt defaults among homeowners and businesses, particularly in "systemically important" regions like the US northeast coast).[16] There is immense uncertainty concerning projected total damages in different mitigation scenarios, though a Swiss Re Institute report—which includes extreme weather impacts on growth that are typically neglected in other modeling studies—projects that the physical risks of 2°C+warming could wipe out 10% of global GDP by 2050, while they will "increasingly puts the break on economic growth in the latter half of this century" if warming continues unchecked.[17] These projections are of course highly uncertain and should be taken with a grain of salt: near-term investments in adaptation would soften the impacts, though the model's inability to account for complex cascading risks across the interlinked realms of climate, finance, agriculture, and energy suggests the projections could also be a significant underestimate.

Moving to transition risks, Jean-Francois Mercure and company estimate that stranded fossil fuel assets would generate global losses of about $1–$4 trillion, which would be comparable to the write-down suffered during the 2008 financial crisis.[18] However, these account only for losses in the energy sector: when taking into account second-order impacts across the global economy—including hits to the automobile, cement, steel, shipping, aviation, and other industries that reman reliant on fossil fuels—such devaluations may place up to $20 or $25 trillion at risk (i.e., roughly 10% of global GDP).[19] Because of these risks, the Bank of International Settlements (BIS) suggests that "extremely rapid and ambitious [decarbonization] measures may be the most desirable from the point of view of climate mitigation, but not necessarily from the perspective of financial stability."[20] However, it emphasizes that "delayed and weak action to mitigate climate change would lead to higher and potentially catastrophic physical risks, without necessarily entirely eliminating transition risks," whereas "delayed actions followed by strong actions in an attempt to catch up would probably lead to both physical *and* transition risks."[21]

In sum, even just focused on the climate problem alone, we can see that global capitalism must navigate a tight catwalk between the pitfalls of physical and transition risks, which gets more and more challenging the longer that ambitious mitigation is delayed. And we should remember, as discussed in chapter 1, that capitalism is already—even before bringing in the climate problem—ensnared in a structural crisis driven by the reinforcing dynamics of inequality, stagnation, financialization, and skyrocketing debt.[22] Collectively this forms a more destabilizing crisis architecture than would be the case if we focused on climate or political-economic crises in isolation.

ENERGY ⟵→ POLITICAL ECONOMY ⟵→ CLIMATE

But while the earth system/political economy nexus is central to the SEP, it does not take us far enough: energy is a relatively autonomous parameter that creates an even more dangerous polycrisis architecture, as the 2022 energy shock made clear.

Starting with the political economy→energy relation, we know that different hegemonic trajectories will entail different energy consumption profiles for the world-system. For instance, if we follow IEA projections, neoliberal drift would likely mirror the "stated policies" scenario in which fossil fuels (FF) continue to take up 74% of the global energy mix in 2030 and 61% in 2050 (down from roughly 80% today), and things would be even worse in a fossil nationalist trajectory.[23] A global green Keynesian transition could bend the curve toward the announced pledges scenario, in which unabated FF takes up 69% of the global energy mix by 2030 and 34% in 2050, though more rapid innovation in and diffusion of RE technologies could plausibly phase out FF more rapidly in this scenario.[24] Furthermore, we can expect with high confidence that all three capitalist trajectories will entail rising total energy consumption: as we saw in chapter 1, the evidence suggests that GDP growth cannot be absolutely decoupled from energy use at the global scale—particularly once we account for rebound effects, as well as the rapidly rising energy demands of the global south.[25] This puts a damper on hopes that even green Keynesian trajectories would be able to meet the 1.5°C target, since this would require unrealistic expectations about absolute decoupling (e.g., as in the IEA's net zero by 2050 scenario), though it does not foreclose the potential that it could be compatible with 2°C trajectories.

Shifting to the energy→political economy relation: as discussed in chapter 1, because of the looming contradiction between "structural underinvestment" and projected rising demand for oil and gas, global capitalism will remain highly vulnerable to energy price shocks in the coming years. Furthermore, if predictions of a nonlinear "net energy cliff" indeed prove to be accurate, then such shocks could be even deeper, more protracted, and intransigent than anticipated by mainstream energy analysts.[26] But as the 2022 energy shock made clear, energy crises are never caused by geological factors alone. Net energy decline can be thought of as a "secular" or long-run trend that (analogous to rising temperatures) "loads the dice" by raising the risks of supply shocks, but any particular shock is always the result of specific proximate causes that combine in a given conjuncture. These include investment trends, economic growth rates, OPEC decision-making (e.g., lowering output even when prices are high), geopolitical tensions (including war, blockades, sanctions regimes), and even anti-extractivist activism (e.g., by preventing multi-gigaton "carbon bomb" projects from coming on line,[27] which is absolutely essential from a climate perspective, though the possible consequences for energy security in a context of rising FF demand must be anticipated). In turn, upstream supply shocks, in conjunction with downstream profiteering by energy companies, would feedback on political-economies by fueling inflation and dampening growth if not causing an outright recession, with uncertain ramifications for debt and financial stability. At the same time, they would also feedback on the climate crisis in uncertain and potentially contradictory ways depending on how states respond: for example, by ramping up coal production and extending new licenses for oil and gas extraction to meet energy security objectives, or by accelerating the RE transition. "All-of-the-above" energy strategies—ramping up FF, nuclear, *and* RE production—were the dominant response to the 2022 energy shock, and a key question is whether we will witness more of the same during future energy crises, or whether a more rapid RE transition and FF phasedown might occur.

In an era of rising temperatures, the proximate causes of energy crises will also increasingly include climate shocks. This brings us to the climate → energy crisis relation, which has three main components: (1) the impacts of climate policy on energy security; (2) the direct physical impacts of climate change on energy infrastructure; and (3) the additional energy demands created by adapting to climate change. First, as noted in chapter 1, there is (sadly) not yet clear evidence that net zero pledges have played an important role in dampening new investment in oil and gas.[28] But these pledges, and the risk of more ambitious climate policies to come, add to future demand uncertainties and thus could be a secondary contributing factor to future FF supply shocks.

Second, the direct impacts of climate on energy infrastructure can manifest in different ways. For one, scholars of the "food-water-energy" nexus illuminate how energy production relies on water, which means the intensification of drought driven by climate change may become a constraint on energy projects. Shale oil projects in particular are highly water-intensive, since large quantities of water and chemicals must be injected into wells to force oil and gas out of these porous rock formations.[29] This means that water stress—already a problem in the major shale-producing regions of the US, including the Permian Basin—could constrain shale oil and gas potential in the US, China, and worldwide.[30] The same is true for mining: the IEA projects that about half of global lithium and cobalt production is located in areas of high water stress, which could form another stressor that constrains the pace of RE expansion.[31] Climate shocks can also damage energy infrastructure in other ways. For one, electricity grids will be subject to worsening extreme weather shocks that can leave hundreds of thousands of homes (or more) without power for days on end.[32] In the FF sector specifically, one report suggests that 40% of oil and gas reserves are threatened with sea level rise, heat stress, flooding, hurricanes, and other extreme weather events—with Saudi Arabia, Iraq, Nigeria, and the United States (particularly its Gulf Coast) among the most vulnerable.[33] (Coincidentally, these are the same countries that the IEA expects to play a leading role in raising oil production to meet rising demand by 2030, a point I return to later). Additionally, as seen during the 2021–2022 energy shock, droughts and water stress can also amplify energy crises by constraining hydropower, coal, and nuclear power production. The World Meteorological Association (WMO) shows that 87% of coal, nuclear, and hydroelectric systems depend on water availability (for cooling purposes in the case of coal and nuclear plants); furthermore, more than a third of the world's coal plants, and nearly a quarter of its nuclear and hydropower plants, are expected to face medium to very high risks of water stress in the coming decades.[34] To make things worse, the climate crisis may even reduce wind power potential through the phenomena of "global stilling," which some scientists believe to have been a contributing factor to Europe's 2022 energy crisis—due to lower-than-average wind speeds in 2021—though the long-term impacts of climate on average wind speeds remain uncertain.[35] Taken together, these risks suggest that the climate crisis may threaten energy security in a way that is "no less serious" than Putin's war on Ukraine.[36]

Third, adapting to climate change will most likely increase energy demand *on top of* that projected by rising economic growth—though this will be globally uneven. One study, for instance, estimates that rising demand for air conditioning and refrigeration could increase energy demand by an additional 25%–58% by 2050—with the highest increases occurring in the tropics as well as southern regions in the United States, Europe, and China—though others estimate much smaller but still significant increases (e.g., 7% by 2050).[37] Furthermore, these energy demands would expand significantly in the case of a rapid scale-up of direct air capture (DAC), which could take up 9%–14% of global electricity use by 2075.[38] The expansion of seawater desalination in drought-prone regions like California, the Middle East, and Southern China—which is highly energy-intensive—may exacerbate these rising energy demands even more.[39] Rising energy demands will no doubt be moderated to some extent by reduced demand for heating in the milder winters of the future, at least in the global north (a dampening feedback that helped Europe cope with the Putin shock during the 2022–2023 winter). But winter temperatures on average have been warming more slowly than summers are heating up, and the still poorly understood phenomena of the "wavy" polar vortex— bringing arctic temperatures and "bomb cyclones" to the midlatitude regions—may counteract this respite to heating and energy demand.[40] On the whole, the most likely scenario is that climate change adds to rising global energy demand, which would not only create a positive feedback on the earth system crisis—for example, by burning more fossil fuels to adapt to climate impacts, increasing the electricity demands that must be met by renewables, and making global-scale absolute decoupling of GDP from energy even more of a pipedream—but also exacerbate already-worsening vulnerabilities to future energy crises.

In sum, the convergence between the climate crisis and net energy decline will create a major source of systemic risk and weakening resilience for the capitalist world-system that is overlooked by most analysts. But again, this will be contingent on the uncertain course of the RE transition, since an accelerated transition would simultaneously dampen the risks of climate change and FF supply shocks. But, as we saw earlier, a rapid RE transition would also mean increased risks of "greenflation," financial instability, and right-wing populist backlash (which I elaborate in the green Keynesian scenario below).

FOOD ←→ CLIMATE/BIODIVERSITY ←→ POLITICAL ECONOMY ←→ ENERGY

In my rendering, the earth system ←→ political economy ←→ energy nexus is the core constellation with the most influence on the possible trajectories of the SEP as a whole. But food systems are also a critical dimension of the SEP, and global food crises in the coming decades may reach historically unprecedented proportions with the capacity to provoke world-system breakdown.[41]

In chapter 1 we covered the current and projected impacts of the climate crisis on agriculture and vice versa, so here I just briefly review some of the key feedbacks. Starting with the direct physical impacts of climate change on food systems, we know that the climate crisis is already reducing potential agriculture yields and will continue to do so, but crop model projections suffer from major limitations. On one side is their limited ability to simulate the intersecting impacts of drought, pests, weather extremes, groundwater depletion, soil degradation, and climactic variability; on the other side is uncertainty about adaptation and technological innovation—such as shifting to more drought-tolerant crop varieties, as well as the potential for increased yields in the upper latitude regions (e.g., Canada, Northern Europe, Siberia) to make up for shortfalls elsewhere. But given the limited capacities of models to capture complex intersecting risks to agriculture in a warming world, the difficulties of expanding agricultural northward where soil is often unsuitable, and evidence that northern agricultural regions will suffer increased production failures from unfamiliar pathogens and other extreme events as the climate warms, the balance of evidence suggests that current projections significantly underestimate the risk of major food shocks in the coming decades.[42] We can speculate that on a current-policies trajectory with limited adaptation, we will likely experience at least 10%–25% yield declines (relative to a world without warming) in key staples for each 1°C rise.[43] This would mean that, rather than world food production increasing 50%–70% between now and 2050—which the FAO projects is needed to adequately feed a population of 9–10 billion, at least in the absence of radical redistribution[44]—it would at best meekly expand beyond contemporary levels. And if/when we near 2.5°C and beyond in the later part of this century, as Julian Cribb warns, world food production would most likely be declining "at the very time we are trying to double it."[45] No doubt we would be witnessing a period of dramatically deteriorating global food security, but just how bad things would get is up for debate.

Shifting to the impacts of agriculture and food system policies on the climate and earth system, we know (as discussed in chapter 1) that agriculture is directly responsible for about 18% of global emissions and is the primary driver of land-use conversion and biodiversity collapse. One key question here is whether and how the global food system can be transformed to provide affordable food for a growing population while becoming carbon neutral and reducing stress on other planetary boundaries. One prominent set of studies, conducted by the EAT-Lancet Commission, suggests that a successful food transition that meets these goals will require the following transformations: (1) feeding humanity with "zero new land-conversion" while using "sustainable intensification" techniques to increase yields on existing agricultural land; (2) ending or at least dramatically reducing use of synthetic fertilizers and insecticides; (3) reducing food loss and waste by 50% to reduce pressure on food demand; and (4) reducing meat consumption in rich countries by 80%–90%.[46] In contrast, apologists of the current food system put less emphasis on reducing meat consumption and synthetic fertilizer use and more on agribusiness-driven technological innovation, whereas food sovereignty activists place less emphasis on the need for yield increases and more on the problem of distribution and local control over agricultural systems.[47] But there is a broad consensus that the global food system must change: the question is how, to what extent, by whom, and in whose interests.

This brings us to the political economy→food relation, since we must highlight, in contrast to mainstream food security analysts, how competing hegemonic projects will shape the future of food in a warming world. An often-neglected question is to what extent the power relations that shape the global food system will constrain efforts to make agriculture more sustainable and resilient to climate shocks. In other words, while it would be unrealistic and unhelpful to assume no technological change or adaptation, we must also be attuned to how hegemonic configurations—such as agribusiness monopoly power and techno-productivist ideologies—constrain adaptive pathways within particular parameters. For instance, while capitalism has always been structurally reliant on "cheap food" to keep labor costs low and sustain political legitimacy, the "corporate food regime" has taken cheap food to new heights.[48] Global market integration under the World Trade Organization means that highly subsidized and capitalized industrial farms in the global north are able to dump cheap grains onto the global south, forcing farmers worldwide to prioritize yields at the expense of sustainability and replicate industrial methods by relying on agribusiness-controlled inputs like fertilizers, pesticides, seeds, and machinery in order to avoid bankruptcy.[49] The result is ever-more concentrated land ownership by a small number of huge farms, with the largest 1% of farms globally controlling over 70% of farmland; small and medium-size farms often struggling on the edge of precarity; and powerful farm lobbies in the United States, Europe, Brazil, and elsewhere resistant to adopting more sustainable practices.[50] Thus there are strong negative feedbacks that pressure farmers around the world to rely on synthetic fertilizers and pesticides while continuing to degrade the earth's soil and biodiversity.

To what extent can food systems plausibly adapt and transform in this context? In complexity theory terms, how wide is the possibility space for the global food system so long as it remains within the corporate food regime attractor—a formation in which agribusiness giants and large-scale industrial farms believe that their "primary function is to provide profit for shareholders"?[51] Buzzwords like "climate smart agriculture," "precision agriculture," and "sustainable intensification," along with technical innovations in genetically modified (GM) seeds, are the main solutions offered by these powerful actors, which they hope will enable them to address the above challenges without relinquishing their control over food systems. It is difficult to anticipate the potential and limits of these approaches, but a closer look at how they are currently being put into practice suggests their transformative potential is limited. As Marcus Taylor shows, these approaches typically involve little more than technical tweaks to existing industrial agriculture practices—such as shifting to no-till agriculture while maintaining "large-scale monocultures of herbicide-resistant soy," which are often primarily used to feed industrial livestock.[52] Haroon Akram-Lodhi also shows that transnational agribusiness firms, driven by the imperatives of delivering short-term shareholder value, undertake "far more investment in mergers and acquisitions" than in R&D strategies that would be needed to drive major innovations in productivity.[53]

All of this suggests that so long as the corporate food regime remains dominant, there will most likely be serious limits to agricultural adaptation. I will thus assume that, in a neoliberal drift trajectory, food system changes would be at best limited to moderate tweaks of existing farming practices and consumption patterns, which would mean the continuation of a global food system with relatively weak resilience to climate shocks, steadily rising agricultural land use, worsening impacts on climate and biodiversity, and increasing rates of hunger and malnutrition over time. Alternatively, ecosocialist trajectories could enable far-reaching agroecological transitions that dramatically reduce the ecological impacts of farming while feeding the world primarily through redistributive rather than techno-productivist strategies.[54] In between these scenarios, green Keynesian trajectories would be able to improve the global food system's sustainability and resilience—for example, by significantly reforming farmer subsidy regimes, rewriting global trade agreements to penalize agricultural imports linked to deforestation (following the EU's lead), and incentivizing reduced meat consumption through a mix of taxes and industrial polices to scale up alternative proteins.[55] But limited redistribution of wealth would mean that food must remain "cheap" in order to prevent worsening food insecurity and political instability,[56] thus making it more challenging for green Keynesian regimes to significantly alter existing industrial farming practices.

In sum, the global food system is being squeezed between the pressures of shifting to more sustainable practices, cultivating resilience to climate shocks, and doing this within the constraints of a transnational corporate-controlled food system structure. Given that climate risks to agriculture are almost certainly being underestimated by most models, and that the corporate food regime will most likely constrain adaptation efforts, the most likely outcome if present trends continue will be worsening food system vulnerabilities over time and a "new era of escalating food commodity price shocks," as Lynas anticipates.[57] Such risks will be further amplified by net energy decline and future energy shocks, since global food supply chains are critically dependent on fossil fuels (particularly oil and gas)—from machinery used on the farm to processing, packaging, refrigeration, transportation, and fertilizer production.[58] Rising biofuel production—which the IEA claims will be necessary to decarbonize transportation by 2050—and demand for BECCS would pose further threats to global food security by diverting agricultural land away from feeding humans toward feeding cars/trucks/planes and drawing down carbon.[59] Furthermore, as discussed in chapter 1, the food system is also a major driver of pandemic risk—a result of land-use conversion as well as the accelerated viral evolution afforded by concentrated livestock operations—and is itself vulnerable to pandemic shocks that disrupt supply chains, sicken agricultural workers, and depress food purchasing power.[60] Each of these feedbacks will contribute to a more destabilizing polycrisis architecture overall.

SOCIOECOLOGICAL PROBLEMATIC ←→ EXISTENTIAL PROBLEMATIC

To finish constructing our "model" of the SEP, we should briefly highlight its key feedbacks with the EP. Solutions to the SEP are not merely constrained by the material interests of investors, fossil capitalists, and agribusiness giants who profit from the status quo: ideological assemblages—structures of meaning, feeling, and belonging—also reinforce BAU pathways. And while crises in these assemblages (i.e., existential crises) can create opportunities for progressive ideological transitions, they can also precipitate surges of reactionary backlash.

Starting with the EP → SEP relation, it has become clear in recent years how investments in whiteness and masculinity are articulated with fossil fuels, cars, meat-heavy diets, and extractivism. Cara Daggett, for example, argues that Trumpian trends in the US highlight how "challenges to fossil-fuelled systems . . . become interpreted as challenges to white patriarchal rule," since the relatively privileged position of the white male working class was historically bound up with FF consumption and jobs reliant on FF systems.[61] Malm and company build on these insights, showing that right-wing imaginaries across the United States, Europe, Australia, Brazil, and elsewhere appear to mythicize fossil fuels and mineral stocks— viewing them as the simultaneously symbolic and material source of the nation's power. Hence the well-documented pattern of stubborn resistance against mitigation policies among far-right parties (even when accepting the reality of anthropogenic climate change), as well as their antipathy to renewable energy sources.[62] Thus, despite falling costs for renewables, investments in racism, nationalism, and masculinity—which, as Malm and company quip, have "not figured in any climate models"[63]—have thus far constrained the RE transition and may very well continue to do so.

Shifting to the SEP → EP relation, we must highlight how socioecological crises can intensify existential crises that reinforce far-right populism, though they will create progressive opportunities as well. As Matthew

Adams writes, the climate crisis is already provoking "existential crises [that] undermine a number of related 'certainties' that have come to provide a taken-for-granted foundation for day-to-day existence," including trust in political institutions, capitalism, consumerism, and liberal democracy.[64] We can see this in diminishing support for capitalism among younger populations in the US and UK,[65] but also in the rising forces of religious fundamentalism and far-right populism. Joshua Jackson and Michele Gelfand even suggest that climate change may be fueling far-right resurgence by provoking "cultural tightening" among populations whose identities are particularly threatened. They fear this "may create a vicious cycle, in which the threat of climate disaster and far-right nationalism encourage one another over time."[66] This argument is further supported by psychosocial research showing that climate change, by threatening the existential security of individuals with deep attachments to the fossil fueled status quo, can "subtly and unconsciously drive people toward developing group-serving, and probably authoritarian attitudes."[67] As Malm and company fear, the result may be that—in conditions of intensifying climate chaos—structures of white supremacy, hegemonic masculinity, and fossil fueled consumption will be "defended with a vehemence never seen before."[68] However, we should also recognize that crises, as Angelos Varvarousis writes, can open up "a field of experimentation with new practices and ideas" that generate new forms of meaning, belonging, and solidarity.[69] Thus we can expect that future crises will continue to destabilize ideological assemblages in ways that intensify polarization, fueling reactionary backlash as well as the emergence of postcapitalist subjectivities based on care, compassion, and solidarity. Whether reactionary or progressive forces will predominate, and in which parts of the world-system, will be the outcome of counter-hegemonic struggles between competing narratives and frames for making sense of the crises to come.

TRAJECTORIES OF THE SOCIOECOLOGICAL PROBLEMATIC

This gives us a rough model of the key dependency relations that structure the SEP. How will they unfold in the coming years and decades? To respond to this question, I start with a set of "what if" questions about the evolution of power relations, and then consider other "what ifs" that would emerge in different crisis conjunctures.

The first question we consider is this: What if the hegemonic configuration of the capitalist world-system remains broadly unchanged over the next five to ten years or longer? Because of the turbulence triggered by COVID-19, the Putin shock, and rising geopolitical tensions, the question of how to conceptualize the currently hegemonic attractor for the world-system is not straightforward. There is no question that the ideological hegemony of neoliberalism has been significantly (if not fatally) weakened in the world-system core. We may even be in the early phases of a "regime shift" away from neoliberalism, with some saying we have already entered a "post-neoliberal" era.[70] For one, "industrial policy" is making a comeback as the United States, the EU, China, and other governments take on a larger role in shaping industries and markets to pursue strategic goals—for example, by reshoring (or "friendshoring") critical industries like semiconductors, RE technologies, and EV batteries.[71] In a speech from April 2023, US national Security Advisor Jake Sullivan spoke of a "New Washington Consensus" that explicitly breaks from core elements of the 1990s neoliberal Washington Consensus—such as "free trade," unrestricted capital mobility, and fiscal discipline. Instead, the United States under Biden aims to "actively steer markets" in order to address domestic and global challenges, including the climate crisis, inequality, labor rights, political polarization, and competition with China.[72] The EU's Green Deal Industrial Plan—conceived in response to the challenge posed by Biden's Inflation Reduction Act—signifies a comparable strategic shift. Meanwhile, China under Xi Jinping has embarked on a more authoritarian and (to a limited extent) state socialist trajectory in order to reduce import-dependence on the West, become a leader in FIR technologies, exert greater control over Chinese tech companies, and promote an agenda of "common prosperity."[73]

However we choose to conceptualize these developments, it would clearly be too simplistic to say that neoliberal hegemony remains entrenched in the world-system core. But we are certainly not yet witnessing a decisive transition to an alternative world-system configuration that can alter the broad "direction of travel" set in motion by the neoliberal era.[74] In other words, certain features of neoliberalism may be coming to an end—including government aversion to industrial policy, knee-jerk adherence to trickle-down economics, and the assumption that the benefits of free trade trump geopolitical considerations—but many continuities remain (seen, for instance, in the persistent influence of monetarist assumptions about inflation and how it must be dealt with, as well as the continued strength of elite coalitions pushing for austerity and "balanced budgets," particularly in the global south). More importantly for our purposes, most of the key socioecological trends set in motion by the neoliberal era—including political-economic turbulence driven by the reinforcing dynamics of inequality, stagnation, debt, and financial systemic risks; massively insufficient climate policies, which are still putting us on pace for roughly 3°C by 2100; still-rising global demand for fossil fuels; and a corporate food regime driving us toward ecological and food system breakdown—remain largely unchanged. We can thus conceptualize our present era as a kind of interregnum in which the ideological hegemony of neoliberalism is in some ways breaking down, but there is not yet a sufficiently powerful hegemonic coalition—both within and across the most powerful states—that is able to shift the world-system toward a new hegemonic regime.

NEOLIBERAL DRIFT

So, in this first scenario, we see a continuation of these trends for the next five to ten years (if not longer). After a period of elevated energy prices, broad-based inflation, interest rate hikes, and weak growth if not recession for most of the world economy, global economic growth slowly recovers as new oil and gas supplies come online, energy and food prices come down, and central banks recommence monetary loosening.[75] But many countries confront lingering headwinds from increased inequality, lingering unemployment, aging populations, huge levels of private and public debt, and a return to austerity.[76] Additional investments in "clean energy" and efficiency driven by the 2022 energy shock boost global RE capacity—with renewables becoming the largest global source of electricity by 2025—while moderating growth rates for oil and gas demand.[77] But the still-limited profitability of RE investments relative to fossil fuels,[78] along with continued permitting delays and limited public investments in new transmission lines, battery systems, and EV charging stations, slows the pace of expansion far below what would be possible with more ambitious policies. Meanwhile, oil and gas demand continues to grow into the 2030s, with oil plateauing around 103 to 105 million barrels per day at least and gas rising to 4,400 billion cubic meters by 2030 before subsequently plateauing.[79] Global emissions from fossil fuels thus continue to rise—reaching at least 38 billion tons in 2025, compared to 37.5 in 2022—before plateauing and very slowly declining (driven mainly by peak coal consumption) but still remaining stubbornly elevated into the 2030s and beyond.[80] Transnational corporate-led efforts to reform the global food system make some progress in improving soil health, input efficiency, and livestock productivity—in part driven by spiking energy, food, and fertilizer prices in 2022. But these remain marginal improvements that are a far cry from the sustainability transition called for by the EAT-Lancet commission. Furthermore, they continue to intensify concentration of land ownership, subject agricultural production decisions to the dictates of short-term profitability for finance capital, expand global meat production, and exacerbate pressures on forests and biodiversity.[81] The biodiversity targets adopted under the Montreal-Kunming Global Biodiversity Framework—like the Aichi targets before them—fail to make a dent in global capital's ecocidal trajectory.[82]

As we are already witnessing, divisions within the capitalist class continue to intensify in this scenario—with the green capitalist factions calling for more ambitious policies to accelerate RE deployment and innovation in low-carbon technologies, the fossil capitalists counseling gradualism and caution to ensure energy and food security, and finance capital continuing to straddle both factions as it reaps short-term profits from fossil fuels while hedging against future uncertainties. Green capitalist factions steadily gain strength thanks to falling costs for solar, wind, and batteries, which begin falling again after the 2022–2023 uptick; worsening climate damages as global temperature increases near 1.5°C; and intensifying geopolitical competition over green industries and supply chains. But a conjunction of forces—including powerful conservative parties in key states (particularly the US Republican Party), fossil capitalists and petro-states like Russia and Saudi Arabia determined to avoid stranded assets, finance capitalists whose overriding priority is short-term profitability no matter the long-term systemic consequences, still-simmering right-wing populist currents, and a global communications ecosystem that allows disinformation to thrive and reactionary forces to sow confusion and polarization[83]—prevent a decisive transition to a new form of hegemony for global capitalism. Rather than the outcome of a coherent hegemonic agenda, the trajectory that emerges would be a kind of "drifting" driven by the short-term interests of powerful capitalist factions, particularly those most aligned with fossil capital, in conjunction with various "entropic" feedbacks like far-right populism and disinformation, while the more "enlightened" factions of the capitalist class are unable to significantly alter the trajectory of the world-system as a whole. Hence my depiction of this scenario with the term neoliberal *drift*, which signifies that it is largely a continuation of the "direction of travel" set in motion during the neoliberal era, but which takes on a self-reinforcing momentum of its own that exceeds the agency or control of a coherent hegemonic coalition.

A key question is at what point this trajectory may reach another bifurcation or crisis point that widens the opportunity-space for counter-hegemonic movements. We can anticipate with high confidence that the continuation of current trends will create the conditions for more intense polycrisis events in the coming years. It is quite possible that the 2022–2023 energy/inflation shock could evolve into an even worse crisis as this book is coming to press—emerging from the conjunction of inflation, interest rate hikes, destabilizing debt defaults, and additional oil and gas shocks. But I focus here first on the potential for even more destabilizing crisis scenarios that could emerge between 2025 and 2035 as net energy decline converges with rising oil and gas demand, worsening climate chaos, an increasingly brittle global food system, and persistent political-economic and financial systemic risks.

As discussed in chapter 1, the IEA shows that a current-policies scenario will make the world economy increasingly vulnerable to oil market volatility by 2030: the conjunction of rising demand, depletion from existing fields, and "underinvestment" in new production means that a 25.9 mb/d gap needs to be met by new sources of supply by 2030—that is, the equivalent of *more than two additional Saudi Arabias*.[84] The IEA assumes that 80% of this gap will be met by increased production in Middle Eastern OPEC countries, US shale, Brazil, and Guyanese offshore oil. In particular, they assume that US production will increase by 4 mb/d—reaching nearly 16 mb/d by 2030—while Saudi production rises from 11 to 13 mb/d.[85]

How realistic are such assumptions? It is impossible to know for sure, but there are good reasons to think they are over-optimistic. To start, many analysts warn that US oil production will likely be unable to expand beyond 12 mb/d, the result of depletion of the pressurized "sweet spots" in many of the most productive regions, demands for capital discipline from investors, labor shortages, and rising input costs (e.g., for steel, diesel, and chemicals).[86] US production could even begin an irreversible decline before 2030 as a result of these conjoined pressures, as Nafeez Ahmed anticipates.[87] Even if not, the expectation that it will be able to deliver an additional 4 mb/d above 2022 levels rests on heroic assumptions. As Justin Mikulka puts it, "If oil prices over $120 a barrel didn't spur production growth in the U.S. shale industry, it is likely nothing will, making 13 million barrels per day an increasingly unrealistic goal"—let alone 16 million.[88] As the IEA recognizes, numerous concerns have also emerged recently about Saudi Arabia's weakening spare capacity, estimated at less than 1 million barrels per day, which means it will be hard-pressed (even if it desires) to ramp up production by another 1 m/bd, let alone 2 m/bd, in response to price spikes.[89] On top of this, as mentioned earlier, 40% of global oil and gas reserves will be highly vulnerable to worsening climate shocks during this time—including water constraints in the US Permian Basin, water plus heat stress in the Middle East, and extreme weather threatening refineries in the US Gulf Coast—which may add further constraints on the capacities of the United States, Saudi Arabia, Iraq, and Iran to significantly boost output in response to future price spikes.[90] The IEA projects that natural gas markets confront lower risks of supply shocks by 2030 compared to oil, due to lower demand growth and major investments to increase production in Qatar and LNG export capacity in the United States.[91] But more-rapid-than-expected declines in US unconventional gas production, higher-than-expected demand in Europe (caused by rebound effects), extreme weather shocks to gas infrastructure, and brutal winters (e.g., from a wavy polar vortex) could still threaten gas security as well.[92]

In sum, by 2030 the world economy will likely confront an oil crisis of unprecedented magnitude—one that would see prices going above $150 and possibly $200 per barrel, though this depends on the uncertain course of electric vehicle uptake, oil demand, and production capacities in the United States, OPEC, and Russia. It is highly uncertain when such a crisis could emerge, which will be contingent on particular proximate causes that combine in a specific conjuncture. But rising global demand in a context of economic recovery—likely driven primarily by China, India, and other "emerging" economies—in conjunction with weak growth or even declining US shale and Saudi production would likely be the key catalysts. Among the major economies, China and India may be the most vulnerable to this crisis, particularly if they can no longer rely on discounted oil from Russia, since they are two of the world's largest net energy importers and will become even more reliant on imported oil by 2030 (even after accounting for recent efforts to boost energy sovereignty).[93] But it would also shock the United States, much of Europe, and most of the global south thanks to resilient car cultures and only incrementalist shifts toward EVs (projected, for instance, to take up just 10% of the US vehicle fleet by 2030, up from 3% today).[94] And it is very likely that this would not just be an oil crisis: oil price spikes would also put pressure on LNG transport costs and RE supply chains, while climate change would continue to strain nuclear, coal, and hydropower production in different regions, leading to another all-of-the-above energy crisis. The result, again, would be an economy-wide inflationary surge, one that puts particular pressure on oil-linked food prices (which will be magnified considerably by worsening climate stress at this time). And if this is followed by interest rate hikes that pummel growth and employment but without addressing the underlying supply shock, then we will witness what I call a "fossil stagflation crisis," or a protracted period of surging inflation, recession, and high unemployment triggered by FF supply shocks. Additional inflationary pressures—such as corporate profiteering, reshoring supply chains, aging populations, rising health-care costs, labor shortages, climate shocks, and (potentially, as I explore in chapter 5) war—would add fuel to the inflationary fire.[95] Indeed, as Roubini warns, this could become "the worst period of stagflation the world has ever seen."[96]

A new set of questions emerge in this conjuncture, which will lead to a subsequent series of alternative scenarios. First, how—and determined by which political coalitions—would states respond to this crisis? Second, would these strategies succeed in bringing down energy prices and reviving economic growth? If no, then what would be the consequences for the world-system? And, if yes, then what further problems may emerge down the road as a result of these strategies?

It seems likely that this would be the sort of crisis that accelerates the RE transition and precipitates the demise of fossil capital. Even more so than today, this would be a crisis in which "all three elements of the energy trilemma—security, affordability and sustainability—are pushing in the same direction"—that is, toward a "clean energy acceleration."[97] Consumers would be fed up with FF price volatility, the case for ambitious climate action would be increasingly obvious, and rising reliance on low-EROI oil and gas would weaken the investment case for expansion.

But we cannot assume that the most rational response will prevail, nor even that this would be the most likely scenario. As we saw when exploring the SEP-EP nexus, an oil crisis of this sort would also reinforce existential crises that trigger right-wing populist, hypermasculine, and ethnonationalist reaction across the world-system. Prolonged fuel and food price spikes would not only intensify economic hardship but also threaten identities with deep attachments to fossil-fueled mobility and consumerism.[98] Like in 2022, rich countries would pursue a suite of policy interventions to try to contain the fallout—for example, subsidies for consumers, windfall taxes on oil and gas companies, releases from the Strategic Petroleum Reserve (SPR) in the United States, and possibly even a coordinated price cap or price controls. These interventions would help dampen populist unrest in many states. But they would also be politically challenging to implement: conservative parties and fiscal hawks would be averse to increasing consumer subsidies at a time when public debt remains at record levels; oil and gas companies will lobby vehemently, and perhaps successfully, against windfall taxes by arguing that such taxes in 2022 deterred upstream investment and set the world economy up for subsequent price shocks; SPR releases would have limited effects and risk depleting emergency reserves to dangerously low levels; and a coordinated price cap—as we saw with EU efforts to impose a cap on Russian oil—would be very difficult to get states to agree on (let alone enforce). Furthermore, the same constraints on the RE transition discussed in chapter 1—particularly the relatively weak returns on RE investments for capitalists; insufficient public investment in transmission lines, EV charging stations, and R&D for decarbonizing the hard-to-abate sectors (exacerbated by higher financing costs from interest rate hikes in 2022–2023); populist resistance to RE projects and persistent permitting delays; and elevated prices for transition minerals—would make many politicians averse to doubling down on renewables while phasing out fossil fuels. And the short-term profitability gains of FF investments for finance capital—like today—would be irresistible, giving many powerful banks and asset managers a continued stake in the perpetuation of fossil capital.

In sum, a "clean energy acceleration" is by no means assured in this scenario. To the contrary, some states might even go the way of fossil nationalism or fascism: right-wing politicians would seize the moment to blame environmentalists, "globalist elites," climate policies, and (with minimal regard for empirics) immigrants for the energy woes of their respective nations. Coalitions of right-wing parties, fossil fuel lobbies, farmers, energy- and emissions-intensive manufacturing capitalists, and conservative middle- and working-class bases might then assume or consolidate hegemony in the United States, UK, Australia, India, Brazil, and parts of the EU. Their main strategy for addressing fossil stagflation and cost-of-living crises would be straightforward: double down on fossil fuel extraction and ecologically damaging industrial agriculture to bolster national energy and food security. And things could get even uglier: fossil fascism, or a far-right regime that deploys "systematic violence against those identified as enemies of the nation" and glorifies the nation's fossil fuel stocks, may assume power in core nations like the United States (e.g., if a Trump-like figure wins the presidency, bolstered by a radicalized Republican Party willing to do whatever it takes to maintain their grip on power).[99] A future fossil stagflation crisis could potentially be the sort of "overwhelming crisis beyond the reach of any traditional solutions" that has historically created the preconditions for fascist regimes coming to power.[100] But it may also predominantly result in less extreme (but still highly dangerous) right-wing populist regimes.

Still, as Mann and Wainwright rightly argue, it would be highly unlikely that "climate behemoth" or fossil nationalism becomes the dominant response across the world-system. Rather, it would more likely form a negative feedback that constrains the world-system within a neoliberal drift trajectory: right-wing populist regimes would gain power in certain states—as would center-left green Keynesian regimes—but neither fossil nationalists or green Keynesians would be able to decisively alter the direction of travel of the world-system. Green Keynesian reformists in the United States, UK, Europe, and elsewhere would remain constrained by the simmering threat of right-wing populist backlash and still-powerful fossil capitalists, but the combination of cheapening renewables and firm commitments to climate mitigation (particularly in a context of worsening climate shocks) would also dampen the appeal of untrammeled FF extraction. Instead, the dominant response to the fossil stagflation crisis would more likely be an all-of-the-above strategy that maintains oil and gas production while expanding solar and wind, hydrogen, nuclear, and (particularly in China and the global south) coal.

We should then turn to another "what if" question: What if such strategies succeed in bringing down energy and food costs and reviving growth, and what if they don't? While we cannot know for sure, these strategies may prove to be self-defeating. For one, global oil and gas demand would still remain stubbornly elevated in this scenario: plateauing between 2030–2035 and then slowly declining until 2050 (but again, demand could be even higher when factoring in rebound effects and additional demands from climate adaptation).[101] And this would set up the world economy for even worse supply shocks in the 2040s for both oil and gas: to make up depleting fields elsewhere, OPEC countries would need to raise production by an additional 7 mb/d at a time when they are already struggling to keep production steady, and worsening water and other climate stressors would dampen their production potential even more.[102] Furthermore, an additional 240 billion cubic meters per year of LNG export capacity beyond what is currently under construction would be needed by 2050 to prevent supply shortfalls. The IEA projects that East Africa would be the "main source of LNG supply growth" at this time, with exports rising by nearly 80 bcm between 2030 and 2050.[103] But production in East Africa would likely be constrained by climate extremes, anti-extractivist activism, and investor anxieties as the investment case for new gas projects steadily deteriorates. Even if these projects move forward, accelerating net energy decline would mean that an increasingly large share of global energy consumption would need to be devoted to the energy sector: if average fossil fuel EROI is somewhere between 5:1 and 4:1 today—meaning that 20%–25% of total energy produced must be devoted to the energy sector, leaving only 75%–80% for the rest of the economy—by the 2030s this would likely fall to between 4:1 and 3:1, and between 3:1 and 2:1 if not lower by the 2040s—meaning that roughly 33%–50% total oil and gas production would need to be devoted to extracting and delivering the increasingly low quality resources that remain, leaving only 50%–67% for the rest of the economy.[104] In essence, more and more energy would be expended to extract and deliver less and less—a process that Louis Delannoy and colleagues call "energy cannibalism."[105]

In this scenario, rather than an eventual return to global economic growth, it is quite possible that an endless recession and cycle of economic and energy contraction would ensue, as Richard Heinberg explains: "Rising energy prices [would] periodically destroy demand by shrinking the economy, thus lowering demand (and prices) temporarily until economies can partially recover; then prices [would] be bid upward once more. The cycle may continue to repeat itself, each time at a lower level of economic activity and energy usage."[106] This pattern is by no means inevitable, since oil and gas demand may peak before we reach peak production (a scenario I explore below). But it is quite possible that future oil and gas production—even if able to meet peak demand around 2030 or 2035—will be unable to sustain sufficient net energy production throughout the 2040s and beyond as demand plateaus and the depletion of conventional oil and gas accelerates.[107] In this case, an irreversible process of energy demand destruction, economic contraction, and relocalization, not unlike what "peak oil" theorists of the past have predicted, is possible.[108]

Many, however, would claim that even if the world economy confronts a structural shortage of oil and gas, the technological and cost advances in RE by this time would be able to more than make up for supply shortfalls. This is certainly possible. But rather than adopting a "dualist" lens that sees RE and FF as separate substances, we must account for how FF production shocks can disrupt the RE transition. As noted in chapter 1, manufacturing, installing, transporting, and mining the materials for RE systems requires the use of FF; and in a slow decarbonization scenario, RE expansion would remain an FF-intensive process for years if not decades to come.[109] As a result, like we saw in 2022, FF supply shocks can disrupt RE supply chains by raising energy, mining, and transport costs. This raises a key question: If an accelerated RE transition is delayed until 2035–2040 when oil and gas shortages become chronic and intractable due to the net energy cliff, would it by this point be too late to build up low-carbon infrastructures? The short answer: not necessarily for countries who are well advanced in their energy transitions, but probably yes for much of the rest of the world econ-omy. Not only would net energy from fossils fuels be declining at a non-linear rate; as discussed in chapter 1, an accelerated transition would also require huge upfront energy expenditures to scale up RE manufacturing, mining, installation, and supply-chain distribution at the needed rate.[110] Thus, by this time, there may be an insurmountable contradiction between rapidly declining net fossil energy and the rapidly rising energy demands of the RE transition, as several scholars anticipate.[111] We would then most likely see rapid cost inflation for all energy sources and intractable transi-tion mineral bottlenecks, especially as depletion forces the mining sector to dig up increasingly diffuse metal reserves that are more energetically costly to extract. This could derail efforts to rapidly scale up low-carbon infrastructures, especially in the global south. And these constraints would be even worse if rising geopolitical tensions between the United States and China—and potentially a war over Taiwan—provoke massive disruptions across RE supply chains (as I explore in chapter 5). Fossil stagflation would then continue unabated, most economies would be mired in a prolonged recession, and there would be no clear end or savior in sight.

At this point, conventional technocratic crisis-management strate-gies would reach their limits, since interest hikes would threaten cascad-ing debt crises and pummel economies even more while doing little to control inflation.[112] While this is highly uncertain, we might then witness an abrupt transition in ideological assemblages across the "advanced" and "emerging" economies simultaneously: collective expectations that growth and profitability will continue indefinitely into the future—that markets and government policies will restore cheap energy, and that stag-flation is merely a temporary blip—would collapse, sending investor and consumer confidence into freefall. A mass sell-off of financial assets and credit crunch would likely ensue as elites try to salvage the value of their fictitious assets. In Wolfgang Streeck's colorful terms, they would "move into endgame mode—cash in, burn bridges, and leave nothing behind but scorched earth."[113] Ruling classes would abandon the objective of eco-nomic growth, intensify police repression of angry populations suffering the double whammy of high unemployment and unprecedented cost-of-living crises, and focus on securing their energy-intensive lifestyles. In con-junction with magnifying food crises and extreme weather shocks as we near 2°C, this could be the polycrisis event that triggers an uneven collapse of the world-system.

In sum, all-of-the-above energy security strategies might very well fail to resolve a 2030s fossil stagflation crisis. But let us now explore a more middle-of-the-road scenario: What if these strategies succeed in moderating such shocks and enable a broad-based global economic recovery? In this scenario, all-of-the-above energy strategies between 2030 and 2035 predominantly favor RE expansion—due to the rising relative power of green capital and popular resistance against new oil and gas extraction. Oil and gas demand thus falls more quickly relative to a stated policies scenario, while the major economies rapidly expand solar and wind, EVs, and green hydrogen production. Policymakers and business leaders also double down on efforts to rapidly scale up carbon-removal techniques like DAC and BECCS, since they recognize (given delayed mitigation) that the 2°C target is now unreachable without massive multidecadal carbon-removal efforts. Together, these additional climate policies bend the global emissions curve toward the NDC trajectory, thereby putting the earth on track for 2.8°C by 2100 in the absence of CDR, and *potentially* for closer to 2°C–2.4°C if an "emergency crash program" for CDR expansion is successful.[114]

We should then ask another "what if" question: What if technological breakthroughs at this point enable solar and wind, nuclear, CDR technologies, green hydrogen, and low-carbon food systems to rapidly scale up? On the other hand, what if innovation remains gradual and incremental? Later I discuss what we can call an "exponential technological breakthrough" scenario, but for now let's explore what would likely happen in the case of an incrementalist innovation trajectory. This would be a technological trajectory similar to that anticipated by Vaclav Smil and Robert Gordon, who expect "evolutionary and continuous" technological changes with relatively mild impacts on growth and productivity, rather than the more "revolutionary" scenarios anticipated by techno-optimists.[115]

In this scenario, RE and FF production is sufficient to meet the still-growing energy demands of a sluggish global economy, though fossil fuels continue to take up a large share of total energy consumption (somewhere between 40%–50% by 2050). The steadily weakening EROI of fossil fuels—and the still-constrained EROI of solar and wind energy—means that a historically high share of global energy consumption and GDP must still be devoted to the energy sector, which slows the pace of RE cost reductions and keeps FF prices elevated.[116] Global electricity demand increases rapidly—roughly doubling if not tripling above contemporary levels—due to the conjunction of economic growth; the electrification of transport, industry, and heating; and increasing demands from climate adaptation.[117] This puts heavy pressure on intermittent RE-based electricity grids, which is made worse by limited breakthroughs in "long duration energy storage." As the IEA warned in 2022, "constant vigilance" among grid operators, and a dramatic expansion of grid storage and new transmission lines, is now required to ensure that rapidly rising electricity demands can be reliably met by intermittent renewables.[118] Furthermore, green hydrogen production by this time begins to scale up significantly and help decarbonize many of the hard-to-abate sectors.[119] But this adds further pressure to electricity grids by taking up a large share of RE-based electricity—with electrolyzers perhaps consuming up to 3,100 gigawatts of electricity by 2050, or "more than twice the total installed generation capacity of solar and wind today" and up to 30% of all electricity generated by 2050.[120] (The problem of electricity demand for green hydrogen would be alleviated if governments institutionalize strong "additionality" requirements, meaning that plants would add new RE capacity rather than subtracting it from the grid, but hydrogen lobbyists are intent on weakening these requirements, and would likely succeed in this scenario).[121] At the same time, mineral bottlenecks make it challenging to rapidly build up new transmission lines and grid storage capacities,[122] and land-use conflicts (particularly in conservative rural regions) remain a stubborn source of permitting delays. As a result, while the energy problem is not a fatal constraint by itself in this scenario, there remains a near-continuous risk of supply crises emerging from rapidly rising electricity demand, mineral bottlenecks (exacerbated by worsening water constraints in mining regions), the challenges of rapidly building out new transmission lines and storage infrastructure, and the intermittency of solar and wind energy—*especially* if "global stilling" and worsening heat stress constrain wind and solar output over time.[123]

Furthermore, as we enter the 2050s, by which time global temperatures would reach 2°C–2.6°C,[124] we will truly be facing a "brave new world" of climate extremes: much of the world's coastlines now face currently once-in-a-century flooding events every year; much of the Middle East and North Africa, sub-Saharan Africa, the southern United States, southern Europe, and South America live under permanent drought conditions; the world's mountain glaciers have lost more than a quarter of their mass, with devastating water security implications for millions of people; and all regions would be experiencing devastatingly regular heat extremes that make today's "record-shattering" events pale in comparison, with India and Pakistan beginning to face sustained temperature extremes that exceed the limits of human survivability.[125] This puts even more stress on energy systems by threatening electricity grids and supply chains with extreme weather; constraining hydro and nuclear (and possibly wind and solar) power generation; and pushing up energy demands for air conditioning, refrigeration, desalination, seawall construction, and energy-intensive DAC facilities.[126] The result is a significant increase in energy demand on top of the expected expansion from continued economic growth—especially in the "emerging" economies and southern regions of the US and Europe—which places further strain on efforts to meet rising energy needs and exacerbates the risks of electricity supply shocks. Physical risks to capital accumulation steadily accumulate, outdoor labor productivity declines under the pressure of heat stress, and "trillion dollar natural catastrophes" with the potential to trigger financial crises begin to strike, all of which converge to stifle and disrupt economic growth.[127] And this scenario would be particularly devastating if CDR technologies prove unable to draw down carbon at scale—for instance, due to weakening land and ocean carbon sinks as it scales up or higher-than-expected carbon leakage from sequestered deposits—which would mean additional climate chaos on top of a colossal waste of energy and financial expenditures.[128]

Additionally, "cheap food" becomes an increasingly distant memory for most of the global population at this time. World food production begins to plateau even as demand rises from a growing population, a still powerful livestock industry with voracious demands for animal feed, and limited efforts to cut down on food waste. Efforts to expand agriculture northward into Canada and Siberia help moderate these shortages to some extent, but they are constrained by poor soil conditions, pathogens, and increasingly unpredictable climate conditions.[129] With a global food system that is more tightly controlled by transnational finance and agribusiness, agriculture adaptation efforts remain limited primarily to those compatible with short-term shareholder returns, with marginal gains for resilience and productivity.[130] The combination of intensifying drought, extreme weather, pests, elevated fertilizer prices, and heatwaves striking the world's major breadbaskets (particularly the American Midwest, China, India, Ukraine, Argentina, and Russia) make historically unprecedented synchronous breadbasket failures a more regular occurrence—which could, as discussed in chapter 1, strike every three to eleven years in a 2°C world.[131] The consequences of any single episode of synchronous breadbasket failure by itself would be catastrophic: a scenario study commissioned by Lloyd's Bank, for instance, projects that this could lead to 7%–10% yield declines, grain price spikes of 400%–500% (compared to 15%–25% average global increases in 2022), "food riots" breaking out across the global south, geopolitical tensions rising as states restrict food exports to protect their own populations, and stock market crashes across the world's major markets.[132] When such shocks happen in a context of plateauing food production and depleting emergency grain reserves, the consequences for global food security would be monumental. And on top of this, if BECCS is dramatically scaled up in an emergency program—deemed necessary by powerful states and capitalist factions in the interests of climate stability, despite its social and ecological consequences—then this would amplify these already-unprecedented food crises while also having detrimental impacts on biodiversity, forests, and water availability at a time when these systems are already under immense stress from 2°C+warming.[133] Thus *even if* CDR works at scale in this scenario, it would still have destabilizing impacts on global food and energy systems that could weaken rather than strengthen the resilience of the global economy as a whole. And in an incremental technological innovation scenario such as this one, their impact on atmospheric carbon concentrations would be moderate at best, and negligible at worst.

To make matters worse: climate tipping points are increasingly activated at this time—particularly forest dieback, permafrost melt, wetland methane release, and arctic ice loss.[134] The Arctic becomes ice-free during the summer for the first time between 2035 and 2045, and the Amazon is well on its way toward a dry savannah, which together cause chaos in global weather systems and intensify both the speed and impacts of global

warming.[135] While these feedbacks remain moderate, they counteract
the climate gains of CDR expansion and cause further stress for political
economies that are already losing resilience because of net energy constraints, rising energy demands, climate shocks to energy infrastructure,
and synchronous breadbasket failures.

In this context, a scientific consensus emerges that a tipping-point cascade might be slowly in the making. Policymakers and capitalist elites are
thus increasingly pressured to turn to "plan B": solar radiation management (SRM), or spraying sulfides into the atmosphere to block out solar
radiation and prevent further temperature increases. The aim, following
proposals by David Keith and the Harvard Solar Geoengineering Research
Program, would be to enact a "temporary, moderate, and responsive"
SRM program that can slow or halt the rate of warming, thereby buying
time for global capitalism to transition beyond fossil fuels while avoiding
the twin threats of accumulating physical risks on one side and stranded
assets on the other.[136] As Kevin Surprise argues, SRM would in this way
serve as a "safety valve—a mechanism that can relieve (for capital) some of
the immediate pressures of the climate crisis and enable a [more gradual]
passive revolution from fossil capitalism to green capitalism."[137] By mid-
century, on a current-policies or NDC pathway, this much-dreaded strategy
will almost certainly see the light of day. In this case, another "what if"
question emerges: What if it works? And what if it doesn't? It is certainly
possible in principle that SRM could work in the ways hoped for by David
Keith and company. However, its feasibility depends not only on questionable assumptions that the climate system could be reliably modified like
a linear mechanistic system; equally problematic is the assumption that a
multidecadal SRM program wouldn't be plagued by the same patterns of
interstate conflict, weak cooperation, polarization, short-sightedness, and
sheer irrationalism that stifled plan A (i.e., reducing emissions).[138] As Catriona MacKinnon forcefully argues, the geographic dispersion of SRM infrastructures across global space and the need to sustain such a program across
many decades means it would require "unprecedented levels of sustained
inter-state and cross-corporation trust, cooperation, and transparency."[139]
If it fails—for example, as a result of unanticipated atmospheric complexities, technical failures, impacts on the ozone layer, cyber-sabotage (either
from states or nonstate actors), supply chain disruptions, and/or interstate

conflict (e.g., if a uni- or mini-lateral US-led program shuts down the South Asian monsoons and triggers catastrophic impacts on food and water security in India)—then the consequences could involve a catastrophic "termination shock": a massive pulse of warming resulting from the buildup of atmospheric CO_2 between the period of initial deployment and termination of SRM.[140] The risks of termination shock remain uncertain and contested, but "are we willing to bet *the climate* that no catastrophe or systemic cascade will trigger [SRM's] downside" over the course of a multidecadal SRM program, as Aaron Tang and Luke Kemp ask?[141] And even a less dramatic failure of SRM would have catastrophic consequences: 2°C+warming and ongoing nonlinear feedbacks would recommence, energy and material resources would be wasted, and the psychological impact on investor confidence could be immense.

Even if SRM succeeds in stabilizing average temperature increases to roughly 2°C, we should remember that material-energy throughput will continue to rise roughly in line with exponential GDP growth, at least doubling if not tripling in size by 2060 and continuing to expand thereafter (at best relatively decoupling from GDP). Incremental innovations in this scenario lead to the steady expansion of lab-grown meat, but cost and cultural barriers keep it confined to a niche market, while livestock farming keeps expanding worldwide to meet globally growing demands for animal products.[142] Relentless land-use changes—in conjunction with 2°C+warming—continue to push the earth toward a wholesale mass extinction. This means pollinator collapse and amplified food system risks, additional pulses of carbon into the atmosphere, and intensifying zoonotic spillover risks. Most of these spillover events remain localized though still potentially devastating epidemics of the Ebola variety, or slower pandemics of the HIV/AIDS or Zika variety. But the world-system will almost certainly be hit by another COVID-19-style pandemic during this period (probably multiple). In particular, while it could come earlier or later, there is a high chance, assuming that concentrated livestock farming practices remain largely unchanged, that an influenza pandemic would strike, likely of the devastating avian flu variety.[143] Imagine a pandemic with a death rate of 10%–20% (or more) hitting at a time when even rich states and the world-system as a whole have even weaker resilience than today: the result of a truly unprecedented polycrisis convergence. The COVID-19 crisis gives us merely a small taste of the synchronous failures across food-energy-finance-public health systems to come—cascading crises in which emergency response agencies and first responders are "deployed across multiple crises simultaneously," including disease outbreaks, wildfires, hurricanes, and flooding events, "putting them under unprecedented strain."[144] In the context of the 2050s, 2060s, or 2070s, if an even more devastating pandemic emerges, it is not clear that a global economic recovery from such an event would be possible. If it occurs in the context of a global SRM program, the resulting supply-chain disruptions and loss of personnel could very well doom the program to collapse—and possibly termination shock.[145] (And remember—we have thus far hardly touched on the feedback of geopolitical tensions and war, which would amplify these crises considerably—a point I return to in chapter 5).

INTERLUDE: COLLAPSE TRAJECTORIES

In sum, while neoliberal drift may persist in some form for a long time, it is highly unlikely that it could form a sustainable attractor for the world-system. Instead, it would probably at some point bifurcate toward a "collapse" trajectory—likely with a detour through fossil nationalism or fascism for some states, since the increasingly relentless and overwhelming polycrisis storm would amplify the existential crises that seed these movements. In a more stubbornly fossil fuel–reliant scenario (i.e., following a current-policies trajectory) this would be triggered by a protracted fossil stagflation between 2035 and 2050. Alternatively, in a more middle-of-the-road variant that is moderated by incremental climate policies (i.e., following an NDC trajectory), this would more likely happen from a longer-term intensification of mutually amplifying stressors in climate-food-energy-economic-public health systems as we near 2.5°C, perhaps with an influenza pandemic, SRM termination shock, Taiwan crisis, or nuclear war to deliver the final blow.

But we should pause to clarify what we mean by "collapse" in this context. In Joseph Tainter's influential work, collapse refers to a "pronounced loss of an established level of sociopolitical complexity" resulting in an irreversible degradation of political-economic integration, governance capacities, standards of living, and (most likely) population levels.[146] In other terms, building on Tainter, we can understand collapse as an irreversible breakdown in the structures, relations, and feedbacks that previously reproduced a particular socioecological system, resulting in a new equilibrium that is less "complex"—that is, more fragmented, less material and energy intensive, more localized and uncoordinated—than what came before.[147]

In the case of global capitalism, a "collapse" of this sort would not necessarily mean that capital accumulation ceases entirely. Rather, energy, food, and water companies would reap record profits, while other "disaster capitalists" would profit handsomely from rising demand for private security services and luxury bunkers.[148] Some states might even continue to grow their GDP (at least for a time) via imperialist practices that drain peripheral regions of their energy and mineral resources. But rich countries are already, in the 2020s, facing secular stagnation. By mid-century on a neoliberal drift trajectory—when 2°C+ is wreaking havoc, making today's 1.2°C world look like a golden age; agriculture is collapsing across the world's major breadbaskets; electricity supplies remain constrained by rapidly rising demand, mineral bottlenecks, and climate shocks; and aging populations put ever-more strain on public finances through surging health-care costs (worsened by climate change) and massively underfunded pension liabilities[149]—GDP growth would at best slow to a crawl and likely cease entirely in today's "advanced" economies. Opportunities for profitable productive investment would steadily vanish, financial speculation and rent-seeking would go into overdrive, political-economic elites would intensify their control over increasingly scarce productive assets (particularly agricultural land, energy, water, seeds, and mineral assets), and living standards would irreversibly decline for the vast majority of the global population.[150] And things would be even worse in the "emerging" economies of China, India, Brazil, Indonesia, and most of the global south, which would be ravaged by a 2°C+ world with insufficient finance for adaptation and loss and damage (practically inevitable in this scenario, given the economic stresses and right-wing populist pressures the global north would be dealing with). Capitalism would steadily, over time, devolve into "rentierism": a mode of political economy that no longer prioritizes growth and innovation but that secures the power and privilege of rentiers, or owners of "scarce assets under conditions of limited or no competition."[151] As Brett Christophers says, rentierism is "capital's logical destination,"[152] and this would be particularly true in late twenty-first-century conditions of worsening socioecological scarcities, plummeting investor and consumer confidence, and the exhaustion of reliable opportunities for profitable productive investment. To punctuate this shift, ruling classes across the world-system would at some point—likely in conditions of severe and intractable polycrises—abandon economic growth as a "core state imperative."[153] And while they may justify this policy shift with reference to ecological limits, in reality it would signal their abandonment of the post–World War II objective of "shared prosperity" in favor of a naked defense of rentier power.

In sum, capitalism need not collapse with a "bang" (though it certainly might) but through the slow whimper of rentierization, the gradual abandonment of economic growth as a core objective, the hollowing out of state institutions, and their steady fragmentation into more localized and improvised structures of governance and economic provisioning.[154] In other words, while a collapse event that rapidly engulfs the world-system is possible (e.g., from an avian flu pandemic or nuclear war), more likely it would be a spatially uneven multidecadal process—affecting different regions at different times with varying intensities. Numerous localized shocks—such as extreme climate events that bring down electricity grids and devastate local infrastructures—would be followed by at least partial recoveries, followed again by even more debilitating shocks, making it ever-harder to build back to a previous state. Government capacities would steadily weaken from the sheer magnitude of overlapping complex emergencies demanding attention and resources, leaving vulnerable communities and cities to fend for themselves more and more over time. The long-term result would be a more fragmented global political-economic landscape in which previous governance structures lose their effective power, global trade dramatically declines, political economies become more localized, living standards deteriorate, food insecurity proliferates, and new structures of territorial rule steadily fill the vacuum left by the collapse or hollowing-out of Westphalian states.[155]

Collapse is in this sense already a reality or ongoing process for many states in the global south, witnessed in so-called "failed states" like Somalia, Afghanistan, Syria, Yemen, and the Democratic Republic of the Congo, whose stability has been eroded by histories of colonialism, imperialist intervention, war, and climate-exacerbated complex emergencies.[156] But while a collapse trajectory would be/is being felt most intensely in the global south at first, the world-system core would be far from immune. The US, for example, may eventually resemble the world described by Octavia Butler in *Parable of the Sower*, one where the "United States" exists in name and imagination only: state capacities are decimated, national elections become ever-more meaningless, law and order breaks down in many parts of the country, and communities are forced to develop their own survival strategies—with the drought-stricken Southwest hit hardest.[157] Similarly, China—as described by Minqi Li—may experience fragmentation and civil war, with ethnic minority regions like Tibet and Xinjiang fighting for autonomy, effective governance devolving to local and regional authorities, and workers potentially taking power in some cities and provinces.[158] But this is not inevitable: these states may also sustain effective governance capacities and relative affluence, forming "bunker" regions heavily fortified from the unemployed, migrants, and other "surplus populations"—or lives deemed disposable in the eyes of the state and capital.[159] "Ecofascist" responses that aim to protect affluent lifestyles at the expense of racialized Others—for instance, by intensifying militarized borders and surveillance, using racialized minorities and migrants as forced labor to serve dominant groups, and potentially engaging in military aggression against energy and mineral-rich states—are also quite possible (a scenario depicted in John Lanchester's gripping climate fiction novel *The Wall*).[160] But sustaining affluent lifestyles would certainly become more challenging if not impossible over time if tipping cascades push global temperatures beyond 3°C toward 4°C over the course of the twenty-second century, which would trigger an even deeper collapse trajectory (and plausibly, with time, human extinction).

Overall, while there is a wide range of possible scenarios of this sort, the concept of "collapse" can effectively describe even the less extreme variants in which economies plateau and gradually contract, capitalism steadily mutates into something like a twenty-first variant of feudalism (via the mechanism of rentier strangulation), and some rich countries are able to sustain relative affluence, at least for an increasingly small class of asset owners. But I acknowledge that this is contestable. As we learn from archaeological studies of collapse, to declare something a "collapse" is an inherently interpretive move—hence ongoing debates on whether the end of the Roman empire, Mayan civilization, and Easter Island should really be considered examples of "collapse."[161] "Rome's collapse," for one, "is still debated in terms of whether it even happened, whether there was a clean break, or whether we should think instead of a period and process of transition and transformation," as Guy Middleton explains.[162] It would likely be no different with a future collapse of the capitalist world-system. Would future historians be able to say for sure when the collapse "began"? More likely (assuming there are future historians) they would debate this question, with some arguing that the collapse began as early as the 2007–2008 financial crisis, and others claiming that the tipping point did not really come until the post-2050 intensification of climate-food-energy-economic polycrises. Some may even question if it was really a "collapse" at all, instead describing it as a process of mutation in which an imperialist world economy slowly gave way to a more diverse mosaic of local and regional socioecological systems—with some retaining many continuities with capitalism, and others looking more like the feudalisms and subsistence economies of the past.

But there is no question that the earth would become a more brutal place during the course of a collapse trajectory. It is possible that some Indigenous and peasant communities, particularly those who retain the skills and community relationships needed to reproduce their livelihoods outside of the global market, would benefit in some ways from a world-system collapse, since this may enhance their autonomy by diminishing the constant assault from agribusiness, logging, and mining companies.[163] New forms of self-organized "commoning" to meet local needs could also emerge, and livelihood provisioning skills can be relearned by "deskilled" populations, enabling a softer collapse to more cooperative neo-agrarian political economies.[164] But the threat of predatory militarism from (formerly) rich countries; deepening control of the earth's land, water, and energy resources by "feudalized" rentier capitalists; the proliferation of predation from warlords, criminal networks, and right-wing militias; and a broader context of 2.5°C+ warming and ongoing tipping points means that a world-system collapse would bring intensified hardship for most of the world's population—and likely also catastrophic loss of life. And while a global collapse trajectory would create opportunities for counter-hegemonic movements, these opportunities would come for progressives as well as reactionary forces—witness, for example, the far-right "accel-erationists" and "three percenter" militias in the US seeking to accelerate the collapse of civilization and dominate a post-collapse world with their white supremacist vision.[165] In sum, we must not romanticize collapse, but better and worse collapse scenarios can be imagined (a point I return to in chapter 5).

GREEN KEYNESIAN TRAJECTORIES

Now let's "rewind the model" (so to speak). Instead of either an indefi-nite continuation of neoliberal drift or fossil nationalist regression, what if the world-system experiences a more decisive transition to a new "green Keynesian" accumulation regime, involving an altered set of power rela-tions and a new "direction of travel" for the world-earth system as a whole? A green Keynesian transition could emerge from a mid-2020s crisis, a 2030s fossil stagflation crisis, or from intensifying socioecological polycrises emerging closer to mid-century. But the longer the delay, the less likely it becomes that green Keynesianism could form a sustainable long-term attractor for global capitalism. There are three reasons for this: a delayed transition would mean (1) exceeding 2°C and forcing states to rely on mas-sive carbon removal plus SRM; (2) pushing fossil fuel EROI further down the slope of the net energy cliff before renewables can expand sufficiently, making it harder and harder to carry out a successful global RE transition; and (3) heightening the risk of stranded assets and financial instability resulting from a "disorderly transition."[166] Let's start by considering the best-case scenario for a green Keynesian transition—one that emerges at least by 2030—and explore where it may lead.

In this scenario, green capitalist reformist efforts from above and popular resistance from below converge to drive more ambitious cli-mate policies in response to a fossil stagflation crisis. The imperatives of energy security, affordability, and climate mitigation would be "push-ing in the same direction,"[167] and in this scenario there would be suffi-ciently powerful counter-hegemonic coalitions that force governments to do the rational thing. Renewed inflation and cost-of-living crises push labor unions, environmental NGOs, and climate justice and antiracist movements to carry out a historic wave of strikes and civil disobedience actions across the United States and Europe; labor unrest similarly magnifies throughout China; and popular uprisings erupt across states in Latin America, Africa, the Middle East, and Southeast Asia suffering from the lingering effects of earlier cost-of-living and debt crises. Meanwhile, green capitalist factions gather strength as solar becomes the cheapest new electricity source in most regions, central bankers issue starker warnings about climate risks to the financial system, shareholder activists force more and more companies to decarbonize their business models, and more of the world's systemically important banks and capital managers are persuaded that ambitious near-term climate action is needed to prevent financial collapse down the road. G20 countries agree to adopt more ambitious green industrial policies, which include coordinated carbon pricing in some form (perhaps reaching \$50–\$100 per ton by 2030 and steadily rising thereafter),[168] phasing out fossil fuel subsidies, coordinating phaseout dates for coal and internal combustion engine vehicles, mobilizing public and private investment to triple "clean energy" spending to \$4.5 billion per year by 2030, reforming agriculture subsidies regimes to reward more sustainable and carbon-sequestering practices, revising free trade agreements to penalize carbon-intensive products and agricultural exports complicit in deforestation, and massively increasing mitigation and adaptation finance for the global south (rising dramatically beyond the annual \$100 billion given mostly in the form of loans, if not reaching the \$1.3 trillion per year called for by African states).[169] Together these policy shifts collectively "drive the World-Earth system into a new basin of attraction,"[170] creating a qualitative break from the trajectory of neoliberal drift. Global emissions begin to fall at an average rate of 3% per year starting around 2030, placing the world-system on an announced pledges trajectory that is too slow for 1.5°C, but fast enough for a shot at 2°C.[171]

This scenario is similar to the "climate Keynesian" transition sketched by Peter Newell and Matthew Paterson, which envisions a global Keynesian regulatory regime that constrains and channels global finance to systematically drive decarbonization.[172] Something like this scenario, while far from perfect, is likely the best we could plausibly hope for in the near term. But could green Keynesianism form a stable long-term attractor or accumulation regime for global capitalism? Following Jason Moore, I argue that this would be possible only if a green Keynesian world-system ensures continuous access to and reproduction of what he calls the "four cheaps"—including cheap energy, food, raw materials, and labor—which have historically been foundational to "long waves" of sustained capital accumulation.[173] Cheap energy in particular is the key challenge, since raw material and food prices will be critically shaped by the trajectory of energy costs, though the challenge of sustaining cheap food while "internalizing" more of its ecological costs and ensuring climate resilience will play an important role as well.

Thus we should return to a critical "what if" question: What if breakthrough innovations in RE technologies, batteries, green hydrogen, CDR technologies, and low-carbon food systems, in conjunction with continuous advance in AI, biotechnologies, 3D printing, nuclear energy, and other elements of the FIR, succeed in unlocking a new era of abundant clean energy and climate-resilient food systems? On the other hand, what if—following the more pessimistic assumptions of Smil and Gordon—these innovations fail to deliver or do not come quickly enough to prevent energy and food price inflation, economic stagnation, and a right-wing populist backlash against the transition?

As discussed in chapter 1, solar and wind no doubt have the potential to unlock a new era of cheap and abundant renewable energy. But deeper attention to the problem of EROI, mineral bottlenecks, land-use conflicts, and the hard-to-abate sectors provides a more complicated picture. To briefly review: one of the key problems is that the high-upfront energy and mineral costs of the RE transition may significantly reduce net energy available for the rest of the world economy in the early to middle phases of the transition. Alojsa Slamersak and company, for instance, project that net energy for the world economy may decline by 34% during an accelerated RE transition, and this doesn't account for the upfront energy investments in manufacturing and mining the materials for batteries and EVs (as they acknowledge).[174] When incorporating a broader range of energy inputs, Capellán-Peréz and company come to even more pessimistic conclusions, projecting that net energy may decline by *up to 75%* compared to contemporary levels.[175] Again, such projections must be taken with a grain of salt. But they lend credence to the concerns of Isabelle Schnabel and others who believe an accelerated RE transition will provoke economy-wide "greenflation" in the form of rising energy, food, mineral, and other prices.[176] Even before taking account of these energy and mineral supply bottlenecks, we can expect that an abrupt shift to more ambitious climate polices—as Jean Pisani-Ferry shows—would amount to an "adverse supply shock": the costs of previously unpriced "externalities" would be "inter-nalized," FF prices would rise (whether from rising carbon taxes or direct regulation to phase down FF production), and consumers and businesses would incur short-term cost increases (e.g., to retrofit buildings and homes, swap gas boilers for heat pumps, and trade in combustion engine vehicles for EVs before the end of their useful life spans).[177] Once we include the consequences of rapid net energy decline and mineral bottlenecks—along with additional inflationary pressures like corporate profiteering, reshor-ing supply chains, and labor shortages—it becomes even more likely that green Keynesian transitions would trigger a major surge of greenflation, and possibly even a "green stagflation crisis" marked by stagnant growth and surging inflation plus high unemployment. The long-run benefits of accelerated decarbonizaton would unquestionably outweigh the short-term costs, and the costs of energy and other consumer goods may "fall dramatically" in the medium-run if green industrial policies trigger a "technology-policy-reinforcement feedback" that fuels rapid innovation in low-carbon technologies.[178] But there is no guarantee that this would occur quickly enough to prevent a populist backlash against the transition.

There are four further problems that, in conjunction with greenflation and the land-use conflicts described in chapter 1, could destabilize a green Keynesian trajectory. The first is ongoing geopolitical tensions between Rus-sia and the West, and the second is ongoing tensions between the United States and China that could spiral into a conflict over Taiwan (both of which I discuss in chapter 5). The third, which I briefly discuss here, is the fallout from job losses in the FF, automotive, and other industries in an accelerated RE transition. The RE transition will most likely be a *net* job creator on the whole, as numerous projections show.[179] But as Helen Thomas says, by focus-ing on aggregate net jobs, optimistic "green jobs" narratives "underplay the churn and dislocation that must be managed" during the transition.[180] Jobs are about more than just income for many people: they are also sources of meaning and cultural identity, which leaves many FF and industrial workers feeling resistant and skeptical toward green jobs discourse. And it does not help that many of the jobs created by the RE transition involve short-term "capex jobs" (e.g., installing renewable energy or retrofitting homes) that don't provide long-term job security, pay lower wages than in the FF sector, are not unionized, and will be under threat from automation and digitization.[181] By itself, the jobs transition is a manageable problem that can be navigated with intelligent policy, such as by investing heavily in worker retraining and incentivizing higher unionization rates. But in conjunction with the other problems discussed above, it could be a source of resentment that would be exploited by fossil capitalists and populist demagogues trying to foment backlash against the transition.

The fourth problem is worsening transition risks. As highlighted earlier, global capitalism, particularly in a green Keynesian form, would need to navigate between a rock and a hard place: intense transition risks from stranded assets if emission reductions accelerate—possibly putting between $5 and $20 trillion in carbon-intensive financial assets at risk—or more intense physical risks over time if emissions reductions are too slow. And if an ambitious mitigation program is delayed until 2030 or beyond, then it may be destabilized by a combination of *both* stranded assets and physical risks.[182] Transition risks, while potentially triggering a major 2008-style financial crisis, would be unlikely on their own to derail a green Keynesian trajectory. But in conjunction with greenflation, simmering right-wing animus toward multiplying solar and wind farms across rural landscapes, and policy failures among states to deliver on green jobs promises, we can see a recipe for bifurcation back toward neoliberal drift if not fossil nationalism or fascism.

Now let's consider how these tensions and feedbacks may play out in practice. Returning to the previous scenario, a green Keynesian transition beginning around 2030 or sooner initially creates a strong stimulus for the global economy—catalyzing an unprecedented wave of investment in RE and other green industrial sectors; creating millions of new jobs; and dramatically increasing demand for transition minerals. But greenflation begins to kick in shortly thereafter, perhaps starting modestly but then intensifying and likely pushing toward the double digits. Mineral prices soar as the relatively slow development of new mining projects is unable to keep up with rapidly rising demand—leading to major supply gaps for lithium, copper, cobalt, and nickel.[183] Proactive investments in battery recycling infrastructure help to alleviate these supply shortages by roughly 5%–10% by 2035, but they are far from sufficient to eliminate the bottlenecks.[184] Efforts to decarbonize long-distance transportation and heat-intensive industries through green hydrogen prove more challenging than expected, forcing these sectors to shift toward higher-cost alternatives that raise prices for steel, aluminum, cement, fertilizers, plastics, shipping, and aviation across the world economy. Adding to the stress, RE costs in the West rise by another 30%–50% (at least temporarily) as the US and Europe bolster efforts to reshore solar PV and battery manufacturing, forcing manufacturers to rely on more expensive domestic labor and energy inputs (alternatively, if they keep labor costs low by investing in automation, then this erodes the "green jobs" promised by politicians and foments populist anger).[185] At the same time, despite rapidly falling demand, FF prices remain a source of inflation from the combination of rising carbon prices, slashed upstream investment, and increasing energy demands from the energy, mining, and manufacturing sectors.[186] Even sulfur shortages emerge that exacerbate greenflation and push up food prices—since sulfur is critical to lithium-ion batteries, electric motors, phosphorous fertilizers, and extracting metals from ores, and rapidly declining oil and gas production (the main source of sulfur) will be reducing supplies "just when the material is needed most."[187]

At best, the result would be a moderate surge of greenflation that amplifies preexisting inflationary trends, and at worst an even more destabilizing stagflationary shock and prolonged recessions across the world economy. And if green Keynesian transitions are delayed until the mid-2030s or 2040, then they would face the same challenges but in an even more intense and condensed form: available net energy from fossil fuels would be even lower, making it more challenging to accelerate the RE transition without provoking energy price spikes; the risk of stranded assets would be higher because of an additional decade's worth of non-2°C-aligned carbon-intensive investments; and physical risks from climate shocks would magnify as well. Thus it is not likely that green Keynesian strategies, by the time we reach 2035 and especially 2040, would be able to resolve a fossil stagflation crisis (at least in a context of slow technological innovation).

In this context, we must again ask: How would political coalitions across the world-system respond to this greenflation or green stagflation crisis? Clearly, fossil nationalist or fascist regression would be a major threat: right-wing populists and FF lobbies would seize the opportunity to denigrate environmentalist "elites," working in tandem with NIMBY opposition to solar and wind farms and workers "left behind" by the transition, to create a powerful reactionary coalition. This would be a Tea Party and Gilet Jaunes–style backlash on an expanded scale across the US, Europe, and elsewhere, given greater force by disinformation operations from Russian troll farms and shadowy PR firms bankrolled by the fossil fuel industry.[188] Fossil fascism is quite possible in this scenario: as Malm and company explain, given that an accelerated RE transition would create a "life-threatening situation" for the FF industry, and an unacceptable affront to its vast network of conservative billionaire donors, these factions of the capitalist class might very well form an alliance with far-right movements in order to restore untrammeled fossil fuel extraction "by any means necessary."[189] Among the major emitters, the US would be most vulnerable to fossil nationalist or fascist backlash, though this could certainly happen in parts of Europe, Asia, or Latin America as well. In most states, if the pressure from capitalist factions from above and populist unrest from below is sufficiently strong, we would see a return to all-of-the-above energy strategies that prioritize energy security, containing inflation, protecting jobs, and rejuvenating economic growth—since this would be the path of least resistance for governments in the short run. Thus the world-system's trajectory would bifurcate back to either a current-policies or NDC energy and emissions trajectory, depending on the severity of the backlash. Again, as described earlier, the most likely result would then be either an energy-cannibalism-driven collapse trajectory, as governments double down on unconventional oil and gas extraction, or (more likely) a longer-term collapse trajectory driven by relentlessly worsening climate-energy-food-pandemic shocks over time.

We can see a pattern unfolding here. If we take seriously the dynamics of net energy decline (that is, in an incremental innovation trajectory), then there is good reason to think that both neoliberal drift as well as green Keynesian trajectories would eventually end up in collapse. Too gradual of a transition would mean increasing risks of socioecological breakdown over time—caused by worsening converging risks of climate chaos, energy insecurity, agricultural collapse, zoonotic spillovers, and earth system tipping points—while a rapid transition would likely provoke negative feedbacks in the form of greenflation, mineral bottlenecks, and populist resistance that force a bifurcation back to more gradualist pathways. It is certainly possible to come to different conclusions by tweaking our assumptions regarding the parameters—for example, by assuming a more gradualist warming trajectory with slower feedbacks, less severe impacts on agriculture in a 2°C world or stronger potential for transnational agribusiness-led adaptation, lower levels of net energy decline and lower risks of greenflation during an accelerated RE transition, higher potential to *absolutely* decouple global GDP from rising material-energy throughput, and/or a more techno-optimistic assessment of CDR and SRM to continuously hold off rising temperatures over the long haul. But in line with the evidence discussed earlier, the assumptions that inform these scenarios, while contestable, are more likely to be proven accurate than the alternatives, and things could be even worse than assumed here (e.g., in the case of more rapid carbon-cycle feedbacks, a sooner-than-expected collapse of the AMOC, or an abrupt disintegration of the West Antarctic ice-sheet that rapidly raises sea levels far beyond adaptation capacities[190]).

However, an important tweak that could make a big difference to how these scenarios unfold involves the technology parameter: What if, as dreamed of by Klaus Schwab of the World Economic Forum and other prophets of "exponential" technological disruption, a series of breakthrough innovations emerge in the context of a nascent green Keynesian hegemony? It is possible that such breakthroughs could also materialize during the course of a neoliberal drift trajectory, which would make rich countries less vulnerable to collapse (a scenario I explore in the book's conclusion). But the expansion of coordinated industrial policies to subsidize green technology manufacturing, research, and deployment would make them much more likely to emerge in a green Keynesian trajectory.[191] Thus I focus for now on the green Keynesian scenario.

In this scenario, green industrial policies succeed in creating a "technology-policy-reinforcement feedback" that stimulates breakthroughs in next-generation solar and wind energy technologies, batteries, green hydrogen, carbon capture, lab-grown meat, modular nuclear reactors, and possibly even fusion energy.[192] Moderate greenflation still emerges in the early phases of this trajectory because of mineral bottlenecks and the high upfront costs of an accelerated transition, but technological breakthroughs shortly bring down costs and give rise to a new era of cheap and abundant clean energy. As the techno-optimists anticipate, FIR technologies converge and reinforce each other, thereby enabling previously unimaginable solutions to formerly intractable engineering and design problems. Breakthroughs in solid-state and other next-generation batteries allow manufacturers to bypass lithium, cobalt, and other mineral shortages while dramatically increasing energy storage capacities.[193] Solar panel efficiencies dramatically advance—leaping from an average 15%–18% for contemporary polycrystalline silicon cells to around 28% with future solar cells based on perovskite and other next-generation materials.[194] Abundant and cheap solar energy makes it possible to cheaply produce green hydrogen at scale, in turn making it possible to decarbonize the hard-to-abate sectors at relatively low cost. Furthermore, advances in synthetic biology enable cheaper and more energetically efficient next-generation biofuels, rapid cost advances for lab-grown meat, and advances in genetically modified seeds capable of boosting agricultural yields and climate resilience. Breakthroughs in modular reactor design bring down costs and throw a lifeline to the nuclear energy industry, and even fusion energy becomes commercially viable around mid-century. The result overall is major expansion of net energy that—in conjunction with the continued "digitalization of everything," increasingly powerful AI systems trained on exponentially growing data streams, and advances in automation—radically increases labor productivity and powers a long wave of "green" accumulation and exponential growth.

While the technological breakthrough scenario may be less likely than expected by the techno-optimists, it is also more plausible than acknowledged by narratives of inevitable energy descent or collapse.[195] But we would be naïve to think that this would necessarily bring forth a world of abundance for all: more likely, as I elaborate in chapter 5, this would be a world of persistent if not worsening inequality, rising material-energy throughput that continuously degrades the biosphere, an unprecedented crisis of automation-induced technological unemployment, the proliferation of cheapening technologies of mass destruction, AI-powered geopolitical conflict and war, and the emergence of ever-more-powerful surveillance assemblages that would make today's surveillance capitalism look like 1960s-era advertising and FBI wire-tapping. In other terms, the world-system would be on the path toward techno-leviathan (elaborated in chapter 5).

To take a step back for a moment: collapse and techno-leviathan are not the only possible futures for the world-system, but they are the most likely. Whether we view one or the other as more likely depends on our expectations about future technological innovation and the success or failure of more "enlightened" political-economic elites. But the different crisis conjunctures described above—particularly, but not solely, the greenflation crisis of green Keynesianism—could also plausibly enable the start of an ecosocialist world-system trajectory. This last part of the chapter therefore shifts from mapping the most likely trajectories of the SEP to the concrete utopian potentials that may populate the possibility space, and the trajectories by which they may emerge.

ECOSOCIALIST TRAJECTORIES

There is no one way to define "ecosocialism," which can be considered one of several postcapitalist "transition discourses."[196] But ecosocialism can be considered a useful umbrella term to capture the range of post-capitalist alternatives seeking to transcend capitalism while also avoiding the ecological irrationalities of prior "actually existing socialisms." We must acknowledge important differences among various ecosocialist currents, and in practice (if we are fortunate), we would find a variety of "actually existing ecosocialisms" that emerge from geographically uneven and combined trajectories of counter-hegemonic struggle in different contexts.[197] But we can say that all these forms of ecosocialism would broadly share three core principles: (1) the prioritization of economic activities that create social use value rather than profit or exchange value; (2) the subordination of markets to collective planning, which does not necessarily mean *abolishing* markets but rather embedding and constraining their sphere of operation (the precise balance between markets and planning would take different forms in different national contexts); and (3) the end of the "growth imperative," with "growth" becoming an option rather than a structural compulsion.[198] Note that with these three principles I am not trying to describe an *ideal* ecosocialist political economy, but rather a minimum program that in practice could take much better or worse (i.e., more or less anti-imperialist, egalitarian, feminist, antiracist, democratic, or authoritarian) forms. I understand that many ecosocialists would prefer to reserve the term only for its most desirable variants. But while this stance makes sense politically, it is more analytically coherent—and strategically useful—to account for the wider range of "actually existing ecosocialisms" that might emerge in the future. Otherwise we may fail to anticipate the different ways that ecosocialist transitions might go down less desirable paths, as has been all-too-common in the history of socialist revolutions, or to develop proactive strategies that may help to prevent these outcomes.

Focusing on the global scale, there is a range of forms an ecosocialist world-system could take—ranging from more imperialist configurations that reproduce some form of core-periphery structure, to more "pluriversal" assemblages that realize the Zapatistas' vision of a "world of many worlds," and various gradations in between. This spectrum can also be conceptualized as having a "degrowth" pole on one side, referring to a world-system configuration in which the rich countries dramatically reduce their material footprints (including domestic material consumption *and* materials embodied in imports), and a "left ecomodernist" pole on the other, in which these countries perpetuate similar-to-today if not rising material footprints. I assume that degrowth transitions in G7 countries would be necessary to enable a more pluriversal ecosocialist world-system, since this is simply the biophysical precondition of global climate justice: as Jason Hickel shows, 40%–60% average material footprint reductions in the global north would be needed to allow the global population to live within Kate Raworth's socioecological "doughnut," or the "safe and just operating space" that simultaneously meets critical development needs and prevents transgression of planetary boundaries.[199] An ecomodernist socialism, on the other hand—one that (like green capitalism) relies more on high-tech solutions than on material footprint reductions to address ecological crises—would be closer to the imperialist pole. This is due to the immense mineral demands it would impose on the global south, which would pressure even well-intentioned rich socialist countries to replicate imperialist practices, and to the entwined pressures of nonstate violence and securitization it would create (discussed in chapter 5).[200] We can thus see that there are challenging trade-offs that ecosocialist movements must navigate, with degrowth currents facing more difficult challenges of political feasibility, while the ecomodernist currents would fall short from the standpoint of global climate justice.

In the discussion that follows, rather than focusing on idealized visions of what ecosocialism should look like in practice—an essential yet one-sided undertaking that risks becoming a form of abstract utopian speculation—I focus instead on the processes and mechanisms through which ecosocialist transitions might plausibly emerge. In this sense, following Kim Stanley Robinson, I am more interested in how we cross the "Great Trench" that separates the present world from the hoped-for future, rather than the precise contours of the destination.

Using E.O. Wright's terminology, socialists often distinguish between "ruptural" and "metamorphosis" paths beyond capitalism. There is sometimes ambiguity in how these and related terms are used. But in my usage, ruptural pathways involve the revolutionary overthrow of existing capitalist states and their replacement by new bottom-up structures of rule and economic planning. In contrast, metamorphosis refers to "incremental modifications" of the state and world economy that "cumulatively transform the system," but without witnessing a revolutionary overthrow and wholesale replacement of existing structures and institutions.[201] In this section I focus on the path of metamorphosis. Revolutionary ruptures may be possible in parts of the periphery and semi-periphery—where state structures are relatively fragile, material deprivation is more intense, and authoritarian repression blocks more democratic reform pathways. But in the world-system core—where state structures are stronger and command broader legitimacy, material security is much greater, security apparatuses are pervasive and powerful, and there is practically zero chance of security forces defecting en masse to join a socialist revolution—ruptural pathways are off the table for the foreseeable future.[202] Yet ecosocialist metamorphosis of the world-system is possible, or scenarios in which strengthening grassroots movements from below and radicalized elite crisis management strategies from above combine to push core countries—and the world-system as a whole—in increasingly ecosocialist directions over time. Metamorphosis does not mean continuous gradualism, since conjunctures of deep capitalist crisis can witness psychosocial tipping points in which popular movements rapidly gain strength and radical reforms move from the fringes to become common sense.[203] *Punctuated* metamorphosis is thus a more fitting term, implying a multidecadal transition process punctuated by periods of relatively rapid change. But there would be no immediate and total overthrow of the capitalist class in the world-system core, much less a simultaneous world revolution. Instead, there would be an uneven and combined transition process in which ecosocialists and allied movements make significant gains in core states, institutionalizing new "equilibria" of class compromise based on strengthening grassroots power and new norms of capitalist governance, followed by periods of capitalist backlash and assault on working class power; in turn, these periods of backlash would be followed either by regression back in the direction of increased capitalist power, or by continuously strengthening popular movements that forcibly push governments further toward decommodification of basic goods and socialization of the means of production.[204]

All of the ecosocialist trajectories described in this section involve variations of this basic pattern, though some may involve a larger role for ruptural strategies (particularly those unfolding after mid-century in the context of world-system collapse). In particular, I suggest there are at least four "ideal-type" ecosocialist trajectories, or simplified representative pathways that are intended to illustrate different possibilities and variations: (1) a near-term degrowth trajectory in G7 states, starting between 2030 and 2045, that emerges from a green-stagflation crisis of green Keynesianism; (2) a near-term left ecomodernist transition emerging from a greenflation crisis of green Keynesianism; (3) a longer-term degrowth trajectory, beginning between 2050 and 2080, emerging in a context of magnifying polycrises and a collapsing capitalist world economy; and (4) a longer-term left ecomodernist transition emerging in a context of magnifying polycrises after mid-century. To further complicate things, these trajectories could involve either anti-imperialist ecosocialisms based on principles of global solidarity, or what I call "fortress ecosocialisms" that reproduce elements of today's militarized global apartheid.[205] I explore these differences more substantively in chapter 5. For now I focus primarily on the near-term, anti-imperialist trajectory of ecosocialist degrowth—which is the most desirable scenario from the standpoint of global climate justice—and then more briefly explore the other trajectories.

In this first scenario, green Keynesian regimes accelerate the RE transition, but the result is an unprecedented surge of greenflation—driven by rapid net energy decline, intractable mineral bottlenecks, and another round of corporate profiteering that exploits upstream supply bottlenecks to amplify profit rates—followed by rising unemployment as central banks hike interest rates in their ideologically constrained efforts to maintain price stability. The conjunction of cost-of-living crises, prolonged recessions, and high unemployment generates an immense wave of popular uprisings and labor strikes across the world-system. As interest rate hikes fail to control inflation and only cause more misery and popular anger, elites in the world-system core recognize that there can be no quick end to the crisis without either backtracking on climate policies or engaging in far-reaching market interventions and social support schemes. The ideological hegemony of green growth—the belief that rapid decarbonization need not come at the expense of economic growth—is thus severely weakened. But in this case, largely because of increasingly organized and powerful "red-green" coalitions composed of labor unions, environmentalists, anti-racist movements, and scientists—who become capable of coordinating disruptive general strikes by this time—fossil fueled backlash is avoided, and a more radical response to the crisis becomes possible. These coalitions succeed in advancing an alternative narrative and set of policy responses to the green-stagflation crisis. In this narrative, the crisis is not simply blamed on the accelerating energy transition, which is by then widely considered a nonnegotiable response to the worsening climate emergency. Rather, these movements successfully frame the crisis as a result of both concentrated corporate power and a growth-dependent economy that makes jobs and economic security contingent on rising GDP, and which fails to equitably share the abundant wealth that already exists. They show that cost-of-living crises are not the result of renewable energy or climate policies per se, but rather of an economic system *in which living has a "cost" in the first place*.[206] In the context of rapidly declining real wages and price volatility and inflation for *all* energy sources (not just renewables), these narratives resonate with a majority of citizens in democratic countries. And after a decade when policy interventions like windfall taxes, price caps, and rationing to protect critical industries reentered public debate in the global north, populations in these countries were primed for more radical state interventions to address this epic and unparalleled polycrisis conjuncture.[207]

As a result, more radical leftwing governments come to power across the world-system: coalitions of radicalized green and social democratic parties are elected across Europe (including in Germany and France—the hegemonic core of the EU); the Democratic and Labour Parties are pushed further leftwards in the United States and UK; Latin America, under the leadership of Brazil and Chile, deepens and cements its progressive "Pink Tide"; and the Chinese Communist Party, whether under an aging Xi or his successor, is emboldened to pursue a more radical ecological agenda. While these governments pursue distinctive policy platforms, they share some general features: (1) price controls, windfall taxes on corporate profits, and in some cases nationalization of energy companies are used to control inflation while simultaneously phasing out fossil fuels; (2) war-like mobilizations are enacted to accelerate deployment of RE technologies, retrofit buildings and homes, improve energy efficiency, and reduce unnecessary forms of energy use to ensure that price controls don't result in shortages; (3) monetary systems are radically reformed—for example, through capital controls, central bank regulations on credit provision, and the nationalization of systemically important banks—to channel finance toward social and ecologically necessary investments; (4) GDP growth is explicitly deprioritized in favor of alternative metrics that more effectively measure social and ecological welfare (e.g., by using Kate Raworth's doughnut economics framework); and (5) a mix of more radical social programs—such as universal basic income (UBI), public job guarantees, and/or universal public services—are enacted to decouple economic security from GDP.[208] These governments also double down on efforts to shift away from synthetic fertilizers and pesticides toward regenerative agroecology, expand public transportation and cycling infrastructure rather than private EV ownership, create denser and more walkable cities, ramp up recycling infrastructure and circular industrial ecologies, and expand alternative proteins while disincentivizing meat consumption. The result is that material-energy throughput falls by 40%–50% on average between 2030 and 2050 in rich countries—as many analysts agree can be done while simultaneously improving living standards—which eliminates transition metal bottlenecks, accelerates the RE transition, and reduces pressure on forests, biodiversity, and Indigenous peoples worldwide.[209] Manufacturing trade unions, while wary of anti-growth rhetoric, are brought on board by the promise of abundant local jobs and a livable UBI to ensure economic security for displaced workers. At the same time, a compromise formation with nationally-based manufacturing capitalists allows them to retain positions of power over industrial operations and within national planning boards (as they did during the US World War II mobilization).[210] Finance capital ruthlessly attacks these regimes via investment strikes and capital flight. But coordinated capital controls, along with radical monetary reforms that abolish the artificial scarcity of money (while controlling inflation through taxation, price controls, and decommodifying critical goods and services), allow these governments to maintain popular support while shifting to a new political-economic equilibria with a radically shrunken financial sector.[211] To deal with NIMBY opposition to rapid RE expansion, policymakers pragmatically agree to incentivize community-owned energy projects that displace centralized investor-owned utilities, since these have been shown to garner more widespread public support for the transition.[212]

The regimes that emerge here could be considered capitalist-socialist hybrids—or post-growth social democracies[213]—that do not entirely displace capitalist power but constrain it within a planning framework that subordinates economic growth to the core objectives of climate stability, social wellbeing, and economic security for all. A transition of this sort may be most likely in continental Europe thanks to its tradition of social democracy, its vulnerability to energy price spikes, and the rising popularity of post-growth ideas among progressive EU policymakers and social movements.[214] But it would need to overcome resistance from staunch fiscal conservatives in Germany and the "Frugal Four,"[215] defeat reactionary backlash from the far-right, and break through the ideological hegemony of ecomodernism and green growth. It is more difficult to imagine in the US, given its more intense culture of individualism, sprawling oil-dependent geographies, and the strength of its Trumpian undercurrents. Even here, such a transition is plausible: polls show that the majority of Americans under 30 prefer socialism over capitalism, and democratic socialist candidates will likely improve their electoral prospects as this group becomes more politically influential over time.[216] But an American state-led mobilization to rapidly transform energy and food systems would spark hysterical conservative backlash, stifling legal challenges from the court system, new thresholds of polarization, and possibly even an insurgency among far-right militia groups leading to something like civil war.[217] As a result, even if a democratic ecosocialist is elected president of the United States, and even if the Democratic Party has control of both houses of Congress, they would most likely face significant constraints on their policy ambitions. Fortunately, an ecosocialist world-system transition might still get underway even without the rise to power of democratic socialists in the United States. China, for instance, may be seen as the best hope for a kind of (authoritarian) ecosocialist transition: as previously noted, its deepening reliance on foreign oil and rapidly rising energy demands make it particularly vulnerable to FF supply shocks (though it may be comparatively unscathed by greenflation, due to its far-reaching control over RE supply chains). In a context of worsening water stress, intensifying labor militancy and social unrest due to cost-of-living crises and spiking youth unemployment, the increasing prominence of ecological Marxism among CCP intellectuals,[218] and concerns about China's energy and food import vulnerabilities, the CCP may plausibly be pushed toward an alternative economic model: a slower, more efficient, and equitable (if still highly authoritarian) post-growth "ecological civilization."[219] As the US intelligence community imagines, could an "unlikely partnership" between the EU and China form the hegemonic foundation of a nascent ecosocialist world-system, perhaps in combination with democratic socialist breakthroughs in Latin America and elsewhere?[220] In conjunction with a soft decline of American power—in which the Democratic Party holds onto power, shifts leftward, and prevents fossil nationalist backlash—this may be our best hope for a more egalitarian postcapitalist future.

Alongside these post-growth social democracy transitions in the world-system core, a suite of "climate reparations" initiatives—including debt cancellation and debt-for-nature swaps; intellectual property reforms to accelerate RE technology transfers; dramatically scaled up finance for mitigation, adaptation, and loss and damage; and a raft of new trade agreements that prioritize sustainability criteria, as well as labor and Indigenous rights—would then facilitate accelerated decarbonization and biodiversity protection across the global south.[221] By canceling debts and providing other compensation mechanisms for states in the global south to forgo profits from fossil fuels and other forms of extractivism, these states would in turn become less dependent on ecologically damaging export-led growth.[222] In effect this would entail something like a "Marshall Plan for the earth," as numerous scholars and activists have called for.[223]

However, adequate finance from the global north is a necessary, but not sufficient, condition for southern producers to keep their "carbon bombs" in the ground.[224] Grassroots struggles against FF extraction across the global south—particularly in key producer states like Venezuela, Brazil, Saudi Arabia, Qatar, Mozambique, and Iran—thus have a critical role to play. Furthermore, political struggles in the global south will also shape how transitions in the world-system core unfold. In particular, given imperialist relations of ecologically unequal exchange, Jason Hickel suggests that southern states have "the power to enforce degrowth in the North, by refusing to be used as a supplier of cheap labour and raw materials for Northern consumption."[225] For instance, if Argentina, Chile, Bolivia, Indonesia, Zimbabwe, and other southern states form a "battery metal OPEC" to exert greater control over the pricing and distribution of transition metals, this could erode the global north's access to these strategic resources.[226] In turn, while this could fan the flames of fossil nationalism in the global north by fueling greenflation, it could also bolster northern struggles for energy demand reduction and a public transport rather than private car-based transportation system (which would require far less mineral extraction).[227] Similarly, if democratic revolutions in North Africa and the Middle East lead to more strident assertions of resource sovereignty—for example, by refusing to liquify and ship their natural gas to Europe and China, or maintaining control of their abundant solar resources rather than sending them northward to gluttonous European markets (whether in the form of electricity exports or green hydrogen)—then they may reinforce degrowth trajectories in the imperial core.[228] The obstacles confronting these efforts are formidable: developing lithium resources in the South American lithium triangle, for instance, currently requires access to Western finance and technology.[229] But if anti-imperialist struggles join forces in South-South partnerships that coordinate trade and industrial strategies, and are bolstered by climate reparations programs from the former colonial powers, then they may succeed in building domestic energy, food, and economic sovereignty while reinforcing degrowth transitions in the world-system core.[230] In this way a *new* "New International Economic Order"—harkening back to the third-world struggles for economic decolonization during the Cold War—may come into being, with the capacity to pursue an agenda of "contraction and convergence" between the material consumption levels of the global north and south.[231]

By collectively escaping from the GDP growth constraint, governments across the global north and south could accelerate decarbonization, agroecological food system transformation, and ecosystem restoration, making it possible to bring down emissions at a 5%–10% annual rate. If this trajectory begins between 2035 and 2045, it would put the world-system on track to keep global temperatures below 2°C and plausibly, through large-scale rewilding and carbon-sequestering agroecology, bring them down to 1.5°C later this century. But this would be merely the beginning. Post-growth social democracies, because of their conflicting capitalist and socialist elements, would be tense hegemonic formations that are vulnerable to capitalist backlash and regression. Many Marxists would say they are not even possible in the first place. But from a complexity theory lens that appreciates the hybridity of actually-existing political economies, these sorts of hybrid regimes in which "hostile elements . . . coexist in shifting uneven equilibria without the system exploding,"[232] are far more plausible than many Marxists would acknowledge. However, it is true that any decisive yet partial movement in the direction of socialism, as E.O. Wright says, would erode "the incentive and information structures that animated economic coordination under capitalism."[233] For instance, policies that make survival less contingent on wage labor—such as UBI and universal public services—could lead to or exacerbate labor shortages, particularly in dangerous and poorly paid occupations.[234] Likewise, while it is plausible that the greener sectors of the capitalist class would initially go along with post-growth social democracy—since this may be seen as necessary to ensure social stability and bolster climate action in a context of deep capitalist crisis—they may eventually turn on these regimes if labor unions are deemed too powerful, wages too high, and profits too low. Meanwhile, the factions of the capitalist class most explicitly targeted and disempowered by these regimes—particularly finance and fossil capital, along with the conservative billionaires and media outlets who support them—would do their best to sabotage and overthrow them, using a mix of smear campaigns, disinformation, cyberattacks, and other means.[235] So long as capitalists are unwilling to accept a shrunken role in the world economy and lower profit rates, then post-growth social democracies would constantly struggle to negotiate a balance between the desires of capital and the goals of ecosocial well-being, and they would be under continuous threat from investment strikes and sabotage.

Thus the struggle for a more deeply democratic, resilient, and globally egalitarian ecosocialist world-system—involving truly bottom-up control over the means of production, and contraction and convergence rather than perpetuation of core-periphery relations—would be an ongoing hegemonic project. Post-growth social democracy would facilitate this longer-term transition, since UBI and/or decommodification of basic goods would liberate more individuals from the discipline of labor markets, allowing them to devote more time to political activism and economic "commoning" initiatives—including worker and consumer cooperatives, community gardens, transition towns, solidarity health clinics, ecological restoration work, and other bottom-up practices of communal care and reproduction.[236] In this way, while a generous UBI might lead to labor shortages in some sectors, it would also free up time and energy for essential forms of care and reproductive labor that are unprofitable for capital, while provoking experimentation with new ways to collectively allocate labor to socially necessary activities experiencing shortages.[237] At the same time, widening participation in these commoning or solidarity economy initiatives, and freedom from labor market competition, would facilitate transitions in ideological assemblages toward collectivist values and postcapitalist conceptions of "the good life." Ecosocialisms-in-transition may in this way deepen their resilience over time. But there is no guarantee that they would ultimately end up in a stable ecosocialist attractor—in other words, no guarantee that negative feedback mechanisms or path dependencies would emerge that entrench ecosocialist hegemony over time and prevent capitalist regression.

Overall, we can identify six mechanisms that, in conjunction with increasingly organized and politically effective red-green coalitions, may facilitate a trajectory of ecosocialist degrowth metamorphosis: (1) labor movements gather strength and momentum in the near-term, bolstered by worker shortages and efforts to reshore manufacturing, which improves the negotiating position of workers;[238] (2) ambitious green Keynesian policies, combined with slow technological innovation and unanticipated supply bottlenecks as renewables rapidly scale up, lead to a deep and protracted green-stagflation crisis that cannot be addressed using conventional crisis management strategies; (3) in this context, with economic insecurity spiking, identities and desires built on neoliberal individualism and consumerism are thrown into crisis. Together with the ideological defeat of green growth narratives, this creates the conditions for ideological tipping points in the direction of mass popular support for post-growth economies that prioritize economic security and "public luxury" rather than private consumption[239] (these tipping points, of course, would not happen automatically, but only through the success of long-term organizing and narrative strategies pursued by grassroots activists, NGOs, and intellectuals); (4) younger populations in the US and Europe, who are more ideologically predisposed to socialism and support ambitious climate action, become more politically influential in the 2030s and 2040s;[240] (5) we witness a "shift in power away from the industrialised west towards mineral-rich nations" in the global south, which is leveraged to pursue a trajectory of contraction and convergence;[241] and (6) "non-reformist reforms" like UBI and decommodification free up time and energy for more and more people to devote to activism and solidarity economy initiatives, which strengthens red-green movements even more and allows them to make further advances toward bottom-up, participatory ecosocialist democracy over time.

To be sure, these mechanisms of transformation are merely potentials, not certainties: capitalist investment in automation to address worker shortages may counteract potential gains for labor, a crisis of Green Keynesianism may be relatively mild rather than historic, resilient cultures of individualism and consumerism may prevent broad-based support for post-growth social democracy, and rich countries may successfully increase domestic mining and recycling efforts to reduce mineral dependence on the global south. Furthermore, it will be challenging to build and sustain broad based red-green coalitions, particularly given the mistrust that many labor unions continue to feel toward environmentalists; the pull of manufacturing workers toward right-wing populism; the tendency toward purist forms of horizontalism among some sectors of the left; and the problem of factionalism, infighting, racism, and sexism across leftwing organizations and movement spaces.[242] An emergent red-green movement would thus be a tense coalition, vulnerable to efforts by police, security agencies, the media, capitalist elites, and autocrats to drive wedges between its factions— for example, by using sophisticated disinformation operations to sow mistrust and exploit preexisting divisions. Ecosocialists and allied movements will need to anticipate and develop strategies to counteract these efforts. No doubt, this concrete utopian scenario is a long shot at best. But the converging crises destabilizing global capitalism mean that the conditions for ecosocialist transitions may be slowing ripening. If leftwing movements can overcome factionalism and build durable red-green coalitions, then a trajectory of ecosocialist metamorphosis could be in the making.

While the near-term G7 degrowth trajectory is the most desirable scenario, it is worth briefly highlighting alternative paths to ecosocialism. The second scenario can be called a near-term *ecomodernist* socialism trajectory, beginning in the 2030s. This scenario would be broadly similar to the G7 degrowth trajectory. But rather than degrowth transitions in the world-system core that reduce material-energy throughput by 40%–50%, instead we would see the emergence of more radical variants of green Keynesianism (e.g., following left-wing Green New Deal proposals).[243] This would most likely happen in the context of a greenflation crisis that is less severe than the green-stagflation described above: one that involves sustained near double-digit inflation, but doesn't trigger a prolonged recession and rising unemployment.[244] But it could also emerge from a carbon bubble shock: if the global financial system is destabilized by the loss of $5–$20 trillion in FF asset values, and red-green movements are strong enough, then center-left governments may be successfully pressured to nationalize the FF sector and other transition laggards, forming another possible mechanism of metamorphosis beyond capitalism. In these more moderate but still intense polycrisis conjunctures, strengthening grassroots movements would amplify popular support for radical inflation fighting measures, nationalization, and public ownership, but (unlike in the degrowth scenario) they would not trigger ideological tipping points toward post-growth and post-consumerist values on a large scale. The leftwing ecomodernist regimes that come to power would dramatically increase public investment to accelerate the energy transition, enact UBI and job guarantees to increase economic security for all, and redistribute wealth and power away from the capitalist class, but they would not bring an end to capitalism's exponential growth dynamic. Instead, they would pursue state-led "mission economy" programs to accelerate innovation in green hydrogen, lab-grown meat, EV batteries, next-generation nuclear energy, and CDR technologies.[245] The goal, like with green capitalist regimes today, would be to rely on technological innovation in order to make current rich-world consumption patterns compatible with net zero. These nascent socialist regimes may over time stabilize or reduce their material footprints, which will be determined by ongoing struggles between ecomodernist and degrowth factions, but this is not guaranteed. The best-case scenario would be a steady-state socialist world-system around mid-century that puts the earth on track for 2°C and achieves some degree of convergence in living standards between the global north and south. This would be a less pluriversal world-system than the G7 degrowth version, due to its expansive mineral demands—particularly for transition minerals, but also uranium for nuclear energy—which would intensify extractivist conflicts with Indigenous and rural communities in both the global north and south (these sorts of conflicts would not be avoided entirely in a G7 degrowth trajectory, which will still require some primary extraction, but they would be significantly less intense in comparison). Still, ecomodernist socialism would no doubt form the basis of a more ecologically rational world-system, so long as these states eschew the ecologically disastrous dream of "fully automated luxury communism."[246] It is also a more realistic scenario than G7 degrowth. But we must be clear-sighted and honest about its limits and faults, rather than clinging to unrealistic win-win-win narratives (as its advocates typically do).

Moving to the third pathway, we can imagine a *longer-term* degrowth trajectory in which capitalist regimes sustain economic growth and political stability beyond mid-century, and red-green movements steadily grow but are not yet strong enough to push for more than reformist policies in coalition with green capitalists. But intensifying polycrises between 2050 and 2070, in conjunction with only weak or incremental gains from technological innovation, severely weakens the resilience of states and capitalist ruling classes. In this context, rapidly strengthening red-green movements catalyze geographically uneven and combined transitions to more local, democratic, and equitable political economies—in some cases involving ruptural pathways, and in others proceeding through metamorphosis.

However, this would happen in the context of 2°C–2.5°C+warming and ecological collapse, which would be particularly devastating for the global south. It is thus highly uncertain whether this global ecosocialist assemblage would be stable or eventually devolve into a deeper collapse trajectory. But political ecologists teach us that political-economic factors, rather than climactic forces alone, are typically much more relevant in shaping patterns of "scarcity" and vulnerability.[247] It is thus possible to envision scenarios in which ecosocialist transitions enable communities across the global north and south to adapt and sustain livelihoods in a 2.5°C world, but this would of course become far more challenging (if not impossible) in a context of tipping point cascades.

Fourth and finally, we can imagine a longer-term ecomodernist socialist transition. Like the longer-term degrowth trajectory, this would be a scenario in which intensifying polycrises in the second half of the century empower red-green movements to catalyze postcapitalist transitions. But it would more likely occur in a context of neoliberal drift or green Keynesianism *plus* dramatic technological innovations, which would moderate the risks of collapse while also driving a nascent crisis of technological unemployment. In this context, ecomodernist socialist regimes may come to power promising to equitably share the fruits of automation while getting ecological crises under control with the aid of advanced technologies. They would enact mission economy programs that mobilize AI, synthetic biology, nanotechnology, and 3D printing to create a more artificialized world capable of feeding and powering a 9–10 billion human population amid 2°C–2.5°C+climate chaos. Ultra-dense cities may be built in the far north as living conditions deteriorate across the global south.[248] If 2.5°C+warming activates tipping cascades, then these regimes would be forced to rely on SRM and CDR on a massive scale, and they would struggle to construct a democratically accountable approach to geoengineering governance.[249] As I show in chapter 5, these states would also confront techno-authoritarian risks because of the diffusion of powerful new technologies of mass destruction and frightening advances in technologies of surveillance and police power. This would be far from an ideal future—but less bad than collapse, and not as dark as techno-leviathan.

In sum, we can speculate that there are at least four ideal-type pathways to an ecosocialist world-system, and more are undoubtedly possible.

Far from a dogmatic prediction about the future (i.e., "this is how it must happen!"), the above should be considered a provisional navigational map that can inform ecosocialist strategy, but one that must be continuously updated and revised as events in the world unfold, new information comes to light, and opportunities for transformative agency arise or evaporate. I will return to these scenarios in chapter 5 and in the book's conclusion in order to elaborate more of their features and variations.

CONCLUSION

In summary, the global SEP is structured by the intersecting crises of capitalism, climate and biodiversity, net energy decline, unsustainable food systems, and pandemic risk. A trajectory of neoliberal drift, at least in the absence of rapid innovations in green technologies, would eventually bifurcate toward a collapse trajectory—whether resulting from a near-term fossil stagflation crisis or a longer-term trajectory of relentlessly intensifying polycrises. Alternatively, a more decisive counter-hegemonic transition to a global green Keynesian regime could plausibly put the world-system on track to meet the Paris targets if it occurs soon enough (i.e., by 2030 or shortly thereafter). But it would likely be an unstable regime thanks to the intersecting risks of greenflation, transition and physical risks to the global financial system, populist resentment, and fossil capitalist strategies to engineer a return to carbon lock-in. Thus it may eventually bifurcate back toward neoliberal drift or fossil fascism and eventually collapse, or (more optimistically) forward toward ecosocialism. However, breakthrough innovations powered by FIR technologies could also help stabilize green Keynesian regimes by creating a new era of abundant clean energy. Yet, as I elaborate in chapter 5, this would also unleash powerful forces of state and nonstate violence that could themselves force a transition to an alternative world-system configuration in which "security," rather than capital accumulation, becomes the ecologically dominant function.

We have not yet explored how the SEP and VP—political economies and security assemblages—may coevolve in the coming decades as the planetary polycrisis unfolds. Thus the collapse, green Keynesian, and ecosocialist trajectories described here remain partial, missing important parameters that will also shape their evolution. These I address in chapter 5.

5

FUTURES OF GEOPOLITICS, SECURITY, AND THE PLANETARY PROBLEMATIC

The SEP may be the key determinant of the possible futures of the world-earth system, but it is certainly not the whole of the planetary problematic. For this we must investigate how the violence problematic (VP)—the problem of regulating and constraining violence, both within and between states—intersects with and shapes the possible trajectories of the SEP.

As argued in chapter 3, the VP is itself a terrain of competing hegemonic projects and counter-hegemonic struggles that is "strategically coupled" with hegemonic projects in the SEP.[1] Global security assemblages are more fragmented relative to the capitalist world-system—with the United States, the EU, China, Russia, and others having relatively autonomous "security empires" based on their own geopolitical positioning, imperialist ambitions, fears, and vulnerabilities—though they are all entangled to some extent through shared technologies, discourses, strategies, and financial linkages.[2] Each state has different factions with competing visions and strategies for pursuing security objectives, which tend to be divided between what Jerry Harris calls "transnational globalist" and "national hegemonist" blocs (though there are overlaps between them): on the globalist side are those who support a cooperative approach to global security that focuses on deepening economic integration while policing various forms of nonstate violence, both domestic and transnational, that threaten capital accumulation. On the national hegemonist side are more hawkish elements that value national protectionism more than integration, prioritize the threats posed by geopolitical rivals more than nonstate actors, and advocate the unilateral pursuit of global hegemony—a position that was clearly articulated in the Trump administration's 2018 National Defense Strategy.[3] But counter-hegemonic movements provide very different articulations of the VP, which include movements against militarism, surveillance, police brutality, xenophobic border regimes, mass incarceration, and racialized counter-terrorism—and *for* alternative practices of security and public safety based on nonviolence, democratic accountability, and restorative justice.[4]

Like with the SEP, the VP can be mapped as a structure of intersecting dependency relations that morphs over time. Whereas chapter 4 mapped the SEP in relative isolation in order to explore its internal complexities, this chapter instead analyzes how the VP and security assemblages coevolve with trajectories in the SEP. To do so, I proceed in the same way as in chapter 4: first describing the dependency relations between key parameters, and then imaginatively constructing different possible trajectories that maintain coherence between these parameters.

To simplify things, the broadest parameters I focus on include political economy, state and nonstate violence, technological change, climate change, energy, and ideology. More specifically, the political economy parameter in this context focuses on the intensity of "structural violence" within a political-economic system. State violence includes interstate conflict as well as military-police repression. But we should emphasize that military-police assemblages include traditional security agencies as well as the privatized military-industrial-surveillance-prison complex—which, at least currently, should be understood more as an *extension* rather than replacement of state functions, though this could change in a collapse trajectory.[5] Nonstate "violence," as discussed in chapter 3, is a similarly wide-ranging category, but I focus primarily on nonstate "terrorism"— understood simply as lethal violence enacted to incite fear among populations in pursuit of political objectives, a tactic used by states and nonstate actors alike—and bottom-up rebellion, which can range from "violent" to "nonviolent" forms of protest (which, again, is an historically unstable and often socially contested distinction). The technology parameter includes advances in AI, robotics, digitalization (particularly the internet-of-things), nuclear energy, synthetic biology, and neurotechnologies. The climate parameter includes future climate impacts on agriculture, water, and critical infrastructures, which can potentially exacerbate scarcities that in some cases reinforce conflict pressures. But we should emphasize that "scarcity" is always a *socio*ecological phenomenon, or an effect of political-economic structures that damage and deplete ecologies while constraining access to means of subsistence.[6] The energy parameter focuses on how geopolitical tensions may impact the RE transition, and how this will impact the climate crisis in turn. Lastly, the ideology parameter includes variables of nationalism, racism, masculinity, and existential crises—all of which shape and constrain patterns of violence and the military-police practices through which communities, cities, and states respond to them.

POLITICAL ECONOMY ←→ STATE VIOLENCE ←→ NONSTATE VIOLENCE

We begin with the basic causal nexus that links the structure of political economies with patterns of state and nonstate violence. Starting with the political economy → nonstate violence relation, this is primarily shaped by the intensity of structural violence inherent in a given political-economic system, defined by Johan Galtung as the indirect violence of material deprivation reproduced through social structures, which reduces human "somatic and mental realizations . . . below their potential realizations."[7] Structural violence operates at different scales, seen in relations of exploitation between owners of capital and workers, national-scale inequalities, and global inequalities driven by processes of ecologically unequal exchange.[8] Generally speaking, while this is not always the case, political economies with higher levels of structural violence will unleash more nonstate violence: this is seen, for example, in the higher prevalence of violent crime and terrorism in countries with high levels of unemployment and inequality; the targeting of states by nonstate terrorists who have historically engaged in imperialism and/or supported repressive regimes; and the obvious correlations between inequality, injustice, and grassroots rebellion.[9] In the words of a common refrain used by Black Lives Matter and other protestors, "No Justice, No Peace!"

The intensity of structural violence within states is also linked with the intensity of geopolitical tensions and patterns of organized violence between states: heightened inequality, precarity, and disruptive economic development often exacerbate both material and existential insecurities that can be exploited by opportunistic elites—particularly from the more ethnonationalist sectors of state managerial and capitalist classes—to drum up nationalist passions and divert attention from underlying economic woes. Hence the frequently drawn parallels between the "thirty years crisis" spanning the first and second world wars—which was largely the product of rapid capitalist development, market liberalization, and destabilizing economic crises—and the recent upsurge in right-wing populism and geopolitical tensions.[10] The drivers of geopolitical tensions and interstate conflict are multidimensional, also encompassing shifts in patterns of political-economic interdependence (e.g., greater or lesser financial and trade linkages between states), economic growth rates, and the interstate balance of power (e.g., the relative decline of US power and the rise of China).[11] But structural violence is arguably the most important factor: stagnant growth, shifts to a more multipolar world, and weakening trade linkages do not necessarily or by themselves increase the likelihood of conflict, which requires the powder keg of relative deprivation, marginalization "without hope of improving one's circumstances," and material and existential insecurities that can be exploited to feed sectarian tensions or bellicose nationalism.[12]

Political economies with higher levels of structural violence and non-state violence will also in turn tend to have higher levels of state violence in the form of more intensive military-police assemblages (greater geopolitical tensions between states will also, of course, lead to increasing military investments). Simply put, to continuously reproduce a hegemonic formation with high levels of inequality and exploitation—whether domestically or globally—larger investments in military-police assemblages will generally be necessary to "keep the lid" on the ensuing violence and rebellion.[13] Political economies with higher levels of structural violence will also tend to have weaker resilience, due to both the violence and rebellion they unleash and the subsequent pressures they face to channel a higher proportion of resources toward security assemblages. This is one reason, for instance, why the South African apartheid regime—which relied on a security apparatus that was "hugely expensive and expansive, draining millions from government coffers"—ultimately collapsed, which has historically been a pattern for authoritarian regimes.[14] Likewise, in a context of neoliberal drift for individual nation-states and the world-system as a whole, we can expect that worsening levels of inequality, exploitation, and uneven development would mean continuously rising investments in security assemblages and weakening resilience over time.

A final political economy→state violence relation we should highlight is the role of profit-driven corporations in shaping national and global security policies. These private companies include the more traditional nationally based arms manufacturers such as Raytheon, Lockheed Martin, and Northrop Grumman, as well as more globalized private surveillance-prison-border-security firms like G4S, Securitas, Dyncorp, and NSO Group.[15] The private military-security industry may enhance the resilience of a neoliberal drift trajectory in at least two ways. First, simply put, it creates a powerful bloc of global capital that profits handsomely from insecurity, war, militarized borders, prisons, and state repression. This bloc encompasses not just private military-industrial companies themselves but also their investors—who include the world's largest capital managers and banks, from Blackrock to Vanguard, Goldman Sachs, Credit Suisse, Morgan Stanley, and Capital Group—as well as elements of fossil capital with close links to military-industrial-border complexes.[16] Second, the private military-security industry creates a lucrative outlet for overaccumulated capital that may be able to sustain accumulation amid the intensifying climate chaos and insecurity that would emerge during a neoliberal drift trajectory, since this would undoubtedly entail rising demand for private security services.[17] As George Rigakos fears, if security can become "productive" for the state-capital nexus, rather than merely an "unproductive" drain on resources, then "the fabrication of an inherently insecure order does not challenge that order, for the preservation of order is an industry in itself."[18] Thus, on the whole, the private military-security industry forms a powerful negative feedback on political economies that will make it even more challenging to escape from neoliberal drift. But, as I argue below, rather than sustaining neoliberal drift indefinitely, at least in the context of a technologically incrementalist trajectory, its continuous expansion would more likely reinforce a spatio-temporally uneven collapse of the world-system.

POLITICAL ECONOMY ←→ TECHNOLOGY ←→
STATE/NONSTATE VIOLENCE

Now let's bring in the technology parameter. Following Deudney,[19] technological change can transform the possibility space of state and nonstate violence in at least three ways: (1) by expanding the capabilities of nonstate actors, whether to engage in terrorism, crime, or insurgencies; (2) advancing state-capitalist powers of surveillance and military-police repression; and (3) changing the nature of military competition and the risks of conflict escalation between states. Later I discuss its impacts on interstate conflict—focusing in particular on the cyber-AI-nuclear nexus—but for now I focus on its implications for nonstate violence and military-police repression.

One of the key issues, as discussed in chapter 1, is that contemporary advances in synthetic biology, AI, robotics, the IoT, and 3D printing are unleashing a "cornucopia of double-edged swords" that can advance human welfare while also democratizing access to more powerful means of destruction.[20] For instance, genetic engineering labs and research facilities, DIY synthetic biology, publicly available databases that store the genetic codes of dangerous viruses, 3D printing and cloud computing platforms that make it easier to modify genomes, cheapening drones, and "smart" IoT systems can be considered technological platforms that "facilitate generative creativity in their users to build and invent new things, new weapons, and new modes of attack."[21] At the same time, these technological advances also enable the creation of global security assemblages with unprecedented powers of surveillance and lethal force projection—involving facial and emotion recognition, big data analytics, drones with "swarming" capabilities, networked IoT sensors, and (with time) neurotechnologies. These technologies can also in some cases empower progressive social movements—for instance, through digital networking and social media campaigns. But given the subjection of progressive activists to ubiquitous surveillance, unprecedented advances in the repressive arsenals of military-police forces, and trends toward automation that may reduce the disruptive power of workers vis-à-vis capital and the state, FIR technologies will most likely empower states, capitalists, and criminal and nonstate terrorist networks far more than progressive social movements (that is, unless creative techniques can be discovered to leverage these technologies toward the ends of progressive change).

All these technologies are critical areas of geostrategic competition between the United States and China: China's Made in China 2025 initiative prioritizes domestic innovation in AI, synthetic biology, robotics, quantum computing, and other FIR technologies; the Biden administration, in turn, has claimed that leadership in these technologies is "a national security imperative."[22] Powerful economic and geopolitical forces are thus converging to drive technological innovations that will enhance the violence capabilities of both states and nonstate actors. But as chapter 4 demonstrates, the continuous ascent of this brave new technological world is not preordained: climate chaos, political-economic decline, and/ or counter-hegemonic ecosocialist struggles could slow this technological trajectory and subject it to enhanced democratic control. Thus there are different possible trajectories for technological innovation, each of which would entail a different structure for the VP. I will assume, for instance, that if technological innovation follows a more incrementalist trajectory, then this would limit both the democratization of weapons of mass destruction and the military-police powers of states. AI and robotics, while making important advances, would fail to deliver on their "revolutionary" promise, as diminishing returns to the "brute force" model of training larger algorithms with ever-more data, and limits to robotic dexterity, constrain their transformative potential.[23] As a result, military-police assemblages would be less powerful, and technological unemployment much less severe. Similarly, synthetic biology, while creating enhanced personalized medicine for the wealthy, would fail to produce game-changing breakthroughs in agriculture, energy, and productivity—but by the same token, next-generation bioweaponization capabilities would remain limited to well-resourced state-military apparatuses. Alternatively, in an exponential technological breakthrough scenario, the technological powers of both nonstate terrorist violence and military-police repression would expand dramatically, which would be less conducive to ecosocialist transformation and would likely (as I argue below) fuel the emergence of techno-leviathan.

CLIMATE ←→ POLITICAL ECONOMY ←→ ENERGY ←→
STATE/NONSTATE VIOLENCE

So far we have focused on how trends in structural violence and technology will shape the future of violence, both between and within states. Now let us explore how the climate crisis may reshape patterns of conflict and insecurity, and how geopolitical tensions and conflict will shape the climate crisis in turn. There can be no climate determinism here: the future of violence will be primarily determined by political and economic processes more than by "natural" forces or scarcities. Thus quantitative studies of climate conflict—such as an oft-cited study which projects that the risks of armed conflict may increase 14% for every half degree of warming—border on the absurd.[24] As critics of climate conflict narratives demonstrate, not only are the findings of these studies consistently contradictory—with past measures of environmental change being just as often correlated with *decreases* in conflict than outbreaks[25]—they also fail to delineate the actual causal mechanisms fueling conflict in specific contexts.[26] But we cannot deny the risk that the climate crisis could exacerbate conflict pressures, particularly if/when it reaches 2°C and beyond. In a world scarred by histories of imperialism, war, mistrust, powerful military-industrial complexes, and an ongoing nuclear "balance of terror," there is no doubt that worsening climate shocks can potentially act as a "threat multiplier" that amplify the political-economic and geopolitical drivers of conflict, state fragility, non-state terrorism, and militant insurgencies.[27]

For example, climate shocks can decimate livelihoods and increase relative deprivation for some groups through drought and crop failures, thereby diminishing the "opportunity costs" of participating in violent rebellion.[28] Furthermore, it can also disrupt water-sharing arrangements between states. The Indus river shared by India and Pakistan is commonly cited as a possible flashpoint: Himalayan glacier melt is projected to reduce water flow by up to 30% by mid-century, which could lead to increasingly severe shortages for agriculture, industry, and hydropower that put pressure on India to cut off water flows to Pakistan.[29] Given that India and Pakistan are nuclear states with a history of animosity and mistrust, the risks of a water conflict going nuclear here cannot be ignored, but neither can the potential for peaceful renegotiation of the Indus Waters Treaty.[30] Conflicts over diminishing fish stocks in the contested waters of the South China

Sea; oil/gas/mineral deposits in the Arctic as the United States, Russia, and other states seek to exploit the opportunities presented by a melting arctic; and diminishing water and agricultural and grazing lands in already war-torn regions like the Middle East, North Africa, and the Sahel are also possible flashpoints.[31] But again, we cannot understand the potential climate impacts on conflict outside the mediation of global political economy: if structural violence remains high, military-security-extractive complexes remain powerful, and opportunities for genuine democratic participation are continuously squashed (the most likely outcome of a neoliberal drift trajectory), then climate change would most likely exacerbate conflict pressures. But if counter-hegemonic struggles succeed in transforming political economies and security assemblages in more egalitarian and sustainable directions, then cooperative peace-building could increase even as the planet warms.[32]

Turning to the state violence → climate relation, we should first focus on the impacts of militarization and war on the climate crisis. The US military, as Neta Crawford shows, is the single largest institutional consumer of FF on the planet: it is responsible for roughly 200 million metric tons of carbon emitted per year between 2001 and 2017, with the Air Force consuming 70% of the total.[33] Data on global military emissions is notoriously sparse and underreported.[34] But one study estimates that *direct* military emissions likely take up about 1% of global emissions (comparable to the annual emissions from the aviation sector), while the total carbon footprint of military activities—accounting for arms manufacturing and military supply-chains—is about 5.5% of global emissions.[35] This is a huge footprint—larger than annual emissions from Russia, the world's fourth-largest emitter—but also almost certainly an underestimate, since it does not include emissions from the impacts of war, such as fires, deforestation, infrastructure damage, and post-conflict reconstruction. The Russian invasion of Ukraine, for instance, likely produced over 100 million tons of emissions during its first seven months, equal to the total emissions from the Netherlands during the same period.[36] The US and NATO have adopted targets of net zero military emissions by 2050, but the odds that these targets will be achieved are close to zero (at least in the absence of carbon offsets with highly questionable social and ecological credentials): there are no technologically mature and cost-effective options for decarbonizing air power, these institutions refuse to commit to transparency on how they calculate their emissions or how they plan to achieve net zero, and the Biden administration explicitly states that decarbonizing the military can only be pursued to the "maximum extent possible and without compromising national security."[37] Military force structures will thus almost certainly continue to be a rising source of emissions in the coming years—not to mention a colossal drain of human, financial, and material-energy resources away from socially useful ends—*unless* military budgets can be shrunk. It goes without saying that this would be impossible in a context of rising geopolitical tensions and strengthening hawkish forces in the United States, China, Russia, Europe, India, and elsewhere, which means that diminishing these tensions is a necessary precondition of military decarbonization.

Beyond military emissions, another interstate conflict → energy → climate relation concerns how geopolitical tensions and war can impact the RE transition. The Putin shock has of course had deep consequences in this regard, and it will likely have a net positive effect on the RE transition by speeding up the shift away from oil and gas (it is more challenging, however, to judge its net impact on the climate overall, since direct emissions from the Ukraine war and its impact on rising military spending may counteract these benefits).[38] For our purposes, however, the key question here concerns the implications of rising geopolitical tensions between the US and China. Experts often debate the relative merits of US-China cooperation versus competition in the realms of climate and energy policy.[39] But the two most consequential implications of US-China tensions will be their impacts on global military emissions (as already discussed), as well as their potential to derail the RE transition and crash the world economy in the case of a conflict over Taiwan. As Hal Brands says, "A major war over Taiwan could create global economic chaos that would make the mess produced by Russia's war in Ukraine look minor by comparison."[40] By disrupting shipping lanes, damaging the Taiwanese semiconductor industry (responsible for more than 50% of global semiconductor production), and accelerating technological and financial decoupling between China and the West, a conflict over Taiwan could plausibly provoke a 5%–10% GDP contraction in the US and a 25%–35% contraction in China (though these economic consequences are of course incredibly challenging to estimate, and could be much higher if the conflict spirals toward nuclear exchange).[41] And the impacts on the RE transition could be massive: China currently manufactures 60% of the world's solar panels, 50% of its onshore wind turbines, 73% of its EV batteries, and controls roughly 85% of its rare earth refining capacity, while also having a large investment presence in battery manufacturing in Europe.[42] Gavin Bade poses the question on the minds of American and European strategists: "If Putin could hold Europe hostage with its gas supplies, what could China do with its even broader dominance of other critical sectors?"[43] A US-China war, even just intensified sanctions in the case of Chinese aggression, would undoubtedly disrupt RE supply chains and at least slow the transition, but the question is how severe such disruptions could become. In the context of a green Keynesian scenario plus rapid technological breakthroughs, I will assume that the consequences would be less dramatic, since the US and China would both be in better position to technologically decouple while meeting their energy and raw material needs. But in the context of a slower and more incremental innovation trajectory, they may dramatically exacerbate a stagflation crisis of green Keynesianism. And in a neoliberal drift trajectory that is made increasingly precarious by oil and gas shortages, worsening climate shocks, and accumulating fragilities in global food and financial systems, the cascading consequences of a conflict over Taiwan would no doubt exacerbate—and potentially trigger—a global collapse trajectory.

CLIMATE ⟵→ NUCLEAR SECURITY ⟵→ CYBERSECURITY

Now let's integrate the "climate-nuclear nexus" and "cyber-AI-nuclear nexus" into our model of the VP. Starting with the climate-nuclear nexus, the IEA projects that nuclear power generation may need to double above current levels to enable a net zero pathway (a contestable assumption to be sure).[44] The global stock of fissile material that would need to be monitored and secured would then increase by roughly a factor of two or more, with the largest increase occurring in countries like China, India, Pakistan, the UK, France, and others planning major nuclear expansions.[45] In this case, the risks of nuclear proliferation and leakage to nonstate actors would increase significantly at a time when worsening climate change (even if held to 2°C) may be amplifying the political-economic and geopolitical drivers of interstate conflict and nonstate terrorism.

The climate → cybersecurity relation is more loosely coupled but still potentially significant. The expansion of digitalization, 5G, AI, the IoT, and "smart everything" is primarily driven by political-economic forces, but the climate crisis provides another motivating factor that may speed up deployment of these technologies. The IoT in particular is widely seen as necessary to create RE-powered smart grids that can monitor and moderate electricity use while transmitting surplus energy from regions with lots of wind and sun at a given time to others experiencing a deficit. As more and more devices are plugged into the IoT—from cars and traffic lights to refrigerators and toasters—this will provide "additional entry points and targets for digital assault," as a report from the International Renewable Energy Agency warns.[46] In this way, the IoT will dramatically expand the "attack surface" that states, criminal organizations, and nonstate terrorists can exploit to hack into electricity grids and critical infrastructures.[47] In a context of rising geopolitical tensions, this may exacerbate the risks of interstate conflict by enhancing opportunities for offensive cyber-operations like sabotage, espionage, and data theft—in IR realist terms, it would tilt the "offense-defense balance" further in favor of the offense—all of which would contain escalatory potential in crisis conditions.[48]

These risks become scarier to contemplate when we bring the cyber-AI-nuclear nexus into the picture. One of the key dangers is that nuclear weapons command, control, and communication (NC3) systems have become increasingly integrated with the civilian communications ecosystem—including satellites, communications networks, and the electricity grids these systems rely on—making them more vulnerable to cyberattack.[49] The key danger is that a cyberattack on these systems, which could hypothetically be intended to disable a state's nuclear surveillance, decision-making, and/or second-strike capabilities, would be (mis)perceived as a precursor to a nuclear attack and put pressure on command authorities to trigger a preemptive nuclear strike before its nuclear forces are destroyed.[50] The problem is deepened by the ongoing development of hypersonic missiles with the capacity to travel five times faster than the speed of sound, which may exacerbate the risks of unintentional nuclear escalation by "compressing the decision-making time frame" of command authorities, as James Johnson warns.[51] Advances in machine learning are already being used by the US, China, and Russia to improve missile targeting systems and are "expected to accelerate progress for hypersonic weapons and other long-range (conventional and nuclear-armed) precision munitions."[52] In turn, this would intensify pressures for these states to program AI systems "with capabilities for making the crucial escalatory choices of when and how to go nuclear," viewed by many generals as necessary to cope with the intensifying pace of twenty-first-century warfare.[53] Furthermore, we have only reached the dawn of the era of "deepfakes," which use deep learning and generative AI to forge realistic images, videos, and audio content that simulate real people and events. As Herbert Lin warns, further advances in AI will enable increasingly realistic forgeries that can be developed by "anyone with imagination, a modicum of technical skill, and a personal computer."[54] And as these capabilities continue to advance, a wider possibility space will emerge for disinformation operations that could further destabilize nuclear deterrence by increasing "misperception, confusion, and uncertainty in a crisis"—for example, by depicting military leaders of a state conspiring to launch a nuclear first strike.[55]

In sum, the combination of nuclear proliferation, rising offensive capabilities relative to defense (driven both by rising cyber-vulnerabilities and hypersonic missiles), compressed decision-making pressures in times of crisis, and an informational environment prone to disinformation and confusion may weaken the future stability of nuclear deterrence. Particularly in a trajectory of neoliberal drift, worsening geopolitical tensions, and 2.5°C+climate chaos, these factors would combine to intensify the risks of nuclear conflict, which could involve India-Pakistan in an Indus River dispute, US-China in a Taiwan crisis, NATO-Russia in a conflict in Eastern Europe, Israel-Iran in a context of plummeting oil and gas revenues and worsening water stress, or North Korea-South Korea in the context of a deepening climate-exacerbated humanitarian emergency on the Korean peninsula. We should not exaggerate the risks, which can become self-fulfilling prophecies within hawkish national security establishments. But given the converging threats of nuclear proliferation, disinformation, bellicose nationalism, AI-distorted decision-making, and the climate emergency, neither should we deny the dangers ahead.

IDEOLOGY AND EXISTENTIAL CRISES ←→ VIOLENCE
PROBLEMATIC ←→ SOCIOECOLOGICAL PROBLEMATIC

To conclude our analysis of the key dependency relations that structure the VP and the planetary problematic as a whole, we must again integrate the EP. The potential for vicious feedback spirals—whether taking the form of climate-AI-cyber-enhanced conflict pressures between states or spirals between nonstate terrorist violence and military-police repression—presuppose reciprocally polarizing ideologies or cognitive-affective dispositions. In other words, such spirals are by no means automatic but rather the product of co-constitutive structures of identity, meaning, and belonging—particularly those constrained by the nexus of nationalism, race, and hegemonic masculinity—that perpetuate sharp self/other divisions.[56] For example, it would be crudely reductionist to expect that intensifying water stress in the Indus river basin will necessarily trigger armed conflict between India and Pakistan, let alone nuclear war. However, given that Hindu nationalism is "intimately tied up with control of the [Indus] river" and wider Kashmir region, and given the Bharatiya Janata Party (BJP)'s proto-fascist tendencies, diminishing food and water availability could indeed get exploited by the BJP to drum up anti-Muslim sentiment and assert control over the Indus.[57] In turn this would exacerbate socioecological scarcities and nationalist anger in Pakistan, creating a situation with dangerous escalatory potential.

Furthermore, ideologies of race, nationalism, and hegemonic masculinity are foundational to how crime, terrorism, and threats posed by other states are perceived and acted on—hence the widespread cognitive-affective associations that link blackness and immigration with criminality, Muslims with terrorism, China with danger, and whiteness with innocence in the global north.[58] In turn, these articulations of self/other and associated military-police responses often produce or exacerbate the insecurity they claim to be merely responding to: for instance, demonization of Muslims as Other to "Western civilization" can reinforce militant Islamic fundamentalism, while constructions of the "China threat" in the US can reinforce Chinese nationalism and militarization.[59] Hegemonic masculinities that desire "toughness"—whether on crime, terrorism, or China—further entrench these dominant military-police "solutions" and make escalatory conflict spirals between states more likely.

Overall, the relations between socioecological crises, violence, and existential insecurities form a potent set of feedbacks running in all directions. And these feedbacks may be further worsened by the rise of what Eleanore Pauwels calls "cognitive-emotional conflicts" between states employing social media platforms, twitter-bots, and deepfakes to sow mistrust, polarization, and confusion among their adversaries.[60] The weaponization of deepfakes is particularly worrisome, which raises the risks of reaching a cognitive-emotional dystopia: a world in which it is near-impossible to instinctively distinguish between the real and the fake, larger fractions of the population completely lose trust in credible sources of information, and AI-generated content is regularly used to incite and manipulate masses of people for violent ends.[61] It is not difficult to see how increasingly sophisticated forms of disinformation may amplify conflict pressures, confuse and misdirect collective responses to polycrisis events, and complicate efforts to build durable counter-hegemonic coalitions that can advance progressive solutions to these crises. A key challenge for progressive movements is thus to develop tactics and strategies that can amplify truth, mutual understanding, and compassion amid a chaotic media-informational landscape in times of crisis. Given the power imbalances that shape the global media landscape, the rise of powerful new tools of cognitive and emotional manipulation, and the threat of corporate-funded and geopolitically motivated disinformation operations, the challenge is indeed daunting.

TRAJECTORIES OF THE PLANETARY PROBLEMATIC

We are now in position to investigate the coevolutionary trajectories of the SEP and VP, and their implications for the futures of the world-earth system. I begin by focusing primarily on the neoliberal drift scenarios discussed in chapter 4, demonstrating how rising geopolitical tensions and investments in military-police assemblages would reinforce an uneven collapse trajectory. Next, I show how a more technologically revolutionary green Keynesian trajectory would lead to techno-leviathan by triggering a feedback between worsening insecurity and techno-authoritarian securitization. I conclude by examining the fortress and abolitionist variants of ecosocialism.

NEOLIBERAL DRIFT, BREAKDOWN, AND NEOFEUDALISM

Let's begin by exploring how the VP may intersect with and reshape a neoliberal drift trajectory and how socioecological crises may in turn shape the evolution of state violence and geopolitical tensions in this scenario. As previously discussed, this would be a trajectory in which the world economy unevenly recovers from the 2022–2023 inflation shock, oil and gas demand continues to rise (likely amplified by the massive expansion of armaments production following the Russian invasion of Ukraine[62]), the share of RE continues to increase but not quickly enough, and net energy decline plus underinvestment put the world on track for another energy and inflation shock. I start by considering how the evolution of the war in Ukraine may impact this trajectory, and then do the same for US-China tensions. After that I explore how the VP may intersect with a longer-term neoliberal drift scenario, and focus on two variants: a breakdown-style scenario, as well as one closer to Raskin's "fortress worlds" archetype (which I call neofeudalism).

Starting with the Russia-Ukraine war, for my purposes the key questions are twofold: How will this impact Russian oil and gas production over the next decade? And relatedly: How will it impact Russia's political economy and geopolitical power, and what might be the geopolitical and planetary consequences of accelerated Russian decline? The Russian oil industry was already struggling before the war, the result of its depleting conventional fields in West Siberia and Western sanctions since 2014, which constrained its access to the finance and technology it needs to develop its unconventional shale and Arctic offshore reserves.[63] This has only been intensified by the tightening sanctions regime following the war—leading the Western oil majors to cease collaborations with Russia—which means these unconventional reserves will almost certainly remain underdeveloped, at least in the near term.[64] The IEA now projects that Russian oil production will fall from 7 mb/d in 2021 to 5 mb/d in 2030, while gas production will be 155 billion cubic meters smaller than in 2021, thus putting increased pressure on the US and OPEC to make up the shortfall (which, as we saw in chapter 4, will be a daunting challenge).[65] If the world-system remains on a current-policies pathway, this will certainly mean heightened risks of a fossil stagflation crisis.

But the situation could be even worse, depending on how the war unfolds. For one, while this is unlikely, a protracted conflict could eventually lead Putin to escalate by using tactical nuclear weapons against Ukraine, which would elicit deeper intervention from NATO, likely provoke a complete cutoff of oil and gas flows from Russia to the West, and (one hopes) elicit worldwide condemnation and isolation of Putin—meaning even China, India, and other trade partners may cut energy ties with Russia. A horrifying nuclear escalation with NATO is not impossible, even assuming NATO responds to a Russian tactical nuke with conventional strikes.[66] But a more likely consequence would be worsening fossil stagflation down the road, making China and India *particularly* vulnerable (though they might weaken their response if the energy security consequences of cutting ties with Russia are deemed too great). Another scenario involves a collapse of the Russian state as it becomes overwhelmed by the cascading consequences of a crashed economy; defeat or protracted bloody stalemate in Ukraine; massive public unrest driven by economic insecurity and military conscription; elite in-fighting; and intensifying successionist struggles in minority regions like Chechnya.[67] According to one poll, nearly half of foreign policy analysts in the US believe something like this will happen before 2033.[68] This may be largely attributable to wishful thinking. But if it does occur, it would rock global energy and food markets: Russian oil and gas production would decline even more precipitously; and wheat, fertilizer, aluminum, and nickel exports would likely plummet (which, due to carve-outs, have been less affected by sanctions so far).[69] Again, if a current-policies trajectory continues, this would magnify a fossil stagflation crisis in the late 2020s or early 2030s, while also intensifying food security vulnerabilities and political instability in North Africa and the Middle East. Such a crisis could be moderated if a post-Putin reformer aiming to rebuild ties with the West comes to power. But as Liana Fix and Michael Kimmage anticipate, the odds of this happening are "vanishingly small," and far more likely would be a new "authoritarian leader in the Putinist mold."[70]

Whichever way the war unfolds, we can be very confident that—even if Putin maintains his grip on power and the state does not fragment—Russia will confront political-economic and geopolitical decline. Even in a current-policies scenario, its share of internationally traded oil and gas could fall

50% by 2030, meaning a deep decline in its export revenues (roughly 40% of which come from oil and gas).[71] To some extent, Putin's war—as Nafeez Ahmed argues—may be interpreted as "the world's first organised state assault on the global climate movement," or a strategy to disrupt the RE transition by stoking energy insecurity and right-wing populism in Europe, while bolstering its own FF export revenues.[72] If so, the strategy has thus far backfired. But we can expect that Putin or his successor would double down on efforts to slow if not derail the RE transition in the context of a 2030s fossil stagflation crisis, and *especially* in the context of a greenflation crisis of green Keynesianism. As many analysts believe, a weakened Russia could be *more* rather than less dangerous, particularly if it simmers with nationalist humiliation from defeat or at best its inability to win decisively in Ukraine.[73] It would thus be primed to exploit a fossil stagflation crisis by ramping up disinformation operations and sabotaging energy infrastructure (e.g., through cyberattacks on electricity grids, or kinetic attacks on gas pipelines, offshore wind farms, and undersea power cables) to inflict more pain on Western states and bolster the forces of far-right populism.[74] At the very least this would form a negative feedback on efforts to pursue a clean energy acceleration in response to future FF supply shocks, and at worst it could help bring fossil nationalism or fascism to power in the US and elsewhere. Furthermore, if a global green Keynesian transition emerges by the mid-2020s—for example, in response to further FF price volatility—then Russia's net income from oil and gas exports would fall even more, making it even weaker come 2030.[75] In the context of a greenflation crisis driven by net energy constraints and mineral bottlenecks as the RE transition accelerates, Russia would be well-placed and incentivized to foment the forces of fossil fascism (and it would likely be joined by Saudi Arabia in this effort, who would also confront collapsing export revenues and an existential crisis for the regime in this scenario). Russian meddling is by no means a necessary precondition of fossil or green stagflation and fossil fueled backlash in the West, but it forms an additional feedback that may amplify these crises while making it harder for Western governments to effectively address them.

Turning to US-China tensions, I focus here on the risks of a conflict over Taiwan (the most likely, but certainly not the only, conflict flashpoint). Kevin Rudd, the former prime minister of Australia and a leading expert on Xi Jinping's strategic thinking, anticipates that Xi will likely attempt to forcibly annex Taiwan before 2035, when he will be 82 and nearing the end of his political career. This is seen as essential both to Xi's personal goal of "political immortality" (i.e., becoming the CCP leader who achieved national unity) and the broader nationalist goal of—in Xi's words—fulfilling the "great rejuvenation of the Chinese nation."[76] Furthermore, in the context of a neoliberal drift trajectory, we can expect that by 2030 China will most likely be confronting deepening political-economic instability and social unrest at home. Rather than successfully transitioning to a more energetically efficient, services-based, and domestic-consumption-driven economy, China in this scenario (at least assuming incremental technological innovation) would be confronting worsening stagnation and financial instability from a shrinking working-age population, US sanctions on its technology sector, the exhaustion of property-bubble-fueled growth, weakening investment from capitalists disillusioned with Xi's authoritarian tendencies, magnifying water stresses, and worsening climate shocks.[77] And this is all before bringing in the fossil stagflation crisis, which—as the world's largest net energy importer—would magnify China's problems considerably (even if it can still cushion itself a bit by purchasing discounted Russian oil and gas, though this will be challenging if Russian production is plummeting). On one hand, by dampening economic growth and heightening its budgetary constraints, this crisis may slow the CCP's efforts to modernize and build up its military capabilities, thereby pressuring Xi to delay plans to forcibly annex Taiwan (and it could also, plausibly, push the CCP in a more ecosocialist direction, a point I return to below).[78] But it could also lead Xi to double down on reunification as a way to drum up nationalist passions and divert attention away from domestic economic problems—*particularly* if he perceives that the US and Europe are bogged down by fossil stagflation, protracted conflict with Russia, and political dysfunction from right-wing populist backlash and worsening polarization at home.[79]

A Chinese blockade or invasion of Taiwan is thus likely to occur in this context, but is by no means inevitable. If it does, the implications for China and the world could be ruinous, though the scale of the damage depends on how the US and its allies respond. To start, because of worldwide dependence on the Taiwanese semiconductor industry, a Chinese blockade that cuts off trade between Taiwan and the world economy would have massive repercussions. As Charlie Vest and company describe,

> Countries around the world would face the risk of spiking inflation and short-ages in key industries. This would range from critical infrastructure inputs, such as medical and telecommunication equipment, to less strategic yet equally vital equipment goods for harvesting or mining, with the potential to disrupt business as usual in countless economies. . . . All these forces could, combined, increase the risks of a global economic recession, sustained inflation, wide-spread sovereign defaults, rising unemployment, and potential social unrest.[80]

These impacts may be moderated depending on how far the United States and Europe succeed in reshoring semiconductor manufacturing. But for a world economy already suffering from energy shocks and inflation, they would undoubtedly send shockwaves and amplify the risks of protracted stagflation. In this context, the economic and military costs of deterring China might be seen as too high by the US and its allies, meaning China would succeed in forcibly annexing the island "without firing a shot"—its best-case scenario.[81] More likely, the US and its allies would at least respond with tightening trade and financial sanctions, and possibly a counter-blockade of China that cuts off the flow of oil and gas from the Persian Gulf (among other critical imports).[82] Given that 63% of China's crude oil imports, and 29% of its gas, come via seaborne shipments, an American counterblockade would inflict significant damage on China's economy—potentially subtracting 17% or more from its GDP, and possibly much more from cascading secondary impacts.[83] Thus, even in the absence of full-blown war, the repercussions of an invasion could crash China's economy and plausibly push it down a trajectory of state collapse. For this reason the CCP is unlikely to take this gamble unless it succeeds in technologically decoupling from the West and moderating its energy import vulnerabilities, but the combined pressures of Xi's desire for glory, nationalism, and hypermasculinity may yet push it toward strategic miscalculation. In turn, if China retaliates by curtailing critical exports of RE technologies, batteries, and rare earths, then this would dramatically exacerbate an ongoing fossil stagflation or greenflation crisis for the West. As a result, the US and its allies would face even deeper headwinds against efforts to rapidly scale up renewables—forming an additional feedback that makes it even more challenging for Western governments to phaseout fossil fuels.

And things could get much uglier: if China undertakes an amphibious invasion, and the US militarily intervenes to defend Taiwan, then there is no telling when or how the conflict would stabilize short of nuclear escalation. As Rudd says, Chinese victory would depend on taking out the US's key military bases in the Pacific—including Guam, which would "constitute an attack on the sovereign territory" of the US—while US victory would depend on taking out China's command and control systems, which would require an attack on the Chinese mainland.[84] For Xi the stakes could not be higher, since defeat in Taiwan could precipitate his downfall and—in a context of mutually amplifying climate, energy, economic, and food crises—possibly even a collapse of the CCP. And if the US is by this time under the leadership of a Trumpian fossil nationalist regime that is thirsty for military glory—as well as a foreign policy distraction to divert the attention of Americans away from their accumulating domestic woes—then we may see a recipe for full-blown great power war with frightening nuclear potential.

In sum, rising tensions between the great powers in a neoliberal drift trajectory would make the world-system even more vulnerable to collapse. The US, Europe, and China by 2030 would all be dealing with an historic series of energy, food, and economic crises; meanwhile, a revanchist Russia would be doing everything it can to destabilize Western democracies and foment the forces of fossil fascism, Ukraine would most likely continue to simmer in high- or low-intensity conflict with continuous escalatory potential, and an aging Xi may seek reunification with Taiwan no matter the costs. Hawkish political coalitions would solidify their power in the US and Europe, and militarization of the European continent and US-China relations would continue unabated. Even if a hot war between Russia-NATO and US-China is avoided, these trends would still amplify the socio-ecological crises discussed in chapter 4: military emissions would increase dramatically, likely pushing back the peak date for total global emissions; and more energy and raw materials would be diverted to military-industrial complexes, thereby exacerbating inflation and constraining energy supplies that could be used for more socially useful purposes (including the RE transition itself).[85] All of this would reinforce fossil fuel–reliant energy security strategies, even in a context of accelerating net energy decline for oil and gas, and make it challenging for the world-system to escape a collapse trajectory. And if nuclear war breaks out in Eastern Europe or Taiwan, then a worst-case "breakdown" scenario may be in the making.

Now let's consider how VP crises might intersect with a longer-term neoliberal drift trajectory in which the great powers successfully moderate a fossil stagflation crisis and continue their growth trajectories into the 2050s. As described in chapter 4, this would be a scenario in which energy security strategies predominantly favor RE expansion and put states on track to meet their NDCs. When integrating the VP, we can imagine two general variants of this scenario. In the first—which can be considered a "regional rivalry" scenario—ruinous hot wars are avoided before 2050, but the combination of worsening socioecological polycrises, the solidifying power of hawkish national security coalitions, and destabilizing technological innovations set the stage for rising geopolitical tensions and mutually destructive wars over time. The second can be called an "ultra-imperialism" scenario of the sort described by Karl Kautsky (comparable to William Robinson's "global police state" thesis): in this scenario, globalist coalitions that prioritize "managed strategic competition" and global cooperation become hegemonic,[86] which produces an oligarchic consortium of states cooperating to maximize exploitation for the capitalist class and keep the lid on the resulting violence and social unrest.[87] Most likely, the actual future would fall somewhere between these poles. But if we assume that higher levels of structural violence entail a more volatile geopolitical landscape (because of the existential crises and hardened self/other relations they tend to provoke), then the "regional rivalry" variant may be more likely.[88]

Starting with the first variant: in this scenario the Russian state, under new authoritarian leadership in the Putinist mold, successfully navigates the 2040s while avoiding regime collapse, but it faces deepening decline by 2050 as its oil and gas rents plummet, melting permafrost generates billions of dollars in infrastructure damages across the country, and it faces harder-than-expected efforts to increase agricultural production in the north as Siberia warms.[89] Thus it remains a dangerous "spoiler" state that simmers with resentment toward the West and is now equipped with more realistic deepfake capabilities, hypersonic missiles, drone swarms, and perhaps even insect-size killer drones (which can operate as undetectable assassins) to sow chaos in increasingly fragile Western democracies.

China realizes its best-case scenario of retaking Taiwan while deterring a US military response, and it successfully navigates the subsequent sanctions regime and fossil stagflation crisis through the combination of increased unconventional oil and gas production at home and new pipeline connections with Russia, Kazakhstan, and other regional trade partners.[90] But it remains economically weakened from still historically elevated energy prices, a steadily aging population, continuously worsening water and climate stressors, deteriorating food security, limited success in creating a domestic advanced semiconductor industry, and slower-than-hoped-for advances in AI and synthetic biology. Rather than pulling back on militarization to focus on domestic problems, ethnonationalist pride—enflamed by continued hostility from the US and its allies—pushes the CCP to continue its pursuit of regional hegemony and military adventurism (especially in the South China Sea, which is seen as an increasingly vital source of oil and protein for China in an age of energy and food insecurity).[91] The US avoids fossil fascism but remains beset by accumulating domestic stressors: an intransigent Republican Party, declining agricultural production across California and the Midwest, a weakening US dollar as other currencies take on a larger role in global trade, and unprecedented budgetary constraints on its capacity to sustain its globe-spanning military footprint. But the "national hegemonist" coalition remains powerful—underpinned by the arms industry and persistent bipartisan concern with the military threats posed by Russia and China—and continues to push through oversized military budgets with heavy investments in military AI, automated weapons systems, hypersonic missiles, and outer space militarization. On all sides, the expansion of the IoT and RE smart grids exacerbate the risks of cyberattacks on critical infrastructure. In conjunction with a new generation of hypersonic missiles, deepfake capabilities, and AI decision-making systems intended to cope with the accelerating pace of war, we see the emergence of a frightening cyber-AI-nuclear nexus (or a cyber-AI-nuclear-climate-existential nexus, once we include the potentially amplifying feedbacks of the climate emergency and hardening self/other relations). Relations between India-Pakistan, India-China, Israel-Iran, and Saudi Arabia-Iran also deteriorate in this scenario, driven by the entrenched hegemonies of ethnonationalist coalitions, hellish heat extremes, and food and water shortages that over time pose increasingly severe existential threats to these regimes. Iran and Saudi Arabia would likely by this time both become nuclear-armed states. And if all or most of these states integrate AI and hypersonic missiles in their nuclear programs—while engaging in mutually destabilizing cognitive-emotional conflicts and deepfake operations—the risks of nuclear war would be further amplified at a time when the US, EU, and other states (facing their own domestic crises) are less capable of playing a mediating role.

It is not difficult to see that this would be a geopolitically unstable landscape of epic proportions. And (to briefly return to the solar geoengineering scenario discussed in chapter 4) something like this would be *the most likely geopolitical environment* in which any attempted SRM intervention would take place. The assumption, implicitly made by SRM advocates, that harmonious global cooperation can be sustained throughout a thirty- to forty-year global SRM program—thus avoiding the risks of interstate war, cyber-sabotage, nonstate terrorism, pandemic disruption, and termination shock—are thus hubristic at best, and dangerously naïve at worst.[92] At best, in this scenario, hawkish hegemonist and ethnonationalist forces would solidify their power, military spending and emissions would reach record levels, the energy and resources devoted to the RE transition and climate adaptation would be constrained (particularly across the global south), and the earth would be on track for 2.8°C by 2100. Even if militaries can be largely decarbonized in this scenario, this would entail further problem-shifting by relying on land-intensive biofuels and/or green hydrogen-based synthetic fuels, which would further contribute to energy and food price inflation by diverting agricultural land and electricity away from meeting critical needs.[93] At worst, the combination of mutually empowering ethnonationalist coalitions in nuclear-armed states, the destabilizing feedbacks of the cyber-AI-nuclear nexus, and the increasingly existential consequences of the climate emergency would destabilize deterrence and make nuclear war become reality. A "breakdown" trajectory is thus possible in this scenario, but a softer world-system collapse would be more likely if the United States, Russia, China, and other states are too overwhelmed by their own domestic crises to get swept up in ruinous hot wars.[94]

Let us now explore a version of this latter scenario. In other words, what if the great powers and global capitalist elites cooperate to reduce geopolitical tensions and focus on managing bottom-up rebellion from the increasingly precarious ranks of "surplus" humanity? In this scenario, something like Robinson's "global police state" would come to fruition. In the face of accelerated economic and geopolitical decline, Russia in the 2040s turns to a post-Putin reformer to restore ties with the West and try diversifying its economy away from oil and gas. The CCP—whether through satisfaction from annexing Taiwan, or from being humbled by US defeat—elects a new leader and breaks from Xi's policy of heavy-handed economic management, aggressive military posturing, and hostility toward the West, which is deemed necessary to revitalize economic growth in an age of worsening stagnation. As a result, we see transnational globalist factions consolidate hegemony in the United States, Europe, China, Russia, and elsewhere. Global fora like the G20, World Economic Forum, and Atlantic Council promote harmony of interests across these states in order to focus on tackling the unprecedented convergence of socioecological crises striking the world-system. But net zero by 2050 is by now a distant utopian dream. Instead, global elites commit to cooperating on CDR expansion and solar geoengineering to stave off the risks of climate tipping-point cascades in a 2°C–2.5°C world. And in a world where elites feel increasingly threatened by intensifying grassroots rebellion, sabotage from radicalized eco-activists, violent insurgencies across Africa and the Middle East, increasing numbers of "illegal" migrants, and nonstate terrorist threats magnified by slowly advancing technologies of mass destruction, they focus on coordinating "security" solutions, technologies, and practices across borders. The private military-security-border-surveillance complex—valued at roughly $431 billion in 2018 and projected to reach $606 billion by 2024, following its recent 5.8% annual growth rate—easily becomes a multi-trillion dollar industry by mid-century.[95] The United States, Europe, and China (to different degrees) would be relying heavily on solar, green hydrogen, LNG, oil, and raw material exports from Africa and the Middle East at a time when these regions confront deteriorating political stability from the still-smoldering legacies of US interventions, authoritarian repression of democratic movements, and socioecologically produced food and water scarcities that make the "food riots" of the 2010s pale in comparison. The imperialist core is thereby forced to ramp up or sustain military-police expenditures to protect these flows of ecologically unequal exchange. Across the world-system, inequality within and between states reaches new heights; security services become increasingly privatized to relieve pressure on fiscally constrained govern-ments; the ranks of surplus populations swell; and vicious spirals between rising levels of structural, state, and nonstate violence ensue.

To what extent or for how long, particularly in a context of worsening and near-relentless polycrises, could such a trajectory for the "advanced" capitalist states—and the capitalist world-system as a whole—be sustained? George Rigakos claims, in contrast to those who anticipate its eventual collapse, that global capitalism may perpetually "stav[e] off its own extinc-tion" through the expansion of a private military-security industry that can simultaneously sustain capital accumulation while pacifying anti-capitalist dissent.[96] I agree that this industry will sustain profits for indi-vidual capitalists, but for the capitalist system *as a whole* this argument overlooks the challenges of continuous compound growth in a context of ever-worsening polycrisis events. As David Harvey highlights, in order to sustain compound growth, capital must locate exponentially rising outlets for accumulation over time—absorbing roughly $160 trillion in profitable goods and services by 2045, $320 trillion by 2070, more than $640 trillion by the century's end, and so on.[97] "The implications," as Harvey says, "are daunting."[98] Thus, even if the private military-security complex becomes a roughly $2 trillion industry by 2050 (extrapolating current trends), possibly rising to $5–$10 trillion by 2070, this would put a mere dent in global capital's surplus absorption problem.[99] More likely, as described in chapter 4, the continuous intensification of socioecological crises would mean steadily weakening investor and consumer confidence, vanishing opportunities for profitable investment, increasing reliance on financial speculation and rent-seeking among capitalists, and accumulating finan-cial fragilities that threaten a systemic crash as debt explodes and growth crawls to a halt. Meanwhile, in a context of intensifying grassroots rebel-lion and racist fears of "illegal" migration, security-minded states would be ramping up military-police-border expenditures in a time of unprece-dented economic and fiscal stress, leaving even fewer resources available to deal with intensifying climate, food system, energy, and pandemic shocks.

In this scenario, if the imperialist powers succeed in simultaneously (1) staving off the near-continuous threat of geopolitical breakdown and great-power war; (2) expanding and sustaining military-police assemblages to protect critical resource flows and pacify increasingly hungry and rebellious populations; and (3) stabilizing global temperatures through a coordinated "temporary and moderate" SRM intervention *plus* a crash program to accelerate CDR expansion—then they might be able to sustain economic growth and rising living standards (at least for privileged segments of their populations, for a time). More likely, we would witness a "softer" trajectory of uneven global collapse. Again, one may come to different conclusions based on different assumptions about key parameters. But over time, the combination of unprecedented climate extremes, energy and raw material supply shocks, declining world food production and relentless breadbasket failures, rising military-police-border expenditures, unprecedented fiscal stress, and mass rebellion from surplus humanity would likely overwhelm the functional governance capacities of most nation-states—even of many currently rich countries. The US, China, and Russia would fragment as a consequence of their sheer size and mounting internal successionist struggles; the EU would collapse into a set of go-it-alone fortress states; and insurgencies and revolutions across Africa, the Middle East, and Latin America would cut off critical resource flows and undermine the capacities of rich countries to sustain their "imperial mode of living."[100] As a result, the imperialist powers would be forced to rely on their own domestic or regional resource base, further inflaming stagflation and cost-of-living crises. In a loosely coordinated effort to protect their accustomed lifestyles, rentier capitalists across the world-system would then enlist the services of private security companies to defend their strangulation of the earth's increasingly scarce productive land, food, water, energy, and mineral resources—fortifying themselves in heavily secured "bunkers."[101] Meanwhile, as capitalist economies gradually slow to a halt or abruptly collapse, rising ranks of unemployed surplus populations would be forced to develop their own survival strategies—whether by developing cooperative networks of subsistence and mutual aid or by exchanging their labor for livelihood protection from rentier elites, thus giving rise to new forms of feudal-esque servitude.

In this way we may begin to see a more fragmented neofeudal or neomedieval geography emerge. States would not necessarily disappear, and some would sustain effective centralized governance while deploying emergency powers to enforce rationing and labor/land conscription—which would be necessary to secure energy and food sovereignty in a world of collapsing trade. But most would be weakened, fragmented, and hollowed out—existing in name and ideology only—and the sun would finally set (for real this time) on the era of the Westphalian state as the dominant form of political organization. In its stead would arise a geographically uneven global landscape composed of feudalized rentier capitalists controlling land, resources, and security services; corporate quasi-state assemblages in which powerful corporate entities, in symbiosis with private security firms, form new territorialized structures of rule (e.g., the post-state floating cities dreamed of by libertarians, or the corporate towns and fortresses envisioned by Butler in *Parable of the Sower* and Atwood in *Oryx and Crake*);[102] increasingly autonomous city-states able to defend and reproduce themselves through deepening socioecological relations with their hinterlands; warlords and "violence entrepreneurs" fighting for control over resources, weapons, and populations; and more egalitarian networks of mutual aid and self-defense able to sustain spaces of care, compassion, and solidarity for those left outside the bunkers.[103] If we think of feudalism as a political-economic formation characterized by competing and to some extent overlapping claims to sovereignty, control of land and productive resources by rentier landlords and warlord classes that extract tribute from subjects in exchange for livelihood protection, and ruling classes that prioritize military-police repression and conspicuous consumption over productive investment and innovation, then neofeudal would indeed be an apt descriptor of this post-collapse future.[104] If positive earth system feedbacks push the climate down a hothouse trajectory, then the result would be deepening collapse and possibly human extinction over time— creating a truly Mad Max–style breakdown scenario. But if these feedbacks remain slow and global temperatures stabilize around 2.5°C—perhaps with the help of planetary rewilding as economies contract and ecosystems expand—then a new historical phase of socioecological regeneration may slowly commence. Collapse, in short, does not necessarily mean the end of history, but also potentially the start of a new era beyond capitalist modernity. From there, the futures to come would be constrained by the parameters of 2.5°C+ climate chaos, continuously rising seas, and depletion of the highest quality nonrenewable resources. But human-earth history would continue—driven by the agency of elites, violence entrepreneurs, social movements, and the quasi-state assemblages of the future to pursue new collective projects (whether imperialist or otherwise) of socioecological reproduction, defense, meaning, and belonging.

GREEN KEYNESIAN TRAJECTORIES: THE SPIRAL OF INSECURITY AND SECURITIZATION

In the scenarios just described, green Keynesian transitions either fail to occur or are unable to establish durable hegemonies through rapid innovation in RE technologies. Even if sufficient technological breakthroughs do indeed emerge, the intersecting challenges described so far—including the fallout from job losses in the FF and other sectors, land-use conflicts over RE expansion, Russian and OPEC efforts to derail RE transitions, and a US-China conflict over Taiwan—could still prevent a global green Keynesian hegemony from stabilizing. But rapid technological innovation would bolster the resilience of green Keynesian regimes, and this would be the best-case scenario from the standpoint of global capital. Let us therefore examine how the VP may unfold in this scenario.

As discussed in chapter 4, a succession of technological breakthroughs in this scenario—driven by green industrial policies and competition between the US and China over the critical technologies of the future—lays the foundation for a long wave of capital accumulation and puts the world-system on track to meet the 2°C target. But the FIR-driven transition has a problem-shifting effect: intensifying the problems of democratized technologies of mass destruction, technological unemployment, and techno-authoritarian securitization.

To start, the means of destruction available to nonstate actors advance in lockstep with FIR-enabled advances in green industry, given that these are dual-use technologies. Mutually reinforcing advances in AI, big data, and synthetic biology continue to bring down the costs of DNA synthesis at a Moore's Law–like rate. In conjunction with advances in automated DNA synthesis and 3D bioprinters, these innovations "reduce the specialist skills needed for design" and fabrication of bioagents while empowering "non-traditional researchers by lowering the threshold for participating in cutting-edge [biotechnology] research."[105] This has progressive consequences by democratizing access to biotechnologies—enabling small farmers, DIY tinkerers, and low-income countries to bypass reliance on bio-tech corporations. But the flip side is vastly expanded access to advanced synthetic biology techniques for nonstate actors with nefarious aims; and, crucially, as the National Academies of Sciences had warned, "the same techniques and knowledge base [e.g., for producing biofuels, pharmaceuti-cals, and genetically modified seeds] would likely prove useful for modifica-tions pursued with a more nefarious intent."[106] Policymakers and security agencies recognize the threat, and a flurry of proposals are made to enhance and harmonize global biosecurity regulations—for instance, by construct-ing a global system to screen orders for DNA sequences and authenticate buyers.[107] But these efforts remain mostly confined to national-scale initia-tives and voluntary self-regulation by the private sector. This is because of (1) the sheer scope and complexity of the actors, materials, and techniques involved; (2) lobbying from powerful actors within the nascent bioecon-omy, who argue that overly intrusive regulation would hinder efforts to address critical health and sustainability challenges; and (3) ongoing ten-sions between the US and China, who both view leadership in synthetic biology as a "national security imperative" and fear the consequences of excessive regulation.[108] Similar problems hamper efforts to regulate the rapidly expanding civilian drone market—since this becomes a huge source of profit for companies like Intel, Verizon, Google, and Dai-Jiang Innovations—which leads to the steady proliferation of "killer robots" as drones become cheaper, more sophisticated, more widely accessible to nonstate actors, and easier to weaponize.[109] (The short film *Slaughterbots*—which depicts killer drone swarms wreaking havoc on civilians, controlled by untraceable nonstate actors—provides a chillingly realistic depiction of how this threat may materialize in this future).

But the diffusion of cheapening technologies of mass destruction does not necessarily mean they will be used with increasing frequency, which depends on the intensity of structural violence in this scenario. Green Keynes-ian regimes would most likely improve on their neoliberal predecessors in reducing inequality and exploitation—at least in their earlier phases—since more progressive taxation and redistribution would be needed to ensure that the costs of an accelerated RE transition don't fall hardest on the working class (necessary to prevent a populist backlash). Furthermore, debt cancella-tion and scaling up climate finance would be necessary to facilitate climate mitigation and biodiversity protection throughout the global south. In this sense, as Beverly Silver and Corey Payne argue, a green Keynesian hegemony must "at least partially [meet] the demands for livelihood protection emanating from mass movements" to be a sustainable hegemonic configuration.[110] It is difficult to gauge how far it could go in this regard. But given the relative weakness of leftist popular movements in the contemporary world-system, we can assume that redistributive concessions from the capitalist class would be limited: like with the post–World War II capital-labor compromise, certain sectors of the global working class would benefit and others would be excluded—likely following race, gender, and core/periphery divisions—but this will be the product of political struggles.

In the later phases of this trajectory (e.g., between 2040 and 2060), mutually reinforcing innovations in AI, robotics, and 3D printing generate an historically unprecedented wave of technological unemployment. This may reach 20%–25% in the 2050s and 2060s, if we follow Kai-Fu Lee's estimates,[111] though it may also unfold more gradually (as Daniel Susskind expects).[112] The result is a convergence of political-economic and existential crises: given that work is not only a source of income but also the "foundation of a meaningful life" for many workers,[113] this would indeed be a time of proliferating anger, existential insecurities, and "tremendous social disorder."[114] This populist anger could plausibly be channeled toward ecomodernist socialist rebellion—as hoped for by Nick Srnicek and Alex Williams, along with other "left accelerationists"[115]—but would also form fertile ground for nonstate terrorism and far-right populism.

At the same time, between 2040 and 2060, even after an accelerated decarbonization trajectory, the planet still reaches 2°C, with increasingly devastating climate extremes hitting the global south hardest. Scaled up climate finance moderates these impacts by improving adaptation capacities, while cheap solar energy makes it easier to diffuse energy-intensive adaptations like air conditioning, seawalls, and desalination on a broader scale. But the beneficiaries mostly remain limited to relatively well-off emerging middle classes in these countries. Poverty and hunger thus remain very difficult to reverse in a 2°C world. And in conjunction with other pressures—for example, intensified extractivism for transition minerals, stranded assets in petro-states, and carbon colonialism via offsets in forest-rich regions of the global south—the result is worsening insecurity and conflict throughout the world-system periphery. Deep grievances felt toward the global north—due to its primary responsibility in creating the problem whose consequences are primarily suffered in the global south, made worse by the north's militarized apartheid response to conflict, migration, and insecurity in the periphery—mean that militant or terrorist violence becomes a predictable form of resistance. In a context of rapidly advancing and cheapening technologies of mass destruction, the conditions are in place for a uniquely destructive new wave of nonstate terrorist violence.

This brings us to the means of organized violence, including for war and police powers. The exponential expansion of "smart everything" not only widens the panoptic eye of the surveillance state but also drives radical improvements in machine learning algorithms—in turn driving further advances in big data analytics, facial and emotion recognition, and other biometric technologies installed in increasingly ubiquitous cameras, sensors, and drones. National and global surveillance assemblages, which today are overwhelmed by the sheer magnitude of accumulated data, become increasingly centralized Orwellian systems capable of seeing and acting on the minutia of individual digital traces as well as the immense social graph that emerges from their spatiotemporal relations.[116] Neurotechnologies introduce another horizon of dystopian potential—from crowd control techniques deploying neurochemicals that render populations more docile (think tear gas canisters, but which release neurochemicals that confuse, disorient, and increase the docility of those who inhale them) to neural implants that are forcibly embedded in at-risk or suspected populations (or possibly all citizens) to enable real-time monitoring of brain activity.[117] We do not yet know the military technologies that may be unleashed by the convergence of AI, robotics, neurotechnologies, and nanotechnology, but they will almost certainly include automated swarming drones to police the land and seas, including migrant routes, and potentially launch rapid military attacks on other states.[118] Robot soldiers—perhaps modeled on Elon Musk's Optimus robot design, unveiled in 2022 with much fanfare—may be fielded by militaries in the 2050s if not sooner.[119] As they become cheaper and their mobility, flexibility, and decision-making powers improve, they become a more ubiquitous asset that steadily diffuses to militaries and police departments around the world. Furthermore, as Paul

Scharre anticipates, the US, China, and Russia begin fielding "billions—yes, billions—of tiny, insect-like drones" to monitor populations and assassinate adversaries, and these capabilities also diffuse to nonstate actors as they get cheaper over time.[120]

In sum, we can identify a vicious feedback loop in which structural violence, technological unemployment, a worsening crisis of violence-interdependence, and the climate crisis combine to spread anger, fear, and existential insecurities among populations, which enables security agencies to surmount legal and technical constraints on their exercise of untrammeled techno-authoritarian power. I refer to this process as a *spiral of insecurity and securitization*, in which emerging nonstate threats bring forth intensified state violence to contain them, which may provoke even more nonstate violence by intensifying state repression.[121] If socialists are able to harness population-wide insecurities to build a mass movement, then a transition beyond green Keynesianism toward ecomodernist socialism is possible. But this would be very challenging, given both the weakening efficacy of labor strikes in an era of mass technological unemployment and the steadily advancing powers of military-police repression they would be up against. More likely, in this scenario, the convergence of political-economic and existential crises—exacerbated by technological unemployment and nonstate terrorist threats—would intensify the politics of fear and allow rightwing politicians and surveillance capitalists to drive a post-9/11-like intensification of military-police power.[122] We should not assume that technological advance in the forces of surveillance would *by itself* trigger such a transition: antisurveillance movements are currently making gains in the US, Europe, and elsewhere by constraining and in some places banning the rollout of facial recognition technologies, while the EU is poised to write up rules for AI intended to prevent the sort of AI-police state feared by many.[123] Even Beijing has exercised some restraint in rolling out AI-surveillance by pushing back against local pilot projects for its "social credit score" system, which were deemed excessively intrusive by the CCP.[124] But if future terrorist groups succeed in harnessing bioweapons, killer drones, the IoT, or increasingly abundant nuclear fissile materials to kill tens of thousands of civilians (if not millions), then the conjunction of rampant population-wide fear and securocratic projects of control would overwhelm efforts by activists and progressive policymakers to restrain the deployment of frightening new technologies of state repression. This would be a time of existential crises—or ideological transitions characterized by heightened feelings of fear, vulnerability, and willingness to trade off liberal freedoms for the promise of "security."

TECHNO-LEVIATHAN

These are the key feedback loops that may catalyze the emergence of something like Mann and Wainwright's climate leviathan during the course of a green Keynesian trajectory, likely between 2050 and 2080 as the intersecting crises of climate, technological unemployment, and violence-interdependence intensify. But I prefer the term techno-leviathan, since climate change would be a contributor but not the primary force fueling its emergence. And more than just a human construction, this would be a technological assemblage: a "cyborgian fusion of body parts, tools, minds, and machines" combining algorithms, drone swarms, biometric cameras, and sensors to create an emergent system that is irreducible to human agency and intentionality.[125] Techno-leviathan would be a global governance assemblage—whether imposed by the hegemony of a single state or by a consortium of states—with the power to "seize command, declare an emergency, and bring order to the Earth, all in the name of saving life."[126] The term "leviathan" is in some ways less than exact, since this would not be a world government modeled on the Westphalian state. But it is also fitting insofar as it signifies a new global order in which states, capitalists, and fearful populations agree to new restrictions on freedom in exchange for the promise of "security."

There are of course many signs, often noted by geopolitical analysts in the West, that China is already in the process of constructing something like techno-leviathan—or a techno-authoritarian world order, with the aim of unseating the Western-led "liberal" international order. A shortlist includes China's worldwide exports of 5G, facial recognition, and other surveillance technologies; its Digital Silk Road initiative, which invests in digital infrastructure across dozens of countries in order to track and extract the data that passes through them; its ambition to harness its massive domestic data resources, and steadily more of the world's as well, to become the world leader in AI by 2030; its particularly intensive adoption of predictive policing, smart city, and biometrics technologies to secure domestic order (especially in Xinjiang); and its efforts to rewrite global internet standards to support a New IP internet structure more amenable to authoritarian controls.[127] If China pursues and is successful in its bid for global hegemony—for example, by defeating the United States in a war over Taiwan, or rapidly advancing as a technological leader in FIR technologies while the US stagnates or collapses from internal political dysfunction—then this is one path to techno-leviathan.

But the emergence of techno-leviathan does not depend on global Chinese hegemony, nor would it be confined to a China-centered bloc based around Chinese platform technologies and standards. Rather, the feedbacks described above show that it would most likely encompass the so-called "free world" as well—which would get steadily less free in this scenario, and over time less capitalist (but not necessarily for the better, a point I return to below). In other words, rather than the liberal counterpoint to an illiberal or autocratic China-led order, the two spheres would become increasingly indistinguishable in this scenario. Individual rights, freedoms, and restraints on surveillance would be steadily watered down as a state-of-emergency response to worsening WMD terrorism is increasingly normalized—allowing military-police forces to detain individuals and mobilize lethal force without legal pretext—while the mobility of people and goods would be tightly constricted. Facial and emotional recognition cameras would be ubiquitous across public and even formerly "private" spaces, while "swarm policing" by drones would become the ever-present condition of life.[128] This would be an even more integrated, automated, and panoptic version of today's militarized global apartheid, which would intensify repression of migrants and racialized minorities (perhaps subjecting them to particularly intrusive genomic or neurotechnological surveillance regimes), cast previously privileged populations into the ranks of the at-risk or always-suspected, and reserve privileged mobility status for an increasingly small elite. More and less totalitarian versions of this scenario are possible—both in China and elsewhere—with the less bad versions involving greater equality, livelihood protection, and rule of law, whereas the even more frightening variants would look like twenty-first-century repetitions of the mid-twentieth-century totalitarianisms described by Hannah Arendt: regimes harnessing AI, big data, and neurotechnologies to police populations and modify human thought and behavior in ways Hitler and Stalin could have hardly dreamed of.[129] Either way, while this could be a world of unprecedented comfort and convenience for privileged classes of citizens with access to livable wages or UBI (as well as one of ecological devastation, ennui, enclosure, and loss of what Shoshana Zuboff calls the "right to sanctuary"[130]), it would most likely be a frightening dystopia for the majority of the world's population. At the very least this would be a "ustopian" future, in Margaret Atwood's sense: a world combining techno-dystopian and utopian elements, with utopian comforts and conveniences made available to privileged classes, while racialized underclasses suffer the brunt of techno-dystopian policing.[131] If techno-leviathan is indeed our future, then political struggles will determine whether its better or worse forms materialize.

Would this future necessarily entail the end or continuation of capitalism? As discussed in chapter 3, if by "capitalism" we mean a world-system in which capital accumulation is the *ecologically dominant* function, or one in which other systems and functions are subordinate to and functionally constrained by limits set by the overriding accumulation function, then it is quite plausible that techno-leviathan would no longer be primarily "capitalist."[132] Again, this does not mean the end of *capital* or accumulation tout court, but rather its constriction and functional subordination to other systemic logics and functions, thereby creating a world-system with a qualitatively novel set of power relations, feedbacks, and emergent patterns. How might such a transition emerge? As Jessop suggests, while capitalism is defined by ecological dominance of the accumulation function, "non-economic" crises (e.g., war, terrorist attacks, pandemics) "can lead to other sub-systems acquiring short-term primacy," which "would happen to the extent that solving these crises becomes the most pressing problem for the successful reproduction of all systems."[133] Such a temporary shift in ecological dominance was clearly witnessed during the early phases of the COVID-19 pandemic, when "nonessential" sectors of the economy (i.e., unnecessary to meet immediate human needs) were abruptly shut down following the overriding priority of public health.[134] The question, then, is whether a techno-leviathan trajectory could witness a *permanent* rather than temporary bifurcation in which capital accumulation is subordinated to the *security* function, thereby constraining capitalist freedom and profits within functional limits set by the overriding systemic imperative of security from WMD terror attacks. In a context of rapidly expanding access to techniques of mass destruction and successive nonstate terrorist attacks with historically unprecedented death tolls, such a transition is clearly possible. But this would require a counter-hegemonic coalition in which militaries and securocrats in leading states, along with elements of the capitalist class (particularly those like the surveillance capitalists and private security firms who would gain positions of privilege in a security-focused techno-leviathan), would succeed in initiating a quasi-permanent state of emergency at national and global scales that subordinates the power of finance capital and others seeking to sustain global capitalist business-as-usual.

In this world, *security*, rather than capital accumulation and economic growth, would become the primary objective of governments and global elites. Transnational corporations would retain much of their control over the planet's productive resources, though they would become servants more than masters of techno-authoritarian "states" (which would be better thought of as governance assemblages, blurring public/private domains, at both national and transnational scales). Technology companies like Google, Meta, and Huawei would become the architects and operators of planetary surveillance assemblages more than private enterprises focused on profit maximization. China, as Jinghan Zeng anticipates, may even "evolve into an AI-driven central planning system that maximizes efficiency in allocating market resources," using ultra-advanced AI to create a new form of techno-authoritarian socialism "with which liberal democracy can hardly compete."[135] If so, then even Western states may be pushed down similar techno-authoritarian socialist trajectories (i.e., via Leon Trotsky's "whip of external necessity").[136] These postcapitalist shifts would be reinforced by the relentless and irreversible trend toward rising technological unemployment, which would steadily diminish the role of wage labor in the global economy. In better-case scenarios, most people would then reproduce their livelihoods through a UBI or free public services. In worst-case scenarios, most people would be considered disposable by elites—since they would no longer be needed as workers or soldiers—and left to develop their own survival strategies.[137] Most likely we would see a combination of both, with richer countries providing a UBI and sustaining reproduction for a privileged class of citizens, while refugees, immigrants, and citizens of poor

countries are largely abandoned and suffer the brunt of intensified surveillance and police repression. Investment patterns and trajectories of technological innovation over time would be shaped less by the profit motive
and more by centralized security-industrial planning boards that prioritize
security and power, in this way subordinating economic production to
security objectives.[138] Growth would likely continue, but capital accumulation, job creation, and the need for tax revenues would no longer be
the primary structural drivers. Instead, technological progress—including
outer space expansionism—would be driven more by the endless "accumulation" of security and power as insatiable ends in themselves.[139] Capitalists would lose direct control over investment and production decisions in
some sectors—particularly those involving potentially dangerous technologies like synthetic biology, nanotechnology, and artificial general intelligence. Something like this occurs, for example, in Ken MacLeod's novel
Star Fraction, in which a global "US/UN" secret police maintains strict control over technological research and development across the world-system,
banning lines of research perceived as threatening and enforcing its dictates through a space-based network of nuclear missiles.[140]

Some may still prefer to describe this world as "capitalist," since continuities would no doubt remain. It would at least be a highly managed and
circumscribed capitalism that is slowly mutating into something very different from its early twenty-first-century form. But a postcapitalist techno-
leviathan is not inevitable in this scenario. On one hand, if no sufficiently
powerful dissident capitalist-securocrat faction emerges to constrain capitalist control over the direction of technological innovation, and continuous
FIR advances lead to the relentless cheapening and diffusion of WMDs to
nonstate actors, then this trajectory could plausibly end up in a breakdown
scenario—for example, through a world-ending bioengineered plague, as
Margaret Atwood depicts in *Oryx and Crake*,[141] or (perhaps) through the
emergence of malevolent and out-of-control artificial superintelligence.[142]
On the other hand, if defensive countermeasures (e.g., screening orders
for DNA synthesis, mass production of universal vaccines, distributed bio-
sensors, totalizing algorithmic surveillance) succeed in containing emerging nonstate terror threats without need of subordinating capitalist power,
then the techno-leviathan that emerges could be considered a particularly
intense version of what Nikos Poulantzas calls "authoritarian statism": a

capitalist state (whether national or transnational) that eviscerates democracy, waters down checks on executive power, and enhances military-police repression of subordinate classes to sustain capital accumulation in conditions of increasing turbulence.[143] But given that we would be simultaneously witnessing a slow but steady end to the era of wage labor through relentless progress in automation, it is more likely that our contemporary vocabulary would become increasingly inadequate to describe this future.

ECOSOCIALISM AND ABOLITIONIST SECURITY ASSEMBLAGES

We have been focusing on some fairly dark futures thus far. Let us now shift back to the concrete utopian mode by considering how the VP may evolve in an ecosocialist trajectory. As discussed in chapter 3, there are at least two ways to frame the challenge of developing ecosocialist security assemblages: one is to follow abolitionist scholars who focus on reducing structural violence and other harms that fuel violent crime, nonstate terrorism, and war, thereby reducing the need for (and eventually abolishing) systems of organized state violence like militaries, police institutions, prisons, and borders.[144] The other is to follow George Rigakos's call for a "socialist police science" that aims to democratize and repurpose existing security assemblages in order to facilitate the transition from capitalism to a democratic socialist world order.[145] Again, while there is some tension between these two frames, they could also be understood as complementary approaches, particularly if we take a *navigational* approach to abolition that views it as a long-term objective requiring careful planning and strategy. The somewhat paradoxical concept of "abolitionist security assemblages" brings these two frames together, which can be understood as practices and techniques for constraining and responding to violence that simultaneously aim to shrink, repurpose, replace, and eventually abolish contemporary military-police institutions. Rather than expecting a utopian world free of violence the moment we transcend capitalism, which would itself be a multidecadal process, ecosocialisms-in-transition would need to navigate a landscape of intersecting security challenges: including nuclear, bio, and cybersecurity threats; far-right terrorism; transnational criminal networks; ongoing regional conflicts and geopolitical tensions; fragile and collapsing states scarred by histories of imperialism, war, and climate change; and military threats posed by other states. All of these problems could potentially derail ecosocialist transitions or take them down the repressive trajectories that have been all too common in the history of socialist revolutions.[146] Therefore, if ecosocialists and allied movements seriously believe that they may gain power one day, then they need to anticipate and develop strategies for addressing these problems as part of a navigational police science or abolitionist agenda.

As explored in chapter 4, there are at least four kinds of ecosocialist pathways. I focus primarily here on the near-term degrowth trajectory, which is most compatible with abolitionist struggles in the VP. But we should first examine the potential for fortress variants of ecosocialism that perpetuate elements of today's militarized global apartheid—including xenophobic border regimes, algorithmic surveillance assemblages deploying biometric technologies, and racialized counterterrorism practices. In short, ecosocialist transformations of political economies in the world-system core would not guarantee that they are conjoined with abolitionist transformations in security and ideological assemblages, which makes it vital that we simultaneously analyze and advance counter-hegemonic struggles on the conjoined yet irreducible terrains of the SEP, VP, and EP.

On one hand, we can expect that ecomodernist socialisms in the global north—those that rely on technological innovation without scaling down material-energy throughput—would find it difficult to pursue abolitionist reforms. Simply put, larger material footprints that exceed rich countries' fair shares of the earth's biogeophysical space would inevitably lead to one of two scenarios: either continuing inequality and exploitation between core and peripheral spaces, and thus a kind of "ecosocialist imperialism," or convergence between the global north and south toward material footprints comparable to or greater than those of rich countries today, which would simply mean ecological disaster.[147] The first would perpetuate relations of uneven development and structural violence that fuel poverty, conflict, terrorism, and grievances toward the global north, whereas the second would make it far more difficult to rapidly reduce emissions, lead to further displacement of peasantries and Indigenous people, and fuel grievances among those displaced by ecomodernist socialist monoculture.[148] Furthermore, both of these scenarios, like green Keynesianism, would entail greater reliance on FIR technologies, thereby creating a higher likelihood of catastrophic nonstate terror attacks and providing states with ever-more-frightening powers of repression and lethal force projection. Thus they may confront a similarly dangerous spiral of insecurity and securitization that, in conjunction with 2°C+climate change, pushes them down techno-authoritarian trajectories.

On the other hand, while degrowth trajectories would be more amenable to abolitionist transformation, they would not automatically ensure an end to militarized global apartheid. For one, the same historically unprecedented polycrises that might make degrowth possible would also magnify domestic distributional conflicts, making it challenging to galvanize public support for global solidarity and redistribution. Thus we can envision a scenario in which accelerated energy and post-growth transitions in the world-system core lead to rapidly declining demand for FF, though this occurs without compensation for FF producers in the global south.[149] In this scenario, as critics of limits-to-growth thinking from the global south have feared for a long time, a post-growth transition cements existing global equalities by limiting the growth prospects of countries still dealing with energy poverty and insufficient basic services for their people. Right-wing populism remains a powerful force across North America and Europe, which pushes many leftists toward a compromise position in which accelerated decarbonization and universal public services are ensured at home in exchange for hard borders, weakened protections for asylum seekers, and muscular counterterrorism. While these ecosocialist states may deploy the rhetoric of global solidarity, in reality they would operate much like rich capitalist countries do today: securing flows of ecologically unequal exchange, supporting authoritarian regimes in critical resource-rich states, collaborating with southern governments on militarized migration control, and deploying military power to fight insurgencies and "terrorist" groups that threaten northern interests.

Given the pull of "lifeboat ethics" thinking in a context of magnified socioecological scarcities—that is, the claim that a nation must "look out for its own" and pull up the drawbridge to avoid sinking with those left outside—it would be very challenging to avoid fortress variants of ecosocialism. Some on the left in Europe and North America would claim that it is the best we can hope for in a grim situation, preferable to the alternative of fossil fueled backlash and climate catastrophe. Yet there are more than just ethical reasons why anti-imperialist and abolitionist ecosocialisms are needed. First, if governments in the global north hope to accelerate global decarbonization and planetary rewilding to keep global temperatures below 2°C, this can only be done through a program of climate reparations involving trillions in debt cancellation, mitigation and adaptation finance, compensation for loss and damage, and RE technology transfers.[150] Second, it is unlikely that perpetuation—let alone expansion—of military-police assemblages in the global north is compatible with accelerated decarbonization, given their energy and emissions intensities. It is almost certainly not compatible with ensuring high quality of life and universal basic services in a context of reduced material-energy throughput, given the intensive labor-material-energy demands of these institutions and the rising opportunity costs of military spending in a context of resource constraints.[151] Thus climate justice activists will be well-positioned to make the argument that a genuinely sustainable solution to the climate and earth system crises requires abolitionist and anti-imperialist forms of ecosocialism. Of course, beyond winning the intellectual argument, the success or failure of this concrete utopia will turn on the strength, size, and coherence of movements and organizations linking struggles for climate justice, economic democracy, demilitarization, decolonization, and police-prison abolition. Given that investments in race, nationalism, and masculinity are foundational to the constitution and reproduction of militarized global apartheid, it will not be possible to escape this attractor unless decolonial transitions from these cognitive-affective patterns can be enacted on a large scale.

So how might this best-case future plausibly emerge? As described in chapter 4, there may be opportunities for ecosocialist transitions between 2035 and 2040 if green Keynesian regimes are struggling with the conjoined problems of greenflation, stagnation, unemployment, stranded FF assets, and populist uprisings. The geopolitical tensions described earlier in this chapter would create a difficult environment for ecosocialist struggles, since they could empower hawkish coalitions in the United States and Europe, stimulate existential anxieties among populations that engender conservative instincts, and reinforce the perspective that economic growth is essential to national security while degrowth is a utopian hair-shirt fantasy. These challenges must be anticipated by ecosocialists, but they are not insurmountable. As noted earlier, the US, China, Russia, and Europe may be facing unprecedented economic headwinds and budgetary pressures caused by aging populations, sustained near-double-digit greenflation, stagnant economies, near 2°C warming, and rising military and policing budgets. China, as we saw, may be far too consumed by domestic crises by this time to engage in military adventurism against Taiwan, particularly if magnifying labor strikes and environmental protests across the country begin to challenge the CCP's grip on power.[152] Likewise, Russia may plausibly transition to a post-Putin reformer or face geopolitical decline with a whimper more than a bang. Given the unprecedented domestic strain that the US and Europe will be simultaneously confronting, geopolitical saber-rattling and ramping up spending on armaments, police, and borders will appear increasingly irrational to more thoughtful citizens and policymakers. Instead, if ecosocialists and climate justice movements are sufficiently popular and well organized by this time, they may be in good position to push green, social democratic, and labor parties closer toward post-growth *and* demilitarization platforms. In place of increased spending on militarized borders and armaments production—which, among rich countries, currently outpaces climate finance for the global south (discounting loans) by a factor of *thirty to one*—climate reparations initiatives would actually mitigate the root causes of state fragility, conflict, migration, and nonstate terrorism in the global south.[153] And domestically—by reducing inequality, ensuring economic security for all, and devoting more resources to mental health and harm reduction—problems like gun violence, violence against women, and drug abuse may decline significantly. In this context, it would become more politically feasible to steadily shrink and replace policing and carceral institutions with restorative justice initiatives and alternative community-based strategies for constraining and responding to interpersonal violence.[154] While the feedback loop that exists today between capitalism, militarization, and policing is difficult to escape, an unprecedented polycrisis storm that is simultaneously striking all of the great powers, combined with increasingly popular and powerful climate justice movements in these states, could ripen the conditions for degrowth and abolitionist transitions.

The above sketch provides a sense of how ecosocialist degrowth in the overdeveloped world and abolitionist strategies can mutually complement and reinforce each other. But we must also consider how ecosocialist regimes might respond to lingering and emerging threats from other states and nonstate actors. Even in a best-case scenario in which the US, China, the EU, and others collaboratively embark on ecosocialist trajectories, other powerful states would likely resist. Russia, as we've seen, would likely pose a threat to ecosocialisms-in-transition because of its reliance on plummeting oil and gas rents, simmering vengefulness, and powerful nuclear, cyber, and info-war capabilities. Thus nascent ecosocialist regimes in Europe and North America may need to sustain military and nuclear force structures while reducing them to the minimum needed to deter aggression, while also committing to clear no-first-use policies, taking nuclear missiles off hair-trigger alert, ending nuclear modernization and hypersonic missile programs, and working with other states to move toward deeper nuclear disarmament and institutionalized mutual constraints over time.[155] Things would of course be far more challenging if the US undergoes Trumpian backlash and remains a resistant outlier to a China-EU-centered ecosocialist bloc. In this case, a global ecosocialist transition may still be possible, but only if US military and geopolitical power declines precipitously. This is possible, since a mass sell-off of US treasuries by China and other states—along with declining demand for US dollars as the global economy transitions beyond oil (thereby undermining the "petro-dollar" nexus, historically foundational to US financial hegemony)—could erode its capacity to sustain its bloated military budget.[156] But the obvious danger is that a US dollar crisis would inflame nationalist passions and bring a Trump-like figure to power promising a return to "greatness" on the back of US military might. Thus it is plausible that great-power war could break out during the course of ecosocialist transitions—particularly if the world splits into competing fossil nationalist and ecosocialist blocs—and it is unlikely that ecosocialisms could survive such a conflagration (at least in their more desirable forms).

Furthermore, even if counter-hegemonic struggles succeed in pushing the US toward democratic ecosocialism, and even if Russia undergoes a social democratic revolution, other threats would remain. In particular, a secure digital communications ecosystem would be critical to the stability of ecosocialisms-in-transition: cybersecurity risks involving disinformation operations and critical infrastructure sabotage could potentially destabilize these regimes by fueling polarization and discord between worker and environmentalist elements of red-green coalitions, particularly in their early phases when their resilience is relatively weak. These risks may come from petro-states like Russia and Saudi Arabia, as well as from far-right groups, fossil capitalists, conservative billionaire networks, and other elements of the capitalist class seeking to restore their power and privilege. Cyberdefense would thus remain critical, which could involve what Ron Deibert describes as collaborative "epistemic communities" of cybersecurity experts across borders—a distributed cybersecurity assemblage that builds up local, national and regional capacities to defend digital infrastructures from state, corporate, and other threats.[157] Similarly, ecosocialisms-in-transition would benefit from open-source synthetic biology and 3D printing, which would allow states and local communities to decouple from far-flung global supply chains, create more localized and less energy-intensive medical infrastructures, and boost efforts to create locally adaptive and climate-resilient crop varieties.[158] Biosecurity risks would therefore remain, which would be lower relative to a world with higher reliance on synthetic biology and more intense levels of structural violence, but significant enough that they would warrant novel institutions for ensuring the safety and benefits of open source synthetic biology. There may be a difficult trade-off between accessibility and biosecurity, since stronger government regulations and intrusive inspection/verification regimes would likely limit access to the benefits of these technologies. But decentralized biosurveillance assemblages, similar to the model for cybersecurity discussed by Deibert, may provide a viable path forward. I do not pretend to have all the answers, which must be developed by bio- and cybersecurity experts and communities of practitioners in the course of ecosocialist transitions. But the questions must first be posed to facilitate the emergence of creative solutions.

This provides merely a brief sketch of the VP challenges that ecosocialisms-in-transition may confront. Again, different states and communities would confront their own relatively autonomous VPs shaped by distinctive problems, histories, and geographies. An ecosocialist regime in the US, for example, would face a particularly difficult challenge from far-right terrorists and insurgents, since there may be hundreds of thousands of participants in armed far-right militias in the US—many of them police and military personnel.[159] Tackling this problem would simultaneously require abolitionist and socialist police science strategies: by addressing the root causes of far-right extremism—including underinvestment in rural regions, agribusiness oligopolies that destroy rural economies, and economic insecurities that fuel compensatory investments in white supremacy[160]—as well as developing more democratically accountable surveillance and public safety practices that can limit and respond to the inevitable far-right violence that does occur. The root drivers of far-right violence would not heal overnight, and ecosocialist security strategies that can limit and respond to this violence would be needed. Otherwise ecosocialisms-in-transition will find themselves beset with reactionary backlash, fear and doubt among populations, and internecine conflicts that risk destabilizing these transitions and forcing them back toward capitalism and its military-police assemblages. These problems remain insufficiently addressed by Marxists and others struggling for egalitarian postcapitalist futures, though a clear-sighted analysis of the possibility space requires that we bring them to the surface, ask difficult questions, and collectively develop creative solutions rather than skirting or downplaying the obstacles these movements would confront.[161]

CONCLUSION

In sum, the VP in a neoliberal drift trajectory would reinforce global collapse by intensifying a fossil stagflation crisis, disrupting the RE transition, accelerating military emissions, and diverting increasingly constrained net energy and mineral supplies toward military-police assemblages. The result would either be a "breakdown" scenario culminating in ruinous great-power wars, or a neofeudalism scenario in which privileged elites cooperate to secure themselves from the expanding ranks of surplus populations. On the other hand, if FIR-driven technological breakthroughs help stabilize an emergent green Keynesian hegemony, then they would most likely trigger a spiral of insecurity and securitization that gives rise to techno-leviathan over time, which could take more or less totalitarian forms in different states. Finally, ecosocialist transitions could potentially perpetuate elements of today's militarized global apartheid, particularly in their ecomodernist forms, whereas G7 degrowth trajectories would be more compatible with abolitionist solutions to the planetary problematic, though they would require abolitionist security assemblages to manage threats posed by states and nonstate actors who would seek to destabilize nascent ecosocialist regimes.

Given the qualitative complexity of the planetary problematic and its solution-space, the need for a "methodology" that combines theory, trans-disciplinary synthesis, history, imagination, and intuition should by now be clear. Quantitative models cannot be ignored by social theorists, social theory and critical political economy cannot be ignored by scientists, and none can deny the inescapable role for intuition and imagination in this effort. This of course entails a research agenda of inexhaustible complexity that must be continuously updated as history unfolds and new data comes to light, and this book can only scratch the surface. But these last two chapters show that by "connecting the dots" between these different forms of knowledge, encompassing theory and data across the natural and social sciences, we can develop new insights into possible future trajectories that would be unthinkable in the absence of transdisciplinary synthesis.

CONCLUSION

Ultimately, we do not know what the future will bring, and there will undoubtedly be numerous surprises. But we cannot proceed headlong into the turbulence of our planetary future without a rough map of where we are headed, the crises we will likely encounter, the forms of problem-shifting that would result from different present and future responses, the opportunities for progressive transformation that will emerge for social justice movements, and the obstacles and dangers these movements would need to overcome. Whether we realize it or not, we all operate with some map of the future, in the sense that we assume particular consequences will flow from our present-day actions.[1] Thus, the question is not whether or not we develop a map of possible futures, but whether or not this is done consciously, systematically, and synthetically, taking account of all the most relevant parameters. I do not claim to have accounted for every possible parameter in this book, or exhaustively integrated the ones I do include. My goal has been more modest: to go further than existing approaches toward a synthetic transdisciplinary analysis of the future possibility space. Planetary systems thinking can be considered a meta-theoretical framework that facilitates transdisciplinary synthesis, in this way helping us construct qualitative models of the planetary problematic and its possible futures. In the years to come, as events in the world unfold and our knowledge of the planetary polycrisis advances, many of the specific scenario trajectories

I discuss in chapters 4 and 5 will become increasingly dated or obsolete. But the theoretical framework and futures "methodology" presented in this book will remain as relevant as ever. I therefore hope that others will continue to build on, enrich, and refine this book's map of the future by deepening its theoretical and methodological foundations, updating its scenarios and developing new ones, integrating new parameters, highlighting other feedbacks or more deeply exploring some of the feedbacks I do address (but insufficiently), bringing in other theoretical perspectives, and developing more fine-grained analyses of the possibility space in different states and regions across the world-system.

It is not easy to encapsulate the trajectories we have explored over the past two chapters into a succinct set of scenarios. Collapse, techno-leviathan, and ecosocialism may be the three main attractors that the planetary problematic is pushing the world-system toward, but numerous variations can be imagined for all three—involving many different timelines, parametric tweaks, and geographically uneven combinations. The future possibility space is indeed a messy multiplicity of overwhelming complexity, and to highlight representative scenarios is inherently selective and liable to occlude other potentials. Still, I suggest that we can identify seven main scenarios based on the trajectories explored in the previous chapters. Call them the uneven and combined world-system pathways, since each world-system trajectory will be the outcome of geographically uneven and combined struggles, though I will subsequently refer to them as the WSPs (which is a less-monstrous acronym). Like the SSPs, I call these *world*-system (rather than *world-earth* system) pathways to signify that each WSP could in principle be paired with different climate and earth system trajectories (e.g., because of variable assumptions about solar geoengineering, CDR deployment, and earth system feedbacks). But, like the IPCC, I will assume that each one would most likely follow a particular planetary pathway.[2] Furthermore, I should emphasize that the WSPs should not be understood as "ends of history" (with the possible exception of breakdown, if it leads to human extinction). Rather, they are more like provisional attractor states for the world-system that would be subject to further evolution over time, and critical transitions between them are possible. For instance, volatile techno-leviathan may eventually shift into neo-feudalism, neofeudalism into breakdown, abolitionist ecosocialism into

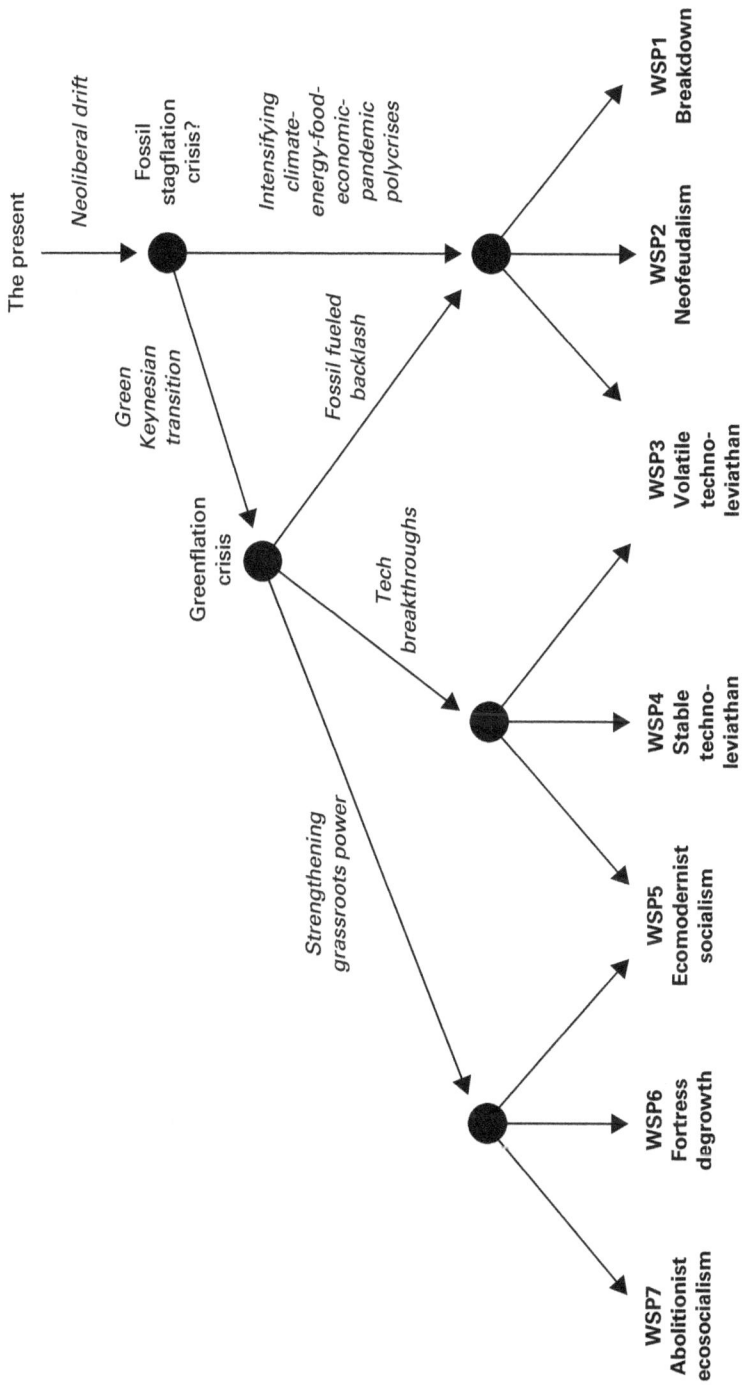

The world-system pathways (WSPs)

The present

Neoliberal drift

Fossil stagflation crisis?

Intensifying climate-energy-food-economic-pandemic polycrises

Green Keynesian transition

Greenflation crisis

Fossil fueled backlash

Tech breakthroughs

Strengthening grassroots power

WSP1 Breakdown

WSP2 Neofeudalism

WSP3 Volatile techno-leviathan

WSP4 Stable techno-leviathan

WSP5 Ecomodernist socialism

WSP6 Fortress degrowth

WSP7 Abolitionist ecosocialism

6.1

ecomodernist socialism, ecomodernist socialism into one or other variant of techno-leviathan, and so forth. Together these scenarios give us a provisional navigational map of the world-system's possibility space—one that will need to be updated and modified as we proceed ever-deeper into the future.

THE UNEVEN AND COMBINED WORLD-SYSTEM PATHWAYS

WSP1 (breakdown). Starting with the worst-case collapse scenario, WSP1 tracks closely with what Raskin calls "breakdown."[3] In this scenario, a global collapse trajectory, whether triggered by a near-term fossil stagflation crisis or longer-term convergence of magnifying socioecological crises, inflames ethnonationalist reaction, fuels geopolitical tensions, and intensifies polarization and conflict within and between states. A vicious spiral between socioecological crises, state and nonstate violence, and war, leading to further socioecological breakdown, ensues. This is more likely to occur in a trajectory of slow and incremental technological innovation. But it could also happen in a context of exponential technological breakthroughs—which could be the result of destabilizing innovations in the cyber-nuclear-AI nexus, or the relentless advance and democratization of WMD capabilities (or, perhaps, the emergence of malevolent artificial superintelligence). Existential crises and hardened self/other relations are key to this scenario, since socioecological crises and technological risks would not *by themselves* lead to breakdown. But by inflaming existential anxieties that get exploited by opportunistic elites to sow division and drum up nationalist passions, and which motivate WMD terrorism by nonstate actors, socioecological crises can indeed trigger vicious spirals that lead to worsening violence, war, and planetary breakdown. If this happens in the course of a neoliberal drift trajectory, then a 3.5°C+ hothouse earth trajectory would likely be in the cards. Eventually, we would witness a world composed of pockets of surviving communities in the upper latitudes, with the human population perhaps numbering in the millions—as James Lovelock imagines in one of his eco-dystopian warnings[4]—though human extinction is possible over the course of the twenty-second and subsequent centuries. This is not the most likely scenario, but one that cannot be ignored.

WSP2 (neofeudalism). This collapse scenario is similar to Raskin's "fortress worlds" archetype, though the term neofeudalism gives us a more precise articulation of its geopolitical and economic structure. In this scenario, world-system breakdown—whether resulting from near-term fossil stagflation or longer-term polycrisis amplification—leads to cooperation among global capitalist elites to manage geopolitical tensions and contain the "real and potential rebellion" of surplus humanity.[5] But the relentless intensification of cascading polycrises over time, in conjunction with worsening WMD terrorism, leads to a softer breakdown of the capitalist world-system into a multiplicity of regional, national, and local political economies and security assemblages. Some nation-states may retain effective governance capacities, but most would eventually fragment and give way to a complex neofeudal geography composed of political-economic and security assemblages cooperating and competing over territory and resources—including corporate quasi-states, city-states, feudalized rentier capitalists and warlords that offer livelihood protection in exchange for tribute, and numerous communities of surplus populations left to develop their own survival strategies. No doubt there are neofeudal tendencies already operative in the contemporary world, just as there were capitalist tendencies at work in the thirteenth and fourteenth centuries in Europe.[6] But this would be a future in which a collapsing world economy leads to the steady demise of capitalist social relations and their historical "laws of motion," while neofeudal structures become ecologically dominant across the planet. This future could bifurcate into a deeper collapse trajectory over time if 2.5°C+ warming triggers tipping-point cascades. Alternatively, a combination of successful imperial projects and technological breakthroughs could potentially lead to world-system reintegration and regeneration over the course of the twenty-second century and beyond (e.g., if carbon-cycle feedbacks remain muted and planetary rewilding helps stabilize global temperatures), perhaps giving rise to a twenty-second-century variant of sixteenth-century mercantile capitalism.[7] Or, more optimistically, rebellion from below—at least in certain regions—may eventually overwhelm and defeat these neofeudal bunkers, creating more egalitarian ecosocialist worlds.

WSP3 (volatile techno-leviathan). We can imagine numerous variants of techno-leviathan that combine different hegemonic configurations (e.g., a

China-led world order, a US- or G7-led order, or a bipolar world of "competitive coexistence"), varying degrees of success in managing the climate and biodiversity crises, varying degrees of success in containing the threats posed by democratized WMDs, different levels of domestic and global inequality, and different degrees of capitalist or statist control of the economy. But I focus here on two ideal types. The first I call volatile techno-leviathan, which is a particularly dark and unstable variant that would be quite vulnerable to neofeudalist regression and breakdown over time. This scenario could be considered an answer to the following "what if" question: What if the world-system undergoes continuous neoliberal drift *plus* dramatic technological breakthroughs? In this scenario, technological breakthroughs allow states in the world-system core and semi-periphery to "muddle through" worsening polycrises over time while avoiding collapse. But the result is a volatile cocktail of stressors: geopolitical tensions between the United States, China, and Russia remain elevated; 2.5°C+ warming forces governments to rely on SRM and CDR expansion to ward of tipping-point cascades; breakthroughs in AI and robotics lead to 15%–25% technological unemployment in the second half of the century, meaning unprecedented inequality and populist anger; the same innovations lead to destabilizing advances in both democratized WMD technologies and the military AI-nuclear-robotic arsenals of states; and global governance of dangerous new technologies remains weak to nonexistent. As a result, the ranks of racialized surplus populations swell; a new wave of WMD nonstate terrorism ensues, fueling a spiral of insecurity and techno-authoritarian securitization; worsening geopolitical rivalries and destabilizing AI-nuclear-cyber technologies create a near-continuous threat of ruinous hot wars; SRM interventions are ungovernable and unstable; and global economic growth stagnates and plateaus from the combination of weakening consumer demand, climate chaos, and rentier strangulation. The world-system slowly mutates from capitalism into a bipolar or multipolar configuration of competing techno-leviathans that prioritize security, power, and geopolitical competition more than economic growth. This scenario forms a sort of middle way between neofeudalism and *stable* techno-leviathan—with more rapid technological innovation compared to the former and more intense inequality, geopolitical rivalry, and climate chaos relative to the latter. It may not form a stable attractor for the world-system. On one hand, an out-of-control technological arms race, rampant WMD terrorism, an increasingly unstable nuclear balance of terror, and climate tipping points may push it toward breakdown. On the other, if global elites cooperate over time to reduce geopolitical tensions and successfully deploy SRM and CDR to ward off climate tipping points, then this scenario would become more like stable techno-leviathan—but a particularly brutal and unequal version of it, with only a small elite reaping the fruits of continuous technological advance. The film *Elysium*—which envisions a world of poverty and techno-authoritarian oppression for most of the global population, combined with techno-luxury, transhumanist experimentation, and outer space expansion for global elites—may be an apt (if slightly extreme) depiction of this future.

WSP4 (stable techno-leviathan). This scenario can be considered a more politically and ecologically stable form of techno-leviathan, one in which green Keynesian transitions combined with FIR-driven innovations power a long wave of exponential growth and stabilize global temperature increases around 2°C. Geopolitical tensions are contained—most likely following a "competitive coexistence" scenario between the US and China-led blocs, though a "renaissance of democracies" leading to a renewed G7-led order is also plausible.[8] Efforts to regulate synthetic biology and other dangerous emerging technologies have more success but remain limited due to concerns about hindering innovation. Within-country inequality is initially moderated by redistributive reforms, but over time relentless automation intensifies polarization by increasing technological unemployment, suppressing wages, and heightening precarity for most workers. Extractivist sacrifice zones proliferate across peripheral regions of the world-system, and the mass extinction crisis continues unabated as material-energy throughput continues to rise. But ultra-dense megacities, abundant solar and nuclear (and possibly fusion) energy, vertical farming, alternative proteins made from precision fermentation, and the plundering of mineral reserves from the Arctic and deep sea support lifestyles of unprecedented comfort and convenience—as well as ennui and digital enclosure—for perhaps between 20%–50% of the world's population (though such percentages are impossible to determine in advance, which will be contingent on political struggles over wages, UBI access, income distribution, and adaptation plus loss and damage finance for the global south). The rest of the population, on the other hand, would form a racialized underclass suspected of WMD terrorism, and would thus be subject to particularly intensive surveillance and mobility constraints. Genetic modification and transhumanist experimentation among privileged classes—to enhance longevity, health, cognitive faculties, and physical capabilities—would over time reinforce these racialized divisions.[9] In short, this would be a far more powerful, panoptic, and (over time) transhumanist version of today's militarized global apartheid. Would "growth" go on forever? In a sense yes, though GDP would become an increasingly irrelevant indicator as automated abundance, technological unemployment, UBI, and rising concerns with security from democratized WMD terrorism alter the priorities of ruling classes. With the opening of the outer space frontier, there may be no fundamental limit to how far this technological civilizational assemblage could expand in terms of its geographic extensity and material-energy throughput, but the earth and its less fortunate inhabitants would undoubtedly be devastated.

WSP5 (ecomodernist socialism). The last three WSPs represent different ecosocialist scenarios. WSP5 can be understood as an ecomodernist and *non*abolitionist socialist trajectory. To some extent this scenario overlaps with WSP4—particularly in the Chinese context, where techno-leviathan would most likely take an authoritarian socialist form. But at least within the democratic sphere of the world-system, ecomodernist socialisms would be more egalitarian political economies that harness a mix of democratic and algorithmic planning to redistribute the fruits of capitalist abundance, accelerate technological innovation in "green" industries, and prioritize the expansion of social welfare (rather than security and power). Transitions to ecomodernist socialism could emerge from a greenflation or carbon bubble crisis of green Keynesianism in an incremental innovation trajectory, a longer-term crisis of technological unemployment in an exponential innovation trajectory, or even a mid- to late-century crisis of neoliberal drift. More or less technologically revolutionary versions of this scenario are possible, from "fully automated" to more sober varieties. They can also be more or less globally egalitarian—including scenarios in which rich countries eventually stabilize their material throughputs while emerging economies "catch up," or varieties in which large inequalities in material and energy consumption are sustained. Either way, all of these scenarios would entail expansive extractive demands that reproduce a core-periphery structure—not necessarily between the global north and south as traditionally understood, but between wealthy urbanized regions and their extractive frontiers or "green sacrifice zones."[10] And the pressures that ecomodernist socialist regimes face as a result of core-periphery exploitation, biosphere degradation even if warming is stabilized around 2°C, worsening violence-interdependence, and technological advance in the forces of military-police repression may eventually push them in more techno-authoritarian directions. In this way, over time, they might become indistinguishable from techno-leviathan, which would especially be the case with "fully automated" variants of ecomodernist socialism.[11] Alternatively, we could envision a scenario in which core countries shift to a steady-state material throughput by mid-century, relations of ecologically unequal exchange between the north and south are brought to an end, all or most countries eventually reach European-esque consumption levels, and material-energy demands are to some extent moderated through massive expansions of recycling infrastructure.[12] This would probably still be a world of biospheric depletion and modernist monoculture,[13] but a much better future than most of the others on offer.

WSP6 (fortress degrowth). This scenario represents a nonabolitionist ecosocialist degrowth trajectory in core regions of the world-system. It would most likely emerge in the context of a world in the throes of collapse from a neoliberal drift trajectory (likely between 2050 and 2080 as the polycrisis storm reaches epic proportions), but could also emerge in the context of a particularly severe stagflation crisis of green Keynesianism. Strengthening ecosocialist movements would catalyze egalitarian degrowth transitions in the core, but compromise formations with conservative blocs—who would be fueled by fears of ecological scarcity and excessive migration—would force them to sustain militarized borders and racialized counterterrorism toward the periphery. Given that ecosocialist degrowth trajectories would almost certainly emerge in a context of deep crisis that intensifies material and existential insecurities, it would indeed be challenging to prevent these regimes from devolving into fortress or lifeboat-style ecosocialisms. Ecofascist variants led by far-right blocs—some of whom, at least in Europe, support certain aspects of degrowth platforms—can be imagined.[14] Most ecosocialist degrowthers would (understandably) refuse to call this a variant of degrowth. But regardless of what we choose to call it, ecosocialists must proactively strategize on how to prevent degrowth transitions—which would almost certainly, if at all, occur in the context of an epic and unparalleled polycrisis storm—from devolving into lifeboats for the privileged.

WSP7 (abolitionist ecosocialism). Finally, as extensively discussed in chapters 4 and 5, WSP7 represents the ideal resolution of the planetary problematic: an ecosocialist world-system that combines degrowth in the global north, abolitionist security assemblages, and a *new* "New International Economic Order" that purses contraction and convergence between north and south. I assume that abolitionist ecosocialism would most likely emerge from a deep and protracted stagflation crisis of green Keynesianism that emerges in the 2030s. But it is also plausibly compatible with longer-term transition scenarios that lead to 2.5°C+warming. This climate trajectory would severely constrict adaptation capacities across much of the global south. But if northern ecosocialist states abolish militarized global apartheid, welcome migrants, develop resettlement programs in collaboration with the governments and peoples of the global south, and build new cities in the increasingly habitable far north, then a more just and livable world for the earth's 9–10 billion human inhabitants may still be possible even as we near 3°C.[15] Alternatively, or in conjunction with cooperative resettlement programs, ecosocialist regimes in a 2.5°C+world may cooperate to bring down temperatures with solar geoengineering—while simultaneously scaling up programs of planetary rewilding, carbon-sequestering agroecology, and DAC in order to ward off hothouse earth and restore atmospheric carbon to safe levels over time.[16] No doubt both of these longer-term scenarios would require "an orchestration so elaborate and requiring so much luck that people may find it a fantastic, utopian dream," as Holly Jean Buck describes the prospect of ecosocialist geoengineering futures.[17] Yet neither should they be completely discounted, which would close our imagination to possible (if less desirable) ecosocialist futures.

IMPLICATIONS FOR COUNTER-HEGEMONIC
NAVIGATIONAL PRAXIS

We should now consider how this provisional map of the planetary future might inform counter-hegemonic navigational praxis. Starting with the concrete utopian aspiration for ecosocialism, I have suggested that the best hope for such transformation would emerge in the context of a greenflation or green-stagflation crisis of green Keynesianism that undermines the ideological hegemony of green growth and enables a tipping point tsunami of support for radical post-growth policy interventions. This suggests two things. First, it is necessary to struggle for green Keynesianism (or a global Green New Deal) as soon as possible, enacting at least the *minimum* objectives of phasing out fossil fuel subsidies; raising and coordinating carbon pricing across the major economies; ramping up spending on green technology R&D, electricity grid modernization, and electrified public transportation; providing as close to $1.3 trillion as possible in climate finance for the global south by 2030; and ensuring domestic redistributive mechanisms are in place and fighting to include as many other social justice objectives as possible.[18] Second, climate justice movements should then anticipate and prepare for a crisis of green Keynesianism emerging from the convergence of greenflation, stagnation, job losses, transition risks, and populist backlash. In this context, how could ecosocialists and climate justice movements successfully prevent fossil fueled backlash while pushing governments in more egalitarian post-capitalist directions? Our best hope is to proactively forge a broad alliance of movements for post-growth social democracy, as described in chapter 4, in order to create the conditions for a very different kind of response to a greenflation or green-stagflation crisis— one based on price controls, reducing energy demand, replacing GDP with alternative indicators of wellbeing, ensuring economic security for all in the absence of GDP growth, and shrinking military budgets. In conjunction with anti-imperialist struggles in the global south, the conditions might then be in place for metamorphosis in the direction of abolitionist ecosocialism and contraction and convergence over time. But this would be a long-term struggle, involving numerous "temporary stations on a continuous, yet rocky journey" toward the hoped-for utopian destination.[19]

On the other hand, if green Keynesian regimes succeed in catalyzing a long wave of accumulation with the aid of FIR-driven breakthroughs, then social justice movements will need to strategize on how to preempt the emergence of increasingly techno-authoritarian regimes over time. Some of the key struggles that could help prevent or at least moderate an incipient techno-leviathan include proactively fighting for a livable and unconditional UBI; ensuring adequate climate finance for the global south; pushing governments to revamp the Biological Weapons Convention or develop new global initiatives to regulate the dangers of synthetic biology, even if this means slower innovation; and fighting to institutionalize restraints on the deployment of facial and emotion recognition, predictive policing, drone swarms, and neurotechnologies by security agencies and police forces. The goal must be to moderate the inequalities and forms of imperialist violence that would fuel terrorism from nonstate actors, force governments to cooperatively restrain the dangers of unchecked FIR innovation, and institutionalize constraints on the efforts of security agencies and police forces to exercise untrammeled techno-authoritarian power.[20]

However, if insecurity-securitization spirals end up pushing liberal democratic states down the techno-authoritarian road, then this is not the end of the story. Rather than simply bowing down to techno-leviathan, counter-hegemonic movements must then struggle to ensure as much democratic oversight, accountability, inclusion, and justice as possible—ideally by pushing governments in more ecomodernist socialist directions (but, as noted previously, this would be quite challenging to pull off in this context). Alternatively, if a decisive green Keynesianism transition never materializes or undergoes backlash and bifurcation back to neoliberal drift—setting us up for a 2.5°C+ world—then this is also not the end of the story. There is a tendency in some sectors of the climate movement to say "we have ten years" to solve the problem—otherwise collapse is imminent and there is nothing more we can do.[21] There is a logic to this way of thinking, but it is also misguided. Warming of 2.5°C could plausibly trigger tipping-point cascades, but this is not inevitable; earth system feedbacks would likely remain moderate and reversible before we reach 3°C, but no doubt this would be a highly uncertain and alarming situation. Ecosocialist transitions later this century are possible, which would be much less ideal given that they would emerge in a context of intensifying socioecological scarcities and existential crises—making it more challenging to avoid the path of fortress degrowth. But ecosocialist geoengineering futures that advance the ends of climate justice, or ecosocialist migration futures that redraw the political map (or a combination of both), can be imagined in a 2.5°C or 3°C world.

Finally, we should not shy away from the navigational dilemmas that would arise in a collapse future. Many analysts across the political spectrum resist talking about the prospect of collapse. Ben Hayes, for instance, calls collapse anticipation "the very worst of foundations for thinking about just and proportionate responses to current insecurities, let alone trying to organize radical politics."[22] Others like Jem Bendell, on the other hand, have come to the conclusion that some form of global collapse is now inevitable.[23] As I have shown in this book, while I do not view global collapse as inevitable, it is nonetheless a very real potential, and a time may come when a path-dependent collapse process is set in motion that would be very challenging to escape. Thus, rather than solely adopting a "revolution or bust" strategy, more careful thinking about the threats, constraints, and opportunities that diverse communities and regions would confront during a world-system collapse is needed. Far-right movements are currently doing the same,[24] and it would be unwise to allow them to monopolize the space of collapse anticipation. We must recognize that, for all the suffering that would emerge during a collapse trajectory, it would continue to pose geographically uneven socioecological, violence, and existential problematics that can be "solved" in better and worse ways. It is even plausible that a world-system collapse could lead to the emergence of more egalitarian ecosocialisms—for example, from transformations of consciousness in the wake of nuclear war,[25] or through ecosocialist insurgencies against neofeudal fortresses. In this sense, the "breakdown of the prevailing system," as Nafeez Ahmed writes, "heralds the potential for long-term post-breakdown systemic transformation."[26]

Even if we fail to avoid the dystopian regions of the possibility space—whether collapse or techno-leviathan—it is still necessary to imagine how social justice movements and communities might sustain spaces of care, compassion, and solidarity in a grim future. Speculation on dystopian futures can aid us in this regard. As Kathryn Yusoff and Jennifer Gabrys describe, dystopian futures force us to imagine "the full range of emotional challenges and difficult choices that have to be made once all the usual landscape markers and reference points have shifted or disappeared . . . to think about what it might be like to endure and survive."[27] Social justice movements in the global north can also learn from what Audra Mitchell and Aadita Chaudhury call "BIPOC futurisms"—written by Black, African, Caribbean, Indigenous, and other authors who have already experienced the end of their ancestral worlds under the yoke of white supremacy—which dramatize the "always-already active labor of world-building and flourishing" in the wake of apocalypse.[28] Following these authors, the point of dystopian futurism is not simply to galvanize preventative action (though this is the ideal outcome), but also to help us prepare cognitively and emotionally to not just survive but also discover new sources of meaning, community, resilience, and perhaps even flourishing within such futures. This is the strength of the Deep Adaptation movement, for instance, which pushes us to explore challenging questions about how we might navigate collapse futures in a way that centers compassion and solidarity.[29] Likewise, we must do the same for techno-leviathan futures—which could be even worse than collapse, at least depending on one's geographic and intersectional positionality. This does not mean we accept such futures as inevitable, simply that we do not remain stubbornly attached to a "revolution or bust" framework. Instead, we need both the intellectual work of analyzing how these futures might unfold and the geographically uneven challenges and opportunities they would present, as well as the more existential work of cognitive-emotional preparation.

BETWEEN PESSIMISM AND HOPE

Antonio Gramsci once remarked that we should maintain an optimism of the will alongside a pessimism of the intellect. Indeed, this stance is as relevant as ever, though we should reflect on what an "optimism of the will" should mean in the context of our twenty-first-century planetary predicament. For centrist liberals and ecomodernists, this takes the form of a "can-do" spirit of apolitical innovation that reminds us of the technological wonders of the modern world and the promise of breakthroughs yet to come. Ecosocialists and degrowthers rightly critique these faith-based analyses while countering with a faith of their own: that mass

social movements can save us. But whether hope is placed in technological innovation or social movements (or both), these optimistic narratives
always require a leap of faith.

Others, on the other hand, are rejecting these faiths and forging new
intellectual, practical, emotional, and (sometimes) spiritual responses to
the planetary predicament. These thinkers aim to go beyond these "green
positivity" narratives and their diverse brands of "hopium," which they critique for constricting our capacities to grieve for the losses we confront and
find new meaning in life beyond the search for "solutions."[30] For example,
Roy Scranton skewers what he calls "fictions" of ecosocial transformation and technological miracles as "farcical daydreams against the coming
chaos, popsicle-stick castles in a hurricane wind." Instead, he counsels us
to confront our fears of death and cultivate a more humble understanding
of our cosmic insignificance.[31] In the context of IR, Jairus Grove calls for
a form of "negative thinking as an alternative to the endless rehearsing
of moralizing insights and strategic foresight," which "celebrates useless
thinking, useless scholarship, and useless forms of life at the very moment
we are told to throw them all under the bus in the name of survival at all
costs."[32] Coming from a more literary angle, the Dark Mountain Project
summons a new practice of "uncivilized" literature that breaks from the
stories of endless progress that capitalist civilization has spoon-fed many
of us from childhood. They ask, "What would happen if we looked down?
Would it be as bad as we imagine? . . . We believe it is time to look down."[33]

It is in some respects easy, and in others challenging, to go the route
of the "new pessimists" (as we might call them). In short, there is a reasonable argument to be made that, as the saying goes, "we're doomed,"
though what that means must be nuanced by appreciating the geographically and intersectionally uneven vulnerabilities that constitute the "we."
At the same time, any proclamation that "we're doomed" must bear the
weight of the incalculable losses in lives, ways of life, species, and ecosystems that would be implicitly accepted as inevitable. I am thus uncomfort-
able with at least certain forms of the new pessimist perspective, which can
become a form of escapism that avoids the grief, pain, terror, and rage that
a genuine reckoning with our predicament must provoke.[34] Just as importantly, as Scranton himself recognizes, the stance of fatalistic pessimism
can often be read as an attempt to remain "above the fray," or to avoid

the "embarrassment" of committing oneself to an erroneous or hopelessly unrealistic future.[35] In other words, rather than risking the fight for a better future, risking the pain and disappointment of failure, the new pessimists can lapse into an apolitical quietism that brings them the cold comfort of likely being proven right in the end. "An enviable position, so high above the fray!"[36]

In contrast, we can navigate a more fruitful path between hope and pessimism. As Elisabeth Grosz suggests, a Deleuzian ethics—inspired by the stoics, a Spinozist love of nature, and Nietzschean *amor fati*—can aid us in these times. The "question of ethics," from this perspective, is "How can I be worthy of the events that await me, how can I enter into events that sweep me up, preexist me, or that I cannot control? . . . What am I capable of doing, what is my degree of power and how can I act to enhance and maintain an active use of it?"[37] These are valuable questions that those of us struggling for more just and sustainable futures should ask ourselves. Taking our bearings from Grosz and Deleuze, the aim is to rigorously determine (as far as possible) what is within our power as movements that could become more than the sum of their parts, how we can take that power to the limit to create the best possible or least bad future, and how we can live well and in solidarity no matter what future ultimately unfolds. On one hand, as noted earlier, this means that we should avoid a revolution-or-bust approach, which is not only likely to end in disappointment and burnout but may also disable the flexibility needed to maximize our collective power to act and flourish within the constraints that limit us. Sadly, if the world's most powerful corporations, capital managers, and governments are hell-bent on protecting their wealth and power at the cost of the earth, and large sections of the global working class remain too constrained by ideologies of capitalism, race, nationalism, and misguided masculinities, then there is only so much that the rest of us can do. Yet, on the other hand, to say that collapse or techno-leviathan is inevitable also limits our praxis and ignores the potentials for transformative agency that will emerge in the coming upheavals. The future is open, and—to paraphrase Deleuze and Guattari—*we do not yet know what a planetary polycrisis can do.*[38] Nonetheless, as Joanna Macy advises, while we remain open to the uncertainty of the future, we should also avoid attaching to the hoped-for results of our actions. "Active hope," in this sense, means we remain steadfast in the struggle for a more just world, not because we think we will succeed but because serving life and reducing suffering is an end in itself.[39] Every iota of harm that our collective efforts are able to reduce, even if only temporarily, is significant. It is not all or nothing.

Perhaps an optimism of the will, understood along these lines, can provide a compass to help us navigate through the unfolding polycrisis. On one hand, democratic ecosocialist transformation during this century of upheaval is possible, and this is a goal worth believing in and fighting for. On the other hand, our optimism should not reside in the belief that we can and *will* create a more sustainable and just world, but that we can collectively discover new ways of life and new sources of meaning, purpose, community—and even joy—no matter what the future brings.

NOTES

INTRODUCTION

1. Adam Tooze, "Welcome to the World of the Polycrisis," *Financial Times*, October 28, 2022, https://www.ft.com/content/498398e7-11b1-494b-9cd3-6d669dc3de33; Neil Turnbull, "Permacrisis: What It Means and Why It's Word of the Year for 2022," *The Conversation*, November 11, 2022, https://theconversation.com/permacrisis-what-it-means-and-why-its-word-of-the-year-for-2022-194306; Thomas Homer-Dixon, Michael Lawrence and Scott Janzwood, "What Is a Global Polycrisis? And How Is It Different from a Systemic Risk?," *Cascade Institute*, September 16, 2022, https://cascadeinstitute.org/technical-paper/what-is-a-global-polycrisis/.

2. Thomas Homer-Dixon, Walker Brian, Biggs Reinette, et al., "Synchronous Failure: The Emerging Causal Architecture of Global Crisis," *Ecology & Society* 20, no. 2 (2015): 1–16; Nafeez Ahmed, *Failing States, Collapsing Systems: Biophysical Triggers of Violence* (Cham: Springer, 2017); Mark Swilling, *The Age of Sustainability: Just Transitions in a Complex World* (Abingdon, UK: Routledge, 2019); Paul Raskin, *The Journey to Earthland: The Great Transition to a Planetary Civilization* (Boston: Tellus Institute, 2016); Tooze, "Welcome to the World of the Polycrisis."

3. Swilling, *Age of Sustainability*.

4. Sander van der Leeuw, *Social Sustainability, Past and Future: Undoing Unintended Consequences for the Earth's Survival* (Cambridge, UK: Cambridge University Press, 2020), 57.

5. Immanuel Wallerstein, *The Modern World-System: Volume I* (Berkeley: University of California Press, 1974), 10.

6. van der Leeuw, *Social Sustainability, Past and Future*, 79.

7. Heikki Patomaki, "A Realist Ontology for Future Studies," *Journal of Critical Realism* 5, no. 1 (2006): 1–30.

8. Jens Beckert, *Imagined Futures: Fictional Expectations and Capitalist Dynamics* (Cambridge, MA: Harvard University Press, 2016), 6.

9. Patomaki, "Realist Ontology for Future Studies," 6.

10. Beckert, *Imagined Futures*; Carl Death, "Climate Fiction, Climate Theory: Decolonising Imaginations of Global Futures," *Millennium: Journal of International Studies* 50, no. 2 (2022): 430–455; Ben Anderson, "Preemption, Precaution, Preparedness: Anticipatory Action and Future Geographies," *Progress in Human Geography* 34, no. 6 (2010): 777–798.

11. Manuel Delanda, *Intensive Science and Virtual Philosophy* (London: Bloomsbury, 2005).

12. Patomaki, "Realist Ontology for Future Studies," 29.

13. Holger R. Maier, Joseph H. A. Guillaume, Hedwig van Delden, et al., "An Uncertain Future, Deep Uncertainty, Scenarios, Robustness and Adaptation: How Do They Fit Together?," *Environmental Modelling & Software* 81 (2016): 155.

14. John Urry, *What Is the Future?* (Cambridge, UK: Polity Press, 2016), 7.

15. Mathias Thaler, *No Other Planet: Utopian Visions for a Climate Changed World* (Cambridge, UK: Cambridge University Press, 2022), 44.

16. Keywan Riahi, Detlef P. Van Vuuren, Elmar Kriegler, et al., "The Shared Socioeconomic Pathways and Their Energy, Land Use, and Greenhouse Gas Emissions Implications: An Overview," *Global Environmental Change* 42 (2017): 153–168; Climate Action Tracker, "Warming Projections Global Update: Massive Gas Expansion Risks Overtaking Positive Climate Policies," *Climate Action Tracker*, November 2022, https://climateactiontracker.org/documents/1094/CAT_2022-11-10_GlobalUpdate_COP27.pdf.

17. Thaler, *No Other Planet*, 249.

18. Ruth Levitas, *Utopia as Method: The Imaginary Reconstitution of Society* (New York: Palgrave Macmillan, 2013), 6.

19. Thaler, *No Other Planet*, 287.

20. Immanuel Wallerstein, *Utopistics: Or, Historical Choices of the Twenty-first Century* (New York: The New Press, 1998), 1–2. See also Hans Baer, *Democratic Ecosocialism as a Real Utopia: Transitioning to an Alternative World-System* (New York: Berghahn Books, 2018).

21. Levitas, *Utopia as Method*, 18–19.

22. Thaler, *No Other Planet*, 72.

23. Quoted in Thaler, *No Other Planet*, 220.

24. Erik Olin Wright, *Envisioning Real Utopias* (London: Verso, 2010), 27.

25. Nick Srnicek and Alex Williams, *Inventing the Future: Postcapitalism and a World without Work* (London: Verso, 2015).

26. Valentine Moghadam, "What Is Revolution in the 21st Century? Towards a Socialist-Feminist World Revolution," *Millennium Journal of International Studies* 47, no. 3 (2019): 470–482.

27. Detlef van Vuuren, Marcel Kok, Bastien Birod, et al., "Scenarios in Global Environmental Assessments: Key Characteristics and Lessons for Future Use," *Global Environmental Change* 22 (2012): 884–895; Geoff Mann and Joel Wainwright, *Climate Leviathan: A Political Theory of Our Planetary Future* (London: Verso, 2018); Riahi et al., "Shared Socioeconomic Pathways"; Raskin, *Journey to Earthland*.

28. Will Steffen, Katherine Richardson, Johan Rockstrom, et al., "Trajectories of the Earth System in the Anthropocene," *Proceedings of the National Academy of Sciences* 115, no. 33 (2018): 8252–8259; William Connolly, *Facing the Planetary: Entangled Humanism and the Politics of Swarming* (Durham, NC: Duke University Press, 2017).

29. Nick Dyer-Witheford, Atle Kjosen, and James Steinhoff, *Inhuman Power: Artificial Intelligence and the Future of Capitalism* (London: Pluto Press, 2019), 28.

30. Brian O'Neill, Elmar Kriegler, Kristie L. Ebi, et al., "The Roads Ahead: Narratives for Shared Socioeconomic Pathways Describing Future Worlds in the 21st Century," *Global Environmental Change* 42 (2017): 169–180.

31. Eduardo Brondizio, Karen O'Brien, Frank Biermann, et al., "Re-conceptualizing the Anthropocene: A Call for Collaboration," *Global Environmental Change* 39 (2016): 318–327.

32. John Bellamy Foster, "Marx's Open-Ended Critique," *Monthly Review* 70, no. 1 (2018): 1–10.

33. Nancy Fraser and Rahel Jaeggi, *Capitalism: A Conversation in Critical Theory* (London: Verso, 2018), 3.

34. David Harvey, *Seventeen Contradictions and the End of Capitalism* (Oxford: Oxford University Press, 2014); John Bellamy Foster, Brett Clark, and Richard York, *Ecological Rift: Capitalism's War on the Earth* (New York: Monthly Review Press, 2011); Bob Jessop, *State Power: A Strategic-Relational Approach* (Cambridge, UK: Polity Press, 2008).

35. Connolly, *Facing the Planetary*.

36. Exceptions to this trend include James O'Connor, *Natural Causes: Essays in Ecological Marxism* (London: Routledge, 1998); Moore, *Capitalism in the Web*.

37. Erika Cudworth and Stephen Hobden, *Posthuman International Relations: Complexity, Ecologism and Global Politics* (London: Zed Books, 2013), 13; David Byrne and Gill Callaghan, *Complexity Theory and the Social Sciences* (Abingdon: Routledge, 2013); Eoin Flaherty, *Complexity and Resilience in the Social and Ecological Sciences* (London: Palgrave Macmillan, 2019); Marten Scheffer, *Critical Transitions in Nature and Society* (Princeton, NJ: Princeton University Press, 2009); Swilling, *Age of Sustainability*; Delanda, *Intensive Science*.

38. Manuel Delanda, *Assemblage Theory* (Edinburgh: Edinburgh University Press, 2016).

39. Edgar Morin, *Homeland Earth: A Manifesto for the New Millennium* (New York: Hampton Press, 1999).

40. Alex Williams, *Political Hegemony and Social Complexity: Mechanisms of Power After Gramsci* (Cham: Palgrave Macmillan, 2020).

41. For discussion, see Flaherty, *Complexity and Resilience*.

42. Ilya Prigogine and Isabelle Stengers, *Order Out of Chaos: Man's New Dialogue with Nature* (New York: Bantam, 1984).

43. Williams, *Political Hegemony*; Scheffer, *Critical Transitions*.

44. Delanda, *Assemblage Theory*.

45. Rana Faroohar, "My Guide to a Deglobalizing World," *Financial Times*, October 20, 2022, https://www.ft.com/content/f4c17c8c-9097-417e-94d6-36825fe85c24.

46. See Delanda, *Intensive Science*, 157–159.

47. Donella Meadows, Dennis Meadows, Jurgen Randers, et al., *The Limits to Growth: A Report for the Club of Rome's Project on the Predicament of Mankind* (New York: Universe Books, 1972).

48. Meadows et al., *Limits to Growth*, 10–11.

49. Morin, *Homeland Earth*, 74.

50. Karl Marx, *The Grundrisse*, trans. Ben Fowkes (New York: Penguin Press, 1993), 146, 145.

51. Delanda, *Assemblage Theory*, 119.

52. Dan Gardner, *Future Babble: Why Pundits Are Hedgehogs and Foxes Know Best* (New York: Dutton, 2012).

53. Ariel Colonomos, *Selling the Future: The Perils of Predicting Global Politics* (Oxford: Oxford University Press, 2016), 40.

54. Martin Wolf, "How to Think About Policy in a Polycrisis," *Financial Times*, November 29, 2022, https://www.ft.com/content/a1918fec-2c8f-4051-ad78-c300b0fc9adb.

55. Death, "Climate Fiction," 434, 441.

56. Alexander Anievas and Kerem Nisancioglu, *How the West Came to Rule: The Geopolitical Origins of Capitalism* (London: Pluto Press, 2015), 61; emphasis original.

57. Stefanie Fishel, Anthony Burke, Simon Dalby, et al., "Defending Planet Politics," *Millennium: Journal of International Studies* 46, no. 2 (2018): 209–219.

58. Which builds on Mann and Wainwright, *Climate Leviathan*.

CHAPTER 1

1. In Deleuzian terms, it is a "multiplicity." See discussion in Michael Albert, "COVID-19 and the Planetary Crisis Multiplicity: From Marxist Crisis Theory to Planetary Assemblage Theory," *Theory & Event* 25, no. 2 (2022): 332–363.

2. E.g. Jason Moore, *Capitalism in the Web of Life*, 1.

3. World Economic Forum, *The Global Risks Report 2023*, 18th Edition (Geneva: World Economic Forum, 2023), 9.

4. We should however emphasize that while the term is relatively new, it partakes in a longer lineage of scholarship on systemic risk and converging crises. E.g. Homer-Dixon et al., "Synchronous Failure"; Ahmed, *Failing States, Collapsing Systems*; Swilling, *Age of Sustainability*; Morin, *Homeland Earth*.

5. Tooze, "Welcome to the World of the Polycrisis."

6. These claims are attributed to Niall Ferguson and Gideon Rachman respectively. Quoted in Thomas-Homer Dixon, Michael Lawrence, and Scott Janzwood, "Dismissing the term 'polycrisis' has one inevitable consequence: reality always bites," *The Globe and Mail*, February 18, 2023, https://www.theglobeandmail.com/opinion/article -dismissing-the-term-polycrisis-has-one-inevitable-consequence-reality/.

7. E.g. Noah Smith, "Against 'Polycrisis,'" *Noahpinion*, November 13, 2022, https:// www.noahpinion.blog/p/against-polycrisis.

8. Homer-Dixon et al, "What Is a Polycrisis?"

9. Albert, "COVID-19 and the Planetary Crisis"

10. James O'Connor, "The Meaning of Crisis," *International Journal of Urban and Regional Research* 5, no. 3 (1982): 301–329.

11. Scheffer, *Critical Transitions*, 104; Immanuel Wallerstein, *World Systems Analysis: An Introduction* (Durham, NC: Duke University Press, 2004); Giovanni Arrighi, *The Long Twentieth Century: Money, Power, and the Origins of Our Times* (London: Verso, 2010).

12. Referring to the nexus of global capitalism and the earth. Adopted from Ilona Otto, Jonathan Donges, Roger Cremades, et al., "Social Tipping Dynamics for Stabilizing Earth's Climate by 2050," *Proceedings of the National Academy of Sciences* 117, no. 5 (2020): 2354–2365.

13. I acknowledge that the US-China rivalry could be viewed as a systemic crisis (e.g., from the perspective of realist hegemonic transitions theory). But barring all-out nuclear war, it is more causally relevant to the future possibility space in terms of how it will shape and constrain the efforts of states to address the core systemic crises of capitalism, ecology, energy, food, and violence-interdependence (as I show in chapter 5).

14. Johan Rockstrom, Will Steffen, Kevin Noone, et al., "A Safe Operating Space for Humanity," *Nature* 461, no. 24 (2009): 472–475.

15. Rockstrom et al., "A Safe Operating Space for Humanity."

16. Will Steffen, Katherine Richardson, Johan Rockstrom, et al., "Planetary Boundaries: Guiding Human Development on a Changing Planet," *Science* 347, no. 6233 (2015): 726–738.

17. Intergovernmental Science-Policy Platform on Biodiversity and Ecosystem Services, *Summary for Policymakers of the Global Assessment Report on Biodiversity and Ecosystem Services* (Bonn: IPBES Secretariat, 2019), 3.

18. World Wildlife Fund, *Living Planet Report 2022: Building a Nature Positive Society* (Gland: WWF, 2022).

19. Francisco Sanchez-Bayo and Kris Wyckhuys, "Worldwide Decline of the Entomofauna: A Review of Its Drivers," *Biological Conservation* 232 (2019): 8–27.

20. Dave Goulson, "The Insect Apocalypse: Our World Will Grind to a Halt without Them," *The Guardian*, July 25, 2021, https://www.theguardian.com/environment/2021 /jul/25/the-insect-apocalypse-our-world-will-grind-to-a-halt-without-them.

21. Matthew Smith, Nathaniel Mueller, Marco Springmann, et al., "Pollinator Deficits, Food Consumption, and Consequences for Human Health: A Modelling Study," *Environmental Health Perspectives* 130, no. 12 (2022): 1–12.

22. Food and Agriculture Organization, *The State of the World's Forests: Forests, Biodiversity and People* (Rome: FAO, 2020), xvii.

23. Luciana Gatti, Luana S. Basso, John B. Miller, et al., "Amazonia as a Carbon Source Linked to Deforestation and Climate Change," *Nature* 595 (2021): 388–408; Tim Lenton, Johan Rockström, Owen Gaffney, et al., "Climate Tipping Points—Too Risky to Bet Against," *Nature* 575 (2019): 592–595.

24. Thomas Lovejoy and Carlos Nobre, "Amazon Tipping Point," *Science Advances* 4, no. 2 (2018): eaat2340; David Lapola, Patricia Pinho, Jos Barlow, et al., "The Drivers and Impacts of Amazon Forest Degradation," *Science Advances* 379, no. 6630 (2023): eabp8622.

25. United Nations Environmental Programme, *Preventing the Next Pandemic: Zoonotic Diseases and How to Break the Chain of Transmission* (Nairobi: UNEP, 2020), 29.

26. United Nations Environmental Programme, *Preventing the Next Pandemic*, 16.

27. David Morens and Anthony Fauci, "Emerging Pandemic Diseases: How We Got to COVID-19," *Cell* 182 (2020): 1077.

28. Walter Willett, Johan Rockstrom, Marco Springmann, et al., "Food in the Anthropocene: The EAT-Lancet Commission on Healthy Diets from Sustainable Food Systems," *The Lancet* 393, no. 10170 (2019): 23.

29. Aruna Chandrasekhar, Daisy Dunne, Orla Dwyer, et al., "COP15: Key Outcomes Agreed at the UN Biodiversity Conference in Montreal," *Carbon Brief*, December 20, 2022, https://www.carbonbrief.org/cop15-key-outcomes-agreed-at-the-un-biodiversity-conference-in-montreal/.

30. Chandrasekhar et al., "COP15."

31. Eileen Crist, Helen Kopnina, Philip Cafaro, et al., "Protecting Half the Planet and Transforming Human Systems Are Complementary Goals," *Frontiers in Conservation Science* 2 (2021): 1–9; OECD-FAO, "Agricultural Outlook 2021–2030," *OECD and FAO*, 2019, accessed December 22, 2022, https://www.oecd-ilibrary.org/agriculture-and-food/oecd-fao-agricultural-outlook-2021-2030_19428846-en.

32. Intergovernmental Panel on Climate Change (IPCC), "Summary for Policymakers," *Global Warming of 1.5°C*, 2018, accessed January 28, 2023, https://www.ipcc.ch/site/assets/uploads/sites/2/2019/05/SR15_Citation.pdf.

33. Climate Action Tracker, "Warming Projections Global Update."

34. Climate Action Tracker, "Warming Projections Global Update."

35. Climate Action Tracker, "Warming Projections Global Update."

36. Hayley Stevenson, "Reforming Global Climate Governance in an Age of Bullshit," *Globalizations* 18, no. 1 (2021): 86–102.

37. Steffen et al., "Trajectories of the Earth System"; Lenton et al., "Climate Tipping Points"; Nico Wunderling, Jonathan Donges, Jurgen Kurths, et al., "Interacting

Tipping Elements Increase Risk of Climate Domino Effects Under Global Warming," *Earth System Dynamics* 12 (2021): 601–619.

38. University of Leeds, "Tropical Forests' Carbon Sink Is Already Rapidly Weakening," *Phys.org*, March 4, 2020, https://phys.org/news/2020-03-tropical-forests-carbon-rapidly -weakening.html?utm_source=nwletter&utm_medium=email&utm_campaign=daily -nwletter. Other scientists fear that we may have already reached a tipping point for the Amazon, or at least parts of it. See Luciana Gatti, Luana Basso, Graciela Tejada et al., "Amazonia as a carbon source linked to deforestation and climate change," *Nature* 595 (2021), 388–393.

39. Katharyn Duffy, Christopher Schwalm, Vickery Arcus, et al., "How Close Are We to the Temperature Tipping Point of the Biosphere?" *Science Advances* 7, no. 1052 (2021): 1–9.

40. Duffy et al., "How Close Are We to the Temperature Tipping Point?" 3.

41. Clive Cookson, "Wildfires in boreal forests release record levels of carbon, satellite study shows," *Financial Times*, March 2, 2023, https://www.ft.com/content/1a24a66d -854a-4c32-859b-b1ef4203e96a.

42. Louise Farquharson, Vladimir Romanovksy, William Cable, et al., "Climate Change Drives Widespread and Rapid Thermokarst Development in Very Cold Permafrost in the Canadian High Arctic," *Geophysical Research Letters* 46 (2019): 1–9; Ayesha Tandon, "Exceptional surge in methane emissions from wetlands worries scientists," *Carbon Brief*, March 20, 2023, https://www.carbonbrief.org/exceptional -surge-in-methane-emissions-from-wetlands-worries-scientists/.

43. Mark Lynas, *Our Final Warning: Six Degrees of Climate Emergency* (London: 4th Estate, 2020), 161.

44. Steffen et al., "Trajectories of the Earth System," 8255.

45. Lynas, *Our Final Warning*, 10–44.

46. Edward Byers, Matthew Gidden, David Leclere, et al., "Global Exposure and Vulnerability to Multi-Sector Development and Climate Change Hotspots," *Environmental Research Letters* 13 (2018): 1–14.

47. Quoted in Leslie Hook, Christian Shepherd, and Nastassia Astrasheuskaya, "Extreme Weather Takes Climate Change Models 'Off the Scale,'" *Financial Times*, July 23, 2021, https://www.ft.com/content/9a647a51-ede8-480e-ba78-cbf14ad878b7.

48. Lynas, *Our Final Warning*, 117, 142.

49. Lynas, *Our Final Warning*, 171–174.

50. Lynas, *Our Final Warning*, ix; see also Daniel Steel, Tyler DesRoches, and Kian Mintz-Woo, "Climate Change and the Threat to Civilization," *Proceedings of the National Academy of Science* 119, no. 42 (2022): 1–4; Luke Kemp, Chi Xu, Joanna Depledge, et al., "Climate Endgame: Exploring Catastrophic Climate Change Scenarios," *Proceedings of the National Academy of Sciences* 119, no. 34 (2022): 1–9.

51. Helmut Haberl, Dominik Wiedenhofer, Doris Virag, et al., "A Systematic Review of the Evidence on Decoupling of GDP, Resource Use and GHG Emissions, Part II: Synthesizing the Insights," *Environmental Research Letters* 15 (2020): 1–42.

52. Haberl et al., "A Systematic Review of the Evidence on Decoupling of GDP, Resource Use and GHG Emissions, Part II."

53. John Asafu-Adaye, Linus Blomqvist, Stewart Brand, et al., "An Ecomodernist Manifesto," 2019, accessed September 13, 2019, http://www.ecomodernism.org.

54. Corinne Le Quere, Jan Korsbakken, Charlie Wilson, et al., "Drivers of Declining CO$_2$ Emissions in 18 Developed Economies," *Nature Climate Change* 9 (2019): 213–217; Andrew McAfee, "Why Degrowth Is the Worse Idea on the Planet," *Wired*, October 6, 2020, https://www.wired.com/story/opinion-why-degrowth-is-the-worst-idea-on-the -planet/.

55. Our World in Data, "Energy Intensity," 2022, accessed January 28, 2023, https://ourworldindata.org/grapher/energy-intensity.

56. International Energy Agency (IEA), *Net Zero by 2050: Roadmap for the Global Energy Sector* (Paris: IEA, 2021), 18.

57. Haberl et al., "Systematic Review of the Evidence"; Giorgos Kallis and Jason Hickel, "Is Green Growth Possible?," *New Political Economy* 25, no. 4 (2020): 469–486; Timothy Parrique, Jonathan Barth, Francois Briens, et al., *Decoupling Debunked: Evidence and Arguments against Green Growth as Sole Strategy for Sustainability* (Brussels: European Environmental Bureau, 2019); James Ward, Paul Sutton, Adrian Werner, et al., "Is Decoupling GDP Growth from Environmental Impact Possible?" *PLoS ONE* 11, no. 10 (2016): 1–14; Thomas Wiedmann, Hanz Schandl, Manfred Lenzen, et al., "The Material Footprint of Nations," *Proceedings of the National Academy of Sciences* 112, no. 20 (2015): 6271–6276.

58. Christian Dorninger, Alf Hornborg, David Abson, et al., "Global Patterns of Eco- logically Unequal Exchange: Implications for Sustainability in the 21st Century," *Ecological Economics* 179 (2021): 1–14.

59. Wiedmann et al., "Material Footprint," 6273.

60. Kallis and Hickel, "Is Green Growth Possible?," 473.

61. United Nations Environment Programme, *Assessing Global Resource Use* (Nai- robi: UNEP, 2017), 42–45. For discussion, see Kallis and Hickel, "Is Green Growth Possible?"

62. Direct rebound effects refer to increases in the consumption of a particular prod- uct (e.g., cars) when efficiency improvements lead to lower costs; indirect rebound effects refer to increased consumption *elsewhere* when efficiency improvements free up resources that can be allocated in other sectors. See Parrique et al., *Decoupling Debunked*.

63. Paul Brockway, Steve Sorrrell, Gregor Semieniuk, et al., "Energy Efficiency and Economy-Wide Rebound Effects: A Review of the Evidence and Its Implications," *Renewable and Sustainable Energy Reviews* 141 (2021): 2.

64. Kallis and Hickel, "Is Green Growth Possible?" 479–481; Kevin Anderson and Alice Bows, "Beyond 'Dangerous' Climate Change: Emission Scenarios for a New World," *Philosophical Transactions of the Royal Society* 369, no. 1934 (2012): 23–41.

65. Laurence Delina, *Strategies for Rapid Climate Mitigation: Wartime Mobilization as a Model for Action?* (Abingdon, UK: Routledge, 2016).

66. IEA, *Net Zero by 2050*, 94.

67. Oxfam, *Tightening the Net: Net Zero Climate Targets—Implications for Land and Food Security* (London: Oxfam, 2021).

68. Oxfam, *Tightening the Net: Net Zero Climate Targets*, 14–15.

69. Vera Heck, Dieter Gerten, Wolfgang Lucht, et al., "Biomass-Based Negative Emissions Difficult to Reconcile with Planetary Boundaries," *Nature Climate Change* 8 (2018): 151–155.

70. Kallis and Hickel, "Is Green Growth Possible?"; International Energy Agency, "Direct Air Capture: Technology Deep Dive," *International Energy Agency*, September 2022, https://www.iea.org/reports/direct-air-capture.

71. Ryan Hanna, Ahmed Abdulla, Yangyang Xu, et al., "Emergency Deployment of Direct Air Capture as a Response to the Climate Crisis," *Nature Communications* 12 (2021): 4–5.

72. Hanna et al., "Emergency deployment of direct air capture," 4.

73. CD Jones et al., "Simulating the Earth System Response to Negative Emissions," *Environmental Research Letters* 11, no. 9 (2016): 95012.

74. Neil Grant, Adam Hawkes, Shivika Mital, et al., "Confronting Mitigation Deterrence in Low-Carbon Scenarios," *Environmental Research Letters* 16 (2021): 1–14.

75. Bronson Griscom, Justin Adams, Peter Ellis, et al., "Natural Climate Solutions," *Proceedings of the National Academy of Sciences* 114, no. 44 (2017): 11645–11650.

76. Willet et al., "Food Systems"; Crist et al., "Protecting Half."

77. Matthew Hayek, William Ripple, Helen Harwatt, et al., "The Carbon Opportunity Cost of Animal-Sourced Food Production on Land," *Nature Sustainability* 4 (2021): 21–24.

78. OECD-FAO, "Agricultural Outlook"; Neil Stephens et al., "Bringing Cultured Meat to Market: Technical, Socio-Political, and Regulatory Challenges in Cellular Agriculture," *Trends in Food Science & Technology* 78 (2018): 155–156.

79. UNEP, *Assessing Global Resource Use*.

80. Kallis and Hickel, "Is Green Growth Possible?"; Christopher Trisos, Cory Merow, and Alex Pigot, "The Projected Timing of Abrupt Ecological Disruption from Climate Change," *Nature* 580 (2020): 496–501.

81. Kallis and Hickel, "Is Green Growth Possible?"; UNEP, *Assessing Global Resource Use*; Haberl et al., "Systematic Review."

82. Wiedmann et al., "Material Footprint"; Parrique et al., *Decoupling Debunked*; Brockway et al., "Energy Efficiency."

83. Matthew Paterson and Peter Newell, *Climate Capitalism: Global Warming and the Transformation of the Global Economy* (Cambridge, UK: Cambridge University Press, 2010), 169–172.

84. Larry Summers, "The Age of Secular Stagnation: What It Is and What to Do About It," *Foreign Affairs* 95, no. 2 (2016): 2–9. Regarding the ongoing slowdown in

China, see Ruchir Sharma, "China's economy will not overtake the US until 2060, if ever," *Financial Times*, October 24, 2022, https://www.ft.com/content/cff42bc4-f9e3 -4f51-985a-86518934afbe.

85. Robert Gordon, *The Rise and Fall of American Growth: The U.S. Standard of Living since the Civil War* (Princeton, NJ: Princeton University Press, 2016); Tim Jackson, "The Post-Growth Challenge: Secular Stagnation, Inequality, and the Limits to Growth," *CUSP Working Paper No 12* (2015): 1–5; Brett Christophers, *Rentier Capitalism: Who Owns the Economy, and Who Pays?* (London: Verso, 2020).

86. Immanuel Wallerstein, "Structural Crisis in the World-System," *Monthly Review Press* 62, no. 10 (2011): 31–39.

87. Martin Wolf, *The Shifts and the Shocks: What We've Learned—and Have Still to Learn—About the Financial Crisis* (New York: Penguin Press, 2014), 173.

88. Adam Tooze, *Crashed: How a Decade of Financial Crises Changed the World* (New York: Penguin Books, 2018), 453.

89. Mohammed El-Erian, "Not Just Another Recession: Why the Global Economy May Never Be the Same," *Foreign Affairs*, November 22, 2022, https://www.foreignaffairs .com/world/not-just-another-recession-global-economy.

90. Tooze, *Crashed*, 453, 316.

91. Oxfam, *Survival of the Richest: How We Must Tax the Super-Rich Now to Fight Inequality* (London: Oxfam International, 2023); John Bellamy Foster, Jamil Jonna, and Brett Clark, "The Contagion of Capital," *Monthly Review* 72, no. 8 (2021): 1–17.

92. International Monetary Fund, *World Economic Outlook: Countering the Cost-of-Living Crisis* (Washington, DC: IMF, 2022).

93. Isabella Weber and Evan Wasner, "Sellers' Inflation, Profits and Conflict: Why can Large Firms Hike Prices in an Emergency?" *University of Massachusetts Amherst Working Paper Series* (2023), 1–51.

94. Weber and Wasner, "Seller's Inflation", 1–2; Also see Josh Bivens, "Corporate Profit Have Contributed Disproportionately to Inflation. How Should Policymakers Respond?" *Economic Policy Institute*, April 21, 2022, https://www.epi.org/blog/corporate -profits-have-contributed-disproportionately-to-inflation-how-should-policymakers -respond/.

95. International Monetary Fund, *World Economic Outlook: A Rocky Recovery* (Washington D.C: IMF, 2023), xiv.

96. Nouriel Roubini, *Megathreats: Ten Dangerous Trends That Imperil Our Future, and How to Survive Them* (New York: Little Brown & Company, 2022).

97. Cedric Durand, "The End of Financial Hegemony?" *New Left Review* 138 (2022): 48, 42.

98. World Bank, *Global Economic Prospects*, 53–54; Roubini, *Megathreats*, 104–107; El-Erian, "Not Just Another Recession."

99. El-Erian, "Not Just Another Recession."

100. Roubini, *Megathreats*, 86.

101. International Energy Agency (IEA), *World Energy Outlook 2022* (Paris: IEA, 2022), 3.

102. IEA, *World Energy Outlook 2022*, 3.

103. David Sheppard, "Gas Shortages: What Is Driving Europe's Energy Crisis?," *Financial Times*, October 10, 2021, https://www.ft.com/content/72d0ec90-29e3-4e95-9280-6a4ad6b481a3.

104. IEA, *World Energy Outlook 2022*, 34–35; The Economist, "The Age of Fossil Fuel Abundance Is Dead," *The Economist*, October 4, 2021, https://www.economist.com/finance-and-economics/the-age-of-fossil-fuel-abundance-is-dead/21805253.

105. Roger Harrabin, "Record Drop in Energy Investment, Warns International Energy Agency," *BBC News*, May 27, 2020, https://www.bbc.co.uk/news/business-52812709.

106. Justin Jacobs, "US Oil Majors Hold Down Spending Despite White House Threats," *Financial Times*, November 3, 2022, https://www.ft.com/content/4192caf1-8626-4131-9777-ceb82860fdb3.

107. Derek Brower, "Chevron Chief Blames Western Governments for Energy Crunch," *Financial Times*, October 20, 2022, https://www.ft.com/content/83d93bdd-659a-47b3-96bf-40884ef46a09.

108. IEA, *World Energy Outlook 2022*, 36.

109. Charles Hall, *Energy Return on Investment: A Unifying Principle for Biology, Economics, and Sustainability* (Cham: Springer, 2017).

110. David Murphy and Charles Hall, "Energy Return on Investment, Peak Oil, and the End of Economic Growth," *Annals of the New York Academy of Sciences* 1219 (2011): 52–72.

111. Murphy and Hall, "Energy Return on Investment."

112. *The Economist*, "Age of Fossil Fuel Abundance Is Dead."

113. Andrew Jackson and Tim Jackson, "Modelling Energy Transition Risk: The Impact of Declining Energy Return on Investment," *Ecological Economics* 185 (2021): 1–27.

114. Hall, *Energy Return*, 93; Todd Gillespie, "Energy Costs Set to Reach Record 13% of Global GDP this Year," *Bloomberg*, March 16, 2022, https://www.bloomberg.com/news/articles/2022-03-16/energy-costs-set-to-reach-record-13-of-global-gdp-this-year?leadSource=uverify%20wall.

115. Jackson, "Post-Growth Challenge"; Ahmed, *Failing States*, 27.

116. Paul Brockway, Anne Owen, Lina Brand-Correa, and Lukas Hardt, "Estimation of Global Final-Stage Energy-Return-on-Investment for Fossil Fuels with Comparison to Renewable Energy Sources," *Nature Energy* 4 (2019): 612–621.

117. Jackson and Jackson, "Modelling Energy Transition Risk," 2.

118. Brockway et al., "Estimation of Global Final-Stage Energy-Return-On-Investment."

119. Brockway et al., "Estimation of Global Final-Stage Energy-Return-On-Investment," 616.

120. Jackson and Jackson, "Modelling Energy Transition Risk."

121. IEA, *WEO 2022*, 51–52.

122. IEA, *WEO 2022*, 61.

123. British Petroleum (BP), *Energy Outlook 2023 Edition* (London: BP, 2023), 40.

124. See Brockway et al., "Energy Efficiency," 14.

125. IEA, *WEO 2022*, 61.

126. Smith, "Against 'Polycrisis.'"

127. Eban Goodstein and Hunter Lovins, "A Pathway to Rapid Global Solar Energy Deployment? Exploring the Solar Dominance Hypothesis," *Energy Research & Social Science* 56 (2019): 1–6; Kingsmill Bond, Harry Benham, and Ed Vaughan, *The Sky's the Limit: Solar and Wind Energy Potential Is 100 Times as Much as Global Energy Demand* (London: Carbon Tracker, 2021).

128. IEA, *Renewables 2022: Analysis and Forecast to 2027* (Paris: IEA, 2022).

129. Bond et al., *Sky's the Limit*.

130. Michael Liebreich, "After Ukraine—The Clean Energy Acceleration," *BloombergNEF*, September 30, 2022, https://about.bnef.com/blog/after-ukraine-the-great-clean-energy-acceleration/.

131. Richard Heinberg and David Fridley, *Our Renewable Future: Laying the Path for One Hundred Percent Clean Energy* (Washington, DC: Island Press, 2016); Inigo Capellán-Peréz, Carlos de Castro, and Luiz Gonzalez, "Dynamic Energy Return on Energy Investment (EROI) and Material Requirements in Scenarios of Global Transition to Renewable Energies," *Energy Strategy Reviews* 26 (2019): 1–26; Vaclav Smil, *How the World Really Works: A Scientist's Guide to Our Past, Present, and Future* (New York: Penguin Books, 2022); Christopher Clack, Staffan Qvist, Jay Apt, et al., "Evaluation of a Proposal for Reliable Low-Cost Grid Power with 100% Wind, Water, and Solar," *Proceedings of the National Academy of Sciences* 114, no. 26 (2016): 6722–6725.

132. Jorg Friedrichs, *The Future Is Not What It Used to Be: Climate Change and Energy Scarcity* (Cambridge, MA: MIT Press, 2013).

133. See discussion in Michael Albert, "The Global Politics of the Renewable Energy Transition and the Non-Substitutability Hypothesis: Towards a 'Great Transformation?'" *Review of International Political Economy* 29, no. 5 (2022): 1766–1781.

134. IEA, *WEO 2022*, 61.

135. IEA, *WEO 2022*, 163–164.

136. IEA, *WEO 2022*, 99.

137. Brett Christophers, "Fossilised Capital: Price and Profit in the Energy Transition," *New Political Economy* 27, no. 1 (2021): 146–159.

138. Christophers, "Fossilised Capital," 2.

139. Mekala Krishnan, Hamid Samandari, Jonathan Woetzel, et al., *The Net-Zero Transition: What It Would Cost, What It Could Bring* (New York: McKinsey Global Institute, 2022), 20.

140. IEA, *WEO 2022*, 23.

141. Maria Sharmina, Oreane Y. Edelenbosch, Charlie Wilson, et al., "Decarbonizing the Critical Sectors of Aviation, Shipping, Road Freight and Industry to Limit Warming to 1.5–2C," *Climate Policy* 21, no. 4 (2021): 455–474.

142. IEA, *Net Zero by 2050*, 96–97.

143. Adrian Odenweller, Falko Ueckerdt, Gregory Nemet, et al., "Probabilistic Feasibility Space of Scaling Up Green Hydrogen," *Nature Energy* 7 (2023): 854–865.

144. Odenweller et al., "Probabilistic Feasibility Space of Scaling Up Green Hydrogen," 861.

145. Quoted in Nathalie Thomas, David Sheppard, and Neil Hume, "The Race to Scale Up Green Hydrogen," *Financial Times*, March 7, 2021, https://www.ft .com/content/7eac54ee-f1d1-4ebc-9573-b52f87d00240?desktop=true&segmentId =d8d3e364-5197-20eb-17cf-2437841d178a#myft:notification:instant-email:content.

146. Smil, *How the World Really Works*, 5.

147. IEA, *The Role of Critical Metals in Clean Energy Transitions* (Paris: IEA, 2022), 8–9.

148. Christos Zografos and Paul Robbins, "Green Sacrifice Zones, or Why Green New Deals Cannot Ignore the Cost Shifts of Just Transitions," *One Earth* 3 (2020): 543–547.

149. IEA, *Role of Critical Metals in Clean Energy Transitions*, 11.

150. IEA, *Role of Critical Metals in Clean Energy Transitions*, 129.

151. IEA, *Role of Critical Metals in Clean Energy Transitions*.

152. Greg Calloway, Cherry Ding, Tim Fitzgibbon, et al., "Could Supply-Chain Issues Derail the Energy Transition?" *McKinsey and Company*, December 5, 2022, https://www.mckinsey.com/industries/oil-and-gas/our-insights/could-supply-chain -issues-derail-the-energy-transition.

153. Smil, *How the World Really Works*.

154. Eric Larson, Chris Geig, Jesse Jenkins, et al., *Net Zero America: Potential Pathways, Infrastructure, and Impacts, Final Report Summary* (Princeton, NJ: Princeton University, 2021), 56.

155. Quoted in Andreas Malm, and The Zetkin Collective, *White Skin, Black Fuel: On the Danger of Fossil Fascism* (London: Verso, 2021), 86.

156. Nichola Groom, "Special Report: US Solar Expansion Stalled by Rural Land-Use Protests," *Reuters*, April 7, 2022, https://www.reuters.com/world/us/us-solar-expan sion-stalled-by-rural-land-use-protests-2022-04-07/.

157. Adam Tooze, "Europe's Decarbonization Challenge," *Social Europe*, March 22, 2021, https://www.socialeurope.eu/europes-decarbonisation-challenge-wir-schaffen -das.

158. Kate Abnett, "EU Plans One-Year Renewable Energy Permits for Faster Green Shift," *Reuters*, May 9, 2022, https://www.reuters.com/business/sustainable-business /eu-plans-one-year-renewable-energy-permits-faster-green-shift-2022-05-09/.

159. Brockway et al., "Final Stage Energy Return."

160. David Murphy, Marco Raugei, Michael Carbakales-Dale, et al., "Energy Return on Investment of Major Energy Carriers: Review and Harmonization," *Sustainability* 14 (2022): 1–20.

161. Carlos de Castro and Inigo Capellán-Peréz, "Standard, Point of Use, and Extended Energy Return on Energy Invested," *Energies* 13 (2020): 1–42.

162. de Castro and Capellán-Peréz, "Standard, Point of Use, and Extended Energy Return," 10–11. Also discussed in Albert, "The Global Politics of the Renewable Energy Transition."

163. Capellán-Peréz et al., "Dynamic Energy Return."

164. Capellán-Peréz et al., "Dynamic Energy Return."

165. Isabel Schnabel, "A New Age of Energy Inflation: Climateflation, Fossilflation and Greenflation," *Speech at The ECB and Its Watchers XXII Conference*, March 17, 2022, https://www.ecb.europa.eu/press/key/date/2022/html/ecb.sp220317_2~dbb3582f0a .en.html.

166. Capellán-Peréz et al., "Dynamic Energy Return"; Jackson and Jackson, "Modelling Energy Transition Risk"; Lewis King and Jeroen C. J. M. van den Bergh, "Implications of Net Energy-Return-On-Investment for a Low-Carbon Energy Transition," *Nature Energy* 3 (2018): 334–340; Ruchir Sharma, "'Greenflation' Threatens to Derail Climate Change Action," *Financial Times*, August 1, 2021, https://www.ft.com/content /49c19d8f-c3c3-4450-b869-50c7126076ee; Alojsa Slamersak, Giorgos Kallis, and Daniel O'Neill, "Energy Requirements and Carbon Emissions for a Low-Carbon Energy Transition," *Nature Communications* 13, no. 6932 (2022): 1–15.

167. King and van den Bergh, "Implications of Net Energy"; Louis Delannoy, Pierre-Yves Longaretti, David Murphy, et al., "Peak Oil and the Low-Carbon Energy Transition: A Net Energy Perspective," *Applied Energy* 304 (2021): 1–17.

168. IEA, *WEO 2022*, 116–117.

169. Food and Agriculture Organization (FAO), *The State of Food Security and Nutrition in the World* (Rome: FAO, 2022).

170. Emiko Terazono and Valentina Romei, "War and Adverse Weather Set to Keep Food Prices High," *Financial Times*, December 4, 2022, https://www.ft.com/content /8fa961a0-1d21-45f6-b15e-3fdc8e16c093.

171. FAO, *State of Food Security*, xv.

172. Hannah Ritche, "How Much of Global Greenhouse Gas Emissions Come from Food?" *Our World in Data*, 2021, accessed February 20, 2022, https://ourworldindata .org/greenhouse-gas-emissions-food.

173. John Foley, "Can We Feed the World and Sustain the Plant?," *Scientific American*, November 2011, https://web.mit.edu/12.000/www/m2019/pdfs/Foley_2011 _ScientificAmerican.pdf.

174. Jason Rohr, Christopher B. Barrett, David J. Civitello, et al., "Emerging Human Infectious Disease and the Links to Global Food Production," *Nature Sustainability* 2 (2019): 445–456.

175. Rob Wallace, *Big Farms Make Big Flu* (New York: Monthly Review Press, 2016).

176. Lester Brown, *Full Planet, Empty Plates: The New Geopolitics of Food Scarcity* (Washington, DC: Earth Policy Institute, 2012); FAO, *The Future of Food and Agriculture: Alternative Pathways to 2050* (Rome: FAO, 2018).

177. Brown, *Full Planet*, 60.

178. FAO, *Future of Food*, 27.

179. Haroon Akram-Lodhi, "The Ties That Bind? Agroecology and the Agrarian Question in the Twenty-First Century," *Journal of Peasant Studies* 48, no. 4 (2021): 693.

180. Philip McMichael, *Food Regimes and Agrarian Questions: Agrarian Change & Peasant Studies* (Halifax: Fernwood Publishing, 2013).

181. IPCC, "Global Warming of 1.5 C," 236.

182. FAO, *Future of Food*.

183. IPCC, "Global Warming of 1.5 C," 237.

184. Curtis Deutsch, Joshua Tewksbury, Michelle Tigchelaar, et al., "Increase in Crop Losses to Insects in a Warming Climate," *Science* 361, no. 6405 (2018): 916–919.

185. John Lienhard, Madramootoo Chandrea, Moniar Erwan, et al., "Climate Change, Agriculture, Water, and Food Security: What We Know, and What We Don't Know," Report of a workshop conducted at the Massachusetts Institute of Technology, May 8–9, 2018, https://jwafs.mit.edu/sites/default/files/imce/publications/Climate_Ag_Report_New.pdf.

186. Monica Caparas, Zachary Zobel, Andrea Castanho, et al., "Increasing Risks of Crop Failure and Water Scarcity in Global Breadbaskets by 2030," *Environmental Research Letters* 16 (2021): 1–13.

187. Anthony Janetos, Christopher Justice, Molly Jahn, et al., *The Risk of Multiple Breadbasket Failures in the 21st Century: A Science Research Agenda* (Boston: Boston University/Pardee Center Research Report, 2017), 5.

188. Caparas et al., "Increasing Risks of Crop Failure."

189. Caparas et al., "Increasing Risks of Crop Failure."

190. Akram-Lodhi, "The Ties That Bind"; Ian Scoones, Rebecca Smalley, Ruth Hall, et al., "Narratives of Scarcity: Framing the Global Land Rush," *Geoforum* 101 (2019): 231–241; Marcus Taylor, "Climate-Smart Agriculture: What Is It Food For?" *Journal of Peasant Studies* 45, no. 1 (2018): 89–107.

191. Klaus Schwab, *The Fourth Industrial Revolution* (New York: Currency, 2017), 1.

192. William Robinson, "Global Capitalism Post-Pandemic," *Race & Class* 62, no. 2 (2020): 3–13.

193. Peter Dauvergne, *AI in the Wild: Sustainability in the Age of Artificial Intelligence* (Cambridge, MA: MIT Press, 2020); Gavin Bade, "'A Sea Change': Biden Reverses Decades of Chinese Trade Policy," *Politico*, December 26, 2022, https://www.politico.com/news/2022/12/26/china-trade-tech-00072232.

194. I expand on this point in Michael Albert, "The Dangers of Decoupling: Earth System Crisis and the 'Fourth Industrial Revolution,'" *Global Policy* 11, no. 2 (2020): 245–254.

195. Kate Crawford, *Atlas of AI: Power, Politics, and the Planetary Costs of Artificial Intelligence* (New Haven, CT: Yale University Press, 2021), 42.

196. E. G. Mohamed Kande and Murat Sonmez, "Don't Fear AI: It Will Lead to Long-Term Job Growth," *World Economic Forum*, October 26, 2020, https://www.weforum.org/agenda/2020/10/dont-fear-ai-it-will-lead-to-long-term-job-growth/.

197. Daniel Susskind, *A World without Work: Technology, Automation, and How We Should Respond* (New York: Metropolitan Books, 2020), 4.

198. Kai-Fu Lee, *AI Superpowers: China, Silicon Valley, and the New World Order* (Boston: HM Harcourt, 2018), 164.

199. Cornelia Daheim and Ole Wintermann, "2050: The Future of Work," *Bertelsmann Stiftung*, 2016, accessed January 28, 2023, https://www.bertelsmann-stiftung.de/fileadmin/files/BSt/Publikationen/GrauePublikationen/BST_Delphi_E_03lay.pdf.

200. Susskind, *World without Work*, 127–129.

201. Lee, *AI Superpowers*, 20–21.

202. Dyer-Witheford et al., *Inhuman Power*.

203. Daniel Deudney, *Bounding Power: Republican Security from the Polis to the Global Village* (Princeton, NJ: Princeton University Press, 2007).

204. Deudney, *Bounding Power*; see also Gabriella Blum and Benjamin Wittes, *The Future of Violence: Robots and Germs, Hackers and Drones: Confronting a New Age of Threat* (New York: Basic Books, 2015); Audrey Cronin, *Power to the People: How Open Technological Innovation Is Arming Tomorrow's Terrorists* (Oxford: Oxford University Press); Albert, "Dangers of Decoupling."

205. Kolja Brockman, Sibylle Bauer, and Vincent Boulanin, *Bio Plus X: Arms Control and the Convergence of Biology and Emerging Technologies* (Stockholm: Stockholm International Peace Research Institute, 2019).

206. Amy Webb and Andrew Hessel, *The Genesis Machine: Our Quest to Rewrite Life in the Age of Synthetic Biology* (New York: Public Affairs, 2022), 92.

207. National Academies of Sciences, *A Proposed Framework for Identifying Potential Biodefense Vulnerabilities Posed by Synthetic Biology: Interim Report* (Washington, DC: The National Academies Press, 2017), 7–8.

208. National Academies of Sciences, *A Proposed Framework*.

209. Jesse Kirkpatrick, Gregory Koblentz, Megan Palmer, et al., *Editing Biosecurity: Needs and Strategies for Governing Genome Editing* (Fairfax, VA: George Mason University, 2018), 54.

210. Filippa Lentzos, "Ignore Bill Gates: Where Bioweapons Focus Really Belongs," *Bulletin of the Atomic Scientists*, July 3, 2017, https://thebulletin.org/2017/07/ignore-bill-gates-where-bioweapons-focus-really-belongs/.

211. NAS, *Biodefense in the Age of Synthetic Biology* (Washington, DC: The National Academies Press, 2018), 18–19.

212. Gaymon Bennett, Nils Gilman, Anthony Stavrianakis, et al., "From Synthetic Biology to Biohacking: Are We Prepared?" *Nature Biotechnology* 27, no. 12 (2009): 1110.

213. Statista, "Internet of Things (IOT) and Non-IOT Active Device Connections Worldwide from 2010 to 2025," *Statista*, September 6, 2020, https://www.statista .com/statistics/1101442/iot-number-of-connected-devices-worldwide/.

214. Seyom Brown, "The New Nuclear MADness," *Survival* 62, no. 1 (2020): 63–88; James Johnson, "Artificial Intelligence: A Threat to Strategic Stability," *Strategic Studies Quarterly* 14, no. 1 (2020): 16–40.

215. Cronin, *Power to the People*, 211–222.

216. Trevor Johnston, Troy Smith, and Luke Irwin, *Additive Manufacturing in 2040: Powerful Enabler, Disruptive Threat* (Los Angeles: RAND Corporation, 2018), 2.

217. Albert, "Dangers of Decoupling."

218. Steven Feldstein, *The Global Expansion of AI Surveillance* (Washington, DC: Carnegie Endowment for International Peace, 2019); Darren Byler, *In the Camps: China's High-Tech Penal Colony* (New York: Columbia Global Reports, 2021).

219. Crawford, *Atlas of AI*, 153.

220. Will Douglas Heaven, "Predictive Policing Algorithms Are Racist. They Need to Be Dismantled," *MIT Technology Review*, July 1, 2020, https://www.technologyreview .com/2020/07/17/1005396/predictive-policing-algorithms-racist-dismantled -machine-learning-bias-criminal-justice/.

221. Heaven, "Predictive Policing Algorithms Are Racist."

222. Byler, *In the Camps*, 31–34, 55–56.

223. Feldstein, *Global Expansion of AI*; Shoshana Zuboff, *The Age of Surveillance Capitalism: The Fight for a Human Future at the New Frontier of Power* (New York: Public Affairs Books, 2019); Ronald Deibert, *Reset: Reclaiming the Internet for Civil Society* (Toronto: House of Anansi Press, 2020); Catherine Besteman, *Militarized Global Apartheid* (Durham, NC: Duke University Press, 2020).

224. Luke Kemp, Laura Adam, Christian Boehm, et al., "Bioengineering Horizon Scan 2020," *eLife*, May 29, 2020, https://www.ncbi.nlm.nih.gov/pmc/articles/PMC72 59952/.

225. Matthew Adams, *Ecological Crisis, Sustainability and the Psychosocial Subject: Beyond Behavior Change* (London: Palgrave Macmillan, 2016).

226. Anne Case and Angus Deaton, *Deaths of Despair and the Future of Capitalism* (Princeton, NJ: Princeton University Press, 2020), 40; Marina Marcus, M. Taghi Yasamy, Mark van Ommeren, et al., *Depression: A Global Crisis* (Geneva: World Health Organization, 2012).

227. Ruth Wodak, *The Politics of Fear: What Right-Wing Populist Discourses Mean* (London: Sage Publications).

228. Michael Kimmel, "Globalization and Its Mal(e)contents: The Gendered Moral and Political Economy of Terrorism," *International Sociology* 18, no. 3 (2003): 603–620.

229. Cara Daggett, "Petro-Masculinity: Fossil Fuels and Authoritarian Desire," *Millennium: Journal of International Studies* 47, no. 1 (2018): 25–44.

230. Wodak, *Politics of Fear*, 2.

231. Wodak, *Politics of Fear*, 35–36.

232. Sophia Siddiqui, "Racing the Nation: Towards a Theory of Reproductive Racism," *Race & Class* 63, no. 2 (2021): 3–20.

233. Malm and the Zetkin Collective, *White Skin, Black Fuel*, 171–175.

234. Albena Azmanova, *Capitalism on Edge: How Fighting Precarity Can Achieve Radical Change without Crisis or Utopia* (New York: Columbia University Press, 2020), 177.

235. Robert Paxton, *The Anatomy of Fascism* (New York: Alfred A. Knopf, 2004), 218.

236. Paxton, *Anatomy of Fascism*, 41.

237. David Neiwert, *Alt-America: The Rise of the Radical Right in the Age of Trump* (Verso: London, 2017).

238. Angelos Varvarousis, "Crisis, Liminality and the Decolonization of the Imaginary," *Environment and Planning E: Nature and Space* 2, no. 3 (2019): 493–512.

239. Azmanova, *Capitalism on Edge*.

CHAPTER 2

1. Colonomos, *Selling the Future*, 9.

2. Bell, *Foundations of Futures Studies*, 182, 73.

3. Silke Beck and Martin Mahony, "The IPCC and the Politics of Anticipation," *Nature Climate Change* 7 (2017): 312; see also Becker, *Imagined Futures*.

4. Meadows et al., *Limits to Growth*.

5. Manuel Delanda, *Philosophy and Simulation: The Emergence of Synthetic Reason* (London: Continuum, 2011), 35.

6. Donella Meadows, Dennis Meadows, and Jurgen Randers, *The Limits to Growth: The Thirty Year Update* (White River Junction, VT: Chelsea Green, 2004), 3–4.

7. Meadows et al., *Limits to Growth*, 102.

8. Meadows et al., *Limits to Growth*, 89.

9. Meadows et al., *Limits to Growth*, 124–125.

10. Meadows et al., *Limits to Growth*, 126–127.

11. Meadows et al., *Limits to Growth*, 132–133.

12. Meadows et al., *Limits to Growth*, 160–163.

13. See discussion in Kerryn Higgs, *Collision Course: Infinite Growth on a Finite Planet* (Cambridge, MA: MIT Press, 2014), 258–261.

14. Meadows et al., *Thirty Year Update*, 51.

15. Tim Jackson and Robin Webster, "Limits Revisited: A Review of the Limits to Growth Debate," *All-Party Parliamentary Group on Limits to Growth*, 2016, accessed January 28, 2023, http://limits2growth.org.uk/revisited/.

16. Jackson and Webster, "Limits Revisited"; Gaya Herrington, "Update to Limits to Growth: Comparing the World3 Model with Empirical Data," *Journal of Industrial Ecology* 25, no. 3 (2021): 614–626.

17. Lisette van Beek, Maarten Hajer, Peter Pelzer, et al., "Anticipating Futures through Models: The Rise of Integrated Assessment Modelling in the Climate Science-Policy Interface since 1970," *Global Environmental Change* 65 (2020): 1–14; William Nordhaus, "Projections and Uncertainties about Climate Change in an Era of Minimal Climate Policies," *American Economic Journal: Economic Policy* 10, no. 3 (2018): 333–360.

18. Steve Keen, "The Appallingly Bad Neoclassical Economics of Climate Change," *Globalizations* 18, no. 7 (2021): 1149–1177.

19. IPCC, *Global Warming of 1.5C*, 100.

20. Beck and Mahony, "IPCC and Politics."

21. Brian O'Neill, Timothy R. Carter, Kristie Ebi, et al., "Achievements and Needs for the Climate Change Scenario Framework," *Nature Climate Change* 10 (2020): 1074–1084.

22. Riahi et al., "Shared Socioeconomic Pathways."

23. Riahi et al., "Shared Socioeconomic Pathways," 158–159.

24. Riahi et al., "Shared Socioeconomic Pathways."

25. Riahi et al., "Shared Socioeconomic Pathways."

26. O'Neill et al., "Roads Ahead," 173–174.

27. O'Neill et al., "Roads Ahead," 174.

28. Riahi et al., "Shared Socioeconomic Pathways," 158–159.

29. Riahi et al., "Shared Socioeconomic Pathways," 155.

30. Inigo Capellán-Peréz, Ignacio de Blas, Jaime Nieto, et al., "MEDEAS: A New Modeling Framework Integrating Global Biophysical and Socioeconomic Constraints," *Royal Society of Chemistry* 13 (2020): 1000–1001.

31. Capellán-Peréz et al., "MEDEAS."

32. IPCC, *Global Warming of 1.5C*, 108–109.

33. Patrick McCully, Lara Cuvelier, Alix Mazounie, et al., "It's not What You Say, It's What You Do: Making the Finance Sector's Net Zero Alliances Work for the Climate," *Reclaim Finance*, November 2021, https://reclaimfinance.org/site/wp-content/uploads/2021/11/FINAL_GFANZ_Report_02_11_21.pdf.

34. Lukas Braunreiter, Lisette van Beek, Maarten Hajer, et al., "Transformative Pathways—Using Integrated Assessment Models More Effectively to Open Up Plausible and Desirable Low-Carbon Futures," *Energy Research & Social Science* 80 (2021): 3.

35. Capellán-Peréz et al., "MEDEAS."

36. Capellán-Peréz et al., "MEDEAS."

37. Capellán-Peréz et al., "MEDEAS"; Keen, "Appallingly Bad Neoclassical Economics."

38. Braunreiter et al., "Transformative Pathways."

39. Malm and the Zetkin Collective, *White Skin, Black Fuel*, xii.

40. Patrick Bolton, Morgan Despres, and Luis Da Silva, *The Green Swan: Central Banking and Financial Stability in the Age of Climate Change* (Basel: Bank of International Settlements, 2020), 10.

41. Bolton et al., *Green Swan*, 23.

42. Bolton et al., *Green Swan*, 26–29.

43. Bell, *Foundations of Futures Studies*, 32.

44. Shell, "40 Years of Shell Scenarios," 2013, accessed June 7, 2023, https://www .shell.com/energy-and-innovation/the-energy-future/scenarios/what-are-the -previous-shell-scenarios/new-lenses-on-the-future/earlier-scenarios/_jcr_content /root/main/section_2095191679/promo/links/item0.stream/1652289755448/a0e75f 042fee5322b72780ee36e5ba17c35a4fc6/shell-scenarios-40yearsbook080213.pdf.

45. K. Campbell, J. Gulledge, J. R. McNeill, et al., *The Age of Consequences: The Foreign Policy and National Security Implications of Global Climate Change* (Washington, DC: Center for a New American Security, 2007), 6.

46. NIC (National Intelligence Council), *Global Trends 2040: A More Contested World* (Washington, DC: National Intelligence Council, 2022), v.

47. NIC, *Global Trends 2040*, v–vi.

48. NIC, *Global Trends 2040*, 110.

49. NIC, *Global Trends 2040*, 111.

50. NIC, *Global Trends 2040*, 113.

51. NIC, *Global Trends 2040*, 114–115.

52. NIC, *Global Trends 2040*, 116.

53. NIC, *Global Trends 2040*.

54. NIC, *Global Trends 2040*, 118.

55. NIC, *Global Trends 2040*, 119.

56. For example, Alexander Cooley and Daniel Nexon, *Exit from Hegemony: The Unravelling of the American Global Order* (Oxford: Oxford University Press, 2020).

57. Quoted in Patrick O'Neill, "Meet the NSA Spies Shaping the Future," *MIT Technology Review*, February 1, 2022, https://www.technologyreview.com/2022/02/01 /1044561/meet-the-nsa-spies-shaping-the-future/.

58. Colonomos, *Selling the Future*, 50.

59. NIC, *Global Trends 2040*, 111.

60. Thomas Ansell and Steve Cayzer, "Limits to Growth Redux: A System Dynamics Model for Assessing Energy and Climate Change Constraints to Global Growth," *Energy Policy* 120 (2018): 514–525.

61. Anna Zalik, "Oil 'Futures': Shell's Scenarios and the Social Constitution of the Global Oil Market," *Geoforum* 41 (2010): 553–564.

62. Nafeez Ahmed, Ben Hayes, and Nick Buxton, "A Permanent State of Emergency: Civil Contingencies, Risk Management and Human Rights," in *The Secure and the Dispossessed: How the Military and Corporations Are Shaping a Climate-Changed World*, ed. Buxton and Hayes (London: Pluto Press, 2015), 87–110.

63. Azmanova, *Capitalism on Edge*, 37.

64. For example, Robert Cox, "Social Forces, States and World Orders: Beyond International Relations Theory," *Millenium: Journal of International Studies* 10, no. 2 (1982): 126–155.

65. Urry, *What Is the Future*, 3–4.

66. Wallerstein, "Structural Crisis," 37.

67. Wallerstein, *World-Systems Analysis*, 87–88.

68. Wolfgang Streeck, *How Will Capitalism End? Essays on a Failing System* (London: Verso, 2017), 13–14.

69. Harvey, *Seventeen Contradictions*, 220.

70. Mann and Wainwright, *Climate Leviathan*, 130, 134.

71. Mann and Wainwright, *Climate Leviathan*, 133.

72. Mann and Wainwright, *Climate Leviathan*, 151.

73. Mann and Wainwright, *Climate Leviathan*, 125.

74. Mann and Wainwright, *Climate Leviathan*, 148.

75. Mann and Wainwright, *Climate Leviathan*, 30.

76. Mann and Wainwright, *Climate Leviathan*, 31.

77. Mann and Wainwright, *Climate Leviathan*, 151–152.

78. Mann and Wainwright, *Climate Leviathan*, 38–39.

79. Mann and Wainwright, *Climate Leviathan*, 44–45.

80. Mann and Wainwright, *Climate Leviathan*, 176.

81. Mann and Wainwright, *Climate Leviathan*, 30.

82. Mann and Wainwright, *Climate Leviathan*, 25–26.

83. For example, Murphy and Hall, "Energy Return"; Ahmed, "Failing States."

84. Wright, *Envisioning Real Utopias*, 6.

85. Mann and Wainwright, *Climate Leviathan*, 194.

86. van Vuuren et al., "Scenarios in Global Environmental Assessments."

87. Raskin, *Journey to Earthland*, 23.

88. Raskin, *Journey to Earthland*, 26.

89. Raskin, *Journey to Earthland*, 42–43.

90. Raskin, *Journey to Earthland*, 27.

91. Raskin, *Journey to Earthland*, 49.

92. Raskin, *Journey to Earthland*, 73.

93. Raskin, *Journey to Earthland*, 74.

94. Raskin, *Journey to Earthland*, 84.

95. Raskin, *Journey to Earthland*, 101–104.

96. Raskin, *Journey to Earthland*, 29.

97. Newell and Paterson, *Climate Capitalism*; Malm and the Zetkin Collective, *White Skin, Black Fuel*; Peter Frase, *Four Futures: Life After Capitalism* (London: Verso, 2016); Heikki Patomaki, *The Political Economy of Global Security* (London: Routledge, 2008); Holly Jean Buck, *After Geoengineering: Climate Tragedy, Repair, and Restoration* (London: Verso, 2018).

CHAPTER 3

1. Bell, *Foundations of Futures Studies*, 81.

2. Quoted in Brondizio et al., "Re-Conceptualizing the Anthropocene," 322.

3. Quoted in Flaherty, *Complexity and Resilience*, 3.

4. Flaherty, *Complexity and Resilience*; Swilling, *Age of Susstainability*; Scheffer, *Critical Transitions*; Prigogine and Stengers, *Order Out of Chaos*; Delanda, *Intensive Science*; Williams, *Political Hegemony*; Cudworth and Hobden, *Posthuman International Relations*.

5. Raskin, *Journey to Earthland*, 45.

6. Cudworth and Hobden, *Posthuman International Relations*.

7. Delanda, *Intensive Science*, 5.

8. Meadows et al., *Limits to Growth*.

9. Delanda, *Assemblage Theory*, 119–120.

10. Delanda, *Assemblage Theory*, 120.

11. Steven Bernstein and Matthew Hoffman, "Climate politics, metaphors and the fractal carbon trap," *Nature Climate Change* 9 (2019), 919.

12. Scheffer, *Critical Transitions*.

13. Albert, "COVID-19 and Planetary Crisis."

14. Wallerstein, "Structural Crisis"; Williams, *Political Hegemony*, 138.

15. Levi Bryant, *Onto-Cartography: An Ontology of Machines and Media* (Edinburgh: Edinburgh University Press, 2014).

16. Williams, *Political Hegemony*, 58–59. See also Albert, "COVID-19 and Planetary Crisis."

17. Williams, *Political Hegemony*.

18. Byrne and Callaghan, *Complexity Theory*, 45.

19. Wallerstein, *World-Systems Analysis*, 24.

20. Jessop, *State Power*, 31.

21. Wright, *Envisioning Real Utopias*, 126.

22. Andreas Malm, *How to Blow Up a Pipeline* (London: Verso, 2021), 68.

23. Wallerstein, *World-Systems Analysis*.

24. Dorninger et al., "Ecologically Unequal Exchange"; Jason Hickel, Christian Dorninger, Hanspeter Wieland, et al., "Imperialist Appropriation in the World Economy: Drain from the Global South through Unequal Exchange, 1990–2015," *Global Environmental Change* 73 (2022): 1–13.

25. Alf Hornborg, "Zero-Sum World: Challenges in Conceptualizing Environmental Load Displacement and Ecologically Unequal Exchange in the World-System," *International Journal of Comparative Sociology* 50, nos. 3–4 (2009): 237–262; Robert Biel, *The Entropy of Capitalism* (Boston: Brill, 2012); Moore, *Capitalism in the Web of Life*.

26. Christopher Chase-Dunn and Thomas Hall, *Rise and Demise: Comparing World-Systems* (London: Routledge, 1997).

27. Neil Smith, *Uneven Development: Nature, Capital, and the Production of Space* (Athens: University of Georgia Press, 2008), 6–7.

28. Bob Jessop, *The Capitalist State: Marxist Theories and Methods* (Oxford: Martin Robertson, 1982), 168.

29. Robyn Eckersley, *The Green State: Rethinking Democracy and Sovereignty* (Cambridge, MA: MIT Press, 2004).

30. Jessop, *State Power*.

31. Bryant, *Onto-Cartography*, 265.

32. Morin, *Homeland Earth*, 131.

33. The distinction between the socioecological, violence, and existential problematics is inspired in part by the work of Kojin Karatani, who identifies three primary "modes of exchange" that structure world history: economic exchange, the exchange of protection, and the exchange of community/belonging. It is also influenced by Michael Mann's work on the sources of social power—particularly economic, military, and ideological power. See Kojin Karatani, *The Structure of World History: From Modes of Production to Modes of Exchange* (Durham, NC: Duke University Press, 2015); Michael Mann, *The Sources of Social Power: Volume 4: Globalizations, 1945–2011* (Cambridge, UK: Cambridge University Press, 2013).

34. Karatani, *Structure of World History*, 224.

35. Fraser and Jaeggi, *Capitalism*.

36. Homer-Dixon et al., "Synchronous Failure."

37. Williams, *Political Hegemony*, 152.

38. Wallerstein, *Modern World-System*; Moore, *Capitalism in the Web*.

39. Beverly Silver and Corey Payne, "Crises of World Hegemony and the Speeding Up of Social History," in *Hegemony in World Politics: Reimagining Power in Global Politics*, ed. Jan Aart Scholte and Tom Casier (Abingdon, UK: Routledge, 2020), 18.

40. Moore, *Capitalism in the Web*, 1.

41. Jairus Banaji, *Theory as History: Essays on Modes of Production and Exploitation* (Chicago: Brill, 2010).

42. Malm, *Fossil Capital*.

43. Elliot Diringer and Bob Perciasepe, "The Climate Awakening of Global Capital," *Bulletin of the Atomic Scientists* 76, no. 5 (2020) 233–237.

44. Reclaim Finance, "Throwing Fuel on the Fire: GFANZ Members Provide Billions in Finance for Fossil Fuel Expansion," *Reclaim Finance*, January 17, 2023, https://reclaimfinance.org/site/en/2023/01/17/throwing-fuel-on-the-fire-gfanz-members-provide-billions-in-finance-for-fossil-fuel-expansion/.

45. K. Surprise and J. P. Sapinski, "Whose Climate Intervention? Solar Geoengineering, Fractions of Capital, and Hegemonic Strategy," *Capital & Class* (2022): 10–11, https://doi.org/10.1177/03098168221114386. Emphasis original.

46. Srnicek and Williams, *Inventing the Future*; Frase, *Four Futures*; Matthew Huber, "Ecosocialism: Dystopian and Scientific," *Socialist Forum*, 2019, accessed November 28, 2022, https://socialistforum.dsausa.org/issues/winter-2019/ecosocialism-dystopian-and-scientific/.

47. Jason Hickel, *Less Is More: How Degrowth Will Save the World* (London: Windmill, 2020); Giorgos Kallis, Susan Paulson, Giacomo D'Alisa, et al., *The Case for Degrowth* (Cambridge, UK: Polity Press, 2020), Max Ajl, *A People's Green New Deal* (London: Pluto Press, 2021); Arturo Escobar, *Pluriversal Politics: The Real and the Possible* (Durham, NC: Duke University Press, 2020).

48. Huber, "Ecosocialism: Dystopian and Scientific."

49. Keith Krause and Michael Williams, eds., *Critical Security Studies: Concepts and Cases* (London: University College London Press, 1997); Deudney, *Bounding Power*.

50. For example, Thomas Szayna, Angela O'Mahony, Jennifer Kavanagh, et al., *Conflict Trends and Conflict Drivers: An Empirical Assessment of Historical Conflict Patterns and Future Conflict Projections* (Santa Monica, CA: RAND Corporation, 2017).

51. Willem de Haan, "Violence as an Essentially Contested Concept," in *Violence in Europe*, ed. Sophie Body-Gendrot and Pieter Spierenburg (Cham: Springer, 2009), 28.

52. Michael Williams, "Global Security Assemblages," in *Routledge Handbook of Private Security Studies*, ed. Rita Abrahamsen and Anna Leander (London: Routledge, 2016), 131–132.

53. The quote is from Mark Neocleous, *War Power, Police Power* (Edinburgh: Edinburgh University Press, 2012), 12; emphasis original. See also Caroline Holmqvist, Jan Bachman, Colleen Bell, et al., "Assemblages of War: Police: An Introduction," in *War, Police and Assemblages of Intervention*, ed. Jan Bachman, Colleen Bell, and Caroline Holmqvist (London: Routledge, 2015), 1–14.

54. Didier Bigo, "Internal and External Aspects of Security," *European Security* 15, no. 4 (2006): 385–404.

55. Giuseppe Zappala, "Killing by Metadata: Europe and the Surveillance-Targeted Killing Nexus," *Global Affairs* 1, no. 3 (2015): 251–258.

56. Williams, "Global Security Assemblages"; Crawford, *Atlas of AI*.

57. Williams, "Global Security Assemblages."

58. Besteman, *Militarized Global Apartheid*, 19.

59. Besteman, *Militarized Global Apartheid*, 120.

60. Besteman, *Militarized Global Apartheid*, 120–121.

61. William Robinson, *The Global Police State* (London: Pluto Press, 2020), 3.

62. Robinson, *Global Police State*, 72.

63. Andreas Bieler and Adam Morton, *Global Capitalism, Global War, Global Crisis* (Cambridge, UK: Cambridge University Press, 2018), 194.

64. Bob Jessop, *State Theory: Putting the Capitalist State in Its Place* (Cambridge, UK: Polity Press, 1990).

65. Bigo, "Internal and External."

66. Peter Phillips, *Giants: The Global Power Elite* (New York: Seven Stories Press. 2018), 91.

67. Jessop, *State Theory*, 336.

68. George Rigakos, *Security/Capital: A General Theory of Pacification* (Edinburgh: Edinburgh University Press, 2016), 99.

69. Angela Davis, *Are Prisons Obsolete?* (New York: Seven Stories Press, 2003); Ruth Gilmore Wilson, *Abolition Geography: Essays Towards Liberation* (London: Verso, 2022).

70. Adam Elliot-Cooper, *Black Resistance to British Policing* (Manchester, UK: Manchester University Press, 2021), 5.

71. Elliot-Cooper, *Black Resistance to British Policing*, 141; see also Movement 4 Black Lives (M4BL), "2020 Policy Platform," 2021, accessed December 4, 2021, https://m4bl.org/policy-platforms/.

72. Arun Kundnani, "Abolish National Security," *Transnational Institute*, May 2021, https://longreads.tni.org/stateofpower/abolish-national-security.

73. Rigakos, *Security/Capital*, 121–122.

74. Stephen Wertheim, "Responses to Aziz Rana," *Dissent Magazine*, Summer 2022, https://www.dissentmagazine.org/article/responses-to-aziz-rana.

75. The Economist, "As Violent Crime Leaps, Liberal Cities Rethink Cutting Police Budgets," *The Economist*, January 15, 2022, https://www.economist.com/united-states/2022/01/15/as-violent-crime-leaps-liberal-cities-rethink-cutting-police-budgets.

76. Mann, *Sources of Social Power*, 1–2.

77. Williams, *Political Hegemony*, 165–166.

78. Althusser, *On the Reproduction*.

79. Thomas Homer-Dixon, Jonathan Leader Maynard, Matto Mildenberger, et al., "A Complex Systems Approach to the Study of Ideology: Cognitive-Affective Structures and the Dynamics of Belief Systems," *Journal of Social and Political Psychology* 1, no. 1 (2013): 337–363.

80. Ashley Bohrer, *Marxism and Intersectionality: Race, Gender, Class and Sexuality under Contemporary Capitalism* (New York: Columbia University Press, 2019), 247.

81. Anievas and Nisancioglu, *How the West*, 123; see also Barry Buzan and George Lawson, *The Global Transformation: History, Modernity, and the Making of International Relations* (Cambridge, UK: Cambridge University Press, 2015).

82. Cedric Robinson, *Black Marxism: The Making of the Black Radical Tradition* (Chapel Hill: University of North Carolina Press, 2000).

83. Sylvia Wynter, "Unsettling the Coloniality of Being/Power/Truth/Freedom: Towards the Human, After Man, Its Overrepresentation—An Argument," *New Centennial Review* 3, no. 3 (2003): 257–337; Escobar, *Pluriversal Politics*; Arrihi, *Long Twentieth Century*.

84. Wynter, "Unsettling the Coloniality"; Buzan and Lawson, *Global Transformation*.

85. Escobar, *Pluriversal Politics*.

86. Escobar, *Pluriversal Politics*; Audra Mitchell and Aadita Chaudhury, "Worlding beyond 'the' 'End' of 'the World': White Apocalyptic Visions and BIPOC Futurisms," *International Relations* 34, no. 3 (2020): 309–332.

87. Protevi and Bonta, *Deleuze and Geophilosophy*.

88. Srnicek and Williams, *Inventing the Future*, 14.

89. Bryant, *Onto-Cartography*, 259–266.

90. Patomaki, *Political Economy of Global Security*, 4.

91. Kathryn Yusoff and Jennifer Gabrys, "Climate Change and the Imagination," *WILEY Climate Change* 2, no. 4 (2011): 519.

92. Mann and Wainwright, *Climate Leviathan*, 134.

93. Swilling, *Age of Sustainability*; Flaherty, *Complexity and Resilience*.

CHAPTER 4

1. Homer-Dixon et al, "What Is a Polycrisis?"

2. Wallerstein, *Modern World-System*, 10.

3. Wunderling et al., "Interacting Tipping Elements."

4. Lynas, *Our Final Warning*, 161; Steffen et al., "Trajectories of the Earth"; Lenton et al., "Climate Tipping Points"; Duffy et al., "How Close to the Temperature Tipping Point."

5. Climate Action Tracker, "Warming Projections Global Update."

6. Trisos et al., "Projected Timing of Abrupt Ecological Disruption."

7. UNEP, *Preventing the Next Pandemic*; Colin Carlson, Gregory Albery, Cory Merow, et al., "Climate Change Increases Cross-Species Viral Transmission Risk," *Nature* 607 (2022): 555–562.

8. Morens and Fauci, "Emerging Pandemic Diseases."

9. IPCC, *Climate Change 2022: Mitigation of Climate Change. Contribution of Working Group III to the Sixth Assessment Report* (Cambridge, UK: Cambridge University Press, 2022), 22–23.

10. Malm and the Zetkin Collective, *White Skin, Black Fuel.*

11. This formation is also similar to what Mann and Wainwright call "climate behemoth." See Mann and Wainwright, *Climate Leviathan*, 44.

12. Michael Lowy, *Ecosocialism: A Radical Alternative to Capitalist Catastrophe* (Chicago: Haymarket Books, 2022); Angus, *Facing the Anthropocene*; Foster et al., *Ecological Rift.*

13. Faster rates of decarbonization are no doubt possible for individual countries, particularly for those who offshore some of their emissions. But for global capitalism *as a whole*, a speed limit of roughly 4% emissions reductions per year on average, sustained over decades, is a reasonable (though contestable) assumption. See Kallis and Hickel, "Is Green Growth Possible?"; Anderson and Bows, "Beyond 'Dangerous' Climate."

14. IEA, *WEO 2022*; Climate Action Tracker, "Warming Projections Global Update."

15. Bolton et al., *Green Swan.*

16. Bolton et al., *Green Swan*; see also Mahalingam et al., *Impacts of Severe Natural Catastrophes on Financial Markets* (Cambridge, UK: Cambridge Centre for Risk Studies, 2017).

17. Swiss Re Institute, *The Economics of Climate Change: No Action Not an Option* (Zurich: Swiss Re Institute, 2021), 12.

18. Jean-Francois Mercure, H. Pollitt, J. E. Vinuales, et al., "Macroeconomic Impact of Stranded Fossil Fuel Assets," *Nature Climate Change* 8 (2018): 588–593.

19. Network for Greening the Financial System (NGFS), "A Call for Action: Climate Change as a Source of Financial Risk," April 2019, https://www.ngfs.net/sites/default/files/medias/documents/synthese_ngfs-2019_-_17042019_0.pdf.

20. Bolton et al., *Green Swan*, 7.

21. Bolton et al., *Green Swan*, 18–19, italics added.

22. Streeck, *How Will Capitalism End?*

23. IEA, *WEO 2022*, 21.

24. IEA, *WEO 2022*, 239.

25. Kallis and Hickel, "Is Green Growth Possible?"; Parrique et al., *Decoupling Debunked*; Brockway et al., "Energy Efficiency"; Haberl et al., "Systematic Review." See also Gregor Semeniuk, Lance Taylor, Armon Rezai, et al., "Plausible Energy Demand Patterns in a Growing Global Economy with Climate Policy," *Nature Climate Change* 11 (2021): 313–318.

26. Brockway et al., "Estimation of Global Final-Stage Energy-Return."

27. Kjell Kuhne, Nils Bartsch, Ryan Tate, et al., "'Carbon Bombs'—Mapping Key Fossil Fuel Projects," *Energy Policy* 166 (2022): 1–10.

28. IEA, *WEO 2022*.

29. Lorenzo Rosa, Maria Rulli, Maria Kyle Davis, et al., "The Water-Energy Nexus of Hydraulic Fracturing: A Global Hydrologic Analysis for Shale Oil and Gas Extraction," *Earth's Future* 6 (2018): 745–756.

30. Rosa et al., "Water-Energy Nexus of Hydraulic Fracturing."

31. IEA, *Role of Critical Metals*, 127–128.

32. World Meteorological Organization (WMO), *2022 State of Climate Services: Energy* (Geneva: World Meteorological Organization, 2022).

33. Will Nichols and Rory Clisby, "40% of Oil and Gas Reserves Threatened by Climate Change," *Verisk Maplecroft*, December 16, 2021, https://www.maplecroft.com /insights/analysis/40-of-oil-and-gas-reserves-threatened-by-climate-change/.

34. WMO, *2022 State of Climate Services*, 5.

35. Anjana Ahuja, "Lazy Winds Could Blow Europe's Renewable Future Off Course," *Financial Times*, November 8, 2022, https://www.ft.com/content/a9a1ee0e-ad7e -416c-85b7-43f70ae44855.

36. As stated by Robert Gross, Quoted in Madeleine Cuff, "Extreme Weather Threat to Energy Security Is as Serious as Ukraine War," *New Scientist*, October 11, 2022, https://www.newscientist.com/article/2341877-extreme-weather-threat-to-energy -security-is-as-serious-as-ukraine-war/.

37. Bas van Ruijven, Enrica De Cian, and Ian Sue Wing, "Amplification of Future Energy Demand Growth Due to Climate Change," *Nature Communications* 10, no. 2762 (2019): 1–13; Francesco Pietro Colelli, Johannes Emmerling, Giacomo Marangoni, et al., "Increased Energy Use for Adaptation Significantly Impacts Mitigation Pathways," *Nature Communications* 13, no. 4964 (2021): 1–12.

38. Hanna et al., "Emergency Deployment of Direct Air Capture."

39. Lex, "Desalination: Worth Its Salt in an Increasingly Water-Scarce World," *Financial Times*, August 21, 2021, https://www.ft.com/content/3cacc3c1-523b-4aa4-80cc -481c2c8a405a.

40. Colelli et al., "Increased Energy Use for Adaptation"; Robert McSweeney, "How IS ARCTIC WARMING LINKED to the 'Polar Vortex' and Other Extreme Weather?," *Carbon Brief*, January 31, 2019, https://www.carbonbrief.org/qa-how-is-arctic-warming -linked-to-polar-vortext-other-extreme-weather/.

41. Lynas, *Our Final Warning*.

42. Thomas Chaloner, Sarah Gurr, and Daniel Bebber, "Plant Pathogen Infection Risk Tracks Global Crop Yields under Climate Change," *Nature Climate Change* 11 (2021): 710–715; Caparas et al., "Increasing Risks of Crop Failure"; Lynas, *Our Final Warning*, 140–142, 195–296.

43. Based on projections by Deutsch et al., "Increase in Crop Losses to Insects."

44. FAO, *Future of Food*.

45. Julian Cribb, *Food or War* (Cambridge, UK: Cambridge University Press, 2019), 78.

46. Willett et al., "Food Systems in the Anthropocene"; Marco Springmann, Michael Clark, Keith Wiebe, et al., "Options for Keeping the Food System within Environmental Limits," *Nature* 562 (2019): 519–525.

47. Scoones et al., "Narratives of Scarcity."

48. McMichael, *Food Regimes*; Moore, *Capitalism in the Web*.

49. McMichael, *Food Regimes*; Moore, *Capitalism in the Web*; Jennifer Clapp and Ryan Isakson, *Speculative Harvests: Financialization, Food & Agriculture* (Rugby: Practical Action, 2018).

50. Ajl, *People's Green New Deal*, 120–121; McMichael, *Food Regimes*, 46.

51. Clapp and Isakson, *Speculative Harvests*, 14.

52. Taylor, "Climate Smart Agriculture," 102.

53. Akram-Lodhi, "The Ties That Bind," 692.

54. Ajl, *People's Green New Deal*; Chris Smaje, *A Small Farm Future* (White River Junction, VT: Chelsea Green, 2020); Troy Vettese and Drew Pendergrass, *Half-Earth Socialism: A Plan to Save the Future from Climate Change, Extinction, and Pandemics* (London: Verso, 2022); Benjamin Bodirsky, David Chen, IIsabelle Weindl, et al., "Integrating Degrowth and Efficiency Perspectives Enables an Emissions-Neutral Food System by 2100," *Nature Food* 3 (2022): 341–348.

55. David Victor, Frank Geels, and Simon Sharpe, *Accelerating the Low Carbon Transition: The Case for Stronger, More Targeted and Coordinated International Action* (London: Energy Transitions Commission, 2019).

56. Moore, *Capitalism in the Web*; Bodirsky et al., "Integrating Degrowth and Efficiency."

57. Lynas, *Our Final Warning*, 142.

58. Homer-Dixon et al., "Synchronous Failure."

59. IEA, *Net Zero by 2050*; Oxfam, *Tightening the Net*.

60. Wallace, *Big Farms Make Big Flu*; Jennifer Clapp and William Moseley, "This Food Crisis Is Different: COVID-19 and the Fragility of the Neoliberal Food Security Order," *Journal of Peasant Studies* 47, no. 7 (2020): 1393–1417.

61. Daggett, "Petro-Masculinity," 29–32.

62. Malm and the Zetkin Collective, *White Skin, Black Fuel*, 275–276.

63. Malm and the Zetkin Collective, *White Skin, Black Fuel*, ix.

64. Adams, *Ecological Crisis*, 112.

65. Felix Salmon, "America's Continued Move toward Socialism," *Axios*, June 25, 2021, https://www.axios.com/2021/06/25/americas-continued-move-toward-socialism.

66. Joshua Jackson and Michele Gelfand, "Could Climate Change Fuel the Rise of Right-Wing Nationalism?," *The Conversation*, September 25, 2019, https://theconversation.com/could-climate-change-fuel-the-rise-of-right-wing-nationalism-123503?mc_cid=d231e3fe5d&mc_eid=0d70a348da.

67. Immo Fritsche, Christsopher Cohrs, Thomas Kessler, et al., "Global Warming Is Breeding Social Conflict: The Subtle Impact of Climate Change Threat on Authoritarian Tendencies," *Journal of Environmental Psychology* 32 (2012): 1–10.

68. Malm and the Zetkin Collective, *White Skin, Black Fuel*, 335.

69. Varvarousis, "Crisis, Liminality," 501.

70. Rana Foroohar, "The New Rules for Business in a Post-Neoliberal World," *Financial Times*, October 10, 2022, https://www.ft.com/content/e04bc664-04b2-4ef6-90f9-64e9c4c126aa.

71. Foroohar, "New Rules for Business"; Bade, "A Sea Change."

72. Kate MacKenzie and Tim Sahay, "A new foreign policy," *Phenomenal World*, 2023, https://www.phenomenalworld.org/series/the-polycrisis/.

73. Kevin Rudd, *The Avoidable War: The Dangers of a Catastrophic Conflict between the US and Xi Jinping's China* (New York: Public Affairs, 2022), 121–126.

74. Williams, *Political Hegemony*, 199.

75. IEA, *WEO 2022*, 21; IMF, *World Economic Outlook 2022*.

76. World Bank Group, *Global Economic Prospects June 2022*, 58–59.

77. IEA, *WEO 2022*, 10.

78. Christophers, "Fossilized Capital."

79. IEA, *WEO 2022*, 24–25; Brockway et al., "Energy Efficiency," 14.

80. IEA, *WEO 2022*, 24–25.

81. Clapp and Isakson, *Speculative Harvests*; OECD-FAO, "Agricultural Outlook."

82. Chandrasekhar et al., "COP15: Key Outcomes."

83. Deibert, *Reset*.

84. IEA, *WEO 2022*, 327; BP, *Energy Outlook 2023*, 40.

85. IEA, *WEO 2022*, 337.

86. David Hughes, *Shale Reality Check: Drilling into the US Government's Rosy Projections for Shale Gas & Tight Oil Production through 2050* (San Francisco: Post Carbon Institute, 2021); Derek Brower and Myles McCormick, "What the End of the US Shale Revolution Would Mean for the World," *Financial Times*, January 15, 2023, https://www.ft.com/content/60747b3b-e6ea-47c0-938d-af515816d0f1.

87. Nafeez Ahmed, "The Great Contraction: How the End of Cheap Money and Energy Will Degrade or Renew Civilization," *Byline Times*, November 28, 2022, https://bylinetimes.com/2022/11/28/the-great-contraction-how-the-end-of-cheap-money-and-energy-will-degrade-or-renew-civilisation/.

88. Justin Mikulka, "Peak US Oil Production Looms as the Domestic Shale Boom Ends," *DeSmog*, December 7, 2022, https://www.desmog.com/2022/12/07/peak-us-oil-production-shale-boom-ends-bakken-permian/.

89. Justin Jacobs and Amanda Chu, "The Oil Futures Price Predicament," *Financial Times*, September 20, 2022, https://www.ft.com/content/7af73416-6963-4b49-994b-29e1ddfcce78.

90. Nichols and Clisby, "40% of Oil and Gas Reserves Threatened."

91. IEA, *WEO 2022*, 383.

92. Hughes, *Shale Reality Check*; Ahmed, "The Great Contraction."

93. BP, *Energy Outlook 2023*, 29.

94. Edison Electric Institute, "26.4 million Cars Will Be on US Roads in 2030," *Edison Electric Institute*, June 20, 2022, https://www.eei.org/News/news/All/eei-projects-26-million-electric-vehicles-will-be-on-us-roads-in-2030.

95. World Bank Group, *Global Economic Prospects*; El-Erian, "Not Just Another Recession"; Roubini, *Megathreats*.

96. Roubini, *Megathreats*, 86.

97. Liebriech, "After Ukraine."

98. Daggett, "Petro-Masculinity."

99. Malm and the Zetkin Collective, *White Skin, Black Fuel*, 235.

100. Paxton, *Anatomy of Fascism*, 291.

101. IEA, *WEO 2022*.

102. IEA, *WEO 2022*, 340.

103. IEA, *WEO 2022*, 382.

104. De Castro and Capellán-Peréz, "Standard, Point of Use, and Extended Energy Return"; Brockway et al., "Estimation of Global Final-Stage Energy-Return"; Delannoy et al., "Peak Oil and the Low-Carbon Transition."

105. Delannoy et al., "Peak Oil and the Low-Carbon Transition," 9.

106. Richard Heinberg, "After the Ukraine Invasion: Sobering New Global Energy-Economic-Political Terrain," *Resilience*, March 18, 2022, https://www.resilience.org/stories/2022-03-18/after-the-ukraine-invasion-sobering-new-global-energy-economic-political-terrain/.

107. Delannoy et al., "Peak Oil and the Low-Carbon Transition"; Brockway et al., "Estimation of Global Final-Stage Energy-Return."

108. Friedrichs, *The Future*; Richard Heinberg, *The Party's Over: Oil, War and the Fate of Industrial Societies* (Gabriola Island: New Society Publishers, 2005).

109. Slamersak et al., "Energy Requirements and Carbon Emissions."

110. Capellán-Peréz et al., "Dynamic Energy Return."

111. Delannoy et al., "Peak Oil and the Low-Carbon Transition"; Lewis and van den Bergh, "Implications of Net Energy-Return-On-Investment"; Ugo Bardi, *The Seneca Effect: Why Growth Is Slow but Ruin Is Rapid* (Cham: Springer, 2018).

112. Roubini, *Megathreats*.

113. Streeck, *How Will Capitalism End*, 68.

114. Climate Action Tracker, "Warming Projections Global Update"; Hanna et al., "Emergency Deployment of Direct Air Capture."

115. Smil, *How the World Really Works*; Gordon, *End of American Growth*.

116. De Castro and Capellán-Peréz, "Standard, Point of Use, and Extended Energy Return"; Jackson and Jackson, "Modelling Transition Risk."

117. IEA, *WEO 2022*, 44.

118. IEA, *WEO 2022*, 30.

119. Odenweller et al., "Probabilistic Feasibility Space of Green Hydrogen."

120. Peter Lovegrove, "Hydrogen at Risk of Being the Great Missed Opportunity of the Energy Transition," *Det Norsk Veritas (DNV)*, June 14, 2022, https://www.dnv.com/news/hydrogen-at-risk-of-being-the-great-missed-opportunity-of-the-energy-transition-226628.

121. See Adam Tooze's excellent discussion in "Carbon Notes #5: Green hydrogen, the 'gas of the future'?," *Chartbook*, May 16, 2023, https://adamtooze.substack.com/p/carbon-notes-5-green-hydrogen-the.

122. IEA, *Role of Critical Metals*.

123. Ahuja, "Lazy Winds"; Guilia Carbonaro, "Solar Panels Are Feeling the Heat too: How Heatwave Temperatures Are Hampering Solar Power," *Euronews*, July 18, 2022, https://www.euronews.com/next/2022/07/18/solar-panels-feel-the-heat-too-how-higher-temperatures-are-undermining-solar-power.

124. IPCC, *Climate Change 2022: Mitigation*, 22.

125. Lynas, *Our Final Warning*, 78–90.

126. WMO, *State of Climate Services 2022*; Colelli et al., "Increased Energy Use"; van Ruijven, "Amplification of Energy."

127. Mahalingam et al., *Impacts of Severe Catastrophes*; Swiss Re Institute, *Economics of Climate Change*.

128. Jones et al., "Simulating the Earth System Response"; Grant et al., "Confronting Mitigation Deterrence."

129. Chaloner et al., "Plant Pathogen Infection Risk"; Lynas, *Our Final Warning*, 195–196.

130. Akram-Lodhi, "The Ties That Bind."

131. Caparas et al., "Increasing Risks of Crop Failure."

132. Trevor Maynard, *Food System Shock: The Insurance Impacts of Acute Disruption to Global Food Supply* (London: Lloyd's Emerging Risk Report, 2015).

133. Heck et al., "Biomass-Based Negative Emissions"; Oxfam, *Tightening the Net*.

134. Lenton et al., "Climate Tipping Points"; Duffy et al., "Is There a Temperature Tipping Point."

135. Lynas, *Our Final Warning*, 67.

136. David Keith and Douglass MacMartin, "A Temporary, Moderate and Responsive Scenario for Solar Geoengineering," *Nature Climate Change* 5 (2015): 201–207.

137. Kevin Surprise, "Preempting the Second Contradiction: Solar Geoengineering as Spatiotemporal Fix," *Annals of the American Association of Geographers* 108, no. 5 (2018): 1228–1244.

138. Olaf Corry, "The International Politics of Geoengineering: The Feasibility of Plan B for Tackling Climate Change," *Security Dialogue* 48, no. 4 (2017): 297–315.

139. Catriona MacKinnon, "The Panglossian Politics of the Geoclique," *Critical Review of International Social and Political Philosophy* 23, no. 5 (2020): 584–599.

140. Aaron Tang and Luke Kemp, "A Fate Worse Than Warming? Stratospheric Aerosol Injection and Global Catastrophic Risk," *Frontiers in Climate* 3 (2021): 1–17.

141. Tang and Kemp, "Fate Worse Than Warming?," 12.

142. OECD-FAO, "Agricultural Outlook"; Stephens et al., "Bringing Cultured Meat to Market."

143. Wallace, *Big Farms*.

144. Carly Phillips, Astrid Caldas, Rachel Cleetus, et al., "Compound Climate Risks in the COVID-19 Pandemic," *Nature Climate Change* 10 (2020): 586–588.

145. Tang and Kemp, "Fate Worse Than Warming?"

146. Joseph Tainter, *The Collapse of Complex Societies* (Cambridge, UK: Cambridge University Press, 1988), 193.

147. Miguel Centeno, Peter Callahan, Paul Larcey, Thayer Patterson, "Globalization and Fragility: A Systems Approach to Collapse," in Miguel Centeno et al (eds.) *How Worlds Collapse: What History, Systems, and Complexity Can Teach Us about Our Modern World and Fragile Future* (New York: Routledge, 2023), 5–24.

148. Craig Collins, "Catabolism: Capitalism's Frightening Future," *Counterpunch*, November 1, 2018, https://www.counterpunch.org/2018/11/01/catabolism-capitalisms -frightening-future/.

149. For a discussion, see Roubini, *Megathreats*, 49–55.

150. Beth Stratford, "The Threat of Rent Extraction in a Resource-Constrained Future," *Ecological Economics* 169 (2020): 1–11.

151. Christophers, *Rentier Capitalism*, xxiv; see also Frase, *Four Futures*; Harvey, *Seventeen Contradictions*, 235–237; Stratford, "Threat of Rent Extraction."

152. Christophers, *Rentier Capitalism*, 421.

153. John Barry, "A Genealogy of Economic Growth as Ideology and Cold War Core State Imperative," *New Political Economy* 25, no. 1 (2020): 18–29.

154. Harvey, *Seventeen Contradictions*, 237.

155. John Michael Greer, *The Long Descent: A User's Guide to the End of the Industrial Age* (Gabriola Island: New Society Publishers, 2003).

156. Branwen Gruffydd Jones, "The Political Economy of Social Crisis: Towards a Critique of the 'Failed State' Thesis," *Review of International Political Economy* 15, no. 2 (2008): 180–205.

157. Octavia Butler, *Parable of the Sower* (New York: Grand Central Publishing, 1993).

158. Minqi Li, *China and the 21st Century Crisis* (London: Pluto Press, 2016), 184.

159. Mark Duffield, "Total War as Environmental Terror: Linking Liberalism, Resilience, and the Bunker," *South Atlantic Quarterly* 110, no. 3 (2011): 757–769.

160. John Lanchester, *The Wall* (London: Faber, 2014).

161. Guy Middleton, *Understanding Collapse: Ancient History and Modern Myths* (Cambridge, UK: Cambridge University Press, 2017).

162. Middleton, *Understanding Collapse*, 211.

163. Glen Kuecker and Thomas Hall, "Resilience and Community in the Age of World-System Collapse," *Nature and Culture* 6, no. 1 (2011): 18–40.

164. See Chris Smaje's discussion of what he calls a "supersedure state," or make-shift modes of local governance cobbled together in the wake of state decline; *A Small Farm Future*, 233–245.

165. Neiwert, *Alt-America*, 153–157.

166. NGFS, "A Call for Action."

167. Liebriech, "After Ukraine."

168. Nicholas Stern and Joseph Stiglitz, *Report of the High-Level Commission on Carbon Prices* (Washington, DC: World Bank, 2017).

169. Victor et al., *Accelerating the Low Carbon Transition*; IEA, *WEO 2022*; Josh Gabbatiss, "Explainer: How Can Climate Finance Be Increased from 'Billions to Trillions'?," *Carbon Brief*, November 4, 2022, https://www.carbonbrief.org/explainer-how-can-climate-finance-be-increased-from-billions-to-trillions/.

170. Otto et al., "Social Tipping Dynamics," 2.

171. Climate Action Tracker, "Warming Projections Global Update."

172. Newell and Paterson, *Climate Capitalism*, 172–175.

173. Moore, *Capitalism in the Web*.

174. Slamersak et al., "Energy Requirements and Carbon Emissions."

175. Capellán-Peréz et al., "Dynamic Energy Return."

176. Schnabel, "A New Age"; Sharma, "Greenflation."

177. Jean Pisani-Ferry, "Climate Policy Is Macroeconomic Policy, and the Implications Will Be Significant," *Peterson Institute for International Economics*, August 2021, pp. 6–7.

178. Pisani-Ferry, "Climate Policy," 7; Sgouris Sgouridis, Christian Kimmich, Jordi Sole, et al., "Visions Before Models: The Ethos of Energy Modeling in an Era of Transition," *Energy Research & Social Science* 88 (2022): 1–15.

179. For example, IEA, *Net Zero*.

180. Helen Thomas, "Workers Need More Than Platitudes about 'Green Jobs,'" *Financial Times*, December 7, 2022, https://www.ft.com/content/8f2212ac-5142-499b-a324-ad18f32065b5.

181. Thomas, "Workers Need More Than Platitudes."

182. Bolton et al., *Green Swan*; NGFS, "Call to Action."

183. IEA, *Strategic Metals*.

184. These numbers are based on IEA projections of recycling potential for transition metals by 2040. See IEA, *Strategic Metals*, 15.

185. This projection of 30%–50% cost increases is based on multiple estimates of how reshoring solar and battery supply chains will raise costs. See Seaver Wang, Juzel Lloyd, and Guido Nunez-Mujica, "Sins of a Solar Empire: Confronting the Solar Manufacturing Industry's Human Rights Problem," *Breakthrough Institute*, November 15, 2022, https://thebreakthrough.org/issues/energy/sins-of-a-solar-empire. Also Yuan Yang, Alice Hancock, and Laura Pitel, "Solar Industry Warns EU Rules Would Hamper Clean Energy Transition," *Financial Times*, March 17, 2023, https://www.ft.com/content/2f876e67-8aa1-4776-a783-bcf5d5ea76eb.

186. As the IEA shows, even an "announced pledges" scenario in which FF demand declines would likely witness rising prices (due to underinvestment). See IEA, *WEO 2022*, 356.

187. Mark Maslin, Liivia Van Heerde, and Simon Day, "Sulfur: A Potential Resource Crisis That Could Stifle Green Technology and Threaten Food Security as the World Decarbonises," *Geographical Journal*, August 21, 2022, https://doi.org/10.1111/geoj.12475.

188. See discussion in Deibert, *Reset*, 117–121.

189. Malmand the Zetkin Collective, *White Skin, Black Fuel*, 286–287.

190. A new study warns that "pulses" of rapid ice-sheet collapse, detected in the earth's past, mean that the level of sea rise "expected over 200 years could actually occur in 20 years," though this remains contested. See Damian Carrington, "Ice sheets can collapse at 600 meters a day, far faster than feared, study finds," *The Guardian*, April 5, 2023, https://www.theguardian.com/environment/2023/apr/05/ice-sheets-collapse-far-faster-than-feared-study-climate-crisis.

191. While green industrial policies are already expanding across the world-system core, spending remains far too low, and policies to actively steer firms towards experimentation with entirely new technologies and production processes remain too weak, to galvanize the necessary technological transformation (at least within the time-frame needed). See IEA, *World Energy Outlook 2022*, 61; also Charles Sabel and David Victor, "Beyond Biden's Climate Plan, A New Industrial Revolution is Needed," *Yale Environment 360*, September 26 2022, https://e360.yale.edu/features/biden-climate-bill-industrial-policy.

192. Sgouris Sgouridis, Christian Kimmich, Jordi Sole, et al., "Visions before Models: The Ethos of Energy Modeling in an Era of Transition," *Energy Research & Social Science* 88 (2022): 1–15.

193. June Yoon, "Lex in Depth: A Solid Case for the Next Generation of Batteries," *Financial Times*, April 6, 2021, https://www.ft.com/content/c4e075b8-7289-4756-9bfe-60bf50f0cf66.

194. Gregory Wilson, Mowafak Al-Jassim, Wyatt K. Metzger, et al., "The 2020 Photovoltaic Technologies Roadmap," *Journal of Physics D: Applied Physics* 53 (2020): 4–48.

195. For example, Heinberg and Fridley, *Our Renewable Energy Future.*

196. Arturo Escobar, "Degrowth, Postdevelopment, and Transitions: A Preliminary Conversation," *Sustainability Science* 10 (2015): 451–462.

197. Michael Albert, "Ecosocialism for Realists: Transitions, Trade-Offs, and Authoritarian Dangers," *Capitalism Nature Socialism* 34:1 (2023), 11–30.

198. Albert, "Ecosocialism for Realists"; Lowy, *Ecosocialism*; Angus, *Facing the Anthropocene*; Baer, *Democratic Ecosocialism.*

199. Jason Hickel, "Is It Possible to Achieve a Good Life for All Within Planetary Boundaries?" *Third World Quarterly* 40 (2018): 18–35; Kate Raworth, *Doughnut Economics: Thinking Like a 21st Century Economist* (White River Junction, VT: Chelsea Green, 2017).

200. Albert, "Ecosocialism for Realists."

201. Wright, *Envisioning Real Utopias*, 321.

202. George Lawson, *Anatomies of Revolution* (Cambridge: Cambridge University Press, 2019), 78–82, 228.

203. Otto et al, "Social tipping."

204. This is comparable to E.O Wright's theory of post-capitalist transformation. See Wright, Envisioning Real Utopias, section III.

205. Besteman, *Militarized Global Apartheid.*

206. Charles Stevenson and Ellen Helker-Nygren, "Degrowth Can End the Cost of Living Crisis," *Resilience*, December 14, 2022, https://www.resilience.org/stories /2022-12-14/degrowth-can-end-the-cost-of-living-crisis/?mc_cid=6615e38c73&mc _eid=cbfbf13f15.

207. Durand, "End of Financial Hegemony?"

208. Hickel, *Less Is More*, chapter 5; Ann Pettifor, *The Case for a Green New Deal* (London: Verso, 2019); Hadas Thier, "What a Socialist Response to Inflation Should Look Like," *Jacobin*, January 6, 2022, https://jacobin.com/2022/01/prices-wages-covid -fed-biden-class.

209. Arnulf Grubler, Charlie Wilson, Nuno Bento, et al., "A Low Energy Demand Scenario for Meeting the 1.5C Target and Sustainable Development Goals without Negative Emissions Technologies," *Nature Energy* 3 (2018): 515–527; Thea Riofrancos, Alissa Kendall, Kristii Dayemo, et al., "Achieving Zero Emissions with More Mobility and Less Mining," *Climate+Community Project*, January 2023, https://www .climateandcommunity.org/more-mobility-less-mining.

210. Delina, *Strategies.*

211. Christopher Olk, Colleen Schneider, and Jason Hickel, "How to Pay for Saving the World: Modern Monetary Theory for a Degrowth Transition," *Social Science Research Network*, July 25, 2022, https://papers.ssrn.com/sol3/papers.cfm?abstract_id =4172005.

212. Vasco Brummer, "Community Energy—Benefits and Barriers," *Renewable and Sustainable Energy Reviews* 94 (2018): 187–196.

213. Comparable to the post-growth economies imagined by Herman Daly and Tim Jackson. See Herman Daly, *Steady State Economics: Second Edition with New Essays* (Washington D.C: Island Press, 1991); Tim Jackson, *Prosperity Without Growth: Economics for a Finite Planet* (Abingdon: Routledge, 2011).

214. This should not be overstated. But the experience of the May 2023 "Beyond Growth" conference organized by EU parliamentarians—which received deeper support and engagement from high-ranking EU officials, at least compared to earlier iterations—suggests that that the ideological hegemony of growth may be slowly weakening in the EU. See Martin Sandbu, "'Degrowth' starts to move in from Europe's policy Fringes," *Financial Times*, May 23, 2023, https://www.ft.com/content/e2f96618 -081f-41de-b7a0-a682017c8d11.

215. Referring to the fiscally conservative grouping of Sweden, the Netherlands, Denmark, and Austria.

216. Salmon, "America's Continued Move Towards Socialism."

217. This would be unlike the first civil war. Rather, it would be a period of distributed far-right insurgencies across the rural US, and deadly clashes between far-right and leftwing protesters in cities, that leads to at least 1,000 fatalities in a given year (the threshold that distinguishes civil strife from civil war). See Stephen Marche, *The Next Civil War: Dispatches from the American Future* (New York: Avid Reader Press, 2022).

218. As Yifei Li and Judith Shapiro show, ecological Marxism provides a key source of inspiration for the CCP's nascent discourse of Ecological Civilization. See Yifei Li and Judith Shapiro, *China Goes Green: Coercive Environmentalism for a Troubled Planet* (London: Polity Press, 2020), 6–7.

219. Li, *China and the 21st Century Crisis*, 183.

220. NIC, *Global Trends 2040*, 119.

221. Olufemi Taiwo and Patrick Bigger, "Debt Justice for Climate Reparations," *Climate+Community Project*, April 2022, https://www.climateandcommunity.org/debt -justice-for-climate-reparations.

222. Albert, "Geopolitics of Renewable Energy."

223. Newell and Paterson, *Climate Capitalism*, 175.

224. Kuhne et al., "Carbon Bombs."

225. Jason Hickel, "How to Achieve Full Decolonization," *New Internationalist*, August 9, 2021, https://newint.org/features/2021/08/09/money-ultimate-decolonizer-fjf.

226. Michael Stott, "State Looms Over Latin America's Hopes to Exploit 'White Gold' of Lithium," *Financial Times*, 2022, accessed January 23, 2023, https://www.ft .com/content/359d5287-d0ab-46ae-9c6b-09517ec9fb0c.

227. Kate Aronoff, Alyssa Battistoni, Daniel Aldana Cohen, and Thea Riofrancos, *A Planet to Win: Why We Need a Green New Deal* (London: Verso, 2019), 142–153.

228. Michael Barnard, "Morocco, Algeria, Egypt: Assessing EU Plans to Import Hydrogen from North Africa," *Transnational Institute*, May 17, 2022, https://www.tni .org/en/publication/assessing-eu-plans-to-import-hydrogen-from-north-africa.

229. Stott, "State Looms."

230. Fadhel Kaboub, "Africa's Path Towards Resilience and Sovereignty: the Real Wakanda is Within Reach," *Tax Justice Network*, March 30, 2021, https://taxjustice .net/2021/03/30/africas-path-towards-resilience-and-sovereignty-the-real-wakanda -is-within-reach/.

231. Max Ajl, "The NIEO in a State of Permanent Insurrection," *Progressive International*, October 1, 2022, https://progressive.international/blueprint/dffe4ca0-4dc6 -478c-9e49-7bc8d18aa989-ajl-the-nieo-in-a-state-of-permanent-insurrection/en.

232. Wright, *Envisioning Real Utopias*, 190.

233. Wright, *Envisioning Real Utopias*, 315.

234. Wright, *Envisioning Real Utopias*, 220–221.

235. Albert, "Ecosocialism for Realists."

236. Wright, *Envisioning Real Utopias*, 373.

237. For a useful discussion of what this might entail, see Robin Hahnel and Erik Olin Wright, *Alternatives to Capitalism: Proposals for a Democratic Economy* (London: Verso, 2016), chapters 1 and 2.

238. See MacKenzie & Sahay, "A new foreign policy"; also Delphine Strauss, "Global economy: will higher wages prolong inflation?," *Financial Times*, May 1, 2023, https://www.ft.com/content/0097fbd7-96ae-4a75-876d-8df4d4379651.

239. Hickel, *Less is More*.

240. Keir Milburn, *Generation Left* (London: Polity, 2019).

241. Harry Dempsey, "China leads rise in export restrictions on critical minerals, OECD says," *Financial Times*, April 11, 2023, https://www.ft.com/content/198b6824 -21d6-4633-9a97-00164d23c13f.

242. Srnicek and Williams, *Inventing the Future*; Moghadam, "What Is Revolution." For an insightful analysis of problems within leftwing organizations, see Maurice Mitchell, "Building resilient organizations," *The Forge*, November 29, 2022, https:// forgeorganizing.org/article/building-resilient-organizations.

243. For examples of this position, see Aronoff et al, *A Planet to Win*; Robert Pollin, "De-Growth vs. a Green New Deal," *New Left Review* 112 (2018): 5–25; Matthew Huber, *Climate Change as Class War* (London: Verso, 2022); Leigh Philips and Michael Roszworski, "Planning the Good Anthropocene," *Jacobin*, August 15, 2017, https://jacobin .com/2017/08/planning-the-good-anthropocene.

244. I assume here that a more severe crisis of capitalism, involving more drastic and prolonged reductions in living standards, would be necessary to facilitate the kind of post-consumerist tipping point needed for degrowth transitions in the world-system core.

245. Mariana Mazzucato, *Mission Economy: A Moonshot Guide to Changing Capitalism* (New York: Penguin, 2020).

246. Aaron Bastani, *Fully Automated Luxury Communism* (London: Verso, 2020).

247. Scoones et al., "Narratives of Scarcity."

248. Gaia Vince, *Nomad Century: How to Survive the Climate Upheaval* (New York: Allan Lane, 2022).

249. Buck, *After Geoengineering.*

CHAPTER 5

1. Jessop, *State Theory.*

2. Besteman, *Militarized Global Apartheid,* 120.

3. Jerry Harris, "The Conflict for Power in Transnational Class Theory," *Science & Society* 67, no. 3 (2003): 329–339.

4. Davis, *Are Prisons Obsolete?*; Kundnani, "Abolish National Security"; Elliot-Cooper, *Black Resistance*; M4BL, "2020 Policy Platform."

5. Richard Godfrey, Jo Brewis, Jo Grady, et al., "The Private Military Industry and Neoliberal Imperialism: Mapping the Terrain," *Organization* 21, no. 1 (2014): 106–125.

6. Scoones et al., "Narratives of Scarcity."

7. Johan Galtung, "Violence, Peace, and Peace Research," *Journal of Peace Research* 6, no. 3 (1969): 167–191.

8. Dorninger et al., "Ecologically Unequal Exchange."

9. Hector Rufrancos et al., "Income Inequality and Crime: A Review and Explanation of the Time Series Evidence," *Sociology and Criminology* 1, no. 1 (2013): 1–9; Ruth Blakeley, Nisha Kapoor, Arun Kundnani, et al., *Leaving the War on Terror: A Progressive Alternative to Counter-Terrorism Policy* (Amsterdam: Transnational Institute, 2019).

10. Patomaki, *Political Economy of Global Security*; Tooze, *Crashed.*

11. Szayna et al., *Conflict Trends.*

12. David Kilcullen, *Out of the Mountains: The Coming Age of the Urban Guerilla* (Oxford: Oxford University Press, 2013), 247.

13. Paul Rogers, *Global Security and the War on Terror: Elite Power and the Illusion of Control* (London: Routledge, 2008).

14. Besteman, *Militarized Global Apartheid,* 126.

15. Godfrey et al., "The Private Military Industry"; Robinson, *Global Police State*; Deibert, *Reset*; Williams, "Global Security Assemblages."

16. Robinson, *Global Police State,* 75–81.

17. Robinson, *Global Police State.*

18. Rigakos, *Security/Capital,* 114.

19. Deudney, *Bounding Power.*

20. Daniel Deudney, "Turbo Change: Accelerating Technological Disruption, Planetary Geopolitics, and Architectonic Metaphors," *International Studies Review* 20 (2018): 223–231.

21. Blum and Wittes, *Future of Violence,* 39, 7–8.

22. Bade, "A Sea Change."

23. Dyer-Witheford et al., *Inhuman Power*, 46; For a useful discussion of diminishing returns in the field of generative AI, see Nafeez Ahmed, "AI Doomers Are Wrong. The 'Existential Threat' Is About Who Controls Information—Not the Singularity," *Age of Transformation*, May 11, 2023, https://ageoftransformation.org/aidoommyth/.

24. Solomon Hsiang, Marshall Burke, and Edward Miguel, "Quantifying the Influence of Climate on Human Conflict," *Science* 341 (2013): 1212.

25. Alexander De Juan and Niklas Hanze, "Climate and Cohesion: The Effects of Droughts on Intra-Ethnic and Inter-Ethnic Trust," *Journal of Peace Research* 58, no. 1 (2021): 151–167.

26. Jan Selby, "Positivist Climate Conflict Research: A Critique," *Geopolitics* 19 (2014): 829–856; Jon Barnett, "Global Environmental Change I: Climate Resilient Peace?" *Progress in Human Geography* 43, no. 5 (2019): 927–936.

27. Campbell et al., *Age of Consequences*.

28. Katharine Mach, Neil Adger, Halvard Buhaug, et al., "Directions for Research on Climate and Conflict," *Earth's Future* 8, no. 7 (2020): 1–7.

29. Michael Klare, "How Rising Temperatures Increase the Likelihood of Nuclear War," *The Nation*, January 13, 2020, https://www.thenation.com/article/nuclear-defense-climate-change/.

30. Muhammah Qamar, Muhammad Azmat, and Pierlugi Claps, "Pitfalls in Transboundary Indus Water Treaty: A Perspective to Prevent Unattended Threats to Global Security," *Nature Clean Water* 2, no. 22 (2019): 1–9.

31. Franscesco Femia and Caitlin Werrell, "Climate Change, the Erosion of State Sovereignty, and World Order," *Brown Journal of World Affairs* 22, no. 2 (2016): 221–235.

32. Barnett, "Global Environmental Change."

33. Neta Crawford, *Pentagon Fuel Use, Climate Change, and the Costs of War* (Providence, RI: Watson Institute, 2019).

34. Olivier Belcher, Patrick Bigger, Ben Neimark, et al., "Hidden Carbon Costs of the 'Everywhere War': Logistics, Geopolitical Ecology, and the Carbon Boot-Print of the US Military," *Transactions of the Institute of British Geography* 45, no. 1 (2020): 65–80.

35. Stuart Parkinson and Linsey Cottrell, "Estimating the Military's Global Greenhouse Gas Emissions," *Conflict and Environment Observatory*, November 2022, https://ceobs.org/wp-content/uploads/2022/11/SGR-CEOBS_Estimating_Global_MIlitary_GHG_Emissions.pdf.

36. Leonard de Klerk, Anatolii Shmurak, Olga Gassan-Zade, et al., "Climate Damage Caused by Russia's War in Ukraine," *Climate Focus*, November 2022, https://climatefocus.com/wp-content/uploads/2022/11/ClimateDamageinUkraine.pdf.

37. Quoted in Mark Akkerman, Deborah Burton, Nick Buxton, et al., *Climate Collateral: How Military Spending Accelerates Climate Breakdown* (Amsterdam: Transnational Institute, 2022), 27.

38. IEA, *WEO 2022*.

39. For example, Michael Davidson, Valerie Karplus, Joanna Lewis, et al., "The Risks of Decoupling from China on Low-Carbon Technologies," *Science* 377, no. 6612 (2022): 1266–1271.

40. Hal Brands, "Economic Chaos of a Taiwan War Would Go Well Past Semiconductors," *Bloomberg*, June 23, 2022, https://www.bloomberg.com/opinion/articles/2022-06-23/economic-chaos-of-a-taiwan-war-would-go-well-past-semiconductors?utm_source=substack&utm_me.

41. Brands, "Economic Chaos of a Taiwan War Would Go Well Past Semiconductors"; Charlie Vest, Agatha Kratz, and Reva Goujon, "The Global Economic Disruptions from a Taiwan Conflict," *Rhodium Group*, December 14, 2022, https://rhg.com/research/taiwan-economic-disruptions/.

42. Michal Meidan, "China: Climate Leader and Villain," in *The Geopolitics of the Global Energy Transition*, ed. Manfred Hafner and Simone Tagliapietra (Cham: Springer, 2020), 75–92.

43. Bade, "A Sea Change."

44. IEA, *Net Zero*.

45. Jurgen Scheffran, Anna Leidreiter, John Burroughs, et al., "The Climate-Nuclear Nexus: Exploring the Linkages between Climate Change and Nuclear Threats," *World Future Council*, November 27, 2015, https://www.worldfuturecouncil.org/climate-nuclear-nexus/.

46. International Renewable Energy Agency (IRENA), *A New World: The Geopolitics of the Energy Transformation* (Abu Dhabi: IRENA, 2019), 57–58.

47. Herbert Lin, *Cyber Threats and Nuclear Weapons* (Palo Alto: Stanford University Press, 2021), 91.

48. James Acton, "Cyber Warfare and Inadvertent Escalation," *Daedalus* 149, no. 2 (2020): 133–149.

49. Lin, *Cyber Threats*.

50. Brown, "New Nuclear MADness"; Acton, "Cyber Warfare."

51. Johnson, "Artificial Intelligence," 17.

52. Johnson, "Artificial Intelligence," 27.

53. Brown, "New Nuclear MADness," 79.

54. Herbert Lin, "The Existential Threat from Cyber-Enabled Information Warfare," *Bulletin of the Atomic Scientists* 75, no. 4 (2019): 187–196.

55. Marina Favaro, *Weapons of Mass Distortion: A New Approach to Emerging Technologies, Risk Reduction and the Global Nuclear Order* (London: Centre for Science and Security Studies, King's College London, 2019), 12; James Johnson, "Artificial Intelligence, Autonomy, and the Risk of Catalytic Nuclear War," *Modern War Institute*, March 18, 2021, https://mwi.usma.edu/artificial-intelligence-autonomy-and-the-risk-of-catalytic-nuclear-war/.

56. Chengxin Pan, "The 'China Threat' in American Self-Imagination: The Discursive Construction of Other as Power Politics," *Alternatives: Global, Local, Political* 29, no. 3 (2004): 305–331.

57. Sam Moore and Alex Roberts, "Ecofascism and Indian Nationalism," *The Ecologist*, February 7, 2022, https://theecologist.org/2022/feb/07/ecofascism-and-indian-nationalism.

58. Kundnani, "Abolish National Security"; Elliot-Cooper, *Black Resistance*; Blakeley et al., *Leaving the War on Terror*.

59. Kundnani, "Abolish National Security"; Pan, "The 'China Threat.'"

60. Eleanore Pauwels, *The New Geopolitics of Converging Risks: The UN and Prevention in the Era of AI* (New York: United Nations University Centre for Policy Research, 2019), 11.

61. Lin, "The Existential Threat."

62. As John Rathbone writes, one of the "big lessons" of the Russian invasion—at least according to military strategists and arms manufacturers—is that "'big war is back' . . . and with that the need for countries to have the industrial capacity and massive weapons stocks to sustain high-intensity fighting." The climate implications are not good. See John Rathbone, "'Big War Is Back': 5 Lessons from Russia's Invasion of Ukraine," *Financial Times*, December 25, 2022, https://www.ft.com/content/b01669cb-5be8-4f69-8d18-8eef0c0c2088.

63. Thane Gustafson, *Klimat: Russia in the Age of Climate Change* (Cambridge, MA: Harvard University Press, 2021), 53–54.

64. Heinberg, "After the Ukraine Invasion."

65. IEA, *WEO 2022*, 337, 366.

66. Matthew Burrows and Robert Manning, "How Will the Russia-Ukraine War End? Here Are Four Scenarios," *Atlantic Council*, 2022, accessed January 29, 2023, https://www.atlanticcouncil.org/content-series/the-big-story/how-will-the-russia-ukraine-war-reshape-the-world-here-are-four-possible-futures/.

67. Liana Fix and Michael Kimmage, "Putin's Last Stand: The Promise and Perils of Russian Defeat," *Foreign Affairs*, December 20, 2022, https://www.foreignaffairs.com/russian-federation/putin-last-stand-russia-defeat.

68. Mary Aylward, Peter Engelke, Uri Friedman, et al., "Global Foresight 2023," *Atlantic Council*, 2022, accessed January 29, 2023, https://www.atlanticcouncil.org/content-series/atlantic-council-strategy-paper-series/welcome-to-2033/.

69. Joseph Glauber and David Laborde, "How Sanctions on Russia and Belarus Are Impacting Exports of Agricultural Products and Fertilizers," *International Food Policy Research Institute*, November 9, 2022, https://www.ifpri.org/blog/how-sanctions-russia-and-belarus-are-impacting-exports-agricultural-products-and-fertilizer#:~:text=Russia%20accounts%20for%20about%2015,compound%20products%20in%20other%20countries.

70. Fix and Kimmage, "Putin's Last Stand."

71. IEA, *WEO 2022*, 56.

72. Nafeez Ahmed, "Putin's War on Net Zero: Controlling 'Europe's Breadbasket' to Prevent Russia's Fossil Fuel Collapse," *Byline Times*, April 21, 2022, https://bylinetimes .com/2022/04/21/putins-war-on-net-zero-controlling-europes-breadbasket-to-prevent -russias-fossil-fuel-collapse/.

73. Andrea Kendall-Taylor and Michael Kofman, "Russia's Dangerous Decline: The Kremlin Won't Go Down Without a Fight," *Foreign Affairs* 101, no. 6 (2022): 28–35.

74. Fix and Kimmage, "Putin's Last Stand."

75. IEA, *WEO 2022*, 366.

76. Quoted in Rudd, *Avoidable War*, 107–108.

77. Hal Brands and Michael Beckley, *Danger Zone: The Coming Conflict with China* (New York: W.W. Norton & Company, 2022), 24–50.

78. Rudd, *Avoidable War*, 359–360.

79. Rudd, *Avoidable War*, 359–360; Brands and Beckley, *Danger Zone*.

80. Vest et al., "Global Economic Disruptions."

81. Rudd, *Avoidable War*, 352–353.

82. Rudd, *Avoidable War*, 354–355.

83. Paul Dabbar, "Potential energy challenges from a China-Taiwan conflict scenario," *Columbia Center on Global Energy Policy*, January 25, 2023, https://www .energypolicy.columbia.edu/publications/potential-energy-challenges-from-a-china -taiwan-conflict-scenario/.

84. Rudd, *Avoidable War*, 354–357.

85. Akkerman et al., *Climate Collateral*.

86. Rudd, *Avoidable War*.

87. Robinson, *Global Police State*; Rogers, *Global Security*.

88. This is also anticipated by Patomaki; see *Political Economy of Global Security*, 154.

89. Gustafson, *Klimat*, 213–215.

90. IEA, *WEO 2022*, 379.

91. Adam Goldstein and Constantine Samaras, "Dire Straits: Strategically-Significant International Waterways in a Warming World," *Center for Climate and Security*, June 2017, https://climateandsecurity.org/wp-content/uploads/2017/06/4_dire-straits.pdf.

92. As also argued by Corry, "International Politics of Geoengineering"; MacKinnon, "Panglossian Politics"; Tang and Kemp, "Fate Worse Than Warming."

93. Leonie Nimmo and Hana Manjusak, "Environmental CSR Reporting by the Arms Industry," *Conflict and Environment Observatory*, December 2021, https://ceobs .org/environmental-csr-reporting-by-the-arms-industry/.

94. This is what Michael Klare anticipates. See "China 2049," *Tom Dispatch*, August 24, 2021, https://tomdispatch.com/china-2049/.

95. Todd Miller, Nick Buxton, Mark Akkerman, et al., *Global Climate Wall: How the World's Wealthiest Nations Prioritise Borders over Climate Action* (Amsterdam: Transnational Institute, 2021); Associated Press, "Global $600+ Billion Homeland Security and Public Safety Market 2020–2024," *Associated Press News*, December 10, 2019, https://apnews.com/press-release/business-wire/technology-middle-east-c23b8f801a e04057aa10a990700eea08.

96. Rigakos, *Security/Capital*, 114.

97. David Harvey, "Value in Motion," *New Left Review* 126 (2020): 103.

98. Harvey, "Value in Motion."

99. Associated Press, "Global $600+ Billion Homeland Security."

100. Ulrich Brand and Markus Wissen, "Global Environmental Politics and the Imperial Mode of Living: Articulations of State-Capital Relations in the Multiple Crisis," *Globalizations* 9, no. 4 (2012): 547–560.

101. Duffield, "Liberalism, Resilience, and the Bunker"; Raskin, *Journey to Earthland*.

102. Butler, *Parable*; Margaret Atwood, *Oryx and Crake* (London: Bloomsbury, 2003).

103. Kilcullen, *Out of the Mountains*, 66; Greer, *Long Descent*.

104. A growing number of leftwing (and rightwing) scholars claim that "neofeudalism" is already a present-day reality, particularly in the digital technology sector characterized by rentier control of platforms. But as Evgeny Morozov rightly says, while we are clearly witnessing limited tendencies toward "re-feudalization," made evident by the rising power of rentiers across the world economy, it is nonetheless the case that "full-blown 'neo-feudalism' is nowhere on the horizon." The world-system today remains capitalist, in the sense that profit and growth remain the driving forces of the economy, and wage labor (at least in the core) is still the dominant mode of survival for proletarianized workers. It would be far more accurate to describe the world-system as neofeudalist only in the context of global collapse. See Evgeny Morozov, "Critique of Techno-Feudal Reason," *New Left Review* 133/134 (2022), 95.

105. Kemp et al., "Bioengineering Horizon Scan," 2.

106. NAS, *Biodefense*, 57–58.

107. Webb and Hessel, *Genesis Machine*, 262–263.

108. Benjamin Trump et al., "Building Biosecurity for Synthetic Biology," *Molecular Systems Biology* 16 (2020): 1–16; Bade, "A Sea Change."

109. As Cronin says, "prices of small [unmanned aerial vehicles] will continue to drop. . . . The private sector is driving this innovation, with strong incentives to offer an array of powerful new features"; see *Power to the People*, 221.

110. Silver and Payne, "Crises of World Hegemony," 18.

111. Lee, *AI Superpowers*.

112. Susskind, *World without Work*.

113. Case and Deaton, *Deaths of Despair*, 4.

114. Lee, *AI Superpowers*, 20–21.

115. Srnicek and Williams, *Inventing the Future*.

116. Kemp et al., "Bioengineering Horizon Scan."

117. Kemp et al., "Bioengineering Horizon Scan," 5–8.

118. Ian Shaw, *Predator Empire: Drone Warfare and Full Spectrum Dominance* (Minneapolis: University of Minnesota Press, 2016).

119. Michael O'Hanlon, *Forecasting Change in Military Technology, 2020–2040* (Washington, DC: Foreign Policy at Brookings, 2019).

120. Quoted in Gregg Allen and Taniel Chan, *Artificial Intelligence and National Security* (Cambridge, MA: Belfer Center Study, Harvard University, 2017), 14.

121. Albert, "Dangers of Decoupling."

122. Wodak, *Politics of Fear*.

123. Melissa Heikkila, "Europe Throws Down Gauntlet on AI with New Rulebook," *Politico*, April 21, 2021, https://www.politico.eu/article/europe-throws-down-gauntlet-on-ai-with-new-rulebook/.

124. Zeyi Yang, "China Just Announced a New Social Credit Law. Here's What It Means," *MIT Technology Review*, November 22, 2022, https://www.technologyreview.com/2022/11/22/1063605/china-announced-a-new-social-credit-law-what-does-it-mean/#:~:text=Initially%2C%20back%20in%202014%2C%20the,figured%20out%20the%20financial%20part.

125. Shaw, *Predator Empire*, 16.

126. Mann and Wainwright, *Climate Leviathan*, 31.

127. Feldstein, *Global Expansion of AI*; Rudd, *Avoidable War*, 293–300; Brands and Beckley, *Danger Zone*, 116–117; Byler, *In the Camps*.

128. Shaw, *Predator Empire*, 239–240.

129. Zuboff, *Surveillance Capitalism*, 414–415.

130. Zuboff, *Surveillance Capitalism*, 478.

131. Thaler, *No Other Planet*, 249.

132. Jessop, *State Power*; Wright, *Envisioning Real Utopias*.

133. Jessop, *State Theory*, 333.

134. Andreas Malm, *Corona, Climate, Chronic Emergency: War Communism in the Twenty-First Century* (London: Verso, 2020).

135. Jinghan Zeng, "Artificial Intelligence and China's Authoritarian Governance," *International Affairs* 96, no. 6 (2020): 1443.

136. In other words: A reversal of the trend by which the Western imperial powers forced capitalist industrialization on the rest of the world; see Anievas and Nisancioglu, *How the West Came to Rule*, 46.

137. Jairus Grove, "From Geopolitics to Geotechnics: Global Futures in the Shadow of Automation, Cunning Machines, and Human Speciation," *International Relations* 34, no. 3 (2020): 432–455.

138. For a comparable argument, see Cronin on the difference between "open" innovation driven by the private sector, and "closed" innovation in which states "control access to major technological developments"; Cronin, *Power to the People*, 11–12.

139. Mark Neocleous, *Critique of Security* (Edinburgh: Edinburgh University Press, 2008).

140. Ken MacLeod, *Star Fraction: A Fall Revolution Novel* (Croydon: Orbit, 1995).

141. Atwood, *Oryx*.

142. Nick Bostrom, *Superintelligence: Paths, Dangers, Strategies* (Oxford: Oxford University Press, 2014).

143. Discussed in Jessop, *Capitalist State*, 170.

144. Kundnani, "Abolish National Security"; Elliot-Cooper, *Black Resistance*.

145. Rigakos, *Security/Capital*, 121–122.

146. As I show in Albert, "Ecosocialism for Realists."

147. Hickel, "Possible to Achieve a Good Life."

148. Escobar, *Pluriversal Politics*.

149. As discussed in Albert, "Geopolitics of Renewable Energy."

150. Taiwo and Bigger, "Debt Justice"

151. Ceyhun Elgin, Adem Elveren, Gokcer Ozgur, et al., "Military Spending and Sustainable Development," *Review of Development Economics* 26, no. 3 (2022): 1466–1490.

152. Li, *China in the 21st Century*; Klare, "China 2049."

153. Akkerman et al., *Climate Collateral*; Blakeley et al., *Leaving the War on Terror*.

154. Davis, *Are Prisons Obsolete?*; Elliot-Cooper, *Black Resistance*; M4BL, "Policy Platform."

155. Deudney, *Bounding Power*, 255–259; Union of Concerned Scientists, "Reducing the Risk of Nuclear War: Taking Nuclear Weapons Off High Alert," February 2016, 2021https://www.ucsusa.org/sites/default/files/attach/2016/02/Reducing-Risk-Nuclear-War-full-report.pdf.

156. Tim Di Muzio, *Carbon Capitalism: Energy, Social Reproduction, and World Order* (London: Rowman & Littlefield International, 2015).

157. Ronald Deibert, "Divide and Rule: Republican Security Theory as Civil Society Cyber Strategy," *Georgetown Journal of International Affairs: International Engagement on Cyber* 3 (2014): 39–50.

158. Thomas Birtchnell and John Urry, "Fabricating Futures and the Movement of Objects," *Mobilities* 8, no. 3 (2013): 388–405.

159. Kundnani, "Abolish National Security."

160. Bill Hogseth, "Why Democrats Keep Losing Rural Counties Like Mine," *Politico*, December 1, 2020, https://www.politico.com/news/magazine/2020/12/01/democrats-rural-vote-wisconsin-441458?mc_cid=988bb52047&mc_eid=0d70a348da.

161. Albert, "Ecosocialism for Realists."

CONCLUSION

1. Bell, *Foundations of Futures.*

2. IPCC, *Climate Change 2022: Mitigation,* 18–19.

3. Raskin, *Journey to Earthland,* 27.

4. James Lovelock, *The Vanishing Face of Gaia: A Final Warning* (Philadelphia: Basic Books, 2010).

5. Robinson, *Global Police State.*

6. Morozov, "Critique of Technofeudal Reason."

7. Arrighi, *Long Twentieth Century,* 208.

8. NIC, *Global Trends 2040.*

9. Webb and Hessel, *The Genesis Engine,* 163, 206–213.

10. Zografos and Robbins, "Green Sacrifice Zones".

11. For example, Bastani, *Fully Automated Luxury.*

12. Matthew Huber's proposals may plausibly enable something like this scenario; see "Ecosocialism: Dystopian and Scientific."

13. Escobar, *Pluriversal Politics.*

14. See Malm and the Zetkin Collective, *White Skin, Black Fuel,* 167–168.

15. As Gaia Vince proposes. See Vince, *Nomad Century,* 105.

16. Buck, *After Geoengineering.*

17. Buck, *After Geoengineering,* 34.

18. Victor et al., *Accelerating the Low Carbon Transition*; Klein, *On Fire.*

19. Thaler, *No Other Planet,* 249.

20. Deibert, *Reset,* 277–299.

21. Jonathan Franzen, "What If We Stopped Pretending?," *New Yorker,* September 8, 2019, https://www.newyorker.com/culture/cultural-comment/what-if-we-stopped-pretending.

22. Ben Hayes, "Colonising the Future: Climate Change and International Security Strategies," in *The Secure and the Dispossessed: How the Military and Corporations Are Shaping a Climate-Changed World,* ed. Buxton and Hayes (London: Pluto Press, 2015), 55.

23. Jem Bendell, "Deep Adaptation: A Roadmap for Navigating Climate Tragedy," IFLAS Occasional Paper 2, July 27, 2018, https://www.lifeworth.com/deepadaptation.pdf.

24. Neiwert, *Alt-America.*

25. As Warren Wagar imagines in *A Short History of the Future* (Chicago: University of Chicago Press, 1989).

26. Ahmed, *Failing States,* 88–89.

27. Yusoff and Gabrys, "Climate Change and the Imagination," 5.

28. Mitchell and Chaudhury, "Worlding Beyond 'the' 'End,'" 327.

29. Bendell, "Deep Adaptation."

30. Bendell, "Deep Adaptation"; see also Carolyn Baker and Andrew Harvey, *Savage Grace: Living Resiliently in the Dark Night of the Globe* (Bloomington, IN: iUniverse, 2017).

31. Roy Scranton, "Beginning with the End," *Emergence Magazine*, April 24, 2020, https://emergencemagazine.org/story/beginning-with-the-end/?mc_cid=5db6ee 138c&mc_eid=0d70a348da.

32. Jairus Grove, *Savage Ecology: War and Geopolitics and the End of the World* (Durham, NC: Duke University Press, 2019), 25.

33. Dark Mountain Project, *Walking on Hot Lava: Selected Works for Uncivilized Times* (White River Junction, VT: Chelsea Green, 2017), 14.

34. Among the pessimists, the work of Carolyn Baker and Andrew Harvey provides one of the deepest and most genuine reckonings with our predicament; see *Savage Grace*.

35. Scranton, "Beginning with the End."

36. Scranton, "Beginning with the End."

37. Elizabeth Grosz, *The Incorporeal: Ontology, Ethics, and the Limits of Materialism* (New York: Columbia University Press, 2017), 151, 134.

38. Gilles Deleuze and Felix Guattari, *A Thousand Plateaus* (London: Continuum, 2004).

39. Joanna Macy and Chris Johnstone, *Active Hope: How to Face the Mess We're in Without Going Crazy* (Novato, CA: New World Library, 2012).

INDEX

Abolitionist, 16, 104–105, 191, 215–218, 219, 222–223, 226–227, 232, 234, 235
abolitionist reforms, 104, 216
abolitionist security assemblages, 16, 215, 223
abolitionist ecosocialism, 218, 226–227, 234–235
Agriculture, 20, 22, 48–49, 51–52, 77, 96–97, 118, 123–126, 136, 143, 147, 152, 158, 183–184
agroecology, 30, 87, 165, 169, 234
climate smart agriculture, 51, 97, 125
genetically modified (GM), 51–52, 125, 159, 206
Ahmed, Nafeez, 133, 194, 237
Anievas, Alex, 13, 106
Anti-extractivist activism, 137
Artificial intelligence (AI), 1, 7, 9, 52–56, 73, 79, 81, 101, 153, 159, 174, 178, 182–183, 187–191, 199–200, 205, 207–209, 211–213, 228, 230
artificial general intelligence, 214
artificial super intelligence, 214, 228
generative AI, 189, 282n23

Assemblage, 11, 95, 101, 106–107
Assemblage theory, 10. *See also* Assemblage
Atlantic Meridional Overturning Circulation (AMOC), 114, 158
Atwood, Margaret, 4, 204, 212, 214
Automation, 19, 53–54, 155–156, 159–160, 171, 174, 182, 215, 231

Bank of International Settlements (BIS), 72, 118
Besteman, Catherine, 101–102
Biden, Joe, 73, 129, 183, 186
Bigo, Didier, 100, 102
Biodiversity crisis, 20, 49
biodiversity collapse, 31, 124
deforestation, 20–21, 26, 126, 152, 185
mass extinction, 1, 22, 115, 145, 231
pollinator collapse, 145
sixth mass extinction, 20
Biofuels, 42–43, 52, 159, 200
Bioenergy plus Carbon Capture and Storage (BECCS), 29, 32, 126, 140, 143

Biosecurity, 55, 206, 221
  bioweaponization, 55, 183
Biotechnology, 52, 54, 73, 206. *See also*
  Synthetic biology
Black Lives Matter, 104, 179
Breakdown, 48, 50–51, 78, 83, 93, 96,
  123, 130, 147, 157, 192, 197, 200,
  202, 204, 214, 223, 226–231, 237.
  See also Collapse
Brockway, Paul, 28, 39, 46
Bryant, Levi, 91, 109
Butler, Octavia, 149, 204

Capellán-Peréz, Iñigo, 46, 153
Carbon dioxide removal (CDR), 29–30,
  43, 69–71, 140, 142–144, 153,
  158, 173, 174, 198, 201, 203, 226,
  230–231
  carbon removal, 22, 29, 116, 140
China, 1, 14, 19, 23, 25, 32, 36, 42,
  48–50, 52, 56–57, 73–76, 80, 93, 101,
  121–122, 129, 134, 137, 139, 143,
  147, 149, 152, 154, 167–168, 177,
  180, 183–184, 186–187, 189–190,
  192–201, 203, 205–206, 209–211,
  213, 219–220, 230
Chinese Communist Party (CCP), 165,
  167, 195–197, 199, 201, 209, 219
  Jinping, Xi, 129, 165, 194–197, 201
Christophers, Brett, 42, 147
Civil disobedience, 99, 152
Clean energy acceleration, 135–136, 194
Climate change, 7, 20, 22–23, 25, 35,
  48–49, 52, 71, 74, 79, 97, 99, 108,
  115, 117–118, 120–123, 127–128,
  134, 147, 178, 185, 188, 210,
  216–217
Climate chaos, 30, 40, 79, 128, 132,
  142, 157, 174, 181, 183, 189, 204
Climate crisis, 2, 20, 22, 25, 28, 59, 76,
  113–115, 120–123, 128–129, 144,
  179, 184–185, 188, 209. *See also*
  Climate change; Climate chaos

Climate reparations, 167, 168, 218–219
Climate tipping points, 144, 201, 231.
  See also Tipping points
  earth system feedbacks, 205, 226,
  236
  hothouse earth, 24–25, 228, 234
  tipping-point cascades, 24, 144, 201,
  229–230, 236 (*see also* Domino-like
  cascade)
Climate Leviathan (CL), 80, 83, 210
  climate behemoth, 80–81, 136
  climate Mao, 80, 82
  climate X, 80–82
Club of Rome, 11, 64, 94–95
Collapse, 4, 7, 15–16, 21, 25, 35, 48,
  55, 65–67, 78, 81, 83–84, 93, 96,
  115, 139, 147–151, 157–160, 163,
  174–175, 178, 181, 187, 193,
  196–198, 200, 202–204, 222, 226,
  228–230, 236–238, 240
Commoning, 150, 170
  solidarity economy, 170–171
Complexity theory, 2, 8, 10, 18, 67,
  87–88, 91, 110, 125, 169
Concrete utopian mode, 15–16, 215
Counter-hegemonic struggle(s), 5, 8, 72,
  77, 93–94, 99, 103, 109–110, 114,
  128, 160, 177, 185, 216, 220
Critical theory, 14, 76–77, 85
Current policies scenario, 4, 23, 117,
  132, 193. *See also* Stated policies
  scenario
Cybersecurity, 55–56, 187–188, 216,
  220
  cognitive-emotional conflicts, 191,
  200
  cyber-AI-nuclear nexus, 55, 182,
  187–188, 199–200
  cyberattacks, 170, 194, 199
  deepfakes, 189, 191
  disinformation, 19, 73–75, 131–132,
  157, 170, 172, 189, 191, 194, 197,
  220

Decoupling, 26–29, 31, 70, 81, 117, 119, 122, 145, 186, 196
  absolute decoupling, 26–28, 70
  relative decoupling, 26–28, 117
Degrowth, 7, 98, 161–163, 168–169, 171–174, 216–217, 218–220, 222, 227, 233–234, 237–238
  ecosocialist degrowth, 163, 170, 219, 233
  fortress degrowth, 227, 233, 237
  post-growth, 26, 70–71, 166–167, 169–171, 217, 219
  post-growth social democracy, 166–167, 169–171, 235
Delanda, Manuel, 10–11, 89
Deleuze, Gilles, 11, 240
Democratic renaissance, 75
Deudney, Daniel, 19, 54, 182
Digital Silk Road initiative, 210
Domino-like cascade, 8, 24
Dystopia(n), 4, 6–7, 32, 73, 77, 191, 208, 212, 228, 237

Earth system crisis, 14, 20, 30, 32, 48, 53, 111, 122
Earth system feedbacks, 205, 226, 236. See also Climate tipping points
  hothouse earth, 24–25, 228, 234
EAT-Lancet commission, 124, 131
Ecologically unequal exchange, 168, 179, 201, 217, 233
Ecomodernism, 26, 127
  fully automated luxury communism, 173
  left accelerationists, 207
  left ecomodernist, 161–163
Ecosocialism, 7, 77, 81–82, 160–162, 163, 170, 172, 175, 191, 215–218, 220–222, 226–227, 233–235, 237
  abolitionist ecosocialism, 218, 226–227, 234–235
  ecomodernist socialism, 162, 172–173, 209, 216, 227–228, 232–233

ecosocialist degrowth, 163, 171, 219, 233–234
  ecosocialist imperialism, 162, 216
  fortress ecosocialism, 163
Energy cannibalism, 138, 157
Energy crisis, 19, 35, 37, 120–121, 134
Energy security, 39–40, 47, 81, 90, 113, 120–121, 140, 151, 157, 193, 196–197. See also Energy crisis; Fossil fuel supply shocks
  electricity, 36, 41–44, 46, 55, 121–122, 130, 141–142, 147–148, 152, 168, 188, 200
  energy crisis, 19, 35, 37, 120–121, 134
  gas, 4, 36–38, 42–44, 67, 119–121, 126, 130–133, 135, 137–140, 154, 156–157, 168, 185–187, 189, 192–196, 198–199, 201, 208, 220
  hydropower, 36, 42–43, 71, 121, 134, 137, 140–142, 153, 156, 159, 168, 173, 184, 200–201
  liquified natural gas (LNG), 36, 133–134, 137, 201
  net energy decline, 1, 9, 14, 38, 41, 46–48, 52, 67, 71, 79, 81, 119, 122, 126, 132, 137, 154, 157, 164, 175, 192, 205.
  nuclear, 9, 42, 52, 54–56, 65, 71, 79, 111, 120–121, 134, 137, 140, 142, 147–148, 153, 159, 173, 179, 182, 184, 187–190, 193, 197, 199–200, 209, 214, 216, 220, 228, 230, 231, 237
  oil, 36–40, 42, 44, 67, 73, 119–121, 126, 130–135, 137–138, 140, 156–157, 167, 185–187, 189, 192–196, 198–199, 201, 220
Existential crises, 14, 19, 57–58, 60, 108, 111, 127–128, 135, 146, 179, 190, 198, 207, 209–210, 228
  fascist regimes, 60, 136
  global epidemic of depression, 58
  religious fundamentalism, 58–59, 128

Existential problematic (EP), 14, 88, 95, 105–107, 109–111, 114, 127, 135, 190, 237

Far-right populism, 1, 7, 59, 76, 108, 127–128, 132, 194. *See also* Politics of fear
Financial crises, 117, 142
2007–2008 financial crisis, 33, 150
FIR technologies, 52, 54, 56–57, 129, 159, 175, 182–183
Food crisis, 9, 19, 48, 51. *See also* Food security
synchronous breadbasket failures, 51, 74, 143–144
Food regime, 49–51, 124–126, 130
corporate food regime, 49, 51, 124–126, 130
neoliberal food regime, 50
Food security, 60, 123–124, 126, 131, 136, 143, 193, 199
Food-water-energy nexus, 120
Fossil capital(ists), 90, 97–98, 116, 127, 131–132, 135–136, 137, 144, 155, 169, 175, 181, 221
Fossil fascism, 116, 136, 157, 175, 194, 199
Fossil fuel supply shocks, 47
Fossil nationalism, 116, 136, 146, 155, 168. *See also* Fossil fascism
Fourth industrial revolution (FIR), 153. *See also* FIR technologies
Future-scenario analysis, 4, 14
Future studies, 4, 63–64, 83

G7, 48, 161, 163, 172–173, 216, 222, 230–231, 234
Gender, 8, 13, 15, 56, 58, 77, 95, 107, 111, 207, 218
feminist, 59, 161
hypermasculine, 58, 107, 135
hegemonic masculinity, 58, 128, 190

Global energy crisis, 19, 35
shale revolution, 36, 81
underinvestment, 36–37, 39–40, 42, 93, 119, 132, 192, 222
Global food system, 1, 31, 48, 50–51, 124–126, 131–132, 142
Global police state, 101, 198, 201
Global problematique, 84, 89
Global stilling, 121, 142
Global Trends reports, 14, 73
Global Trends 2040, 76
Gordon, Robert, 140, 153
Gramsci, Antonio, 238. *See also* Neo-Gramscian
Green capitalism, 81, 144, 162. *See also* Green capitalist
Green capitalist, 22, 26, 32, 52, 97, 131, 152
Green Deal Industrial Plan, 129
Green growth, 26–27, 164, 166, 235. *See also* Ecomodernism
Green hydrogen, 43, 71, 140–141, 153, 156, 159, 168, 173, 200–201
Green Keynesianism, 7, 15, 16, 151, 153, 160, 163, 171–172, 174, 187, 194, 209, 216, 232–235
Green New Deal, 172, 235
Green sacrifice zones, 44, 233

Hard-to-abate sectors, 29, 42–44, 136, 141, 153, 159
Harvey, David, 78, 202
Hickel, Jason, 28, 161, 168
Homer-Dixon, Thomas, 18, 95, 106

Indigenous and peasant communities, 150
Indigenous communities, 22
Indigenous inhabitants, 21
Indigenous people(s), 166, 173, 216. *See also* Indigenous and peasant communities; Indigenous

communities; Indigenous inhabitants; Indigenous rights
Indigenous rights, 167
Industrial Policy, 126, 129, 152, 154, 158–159
 green industrial policies, 152, 154, 159
Inflation, 18, 23, 34–36, 39, 41–42, 47, 120, 129–130, 132, 134, 139, 152–154, 156–157, 164–166, 172, 192, 196–197, 200
 fossil stagflation, 134, 136–137, 139–140, 146, 151–152, 156–157, 175, 192–197
 greenflation, 47–48, 122, 154–160, 163–164, 168, 172, 194, 196, 205, 219, 227, 232, 235
 green stagflation, 154, 157, 163–164, 171–172, 194, 234–235
 stagflation, 35, 134, 136–137, 139–140, 146, 151–152, 154, 156–157, 163–164, 171–172, 175, 187, 192–199, 203, 222, 227–229, 233–235
Integrated assessment models (IAMs), 14, 67–68, 70–72, 75, 87, 109
Intergovernmental Panel on Climate Change (IPCC), 22–24, 28–29, 49–50, 68, 70, 114–116
International Energy Agency (IEA), 27–29, 35, 37, 39–44, 68, 119, 121, 126, 132–133, 137, 141, 187, 192
International Renewable Energy Agency, 188
Internet-of-Things (IoT), 52, 55, 182, 188, 199, 209
Invasion of Ukraine, 1, 18, 35, 185, 192

Jessop, Bob, 92–93, 102–103, 212

Limits to Growth (LtG), 11, 14, 64–67, 70–71, 79, 94
Lovelock, James, 228
Lynas, Mark, 24–25, 114, 126

Malm, Andreas, 72, 127–128, 157
Mann, Geoff, 79–84, 87, 110, 136, 210
Mann, Michael, 90, 106, 265n33
Mapping, 6, 15, 82, 84, 88, 94, 108–110, 160
Marx, Karl, 9, 77
Marxism, 2, 8–10, 67, 167
 ecological Marxism 9, 26, 32, 91
Meadows, Donella, 64–66, 85, 89
Middle of the road variant, 146
Militarized global apartheid, 101, 163, 211, 216–218, 222, 232, 234
Military emissions, 185–186, 197, 222
Montreal-Kunming Global Biodiversity Framework, 22, 131
Moore, Jason, 96, 153
Moore's Law, 55, 205
Morin, Edgar, 10–11, 87

National Academies of Sciences, 54, 206
National Intelligence Council (NIC), 14, 73, 75–76, 80. See also Global Trends reports; Global Trends 2040
 competitive coexistence, 74, 230–231
 renaissance of democracies, 73, 231
  (see also Democratic renaissance)
 separate siloes, 74
 tragedy and mobilization, 74
Nationally Determined Contributions (NDCs), 23, 115–116, 140, 144, 146, 157, 198
NATO, 100, 103, 185, 189, 193, 197
Navigational praxis, 3, 6, 235
Neofeudalism, 192, 222, 226–227, 229–230, 286n104
Neo-Gramscian, 10, 87, 93
Neoliberalism, 78, 116, 129
 neoliberal drift, 116, 119, 125, 130, 132, 136, 146–147, 151–152, 155, 157, 174–175, 181, 185, 187, 189, 191–192, 195, 197–198, 222, 227–228, 230, 232–233

Net energy decline, 1, 9, 14, 38, 41,
   46–48, 52, 67, 71, 79, 81, 119, 122,
   126, 132, 137, 153, 157, 164, 175,
   192, 205
   Energy return on energy investment
      (EROI), 37–39, 41–42, 46–47, 66,
      133, 135, 137, 140, 151, 153
   net energy cliff, 38–40, 67, 119, 138
   peak oil, 138
Neurotechnologies, 179, 182, 208,
   211–212
Newell, Peter, 32, 153
New International Economic Order,
   169, 234
New Washington Consensus, 129
Nisancioglu, Kerem, 13, 106
Nuclear energy, 42, 71, 153, 159, 173,
   179
Nuclear weapons, 9, 55–56, 79, 111,
   188, 193
   cyber-AI-nuclear nexus, 55, 182,
      187–188, 199
   nuclear war, 147–148, 190, 197, 200,
      237

Pandemics, 1, 67, 90, 145, 212
   avian influenza, 49
   COVID-19, 18, 21, 29, 33–36, 54, 57,
      90, 96, 129, 145–146, 212
Paterson, Matthew, 32, 153
Patomäki, Heikki, 3, 109
Physical risks, 117–118, 142, 144, 155,
   157, 175
Planetary boundaries (PBs), 20, 26,
   66–67, 81, 124, 161
   biodiversity crisis, 20, 49
   deforestation, 20–21, 26, 126, 152,
      185
   mass extinction, 1, 20, 22, 115,
      145, 231 (see also Sixth mass
      extinction)
Planetary polycrisis, 12–14, 17–19, 57,
   60–61, 84, 88, 175, 225, 240

Planetary problematic, 12–15, 82, 88,
   94, 107–108, 110–111, 177, 190–191,
   222, 225–226, 234. See also Global
   problematique; World Problematique
Planetary systems thinking, 8, 10, 14,
   85, 88, 91, 93, 108–110, 112, 225
Pluriversal, 161, 173
Policing, 9, 14, 56–57, 99–101, 103–105,
   177, 211–212, 219–220, 236
Politics of fear, 57, 59–60, 209
Population growth, 19, 51, 65–66, 72,
   96
Possibility spaces, 2–8, 12, 15, 41,
   81–82, 84, 87–91, 93–94, 96, 105,
   110, 113, 116, 125, 160, 182, 189,
   222, 225–226, 228, 237
   attractor, 88–91, 105–106, 116, 125,
      129, 146, 151, 153, 170, 218, 226,
      229, 231
Problematique, 11–12, 67, 88, 113

Race, 8, 15, 77, 80, 95, 107, 111, 190,
   207, 218, 231, 240. See also Racism
racial capitalism, 107
Racism, 8, 15, 58, 127, 171, 179
Raskin, Paul, 82–84, 192, 228–229
   conventional worlds, 82, 84
   fortress worlds, 83, 192, 229
Raworth, Kate, 161, 165
Rebound effects, 28, 40, 119, 133, 137
Renewable energy (RE), 15, 25, 30,
   40–41, 69, 79, 97, 127, 155, 164,
   188. See also Renewable energy (RE)
   transition
   EROI question, 46–47
   land-use conflicts, 45
   scaling up finance for renewables,
      42–43
Renewable energy (RE) transition, 15,
   30, 40, 42, 45, 47–48, 117, 120, 122,
   127, 135, 138–139, 151, 153–158,
   164–165, 179, 186–187, 194, 197,
   200, 205–206

Rentierism, 148
Rigakos, George, 103–104, 181, 202, 215
Robinson, Kim Stanley, 5, 162
Robinson, William, 101, 103, 198, 201
Roubini, Nouriel, 34–35, 134
Rudd, Kevin, 194, 197

Scenario analysis, 42, 64, 72, 83. *See also* Future-scenario analysis
Schnabel, Isabel, 47, 154
Schwab, Klaus, 52, 158
Secular stagnation, 32, 38, 147. *See also* Structural crisis of capitalism
Security assemblages, 16, 100–102, 175, 177–178, 180–182, 185, 215, 223, 229, 234
military-police assemblages, 101–103, 107, 178, 180, 183, 191, 202, 218, 222
Security empires, 101, 177
Shared socioeconomic pathways (SSPs), 14, 67–71, 73, 75, 79, 81, 115, 226
fossil fueled development scenario, 69
inequality scenario, 69, 74
middle of the road scenario, 69
(*see also* Middle of the road variant)
regional rivalry scenario, 69, 102, 198
sustainable development scenario, 69
(*see also* Sustainable development trajectory)
Silver, Beverly, 96, 207
Sixth mass extinction, 20
Smil, Vaclav, 44, 140, 153
Socioecological problematic (SEP), 14–15, 88, 95–96, 98–100, 102–103, 108–110, 113–114, 118, 122–123, 127–128, 135, 138, 147, 160, 162, 178, 190–191, 216
Solar geoengineering, 69, 97, 144, 200–201, 226, 234
solar radiation management (SRM), 79, 144–146, 151, 158, 174, 200, 203, 230–231

Srnicek, Nick, 6, 207
Stated policies scenario, 39, 119, 140
Streeck, Wolfgang, 78, 139
Structural crisis of capitalism, 14, 19, 32, 59, 78, 102, 118
Structural violence, 99, 111, 178–180, 184–185, 198, 206, 209, 215–216
Structures of feeling, 8, 106
Surveillance, 9, 56, 81, 101–103, 111, 149, 161, 174, 178, 181–182, 188, 201, 208–211, 213–216, 221–222, 232
antisurveillance movements, 209
emotion recognition, 56–57, 182, 208, 236
facial recognition, 56–57, 101, 209, 236
surveillance capitalism, 159
Sustainable development trajectory, 70
Synthetic biology, 1, 7, 9, 52, 54–55, 79, 81, 159, 174, 179, 182–183, 199, 205–206, 214, 221, 231, 236. *See also* Biotechnology
System dynamics, 15, 64–65, 67, 70–71, 85, 89, 91, 113
World3 model, 65–66, 85

Taiwan crisis, 139, 146, 154, 186–187, 189, 194–197, 205, 211
Techno-authoritarianism, 4, 6, 53, 56–57
Techno-leviathan, 7, 15–16, 84, 160, 174, 183, 191, 210–215, 223, 226, 228–233, 236–238
Technological unemployment, 19, 53–54, 75 76, 160, 174, 183, 205, 207, 209–210, 213, 230–232. *See also* Automation
Technological problem-shifting, 52–53, 75, 98
Techno-optimist(ic), 41, 43, 47, 53, 140, 158–159
Termination shock, 145–146, 200, 230

Terrorism, 14, 58, 99–101, 105, 111,
    178–179, 182, 184, 188, 190, 200,
    207, 211, 215–217, 219, 228–232,
    236
  weapons of mass destruction (WMD)
    terrorism, 211, 228–229, 231–232
3d printing, 52, 55, 153, 174, 182, 207,
    221
Tipping points, 8, 24, 76, 88, 90,
    108, 115, 144, 150, 158, 162,
    171–172
  tipping-point cascades, 24, 144, 201,
    229–230, 236 (*see also* Domino-like
    cascade)
Tooze, Adam, 17–18, 33, 45
Transdisciplinary, 2, 5, 7–8, 12, 14, 76,
    79, 81–84, 87, 114, 223, 225
Transition minerals, 7, 66, 81, 136, 156,
    173, 207
  transition metal(s), 44, 165, 168
  transition mineral bottlenecks, 44–45,
    139
Transition risks, 117–118, 155, 235.
    See also Physical risks
  carbon bubble 172, 232
  stranded assets, 117, 131, 144, 151,
    155–156

Ukraine war, 36, 186, 192. *See also*
    Invasion of Ukraine
United States (US), 27, 49–50, 52,
    56, 59, 74–75, 80, 101, 121, 125,
    127, 129, 133–137, 139, 142, 149,
    152, 154, 165, 167, 177, 183,
    185–186, 189, 196, 200–201, 203,
    205–206, 209, 211. *See also* Biden,
    Joe
Universal Basic Income (UBI), 165–166,
    169–172, 212, 213, 232, 236
Urry, John, 4, 77, 206
Utopia(n), 4–7, 15–16, 73, 80–83,
    97–98, 109, 160, 162, 172, 201, 212,
    215, 218, 234–235

Violence-interdependence (VI), 19,
    53–55, 209–210, 233
Violence problematic (VP), 14, 81, 88,
    95, 98–100, 102–104, 107, 109–111,
    178, 183, 187, 190–192, 198, 205,
    215–216, 222
  nonstate violence, 99, 162, 175,
    177–180, 182, 184, 202, 209, 228
  private military-security industry, 181,
    201–202
  state violence, 99, 104, 178–181, 185,
    192, 209, 215

Wainwright, Joel, 79–84, 87, 110, 136,
    210
Wallerstein, Immanuel, 2, 5, 78, 114
Williams, Alex, 6, 10, 207
Williams, Michael, 100–101
World Economic Forum, 1, 52, 158, 201
World Problematique, 11, 64, 67, 94–95
World Trade Organization, 124
World-earth system, 19, 64–66, 72, 84,
    91–92, 94–95, 110, 114, 151–152,
    177, 191, 226
  core-periphery, 92–93, 170, 233
World-systems theory, 10, 91–92
Wright, Erik Olin, 5, 81, 92, 162, 169

Press
et Rossi
Main Street, 9th floor
02142

edu
tt@mit.edu
253-2882

authorized representative in the EU for product safety and compliance is

 Access System Europe Oü, 16879218
tamäe tee 50,
 10621

.requests@easproject.com
 56 968 939

: 9780262547758
ase ID: 155365110

www.ingramcontent.com/pod-product-compliance
Lightning Source LLC
Chambersburg PA
CBHW022302280326
41932CB00010B/950